PENGUIN BOOKS

THE PORTABLE
THOMAS JEFFERSON

Each volume in The Viking Portable Library either presents a representative selection from the works of a single outstanding writer or offers a comprehensive anthology on a special subject. Averaging 700 pages in length and designed for compactness and readability, these books fill a need not met by other compilations. All are edited by distinguished authorities who have written introductory essays and included much other helpful material.

"The Viking Portables have done more for good reading and good writers than anything that has come along since I can remember."
—Arthur Mizener

Merrill D. Peterson is Professor of History at the University of Virginia and has written several books on Jefferson's life and work, including *Jefferson and the New Nation*.

THE PORTABLE

Thomas Jefferson

Edited and with an introduction by

MERRILL D. PETERSON

PENGUIN BOOKS

PENGUIN BOOKS
Published by the Penguin Group
Penguin Books USA Inc.,
375 Hudson Street, New York, New York 10014, U.S.A.
Penguin Books Ltd, 27 Wrights Lane, London W8 5TZ, England
Penguin Books Australia Ltd, Ringwood, Victoria, Australia
Penguin Books Canada Ltd, 10 Alcorn Avenue,
Toronto, Ontario, Canada M4V 3B2
Penguin Books (N.Z.) Ltd, 182–190 Wairau Road, Auckland 10, New Zealand

Penguin Books Ltd, Registered Offices:
Harmondsworth, Middlesex, England

First published in the United States of America
by Viking Penguin, Inc. 1975
Reprinted 1975, 1976
Published in Penguin Books 1977

15   17   19   20   18   16

LIBRARY OF CONGRESS CATALOGING IN PUBLICATION DATA
Jefferson, Thomas, Pres. U.S., 1743–1826.
The portable Thomas Jefferson.
Bibliography: p. 587.
1. United States—Politics and government—
Revolution, 1775–1783—Collected works. 2. United
States—Politics and government—1783–1865—
Collected works. I. Peterson, Merrill D.
II. United States. President, 1801–1809 (Jefferson)
III. Title
E302.J54   1977   973.4'6'0924   77-4725
ISBN 0 14 015.080 3

Printed in the United States of America
Set in Linotype Janson

Contents

IV

Letters   347

Introduction

THOMAS JEFFERSON came upon the world's stage at the dawn of "the age of the democratic revolution." He helped to make the age as well as the American nation, which was its best achievement. Perhaps no one, certainly no other American, better exemplified the spirit of the age or had a more enduring influence on the shape of things to come. Rising to fame as a leader of colonies in revolt against an empire, penning the charter of American independence in 1776, Jefferson embodied the new nation's aspirations for freedom and enlightenment, and throughout a long life was intellectually and politically engaged not only in American affairs but also in the affairs of a world unhinged by war and revolution.

Jefferson earned his place in history primarily as a statesman identified with the revolutionary experiment in America. But he was much more than a statesman. A prodigy of talents—scientist, architect, musician, agriculturist, lawyer, educator, inventor, philologist, geographer, and so on—he defies simple classification. Posterity has generally comprehended him only in fragments. Jefferson himself, with an aversion to cosmic philosophizing, never reduced his thought to a system. He wrote but one book, *Notes on the State of Virginia*; for the rest his philosophy must be pieced together, like a mosaic, from discrete observations in scattered memoranda, state papers, reports, addresses, and, above all, tens of thousands of letters, which, in their freshness and variety, are an inexhaustible treasure. The letters of a man, Jefferson said, "form the only genuine journal of his life." From the time he became conscious of his fame and of posterity's stake in the events with which he was associated, Jefferson dutifully preserved this journal.

It was a life of seemingly bewildering conflicts and contradictions. By birth, taste, and training he was an aristocrat, yet his principles and politics placed him in the vanguard of modern democracy. One of the first Americans to give authentic expression to the nation's genius—"The Apostle of Americanism" in the judgment of one biographer—he nevertheless seemed more at home in Parisian salons than in the rude American world, more cosmopolitan than national in thought and feeling. He was both philosopher and politician. Despite his mastery in the latter role, he cursed the fate that yoked him to the labors of government rather than to the infinitely more agreeable tasks of the arts and sciences to which he believed he had been born. He was a man of theories and ideals—"visionary" was the favorite epithet of his enemies—yet on the evidence of his work uncommonly hardheaded and practical. Even his dreams proved more substantial than the realities so much insisted upon by conservative-minded men. Outwardly amiable, charming, open to all and sundry, with an effortless talent for drawing men to him, he was nonetheless a man of almost impenetrable emotional reserve, "easy and delightful of acquaintance, impossible of knowledge," as Albert J. Nock observed. Every other American statesman, Henry Adams wrote, could be portrayed with "a few broad strokes of the brush," but Jefferson "only touch by touch with a fine pencil, and the perfection of the likeness depended upon the shifting and uncertain flicker of the semi-transparent shadows."

The shadows, the ironies, and the paradoxes cannot be dismissed, and Jefferson would be a lesser figure if they were. In the final analysis, however, it is the fundamental unity and coherence of his life and thought that impresses the modern student. As in a great watershed, all the tributaries of his mind fed into a mainstream freighted with ideas and projects, hopes and fears, for the culture of free men in America. The selections in this volume are intended to present Jefferson in the fullness of his thought and imagination. From them every reader must draw his own conclusions, but the essential Jefferson is inescapable. The brief biographical commentary that follows aims to provide the necessary orientation to the man and his times.

Thomas Jefferson was born at Shadwell, in Virginia, April 13, 1743. His father, Peter Jefferson, a self-taught surveyor and mapmaker, had been among the earliest settlers of this wilderness country to be called Albemarle. Lying in the hills just east of the Blue Ridge, it would always seem to Jefferson "the Eden of the world," and the freedom, openness, and simplicity of up-country life enforced a sense of man's proper relationship to nature that colored all his values. From modest beginnings Peter Jefferson built a fair estate, and died in 1757 the first citizen of his county. Most of the estate, several thousand acres of land and the slaves to work them, descended to Jefferson. Of his mother, Jane Randolph, though she lived to 1776, the son had little to say, except that she was the daughter of a princely family who "trace their pedigree far back to England and Scotland, to which let every man ascribe the faith and merit he chooses." The Randolph pedigree assured him social position in Virginia, yet Jefferson obviously valued more the enterprising example of his father.

His father had set him on the course of education, for which Jefferson always venerated his memory. At the age of seventeen, having become a proficient classical scholar in the Reverend James Maury's school not far from his home, he left the red hills of Albemarle to attend the College of William and Mary in the provincial capital, Williamsburg. Dr. William Small, of Scotland, the one truly enlightened man on a faculty otherwise composed of Anglican clerics, was his constant teacher, unveiling vistas of "the expansion of science, and the system of things in which we are placed." Nature destined him for the sciences, Jefferson often said, but no careers opened to science in Virginia, and he took the well-traveled path of the law, where his mentor was the good and learned George Wythe. The chain of influence from Small to Wythe was closed by Francis Fauquier, the urbane royal governor, who introduced Jefferson to the life of cultivated taste and sensibility. This Williamsburg trio of philosophers invited the gifted student into their circle. Dinners at the Governor's Palace were followed by spirited conversations, which Jefferson thought nearly sixty years later mingled more wit, learning, and philosophy than he had heard in all his life besides.

Under Wythe's tutelage Jefferson studied law as a branch of humane learning and put five years of effort into it. He acquired a substantial personal library—the first of three he would assemble in his lifetime. Its actual contents are unknown—a fire at Shadwell saw to that—but Jefferson's early book lists suggest that it surveyed a wide field from the sciences to the fine arts and was equally cordial to the ancients and the moderns. A youthful taste for poetry and fiction waned as he matured and set his mind on the track of "useful knowledge." In the black-letter of the law Jefferson began with Sir Edward Coke's formidable *Institutes*, and from there, like a good Whig, pursued English rights and liberties back to their ancient Saxon foundations. Admitted to the bar in 1767, Jefferson was successful, though he never attained the celebrity of his folksy friend Patrick Henry. "Mr. Jefferson," it was said, "drew copiously from the depths of the law, Mr. Henry from the recesses of the human heart." Law led into politics and was finally significant as a preparation for statesmanship. When the onrush of revolution forced Jefferson to abandon his practice in 1774, he did not abandon the law, but turned it to the cause of American liberty.

His political career commenced in 1769 when the freeholders of Albemarle elected him to the House of Burgesses. At the same time he began to build Monticello, the lovely house perched on a densely wooded summit near his birthplace. There were no architects in Virginia, so Jefferson set out to become his own architect. The versatility he demonstrated in this endeavor marked a permanent trait. Learning architecture, as he learned most things, from books, he discovered his master in the Renaissance Italian, Andrea Palladio, who had gone to Roman antiquity for his models. Monticello was a modified Palladian villa, and all of Jefferson's later architectural masterpieces, such as the Virginia Capitol and the University of Virginia, were in the Palladian manner though original creations in their own right. In architecture this scientific modernist returned to ancient forms because there, rather than in the vernacular of his own time and place, he found an aesthetic as universal, chaste, and orderly as the Newtonian laws of motion. Jefferson was a dozen years building Monticello; a decade later he rebuilt it on a more elaborate plan, and the house assumed its ultimate form only about the time he left the Presidency in 1809. It was a lifelong obsession.

Jefferson brought his bride to the "little mountain" in January 1772. Martha Wayles Skelton was an attractive, accomplished, and well-to-do young widow from the low-country around Williamsburg. Legend reports that she favored the rawboned and ungainly Jefferson over more gallant suitors because he shared her fondness for music; but little is actually known of Martha or what she contributed to Jefferson's life during ten years of marriage other than six children and an abiding love. Her death in 1782 desolated him. Only two of the children survived infancy, and only the eldest, Martha, survived her father. For a man who prized domestic felicity above any other, Jefferson received but a small portion of it. He never remarried, and with a possible exception for one brief amorous adventure in France kept his relations with women on the same aloof plane with his mind.

From his entrance into the Virginia assembly, Jefferson was associated with the young militants around Patrick

Henry in the controversy with the mother country. In 1774, after Governor Dunmore dissolved the unruly assembly for its protest against Parliament's "coercive acts," Jefferson was elected to the colony's first revolutionary convention, which, in turn, chose delegates to the First Continental Congress. Illness kept him from Williamsburg, but Jefferson forwarded the "instructions" he had drafted, in a 6500-word paper that was deemed too bold for the convention's approval. It was at once published, however, under the title *A Summary View of the Rights of British America*. Jefferson drew his argument from the Whig tradition of the English constitution but broached the radical conclusion that the Americans possessed the natural right to govern themselves. This appeal to the past in behalf of modern principles, this mingling of the legalism of the English tradition with the rationalism of the natural-rights philosophy, was thoroughly characteristic of him. Although the logic of the argument pointed to independence, Jefferson stopped at the wholesale repudiation of Parliament's authority over the colonies, leaving allegiance to a common king the only bond of empire. By advancing this new theory of empire, which was no more acceptable to Britain than the old theory of colonial subserviency was to America, the *Summary View* opened the final chapter in the polemics leading to the Revolution.

The fighting had begun when in June 1775 Jefferson took one of the Virginia seats in the Second Continental Congress at Philadelphia. He brought with him, John Adams said, "a reputation for literature, science, and a happy talent for composition." Congress at once employed this talent. Jefferson drafted the stinging reply to Lord North's "conciliatory proposition" and shared with John Dickinson the honors of the momentous Declaration of the Causes and Necessity of Taking Up Arms. As hopes of reconciliation faded, Virginia, like several of the other colonies, proceeded to establish an independent government and in May 1776 called upon Congress to speak for the united colonies. On June 11 Jefferson found himself appointed at the head of a five-man committee to prepare a declaration of independence. Either of the committee's two most distinguished members, Benjamin Franklin and John Adams, might have been expected to draft the document, but the task fell to the young Virginian for political reasons and also because he possessed that "peculiar felicity of expression" so much wanted in a state paper of this kind. He showed a preliminary draft to Franklin and Adams, who suggested only minor changes, revised it to his own satisfaction, gave it to the committee, and from there it went unaltered to Congress. After adopting the Virginia resolution for independence on July 2, Congress debated the proposed declaration for two and one-half days. Many changes were made, mostly stylistic, some of substance, especially in the body of the work, the indictment of George III, but as adopted on July 4 the Declaration of Independence bore unmistakably the stamp of Jefferson's genius.

That genius was literary as well as philosophical. Without literary pretensions, seemingly without a trace of literary artifice, Jefferson had matured a prose style distinguished for its moral earnestness, its felicitous diction, rhythmic cadence, and crisp clarity and precision. In literature as in architecture the Romans offered "the purest models," and he particularly recommended the writings of Livy, Sallust, and Tacitus as "pre-eminent specimens of logic, taste, and sententious brevity." He was a superb rhetorician, in the ancient usage of that term, interested in the communication of ideas rather than in beauties of expression. This went along with his trust in reason, his scientific penchant for the matter-of-fact, and his neoclassical taste in painting. Yet Jefferson's fundamentally utilitarian prose, never dawdling but striking to the heart of the subject, possessed warmth, grace, imagination, and that lofty eloquence that gave unique charm and power to his writings. The Declaration of Independence, the most carefully wrought of all Jefferson's productions, epitomized the style with the man. Its lan-

guage was bold yet elevated, plain and direct yet touched
with philosophy, befitting a solemn appeal to the reason of
mankind. In rhythmic strides from the first nobly turned
phrase to the last, the argument inspired conviction in the
cause of American freedom.

The achievement of the Declaration consisted chiefly
in this: it gave timeless symbolization in words to a
philosophy of human rights and self-government. Jefferson
subordinated the recondite legalism of the English constitution to fundamental human values expressed in lan-
gauge all might understand. He encapsulated a cosmology,
a political theory, and a national creed in the celebrated
second paragraph. The truths there declared to be "self-
evident" were not new; they derived from John Locke,
dissident English Whigs, and philosophers of the Enlightenment, and were so much a part of American opinion that
Jefferson himself later said he had only attempted "to place
before mankind the common sense of the subject." Equality, the natural rights of man, the sovereignty of the
people, the right of revolution—these principles endowed
the American Revolution with high moral purpose united
to a theory of free government. For the first time in
history "the rights of man," not of rulers, were laid at the
foundation of a nation. The first great colonial revolt of
the modern age perforce became the first great democratic
revolution as well.

The framework of Jefferson's thought was well settled
by 1776. Of paramount importance in accounting for it
was the scientific rationalism of the Enlightenment. Bacon,
Newton, and Locke made up his trinity of heroes. From
his early exposure to English and Scottish rationalists, Jefferson turned to the Continental representatives of the
Enlightenment—Montesquieu, Voltaire, Diderot, Holbach,
Beccaria, and others—and later, when he went to France,
became something of a *philosophe* himself. The mission of
philosophy was no longer to reflect the world but to
change it. By relentless inquiry into nature, its laws and
truths, after being so long buried under the rubble of

bigotry and superstition, might be discovered and put to the service of mankind. Jefferson's heretical natural religion, his commitment to untrammeled inquiry, his belief in the moral identity of all men and in the illimitable progress of the human mind were all anchored in the thought of the Enlightenment. Ancient philosophy, another source of Jefferson's ideas, was very much a part of the modern intellectual world. With other enlightened men he found in pagan Greece and Rome a basis of perspective on his own age, one that exhibited ideals of learning, beauty, and virtue and furnished a whole armory of weapons for the assault on mystery and authority. The ancients were important to Jefferson's political thought only as monitors against tyranny. Here, in political theory, he was mainly influenced by the history of the English constitution, which he traced to the primitive Saxons. That constitution had been repeatedly corrupted, from the feudal Normans through George III, though its best elements of liberty and self-government might be preserved in America. In 1776, of course, Jefferson shifted the basis of these elements from history to reason and nature, and gradually, as the shadow of the English heritage lifted, he combined them into a new amalgam, American and democratic. His sense of nationality, of Americanism, was still inchoate, but it developed rapidly during the Revolutionary War and in due time completed the intellectual framework. With Jefferson as with all Americans, to paraphrase Robert Frost, the land was theirs before they were the land's. Increasingly, however, the freed colonials began to think of themselves as a new order of men, to study out their land, to differentiate it from the Old World, and to define its unique promise. Jefferson was not only important in this work but almost the embodiment of its spirit.

Jefferson returned to Virginia in September 1776 with plans to reform the old order. A constitution had been adopted for the commonwealth, but it was distressingly less democratic than the one he had drafted in Philadelphia and dispatched to Williamsburg. Repeatedly over the next fifty years Jefferson rode full tilt against the Virginia constitution, each charge more democratic than the last, yet it withstood every blow. Now, in 1776, from his seat in the House of Delegates (successor to the Burgesses), he sought far-reaching reforms by ordinary legislation. Most of these were contained in the comprehensive Revision of the Laws which occupied Jefferson for several years. The rational aim of a revised code miscarried, although the legislature eventually adopted or rejected the 126 bills of the revisal one by one.

Among the major reforms was the abolition of entail and primogeniture—vestiges of feudalism—and the establishment of a uniformly individualistic system of land tenure. If the change was not as great as Jefferson supposed, it nevertheless tended to break the pride and opulence of aristocratic families and contributed to that "revolution of property" from generation to generation which Alexis de Tocqueville later named one of the foundations of American democracy. Jefferson took special pride in his Bill for Religious Freedom, finally enacted in 1786 after a decade-long campaign against the Anglican establishment. Religious freedom was an absolute right in his philosophy. Its exercise being wholly a matter of private conscience, it injured no one and admitted neither protection nor support from the state. Rejecting Lockean toleration as insufficient, since it implied an official or preferred religion, Jefferson demanded full religious freedom and entire separation of church and state. The tone of the argument was anticlerical, yet Jefferson, unlike his philosophical allies in Europe, professed to be a friend of true religion which had freedom for its element. The celebrated statute became a powerful directive for the unique relationship of church and state in America, and, by its bold assertion that the opinions of men are beyond the reach of civil authority, one of the great charters of the free mind as well.

The Virginia oligarchs stubbornly resisted other major reforms of Jefferson's "system." A bill to replace Virginia's bloody criminal code by enlightened and humane standards of criminal justice was at last defeated. So too was the Bill for the More General Diffusion of Knowledge. Jefferson's faith in freedom and self-government was at bottom a faith in education, which therefore became a paramount responsibility of the state. He proposed a complete plan of public education from elementary schools to a university, with a state library as well. In its comprehensiveness, in its substitution of the citizen-republicanism of the new nation for the religious ideal of New England education, and in its social aim of replacing the "pseudo aristocracy" of wealth and privilege with the "natural aristocracy" of talent, Jefferson's plan was a landmark in the history of American education despite its rejection in Virginia. Slavery, like ignorance and the inhumanity of the laws, was still another obstacle to the hopes of republicanism. A plan of gradual emancipation was part of Jefferson's reform system, but it was held back on the plea of expediency. Convinced that "the public mind would not yet bear the proposition," and unwilling to martyr himself uselessly, Jefferson looked to the younger generation to turn the fate of this question.

On balance, Jefferson's achievement in this Revolutionary endeavor fell well short of the goal. The mass of Virginians seemed not to share his vision. He was successful with reforms that uprooted institutionalized privilege, while his more constructive measures, such as public education, were defeated. The new order was incomplete and fouled by the remains of the old.

On June 1, 1779, Jefferson was elected governor of Virginia. The republican convictions, easy temperament, and philosophical turn of mind that had served him so well in the legislative forums of the Revolution would prove less serviceable to executive leadership in a situation fraught with disaster. The British, unable to destroy General Washington's army in the North, had begun "to unravel the thread of rebellion from the southward." If their attempt was successful, Virginia must become the crucial battleground. At the risk of the state's meager defenses, Jefferson rushed all possible assistance to the Carolinas. But he labored under mounting difficulties. Inflation, shortages of arms, stores, and fighting men, Indian warfare on the frontiers, sagging morale in the counties —these problems were serious when Jefferson took office, and they rapidly passed beyond the power of government to solve. Early in January 1781, the traitor-general Benedict Arnold invaded the state from the coast, marched through the low-country to Richmond, now the capital, and put the government itself to flight. Jefferson met the crisis bravely, though not without censure, and upon his return to the capital acted with more vigor than before, still to no avail. In the spring General Cornwallis marched his southern army into the defenseless state. The government took refuge in Charlottesville, near Jefferson's home, and on June 2, after his term of office had expired but before a successor could be named, the redcoats chased him from Monticello. At this crisis of humiliation and defeat the House of Delegates voted an inquiry into the conduct of the executive. But no inquiry was held, and in December 1781, months after the British surrender at Yorktown— the happy outcome of these unhappy events—the assembly voted Jefferson a resolution of thanks for his services.

Exhausted by the ordeal, wounded by criticism, and disgusted that his exertions had been of so little account, Jefferson vowed to quit the public stage forever. Personal tragedy struck in September 1782 when his wife died, plunging him into the deepest gloom of his life. The idyll he had sought at Monticello was suddenly shattered. "Before that event my scheme of life had been determined," he wrote in November. "I had folded myself in the arms of retirement, and rested all prospects of future happiness on domestic and literary subjects. A single event wiped away all my plans and left me a blank which I had not the spirit to fill up." Fortunately, Congress came to his rescue, renewing the commission previously declined to negotiate peace in Paris. Peace came before he could sail, however, and Jefferson wound up in Congress instead.

During his retirement he wrote most of what would become *Notes on the State of Virginia*. It was not begun as a book, or with any view to publication, but as a response to a series of questions posed by the secretary of the French legation in Philadelphia. Becoming fascinated with these matter-of-fact questions, Jefferson converted the task into an intellectual discovery of his native country, the greater Virginia of that day. A mélange of information and opinion on many subjects, from rivers and mammoths to laws and aborigines, the *Notes on Virginia* is uniquely interesting as a guide to Jefferson's mind. It reveals the man of science eager to possess nature for the mind, but also the man of almost romantic sensibility enraptured by the grandeur of the American environment even in his quest for useful knowledge.

The work belonged to the two realms of natural and civil history. Taking his cue from the Baconian faculties of the mind—memory, reason, and imagination—Jefferson divided all knowledge into three great branches, history, philosophy, and fine arts, then subdivided each of these until every species of knowledge found its logical place. Such was the system of classification he employed in his library. Natural history, always the principal field of Jefferson's scientific investigations, comprehended the earth as a scene of life. Nothing was more interesting in the *Notes* than his refutation of current European theories advanced by the great Buffon and others of biological impotence and decay in the New World. In the course of offering a scientific vindication of American nature, Jefferson also gave voice to an incipient American nationalism. Other parts of the book belonged to civil history, still others to philosophy and the fine arts. It was a virtual manual of Jefferson's political opinions. Several of its passages—on slavery, on the virtues of husbandry and the vices of cities, on the Virginia constitution—became so well known that they were said to be "stereotyped in the public voice." Many of the opinions were controversial; at least one of them, in which Jefferson "hazarded" the racial inferiority of the Negro, proved embarrassing to his philosophy. The book whetted the appetite of the tiny community of American philosophers, and upon its publication in 1785 ensured Jefferson a scientific and literary reputation on both sides of the Atlantic.

In Congress from November 1783 to the following May, Jefferson laid the foundations of national policy in several areas. He proposed the decimal system of coinage on the dollar unit. (At a later time, in 1790, he would propose a decimal system of weights and measures founded on a natural and universal standard, but this enlightened measure was not adopted.) After Virginia ceded her western lands to Congress, Jefferson prepared the first plan of government for the immense trans-Appalachian domain. The Ordinance of 1784 created a number of territories bounded by latitudinal and longitudinal lines, and established the principle of raising new, free, and equal self-governing states out of the wilderness. This plan of empire—"an empire of liberty" in Jefferson's happy phrase—reversed European theories of colonial dependency. Unfortunately, Congress eliminated Jefferson's provision to bar slavery from the West, though the error was later rectified in part by the Northwest Ordinance of 1787. The nation's first land law also bore the imprint of Jefferson's mathematical mind. The effects of the land survey system he proposed are visible even today to anyone who flies over the prairies and plains and views the linear patchwork of the fields below. Jefferson would never know at first hand the sprawling country beyond the mountains, but the West constantly tugged at his imagination, and he showed notable vision in planning for it.

In May 1784 Congress appointed him to a three-man commission to negotiate treaties of commerce with European states. The commission met with indifferent success and expired, but Jefferson continued his efforts for

American commerce when, in 1785, he succeeded Franklin as Minister to France. Usually portrayed as a narrow "agrarian" in his economic outlook, Jefferson was actually, sentiment aside, an ardent commercial expansionist. Several considerations were involved. First, the conditions did not exist for an American "home market," hence national wealth and power depended on the growth of foreign navigation and commerce. Second, cut adrift from the British trading empire in 1776, the nation must open new markets to American ships and productions. Third, the American Revolution in its bearings for political economy pitted the emerging liberal tenets of free trade against the jealous mercantilist policies of European courts. Jefferson subscribed to this economic liberalism both as a philosopher and as an American. His persistent hostility to Britain, whatever its sources in the psyche of the freed colonial, rested on the belief that Britain aimed to hold the Americans in economic bondage after their political bondage was broken. She was succeeding, too. The solution, Jefferson thought, lay in retaliation against Britain and the development of a free commercial system centered on France, the friend and ally of the United States. In negotiations at Versailles, where he was assisted by the Marquis de Lafayette, Jefferson won valuable concessions for American commerce, yet he could not shake British monopoly. Without abandoning the ambitious goal of throwing American commerce into a new orbit, he looked increasingly to the progress of reform in Europe and a strengthened national government at home to secure it.

The five years Jefferson spent in France were among the happiest of his life. Paris was the acme of civilization, and such were its delights that Jefferson seemed to walk with an extra spring in his step and speak with a special lilt in his voice throughout his sojourn there. He haunted the bookstalls, frequented the fashionable salons, and indulged his starved appetite for art and music and theater. He was excited by ingenious inventions, smitten by the beauties of architecture, and captivated by the French cuisine. For one glorious season in 1786 he was swept up in a romance with Maria Cosway, the lovely and talented wife of an English painter and the nonplused recipient of Jefferson's "Dialogue between My Head and My Heart." He traveled in the south of France, in Italy, in England, where his friend John Adams was minister, and in the Rhineland, not alone for personal pleasure but that, from all this activity, he might return home "charged, like a bee with the honey gathered on it," for the improvement of his own country. He interpreted the New World to the Old and presided over the two-way intercourse in the arts and sciences. Some of this would have profound effects, as in his design for the Virginia Capitol, which inaugurated the Roman style in the architecture of the young republic, and, of course, in his transmission of revolutionary ideas to the French. About France, and Europe generally, Jefferson expressed ambivalent feelings. On balance, the more he saw of Europe the dearer his own land became. Like many of the countrymen who would follow him, he came into full possession of his Americanism in Europe.

As the French Revolution came on, Jefferson's liberal friends in Paris looked to him for counsel. He advocated reform of the Bourbon monarchy, establishment of representative assemblies, guarantees of certain individual liberties, and removal of the most objectionable feudal privileges. He did not think the French people, who knew nothing even of habeas corpus, were ready for revolution on the American plan, and he feared a conservative reaction if things were pushed too far. Yet as the revolutionary wave rolled upon him, Jefferson rode with it. When he returned to the United States in the fall of 1789— after the ascendancy of the National Assembly, the so-called abolition of feudalism, and the adoption of the Declaration of the Rights of Man and Citizen—Jefferson viewed the French Revolution as an extension of the American and believed his own country had a vital stake in its future. "Here," he said, "is but the first chapter in the history of European liberty."

Jefferson returned home on leave, but President Washington had other plans for him, and so he became Secretary of State in the new government. He was cordial to the experiment launched by the Constitution. He had, after all, seen the Confederation kicked and scoffed abroad and had gone begging to Dutch bankers to keep its treasury afloat. Nevertheless, as Jefferson pondered the Constitution in Paris, where tyranny, not anarchy, was the problem, he felt that it had been too much influenced by disorders like Shays's Rebellion and general disenchantment with the democracy released in 1776. He objected, in particular, to the perpetual re-eligibility of the chief magistrate, fearing that the office would degenerate into a corrupt monarchy, and to the omission of a bill of rights. Partly because of his intervention, especially with his great friend James Madison, the Federalists consented to amendments which became the Bill of Rights. Neither Federalist nor Anti-Federalist, as he said, but anxious for the success of the new government, Jefferson took up his duties in New York, the temporary capital, in March 1790.

The tall, soft-spoken, and self-possessed Virginian held impressive credentials for the conduct of the nation's foreign affairs. His main objectives were, first, the liberation and expansion of American commerce, which he associated with the French alliance; second, the redemption of the West from European colonialism, that of the Spanish on the border to the south and of the British to the north, together with pacification of the Indians; and third, the manipulation of American neutrality to take advantage of any war among the European powers. Hopes of progress with France suffered a setback when the National Assembly, far from freeing trade in accordance with Jefferson's scenario for revolution, turned toward protectionism. With Spain Jefferson sought to fix the southern boundary and secure the navigation of the Mississippi River through Spanish territory to the Gulf. Spain was in her dotage. So long as she held the Floridas and New Orleans, they were

America's for the taking, but Jefferson wished to obtain them peacefully and would have been quite patient except for the danger that they would again become pawns on the chessboard of European politics, falling to Britain or France. The problem would not be resolved for many years.

In the first serious negotiations with Britain since 1783, Jefferson sought removal of His Majesty's troops below the Great Lakes and settlement of other issues left over from the treaty of peace. Britain was vulnerable, Jefferson believed, to the most potent weapon in the American armory —commercial discrimination. She could be made to pay for her monopoly of the American market, and if this was not enough to extort concessions, then her dependence in war on American provisions, both at home and in the West Indies, would be. But in dealing with Britain, Jefferson was checked by the Secretary of the Treasury, Alexander Hamilton. Hamilton's fiscal system turned on British trade, credit, and power. The treasury coffers were filled with revenue from British trade—revenue that was mortgaged to servicing the huge funded debt. Jefferson's system, on the other hand, turned on commercial liberation, alliance with France, and the progress of democratic revolution abroad. His commitment to the French Revolution was more than philosophical. The American experiment was still precarious; buffeted on treacherous seas with no friend in sight but France, vulnerable to every "monarchical" breeze, its future depended on the outcome of the struggle for liberty in the Atlantic world.

But Jefferson's quarrel with Hamilton went beyond foreign policy. The New Yorker's measures to fund the debt, establish a national bank, and subsidize manufactures enriched the few at the expense of the many, excited speculation and fraud, corrupted the Congress, and broke down the restraints of the Constitution. Not only was it a system of privilege; Jefferson associated it with counter-revolutionary opinions he heard from Hamilton and his friends—the very speculators in funded debt and bank stock—and even from the Vice President, John Adams. To combat these tendencies, which he labeled "Anglican" and "monarchical," Jefferson silently cooperated with the incipient party opposition in Congress. In 1791 he helped to persuade Philip Freneau to come to the capital in Philadelphia to edit a national newspaper devoted to republicanism. The feathers were soon flying between Freneau's *National Gazette* and John Fenno's administration mouthpiece, *The Gazette of the United States*. As the party division between Federalists and Republicans took form in Congress and the press, Jefferson was publicly denounced by Hamilton and company as the "generalissimo" of the Republicans and the real enemy of the administration he pretended to serve. His role was not an easy one—a Janus in the cabinet according to the Hamiltonians—and but for his loyalty to President Washington he would have resigned his office.

War between France and Britain in 1793 menaced American peace and polarized the parties between the belligerents. Hamilton, in the cabinet, took a high tone toward the new French republic, holding that the death of the Bourbon monarchy negated the Franco–American alliance. Jefferson sustained the alliance both on the authority of international law and on his own novel test of the legitimacy of a foreign government: "the will of the nation substantially declared." The President sided with Jefferson on this issue, but his Proclamation of Neutrality seemed to play into Hamilton's hand. Jefferson acquiesced, grudgingly, then attempted to use the policy to force concessions from Britain and improve the French alliance. Again checked by Hamilton, he was further embarrassed by the firebrand French minister, Edmond Genêt, whose warlike antics spoiled everything. To preserve peace, and to preserve the Republican party from the recoil of the threatened explosion, Jefferson was forced to destroy Genêt. Successful in this, he also deftly restored Britain as the chief enemy of American neutrality before leaving the government at the year's end. Yet the deterioration of Franco–American relations did irreparable damage to his political system, and John Jay's treaty with Britain a year later would complete the Federalist triumph.

"My farm, my family and my books call me to them irresistibly," Jefferson wrote upon his retirement; nor did he expect to be called from them again. From his little mountain he portrayed himself as a plain farmer, a patriarch among his children, reading not a single newspaper, and while still capable of feeling outrage against the enemies of liberty, "preferring infinitely to contemplate the tranquil growth of my lucerne and potatoes." As before, however, the pastoral idyll he had envisioned eluded his grasp, and he yielded in 1796 to pressures drawing him back into the political inferno. The Republicans made him their presidential candidate against John Adams. Adams won in a close contest, and Jefferson succeeded him as vice-president, the post he actually preferred at this critical juncture in the nation's affairs. The prolonged partisan battle over the Jay Treaty had, as Henry Adams said, "plunged a sword into the body politic." Cordial to Adams, Jefferson longed for a political truce. But this was not to be. He was thrust into the leadership of the Republican party, and with the publication in May of his year-old letter to Philip Mazzei—a thinly veiled attack on Washington—all the wrath of Federalism descended upon him.

The crisis with France, matured by the British treaty, culminated in the XYZ Affair of 1798. This clumsy attempt by agents of Foreign Minister Talleyrand to extort money from the American envoys sent to negotiate for peace drove the administration toward war. In the enveloping hysteria Jefferson made the best excuses he could for France and rallied the battered Republicans in opposition to the Federalist "war system." Passage of the repressive Alien and Sedition Acts convinced him that the Federalists aimed under the smokescreen of war to annihilate the Republican party. The Alien Law provided for the summary deportation of undesirable aliens—Frenchmen and

Irishmen in Republican ranks—while the Sedition Law punished false, scandalous, or malicious writing against the government. Because the Federalists controlled all branches of the government, they had the power, unchecked, to intimidate the press and clog the wheels of public opinion. The first Amendment and all the restraints of the Constitution were of little account. The only salvation, Jefferson reluctantly concluded, lay in the intervention of the state authorities.

Thus it was that Jefferson secretly drafted the Kentucky Resolutions of 1798. They advanced the theory of the Union as a compact among the several states, declared the Alien and Sedition Laws unconstitutional, and prescribed the remedy of "nullification" (Jefferson's word, omitted by Kentucky) for such usurpations by the national government. The Virginia assembly adopted similar resolutions drafted by Madison. Whatever the later significance of the Virginia and Kentucky Resolutions for the issue of state rights and union—the constitutional issue on which the Civil War would be fought—they originated in a desperate struggle for political survival and addressed the fundamental issue of freedom and self-government descending from the American Revolution. Without forcing repeal of the repressive laws—and the Sedition Law was widely enforced—the Resolutions of '98 contributed to the rising public clamor against the administration that led to its defeat at the polls in 1800.

The election of 1800 was the first national contest between organized political parties. Around Jefferson, "the man of the people," the Republicans achieved unprecedented unity of action and feeling. They exploited the popular reaction against the "quasi war" with its standing army, debts and taxes, delusions and persecutions. The Federalists, badly split between Adams, who had finally made peace with France, and the warmongering Hamiltonians, united in vilifying Jefferson as a hard-hearted infidel, Jacobin incendiary, visionary, demagogue, and enemy of Washington, the Constitution, and the

Union. While personally hurt by this smear campaign, Jefferson nursed his wounds in private. He had long since learned that for every libel put down another rose in its place; besides, he was committed to the widest latitude of public discussion on the principle he would state in the First Inaugural Address: "that error of opinion may be tolerated where reason is left free to combat it." Jefferson defeated Adams by a comfortable margin. However, his running mate, Aaron Burr, received an equal number of electoral votes, which threw the final decision into the House of Representatives. (The Twelfth Amendment had yet to be enacted.) There the lame-duck Federalist majority, defiant to the end, supported Burr. Only after thirty-six ballots was Jefferson elected.

Inaugurated in Washington, the embryo capital on the Potomac he had himself helped to plan, Jefferson wished to quiet the political turbulence of the past decade and introduce into government that serene and noiseless course which, he said, was the mark of a society going along in happiness. His inaugural address—a political touchstone for a century to come—combined a lofty appeal for the restoration of harmony and affection with a brilliant summation of the Republican creed. Its meaning was double. Jefferson hoped to convert the mass of Federalists to Republicanism, thereby making the party virtually identical with the nation. For this reason he planned to limit removals of Federalist officeholders to exceptional cases. Even when partisan pressures forced him to revise this strategy, as he explained in reply to the New Haven Remonstrance, moderation characterized his course.

But conciliation did not exclude reform. Interpreting his election as "the revolution of 1800," Jefferson aimed to dethrone "tory" politics, elitist, privileged, distrustful of the people, centralizing and monarchical in tendency, and to restore the "whig" principles of 1776. Under his leadership the Republicans revived freedom of the press, returned the naturalization law to five years (Federalists had raised it to fourteen), drastically reduced the army and

navy (despite a successful war on Barbary piracy), repealed the partisan Judiciary Act of 1801, abolished internal
taxes, replaced courtly forms and ceremonies with "Jeffersonian simplicity," and began planned retirement of the
swollen debt in sixteen years. Contracting the means with
the powers of government, Jefferson set his administration
on the track of peace and freedom. Yet he did not dis-
mantle all the machinery of his predecessors. The judiciary,
a Federalist stronghold, was contained and intimidated
but not reformed—a matter of some regret to Jefferson in
later years. He prudently tolerated Hamilton's bank. "It
mortifies me to be strengthening principles which I
deem radically vicious, but the vice is entailed by the first
error," he said, adding philosophically, "What is practicable must often control pure theory." He pleased neither
the purists in his own party nor the madcap Federalists.
But the mass of the nation approved his leadership, and he
was overwhelmingly re-elected in 1804, only Connecticut
and Delaware voting against him.

Jefferson's greatest triumph, and his greatest defeat,
came in foreign affairs. The clouds of war were lifting in
1801, and Jefferson dared to hope that the American Republic, now securely anchored on its Atlantic shore, need
no longer concern itself with Europe. The French Revolution was dead, assassinated by "the beast" Napoleon. So,
too, was the old alliance. And Jefferson looked to a foreign
policy that was detached, evenhanded, and free of subservience. Immediately "the embryo of a tornado" appeared
on the western horizon. Spain's retrocession of Louisiana
and the great port of New Orleans to France threatened
American peace. Louisiana in the hands of Spain was one
thing, but Louisiana, perhaps the Floridas too, for this was
suspected, in the hands of France was quite another,
signaling the rebirth under Napoleonic auspices of French
empire in the New World. For two years Jefferson and
Madison, his able Secretary of State, skillfully negotiated
the crisis. The purchase treaty was signed in Paris on May
2, 1803. It was not exactly the bargain Jefferson had sought.

It included the whole of Louisiana but not the Floridas, which remained Spanish, for a price of under fifteen million dollars. Doubtless the Louisiana Purchase owed more to the vagaries of Napoleon's ambition than to Jefferson's diplomacy. Still it could not be denied that he had made the right calculations from the beginning. He had correctly weighed the imponderables of the European balance of power, shrewdly threatened to throw his weight into the British scale, anticipated the rebel blacks' decimation of French armies in Santo Domingo, gauged the effect of renewed war in Europe on Napoleon's imperial design, and prepared to take advantage of the *démarche* when it came. Altogether it was an impressive vindication of the ways of peace in American diplomacy.

The Louisiana Purchase altered the timetable of American expansion but not its destination. Long before the treaty was signed Jefferson had planned an expedition to the sources of the Missouri River and westward to the Pacific. Conceived primarily for scientific and commercial objects, the Lewis and Clark Expedition assumed greater importance with the acquisition of Louisiana. The addition of some 820,000 square miles to the American Union, almost doubling its size, presented a host of problems to the President. Did the Constitution allow it? He thought not and drafted an amendment to sanction the acquisition, then buried it on congressional pleas of expediency. A revolution in the Union perforce became a revolution in the Constitution as well. What should be done with this distant land? Jefferson proposed to limit settlement to the lower part, "lock up" the rest, and turn it into an Indian reserve to which the eastern tribes, pressed for their lands, might remove. Jeffersonian policy had always looked to the civilization and amalgamation of the Indians; now they were invited to renew the hunt and the chase beyond the Mississippi. How was the "foreign" populace of lower Louisiana to be governed? Jefferson thought the territory should be Americanized demographically and in its laws and institutions before admission into the estate of self-government and partnership in the Union. Only after the western conspiracy of Aaron Burr was crushed in 1807 could he feel confident that the expanded nation would mature in common freedom and union. Finally, what were the boundaries of Louisiana? No one knew. Making the most of the obscurity, Jefferson put in a claim to West Florida, and he offered Spain two million dollars and half of Texas, also claimed, for East Florida. He got neither, in the process expending much of his diplomatic capital abroad and opening himself to attack at home for the next five years.

Jefferson's first term was such a success that he seemed almost to enjoy the "splendid misery" of the Presidency. A self-congratulatory tone pervaded his Second Inaugural Address. His "experiment" in unlimited freedom of public discussion had been proved, he said, for truth and reason had triumphed over defamation and falsehood. He noted the progress toward retirement of the debt and looked forward to the day when the federal revenues might be applied to internal improvements, later detailed in his Sixth Annual Message to Congress. Playfully, by metaphorical analogy to Indian savages, Jefferson rebuked ancestor-worshiping Federalists who had dared to call him "visionary" and dismiss his doctrines as "philosophism." He repeatedly complained in private that affairs of state left him little time for philosophy. Perhaps, but his letters still burst with ideas and his busy dinner table at the White House was a perpetual feast of philosophical conversation. Throughout these years, indeed from 1797 to 1815, he was also President of the American Philosophical Society, the citadel of the American Enlightenment; thus the first magistracy of the nation's government and the first magistracy of the nation's science were combined in one person. He continued his scientific exchanges with European savants, in fact would not permit this traffic in knowledge to be interrupted even when his own embargo law later prohibited anything to leave the country. Except in paleontology, Jefferson's scholarly contributions were modest, but he lent great prestige and encouragement to American science in its infancy.

Jefferson's second term was less a triumph than an ordeal. His method of working with Congress through unofficial channels of personal and party leadership broke down. The Republicans began to quarrel among themselves, and the Federalists grew more desperate as their numbers shrank. The Burr Conspiracy made Jefferson angry, so angry that he almost turned the ensuing trial for treason into a personal vendetta against Burr and the presiding judge John Marshall. But his heaviest burden was in foreign affairs. With the formation of the Third Coalition against Napoleon in 1805, all Europe was ablaze. The United States became the last neutral of consequence. Each side, the French and the British, demanded American trade on its own terms, and neither feared war with the country whose President boasted "peace is my passion" and who had neither army nor navy to speak of. In Jefferson's eyes Britain was the chief aggressor. She impressed thousands of American seamen into her service, thereby assaulting the very existence of American nationality. Her ships infested American waters and plundered American trade, not, Jefferson was convinced, to cut off supplies from Britain's enemies, which she herself supplied, but to destroy a dangerous rival in the Atlantic trade. American diplomatic initiative to settle these issues of "neutral trade and seamen's rights" failed. The inflammatory *Chesapeake-Leopard* affair followed in June 1807. The arrogance and brutality of the HMS *Leopard*'s attack on the American frigate united the country against Britain. War awaited only Jefferson's signal. But he cooled the crisis and attempted to use it as a lever in further negotiations, to no avail. New orders in council in the fall closed the entire continent to American carriers except on monopolistic British terms. Napoleon reciprocated by extending his Berlin Decree to the Americans. Between the Emperor's Continental System and the British orders, American commerce was caught in a vise—a maniacal war of blockades—

from which there seemed to be no appeal to reason or justice.

Thus it was that Jefferson proposed and Congress legislated on December 22, 1807, the embargo of American commerce and navigation. More than an alternative to war, this most ambitious act of Jeffersonian statecraft was an experiment to test the effectiveness of "peaceable coercion" in international disputes. Jefferson had long felt that the United States might, by withholding its commerce and closing its markets (a nonimportation act was also put in force) exact justice from European powers, especially Britain. He labored like Sisyphus to enforce the embargo, stretching the capacities of the government to the limit—in time beyond the constitutional limits he had always advocated. While not without effect abroad, the privations and the discontents produced by the law at home proved more compelling. Finally, in the waning hours of Jefferson's Presidency, the embargo was repealed. The sequel, eventually, was the War of 1812. Jefferson always believed that this unhappy outcome would have been avoided if the nation had shown the unity and the courage to persevere in the embargo. He may have erred in this judgment; if so, it was the error of a statesman who hoped for too much from mankind.

The lives of most great men in retirement merit little more than a footnote on the page of history, but Jefferson's seventeen years' retirement at Monticello is almost a life story in itself. Monticello was not just a home; it was a monument. (It was a museum, too: the walls hung with New World curiosities and some fifty paintings, most of them acquired in Europe, which, with the sculptures, constituted one of the largest art collections in the United States.) Men came from far and near, the great and the ordinary, to see the Sage of Monticello. His daughter Martha managed the household filled with adoring grandchildren. "My mornings are devoted to correspondence," he wrote in 1810. "From breakfast to dinner [mid-afternoon], I am in my shops, my garden, or on horseback among my farms; from dinner to dark, I give to society and recreation with my neighbors and friends; and from candle light to early bed-time, I read." Books were the essential nutriment of his mind—he could not live without them. He sold his great library of more than six thousand volumes to Congress in 1815, where it became the nucleus of the Library of Congress; he then at once commenced another. His correspondence was immense. Deluged with letters seeking his views on subjects as varied as Indian languages, hopper-boys, Plato, and the Bible, Jefferson could neither turn aside these appeals nor resist their intellectual challenge, with the result that what was a daily drudgery for him remains an unfailing delight to posterity. Its best fruit was the correspondence with John Adams, the Revolutionary comrade with whom he was reunited in friendship in 1812.

Jefferson's thinking about religion had found expression almost entirely in writings on religious freedom. Sometime before his death, however, he completed a task begun in 1803 (in a letter to Dr. Benjamin Rush) and which has since become widely known as the Jefferson Bible. Through a rough sort of New Testament criticism, he attempted to identify the *real* teachings of Jesus amid the Platonized corruptions of the priests and theologians. In his youth he had gone to the ancients for moral instruction; now, in the ripeness of years, after penetrating the fog of supernaturalism, Jefferson concluded that the plain, unsophisticated teachings of Jesus made the best of all moral systems. He called his bible distilled from the gospels "The Life and Morals of Jesus of Nazareth," and offered it as proof that he whom the priests and Pharisees called infidel was "a true Christian" in the only sense that mattered, the love of man taught by Jesus. Of course, religion belonging wholly to the private conscience, Jefferson disdained public profession and disapproved proselytization. The work was intended for himself, his family, and his dearest friends. But clearly he was on the track of a unifying religion of humanity, morally earnest but stripped of supernaturalism, of which he saw anticipations in Unitarianism.

Several items of unfinished business from the Revolution claimed Jefferson's attention. He again championed reform of the Virginia constitution. But this would come only after his death. As for emancipation of the slaves, it would not come at all, short of the catastrophe he increasingly feared. The younger generation to whom he had committed this cause showed no more willingness to assume it than had the fathers. In the end, though he adhered to his Revolutionary plan of gradual emancipation with the conditions of compensation and colonization, Jefferson seemed to despair of any solution.

The cause to which he gave himself in his old age was public education. In 1814 he revived his general plan of education. Again the legislature rejected the plan, though it approved one part, the state university. Jefferson wondered at the folly of raising the apex of the pyramid before laying the foundations in the primary and secondary schools. As he wrote, "it is safer to have the whole people respectably enlightened than a few in a high state of science and the many in ignorance. This last is the most dangerous state in which a nation can be. The nations and governments of Europe are so many proofs of it." Nonetheless, Jefferson rejoiced in the university. He had become associated with a local group seeking to found an academy in Charlottesville. Taking hold of the project, he at once escalated the academy into a college, Central College, chartered in 1816, and then escalated this private college into the University of Virginia, chartered in 1819. He was the master builder of the university in all its parts. His design of an "academical village" was strikingly original, marvelously attuned to his purpose, and beautifully executed in brick and mortar and wood under his constant care. He sent abroad for the faculty, formed the curriculum, acquired the library, and attended to literally hundreds of small details. Secular and modern in conception, raised against massive obstacles—legislative parsimony, sectarian fanaticism, and public indifference—the University of Virginia finally opened its doors a year before Jefferson's death. When it came time for him to write his epitaph, it was one of the three achievements, along with the Declaration of Independence and the Virginia Statute of Religious Freedom, for which he wished to be remembered.

The serenity and optimism that were so much a part of Jefferson's personality took some punishing blows during his declining years. He was deeply troubled by the course of national affairs. The Missouri Compromise "fanaticized" politics on a sectional line, dividing free and slave states; the Supreme Court became "a subtle corps of sappers and miners" of the Constitution; and the drift toward consolidation—national bank, national internal improvements, protective tariff—menaced individual liberty and the federal balance on which the Union depended. Jefferson retreated to the safety of the "principles of '98" and gave aid and comfort to the revival of state-rights politics in Virginia. At the same time, his personal fortune was doomed. Years of embargo, nonintercourse, and war had crippled all Virginia agriculture, and recovery had only begun when the Panic of 1819 struck. The panic piled new debts upon old, some descending from before the Revolution, and sank Jefferson into bankruptcy. In the end not even Monticello could be saved from the wreckage.

Jefferson died at Monticello on the fiftieth anniversary of American independence, July 4, 1826. It almost seemed that he had appointed the hour of death to embellish his legend. Posterity would remember him, not always with affection, less for himself than for what he stood for politically. Among the nation's founders he above all others was identified with the destiny of democracy. Through the generations his name, his principles and ideals were implicated in the successive crises of the democratic experiment. Indeed, in retrospect American history has sometimes seemed little more than a protracted litigation

—hearings, negotiations, trials, and appeals in endless number—on Thomas Jefferson. He was a great rhetorician
and would survive more on the spiritual capital of his
words than on the tangible rewards of his work. Because
he never codified his thought but let stand the existential
record of "man thinking" in all its shapes and hues, it has
been easy for men of different persuasions to seize upon
some fragment, eminently quotable, and impute to it the
character of the whole. So it is that Jeffersonian political
craft have sailed under many colors: Democracy, State
Rights, Agrarianism, Anti-Statism, Civil Libertarianism,
Isolationism, One Worldism, Welfare Statism. None of
these flags is entirely fraudulent. Yet the rage surrounding
the political symbol has tended to obscure the unity and
balance and civilizing thrust which Jefferson's life, like his
buildings, actually had. As Woodrow Wilson once said,
"It is the spirit, not the tenets of the man, by which he
rules us from his urn." That spirit is freedom, not alone in
its political references but in all that concerns the questing
human spirit. When so many of Jefferson's political tenets
have fallen into disuse before the march of history, the
dominant motif of his life remains valid and challenges
understanding in all the avenues of his thought and
imagination.

A Note on the Selections

Weighed in the balance with the vast corpus of Jefferson's writings, those published during his lifetime were but a small portion. Both *A Summary View of the Rights of British America*, his first published work, and *Notes on the State of Virginia* appear in this volume. Other American imprints entirely of Jefferson's authorship include *A Manual of Parliamentary Practice* (Washington, 1801), still in use in the United States Senate, and a lengthy law argument with the short title, *Proceedings in the Government of the United States in Maintaining the Public Right to the Beach of the Mississippi* (New York, 1812). His most important scientific paper is "A Memoir on the Discovery of Certain Bones of a Quadruped of the Clawed Kind in the Western Parts of Virginia," American Philosophical Society *Transactions*, v. IV (Philadelphia, 1799). The *Report of the Committee of Revisors* (Richmond, 1784), largely Jefferson's work, was prepared in collaboration with George Wythe and Edmund Pendleton. Jefferson often contributed to the work of others, for instance *Essai sur les États-Unis* (Paris, 1786) prepared by Jean Nicolas Démeunier for the *Encyclopédie Méthodique*. His biography of Meriwether Lewis appeared in the *History of the Expedition under the Command of Captains Lewis and Clark . . .* (Philadelphia, 1814). Of course, letters of Jefferson's authorship often found their way into the press, and his numerous state papers were printed in both official and unofficial versions. Among the more important of Jefferson's writings published since his death are the

Autobiography, a brief chronicle of his early career, written in 1821; *Essay on Anglo-Saxon Grammar*, first published by the University of Virginia in 1851; and *The Life and Morals of Jesus of Nazareth*, first published in 1902 and printed by the United States Congress in 1904. The first collected edition of his writings, *The Memoirs, Correspondence and Private Papers of Thomas Jefferson*, appeared in four volumes in 1829.

Except for the *Notes on Virginia*, most of the selections that follow have been taken from the three principal editions of Jefferson's writings. These are Paul L. Ford, *The Writings of Thomas Jefferson*, 10 vols. (New York, 1892–99); A. A. Lipscomb and A. E. Bergh, *The Writings of Thomas Jefferson*, 20 vols. (Washington, 1903); and Julian P. Boyd and others, *The Papers of Thomas Jefferson*, 18 vols. to date (Princeton, 1950–72). The Boyd edition is definitive, and I have relied upon it as far as it goes, to March 1791, the terminal date of the last published volume. The Ford edition is generally more reliable but less complete than the Lipscomb and Bergh, so while I have given preference to the former, I have selected from the latter as well.

The section "Public Papers and Addresses" includes writings of considerable range and variety, from Jefferson's most famous state papers to things he might have judged ephemeral. No American statesman of the time drafted as much legislation, wrote as many reports and memoranda, or contributed as much to the public record as Jefferson. The artists who have portrayed him with pen in hand have not been mistaken. In addition to the monuments, which select themselves, I have chosen papers that have historical or philosophical importance and yet should be comprehensible to the general reader without technical guidance beyond that supplied in the Introduction. On this rule of exclusion certain papers of a highly specialized nature have been omitted, for example *Observations on the Whale Fishery* (1788), the Report on Weights and Measures (1790), and the Report on Commerce (1793). The category "public" as applied to Jefferson's writings is far from exact. His little address to his neighbors on accepting the post of Secretary of State does not strictly merit this designation, while some of his letters clearly do. In these matters I beg the reader's indulgence.

Jefferson expressed himself primarily through his letters. The personal letter was his genre. Many of his letters are in effect essays and should be read as such. To select a mere handful of letters from the mass that he wrote has been exceedingly difficult. It is an embarrassment of riches. I have tried to make a balanced selection of letters possessing significant intellectual content, literary excellence, and transcendent human interest. Several of these have not previously been published and are taken directly from the manuscript copies in the Library of Congress collection of Jefferson's papers. Collectively, the letters accurately portray Jefferson as "a man for all seasons," yet no claim can be made that every phase of his experience or every facet of his mind is represented. I have avoided short extracts despite the temptation to sift out the axioms and aphorisms that appear like nuggets in the ore of Jefferson's writings. And I have excluded letters judged to be incomprehensible without labored historical or biographical explanation.

Editing has been kept to the minimum compatible with the objectives of the volume. Ellipses have been used where merely personal or extraneous parts of letters have been omitted. Where I have resorted to extracts, as with Jefferson's executive messages to Congress, this is clearly indicated. Different editors have followed different practices with respect to modernization of spelling and punctuation in Jefferson's writings. I have allowed these variations, which will scarcely be noticed by the general reader, to stand.

I

*A Summary View
of the Rights of
British America*

A Summary View
of the Rights of British America[1]

[*July 1774*]

RESOLVED that it be an instruction to the said deputies when assembled in General Congress with the deputies from the other states of British America to propose to the said Congress that an humble and dutiful address be presented to his majesty begging leave to lay before him as chief magistrate of the British empire the united complaints of his majesty's subjects in America; complaints which are excited by many unwarrantable incroachments and usurpations, attempted to be made by the legislature of one part of the empire, upon those rights which god and the laws have given equally and independently to all. To represent to his majesty that these his states have often individually made humble application to his imperial throne, to obtain thro' it's intervention some redress of their injured rights; to none of which was ever even an answer condescended. Humbly to hope that this their joint address, penned in the language of

[1] The text is from a manuscript based upon Jefferson's draft. It varies slightly from the pamphlet published in Williamsburg in 1774 and reprinted in both Philadelphia and London before the end of the year. The full title of the pamphlet is *A Summary View of the Rights of British America. Set Forth in Some Resolutions Intended for the Inspection of the Present Delegates of the People of Virginia. Now in Convention.* It is ascribed to "A Native, and Member of the House of Burgesses." Marginal glosses on the manuscript have been omitted. [Ed.]

truth, and divested of those expressions of servility which would persuade his majesty that we are asking favors and not rights, shall obtain from his majesty a more respectful acceptance. And this his majesty will think we have reason to expect when he reflects that he is no more than the chief officer of the people, appointed by the laws, and circumscribed with definite powers, to assist in working the great machine of government erected for their use, and consequently subject to their superintendance. And in order that these our rights, as well as the invasions of them, may be laid more fully before his majesty, to take a view of them from the origin and first settlement of these countries.

To remind him that our ancestors, before their emigration to America, were the free inhabitants of the British dominions in Europe, and possessed a right, which nature has given to all men, of departing from the country in which chance, not choice has placed them, of going in quest of new habitations, and of there establishing new societies, under such laws and regulations as to them shall seem most likely to promote public happiness. That their Saxon ancestors had under this universal law, in like manner, left their native wilds and woods in the North of Europe, had possessed themselves of the island of Britain then less charged with inhabitants, and had established there that system of laws which has so long been the glory and protection of that country. Nor was ever any claim of superiority or dependance asserted over them by that mother country from which they had migrated: and were such a claim made it is beleived his majesty's subjects in Great Britain have too firm a feeling of the rights derived to them from their ancestors to bow down the sovereignty of their state before such visionary pretensions. And it is thought that no circumstance has occurred to distinguish materially the British from the Saxon emigration. America was conquered, and her settlements made and firmly established, at the expence of individuals, and not of the British public. Their own blood was spilt in acquiring lands for their settlement, their own fortunes expended in making that settlement effectual. For themselves they fought, for themselves they conquered, and for themselves alone they have right to hold. No shilling was ever issued from the public treasures of his majesty or his ancestors for their assistance, till of very late times, after the colonies had become established on a firm and permanent footing. That then indeed, having become valuable to Great Britain for her commercial purposes, his parliament was pleased to lend them assistance against an enemy who would fain have drawn to herself the benefits of their commerce to the great aggrandisement of herself and danger of Great Britain. Such assistance, and in such circumstances, they had often before given to Portugal and other allied states, with whom they carry on a commercial intercourse. Yet these states never supposed that, by calling in her aid, they thereby submitted themselves to her sovereignty. Had such terms been proposed, they would have rejected them with disdain, and trusted for better to the moderation of their enemies, or to a vigorous exertion of their own force. We do not however mean to underrate those aids, which to us were doubtless valuable, on whatever principles granted: but we would shew that they cannot give a title to that authority which the British parliament would arrogate over us; and that they may amply be repaid, by our giving to the inhabitants of Great Britain such exclusive privileges in trade as may be advantageous to them, and at the same time not too restrictive to ourselves. That settlements having been thus effected in the wilds of America, the emigrants thought proper to adopt that system of laws under which they had hitherto lived in the mother country, and to continue their union with her by submitting themselves to the same common sovereign, who was thereby made the central link connecting the several parts of the empire thus newly multiplied.

But that not long were they permitted, however far they thought themselves removed from the hand of oppression, to hold undisturbed the rights thus acquired at the hazard of their lives and loss of their fortunes. A family of princes was then on the British throne, whose treasonable crimes against their people brought on them afterwards the exertion of those sacred and sovereign rights of punishment, reserved in the hands of the people for cases of extreme necessity, and judged by the constitution unsafe to be delegated to any other judicature. While every day brought forth some new and unjustifiable exertion of power over their subjects on that side the water, it was not to be expected that those here, much less able at that time to oppose the designs of despotism, should be exempted from injury. Accordingly that country which had been acquired by the lives, the labors and the fortunes of individual adventurers, was by these princes at several times parted out and distributed among the favorites and followers of their fortunes; and by an assumed right of the crown alone were erected into distinct and independent governments; a measure which it is beleived his majesty's prudence and understanding would prevent him from imitating at this day; as no exercise of such a power of dividing and dismembering a country has ever occurred in his majesty's realm of England, tho' now of very antient standing; nor could it be justified or acquiesced under there or in any other part of his majesty's empire.

That the exercise of a free trade with all parts of the world, possessed by the American colonists as of natural right, and which no law of their own had taken away or abridged, was next the object of unjust incroachment. Some of the colonies having thought proper to continue the administration of their government in the name and under the authority of his majesty king Charles the first, whom notwithstanding his late deposition by the Commonwealth of England, they continued in the sovereignty of their state, the Parliament for the Common-wealth took the same in high offence, and assumed upon themselves the power of prohibiting their trade with all other parts of the world except the island of Great Britain. This arbitrary act however they soon recalled, and by solemn treaty entered into on the 12th. day of March 1651, between the said Commonwealth by their Commissioners and the colony of Virginia by their house of Burgesses, it was expressly stipulated by the 8th. article of the said treaty that they should have 'free trade as the people of England do enjoy to all places and with all nations according to the laws of that Commonwealth.' But that, upon the restoration of his majesty King Charles the second, their rights of free commerce fell once more a victim to arbitrary power: and by several acts of his reign as well as of some of his successors the trade of the colonies was laid under such restrictions as shew what hopes they might form from the justice of a British parliament were its uncontrouled power admitted over these states. History has informed us that bodies of men as well as individuals are susceptible of the spirit of tyranny. A view of these acts of parliament for regulation, as it has been affectedly called, of the American trade, if all other evidence were removed out of the case, would undeniably evince the truth of this observation. Besides the duties they impose on our articles of export and import, they prohibit our going to any Markets Northward of cape Finesterra in the kingdom of Spain for the sale of commodities which Great Britain will not take from us, and for the purchase of others with which she cannot supply us; and that for no other than the arbitrary purpose of purchasing for themselves by a sacrifice of our rights and interests, certain privileges in their commerce with an allied state, who, in confidence that their exclusive trade with America will be continued while the principles and power of the British parliament be the same, have induldged themselves in every exorbitance which their avarice could dictate, or our necessities extort: have raised their commodities called for in America to the double and treble of what they sold for before such exclusive privileges were given them, and of what better commodities of the same kind would cost us elsewhere; and at the same time give us much less for what we carry thither, than might be had at more convenient ports. That these acts prohibit us from carrying in quest of other purchasers the surplus of our tobaccoes remaining after the consumption of Great Britain is supplied: so that we must leave them with the British merchant for whatever he will please to allow us, to be by him reshipped to foreign markets, where he will reap the benefits of making sale of them for full value. That to heighten still the idea of parliamentary justice, and to shew with what moderation they are like to exercise power, where themselves are to feel no part of it's weight, we take leave to mention to his majesty certain other acts of British parliament, by which they would prohibit us from manufacturing for our own use the articles we raise on our own lands with our own labor. By an act passed in the 5th. year of the reign of his late majesty king George the second an American subject is forbidden to make a hat for himself of the fur which he has taken perhaps on his own soil. An instance of despotism to which no parrallel can be produced in the most arbitrary ages of British history. By one other act passed in the 23d. year of the same reign, the iron which we make we are forbidden to manufacture; and, heavy as that article is, and necessary in every branch of husbandry, besides commission and insurance, we are to pay freight for it to Great Britain, and freight for it back again, for the purpose of supporting, not men, but machines, in the island of Great Britain. In the same spirit of equal and impartial legislation is to be viewed the act of parliament passed in the 5th. year of the same reign, by which American lands are made subject to the demands of British creditors, while their own lands were still continued unanswerable for their debts; from which one of these conclusions must necessarily follow, either that justice is not the same thing in America as in Britain, or else that the British parliament pay less regard to it here than there. But that we do not point out to his majesty the injustice of these acts with intent to rest on that principle the cause of their nullity, but to shew that experience confirms the propriety of those political principles which exempt us from the jurisdiction of the British parliament. The true ground on which we declare these acts void is that the British parliament has no right to exercise authority over us.

That these exercises of usurped power have not been confined to instances alone in which themselves were interested; but they have also intermeddled with the regulation of the internal affairs of the colonies. The act of the 9th. of Anne for establishing a post office in America seems to have had little connection with British convenience, except that of accomodating his majesty's ministers and favorites with the sale of a lucrative and easy office.

That thus have we hastened thro' the reigns which preceded his majesty's, during which the violation of our rights were less alarming, because repeated at more distant intervals, than that rapid and bold succession of injuries which is likely to distinguish the present from all other periods of American story. Scarcely have our minds been able to emerge from the astonishment into which one stroke of parliamentary thunder has involved us, before another more heavy and more alarming is fallen on us. Single acts of tyranny may be ascribed to the accidental opinion of a day; but a series of oppressions, begun at a distinguished period, and pursued unalterably thro' every change of ministers, too plainly prove a deliberate, systematical plan of reducing us to slavery.

That the act passed in the 4th. year of his majesty's reign intitled 'an act [for granting certain duties],'[2] one other act passed in the 5th. year of his reign intitled 'an act [for applying certain stamp duties],' one other act passed in the 6th. year of his reign intitled 'an act [declaring the right of Parliament over the colonies],' and one other act passed in the 7th, year of his reign intitled 'an act [for granting duties on paper, tea, etc.]' form that connected chain of parliamentary usurpation which has already been the sub-

[2] The brackets in this section are mine. [Ed.]

ject of frequent applications to his majesty and the houses of Lords and Commons of Great Britain; and, no answers having yet been condescended to any of these, we shall not trouble his majesty with a repetition of the matters they contained.

But that one other act passed in the same 7th. year of his reign, having been a peculiar attempt, must ever require peculiar mention. It is intitled 'an act [suspending the legislature of New York].' One free and independent legislature hereby takes upon itself to suspend the powers of another, free and independent as itself, thus exhibiting a phaenomenon, unknown in nature, the creator and creature of it's own power. Not only the principles of common sense, but the common feelings of human nature must be surrendered up, before his majesty's subjects here can be persuaded to believe that they hold their political existence at the will of a British parliament. Shall these governments be dissolved, their property annihilated, and their people reduced to a state of nature, at the imperious breath of a body of men whom they never saw, in whom they never confided, and over whom they have no powers of punishment or removal, let their crimes against the American public be ever so great? Can any one reason be assigned why 160,000 electors in the island of Great Britain should give law to four millions in the states of America, every individual of whom is equal to every individual of them in virtue, in understanding, and in bodily strength? Were this to be admitted, instead of being a free people, as we have hitherto supposed, and mean to continue, ourselves, we should suddenly be found the slaves, not of one, but of 160,000 tyrants, distinguished too from all others by this singular circumstance that they are removed from the reach of fear, the only restraining motive which may hold the hand of a tyrant.

That by 'an act to discontinue in such manner and for such time as are therein mentioned the landing and discharging lading or shipping of goods wares and merchandize at the town and within the harbor of Boston in the province of Massachusett's bay in North America' which was passed at the last session of British parliament, a large and populous town, whose trade was their sole subsistence, was deprived of that trade, and involved in utter ruin. Let us for a while suppose the question of right suspended, in order to examine this act on principles of justice. An act of parliament had been passed imposing duties on teas to be paid in America, against which act the Americans had protested as inauthoritative. The East India company, who till that time had never sent a pound of tea to America on their own account, step forth on that occasion the asserters of parliamentary right, and send hither many ship loads of that obnoxious commodity. The masters of their several vessels however, on their arrival in America, wisely attended to admonition, and returned with their cargoes. In the province of New England alone the remonstrances of the people were disregarded, and a compliance, after being many days waited for, was flatly refused. Whether in this the master of the vessel was governed by his obstinacy or his instructions, let those who know, say. There are extraordinary situations which require extraordinary interposition. An exasperated people, who feel that they possess power, are not easily restrained within limits strictly regular. A number of them assembled in the town of Boston, threw the tea into the ocean and dispersed without doing any other act of violence. If in this they did wrong, they were known, and were amenable to the laws of the land, against which it could not be objected that they had ever in any instance been obstructed or diverted from their regular course in favor of popular offenders. They should therefore not have been distrusted on this occasion. But that ill-fated colony had formerly been bold in their enmities against the house of Stuart, and were now devoted to ruin by that unseen hand which governs the momentous affairs of this great empire. On the partial representations of a few worthless ministerial dependants, whose constant office it has been to keep that government embroiled, and who by their treacheries hope to obtain the dignity of the British knighthood, without calling for a party accused, without asking a proof, without attempting a distinction between the guilty and the innocent, the whole of that antient and wealthy town is in a moment reduced from opulence to beggary. Men who had spent their lives in extending the British commerce, who had invested in that place the wealth their honest endeavors had merited, found themselves and their families thrown at once on the world for subsistence by it's charities. Not the hundredth part of the inhabitants of that town had been concerned in the act complained of; many of them were in Great Britain and in other parts beyond sea; yet all were involved in one indiscriminate ruin, by a new executive power unheard of till then, that of a British parliament. A property of the value of many millions of money was sacrificed to revenge, not repay, the loss of a few thousands. This is administering justice with a heavy hand indeed! And when is this tempest to be arrested in it's course? Two wharfs are to be opened again when his majesty shall think proper: the residue which lined the extensive shores of the bay of Boston are forever interdicted the exercise of commerce. This little exception seems to have been thrown in for no other purpose than that of setting a precedent for investing his majesty with legislative powers. If the pulse of his people shall beat calmly under this experiment, another and another will be tried till the measure of despotism be filled up. It would be an insult on common sense to pretend that this exception was made in order to restore it's commerce to that great town. The trade which cannot be received at two wharfs alone, must of necessity be transferred to some other place; to which it will soon be followed by that of the two wharfs. Considered in this light it would be an insolent and cruel mockery at the annihilation of the town of Boston.

By the act for the suppression of riots and tumults in the town of Boston, passed also in the last session of parliament, a murder committed there is, if the governor pleases, to be tried in the court of King's bench in the island of Great Britain, by a jury of Middlesex. The witnesses too, on receipt of such a sum as the Governor shall think it reasonable for them to expend, are to enter into recognisance to appear at the trial. This is in other words taxing them to the amount of their recognisance; and that amount may be whatever a Governor pleases. For who does his majesty think can be prevailed on to cross the Atlantick for the sole purpose of bearing evidence to a fact? His expences are to be borne indeed as they shall be estimated by a Governor; but who are to feed the wife and children whom he leaves behind, and who have had no other subsistence but his daily labor? Those epidemical disorders too, so terrible in a foreign climate, is the cure of them to be estimated among the articles of expence, and their danger to be warded off by the almighty power of a parliament? And the wretched criminal, if he happen to have offended on the American side, stripped of his privilege of trial by peers, of his vicinage, removed from the place where alone full evidence could be obtained without money, without counsel, without friends, without exculpatory proof, is tried before judges predetermined to condemn. The cowards who would suffer a countryman to be torn from the bowels of their society in order to be thus offered a sacrifice to parliamentary tyranny, would merit that everlasting infamy now fixed on the authors of the act! A clause for a similar purpose had been introduced into an act passed in the 12th. year of his majesty's reign entitled 'an act for the better securing and preserving his majesty's dock-yards, magazines, ships, ammunition and stores,' against which as meriting the same censures the several colonies have already protested.

That these are the acts of power assumed by a body of men foreign to our constitutions, and unacknowledged by our laws; against which we do, on behalf of the inhabitants of British America, enter this our solemn and determined protest. And we do earnestly intreat his majesty, as yet the only mediatory power between the several states of the British empire, to recommend to his parliament of Great Britain the total revocation of these acts, which however nugatory they be, may yet prove the cause of further discontents and jealousies among us.

That we next proceed to consider the conduct of his majesty, as holding the executive powers of the laws of these states, and mark out his deviations from the line of duty. By the constitution of Great Britain as well as of the several American states, his majesty possesses the power of refusing to pass into a law any bill which has already passed the other two branches of legislature. His majesty however and his ancestors, conscious of the impropriety of opposing their single opinion to the united wisdom of two houses of parliament, while their proceedings were unbiassed by interested principles, for several ages past have modestly declined the exercise of this power in that part of his empire called Great Britain. But by change of circumstances, other principles than those of justice simply have obtained an influence on their determinations. The addition of new states to the British empire has produced an addition of new, and sometimes opposite interests. It is now therefore the great office of his majesty to resume the exercise of his negative power, and to prevent the passage of laws by any one legislature of the empire which might bear injuriously on the rights and interests of another. Yet this will not excuse the wanton exercise of this power which we have seen his majesty practice on the laws of the American legislatures. For the most trifling reasons, and sometimes for no conceivable reason at all, his majesty has rejected laws of the most salutary tendency. The abolition of domestic slavery is the great object of desire in those colonies where it was unhappily introduced in their infant state. But previous to the infranchisement of the slaves we have, it is necessary to exclude all further importations from Africa. Yet our repeated attempts to effect this by prohibitions, and by imposing duties which might amount to a prohibition, have been hitherto defeated by his majesty's negative: thus preferring the immediate advantages of a few British corsairs to the lasting interests of the American states, and to the rights of human nature deeply wounded by this infamous practice. Nay the single interposition of an interested individual against a law was scarcely ever known to fail of success, tho' in the opposite scale were placed the interests of a whole country. That this is so shameful an abuse of a power trusted with his majesty for other purposes, as if not reformed would call for some legal restrictions.

With equal inattention to the necessities of his people here, has his majesty permitted our laws to lie neglected in England for years, neither confirming them by his assent, nor annulling them by his negative: so that such of them as have no suspending clause, we hold on the most precarious of all tenures, his majesty's will, and such of them as suspend themselves till his majesty's assent be obtained we have feared might be called into existence at some future and distant period, when time and change of circumstances shall have rendered them destructive to his people here. And to render this grievance still more oppressive, his majesty by his instructions has laid his governors under such restrictions that they can pass no law of any moment unless it have such suspending clause: so that, however immediate may be the call for legislative interposition, the law cannot be executed till it has twice crossed the Atlantic, by which time the evil may have spent it's whole force.

But in what terms reconcileable to majesty and at the same time to truth, shall we speak of a late instruction to his majesty's governor of the colony of Virginia, by which he is forbidden to assent to any law for the division of a county, unless the new county will consent to have no representative in assembly? That colony has as yet affixed no boundary to the Westward. Their Western counties therefore are of indefinite extent. Some of them are actually seated many hundred miles from their Eastern limits. Is it possible then that his majesty can have bestowed a single thought on the situation of those people, who, in order to obtain justice for injuries however great or small, must, by the laws of that colony, attend their county court at such a distance, with all their witnesses, monthly, till their litigation be determined? Or does his majesty seriously wish, and publish it to the world, that his subjects should give up the glorious right of representation, with all the benefits derived from that, and submit themselves the absolute slaves of his sovereign will? Or is it rather meant to confine the legislative body to their present numbers, that they may be the cheaper bargain whenever they shall become worth a purchase?

One of the articles of impeachment against Tresilian and the other judges of Westminster Hall in the reign of Richard the second, for which they suffered death as traitors to their country, was that they had advised the king that he might dissolve his parliament at any time: and succeeding kings have adopted the opinion of these unjust judges. Since the establishment however of the British constitution at the glorious Revolution on it's free and antient principles, neither his majesty nor his ancestors have exercised such a power of dissolution in the island of Great Britain; and when his majesty was petitioned by the united voice of his people there to dissolve the present parliament, who had become obnoxious to them, his ministers were heard to declare in open parliament that his majesty possessed no such power by the constitution. But how different their language and his practice here! To declare as their duty required the known rights of their country, to oppose the usurpation of every foreign judicature, to disregard the imperious mandates of a minister or governor, have been the avowed causes of dissolving houses of representatives in America. But if such powers be really vested in his majesty, can he suppose they are there placed to awe the members from such purposes as these? When the representative body have lost the confidence of their constituents, when they have notoriously made sale of their most valuable rights, when they have assumed to themselves powers which the people never put into their hands, then indeed their continuing in office becomes dangerous to the state, and calls for an exercise of the power of dissolution. Such being the causes for which the representative body should and should not be dissolved, will it not appear strange to an unbiassed observer that that of Great Britain was not dissolved, while those of the colonies have repeatedly incurred that sentence?

But your majesty or your Governors have carried this power beyond every limit known or provided for by the laws. After dissolving one house of representatives, they have refused to call another, so that for a great length of time the legislature provided by the laws has been out of existence. From the nature of things, every society must at all times possess within itself the sovereign powers of legislation. The feelings of human nature revolt against the supposition of a state so situated as that it may not in any emergency provide against dangers which perhaps threaten immediate ruin. While those bodies are in existence to whom the people have delegated the powers of legislation, they alone possess and may exercise those powers. But when they are dissolved by the lopping off one or more of their branches, the power reverts to the people, who may use it to unlimited extent, either assembling together in person, sending deputies, or in any other way they may think proper. We forbear to trace consequences further; the dangers are conspicuous with which this practice is replete.

That we shall at this time also take notice of an error in the nature of our landholdings, which crept in at a very early period of our settlement. The introduction of the Feudal tenures into the kingdom of England, though antient, is well enough understood to set this matter in a proper light. In the earlier ages of the Saxon settlement feudal holdings were certainly altogether unknown, and very few, if any, had been introduced at the time of the

Norman conquest. Our Saxon ancestors held their lands, as they did their personal property, in absolute dominion, disencumbered with any superior, answering nearly to the nature of those possessions which the Feudalists term Allodial: William the Norman first introduced that system generally. The lands which had belonged to those who fell in the battle of Hastings, and in the subsequent insurrections of his reign, formed a considerable proportion of the lands of the whole kingdom. These he granted out, subject to feudal duties, as did he also those of a great number of his new subjects, who by persuasions or threats were induced to surrender them for that purpose. But still much was left in the hands of his Saxon subjects, held of no superior, and not subject to feudal conditions. These therefore by express laws, enacted to render uniform the system of military defence, were made liable to the same military duties as if they had been feuds: and the Norman lawyers soon found means to saddle them also with all the other feudal burthens. But still they had not been surrendered to the king, they were not derived from his grant, and therefore they were not holden of him. A general principle indeed was introduced that 'all lands in England were held either mediately or immediately of the crown': but this was borrowed from those holdings which were truly feudal, and only applied to others for the purposes of illustration. Feudal holdings were therefore but exceptions out of the Saxon laws of possession, under which all lands were held in absolute right. These therefore still form the basis or groundwork of the Common law, to prevail wheresoever the exceptions have not taken place. America was not conquered by William the Norman, nor it's lands surrendered to him or any of his successors. Possessions there are undoubtedly of the Allodial nature. Our ancestors however, who migrated hither, were laborers, not lawyers. The fictitious principle that all lands belong originally to the king, they were early persuaded to beleive real, and accordingly took grants of their own lands from the crown. And while the crown continued to grant for small sums and on reasonable rents, there was no inducement to arrest the error and lay it open to public view. But his majesty has lately taken on him to advance the terms of purchase and of holding to the double of what they were, by which means the acquisition of lands being rendered difficult, the population of our country is likely to be checked. It is time therefore for us to lay this matter before his majesty, and to declare that he has no right to grant lands of himself. From the nature and purpose of civil institutions, all the lands within the limits which any particular society has circumscribed around itself, are assumed by that society, and subject to their allotment only. This may be done by themselves assembled collectively, or by their legislature to whom they may have delegated sovereign authority: and, if they are allotted in neither of these ways, each individual of the society may appropriate to himself such lands as he finds vacant, and occupancy will give him title.

That, in order to inforce the arbitrary measures before complained of, his majesty has from time to time sent among us large bodies of armed forces, not made up of the people here, nor raised by the authority of our laws. Did his majesty possess such a right as this, it might swallow up all our other rights whenever he should think proper. But his majesty has no right to land a single armed man on our shores; and those whom he sends here are liable to our laws for the suppression and punishment of Riots, Routs, and unlawful assemblies, or are hostile bodies invading us in defiance of law. When in the course of the late war it became expedient that a body of Hanoverian troops should be brought over for the defence of Great Britain, his majesty's grandfather, our late sovereign, did not pretend to introduce them under any authority he possessed. Such a measure would have given just alarm to his subjects in Great Britain, whose liberties would not be safe if armed men of another country, and of another spirit, might be brought into the realm at any time without the consent of their legislature. He therefore applied to parliament who passed an act for that purpose, limiting the number to be brought in and the time they were to continue. In like manner is his majesty restrained in every part of the empire. He possesses indeed the executive power of the laws in every state; but they are the laws of the particular state which he is to administer within that state, and not those of any one within the limits of another. Every state must judge for itself the number of armed men which they may safely trust among them, of whom they are to consist, and under what restrictions they are to be laid. To render these proceedings still more criminal against our laws, instead of subjecting the military to the civil power, his majesty has expressly made the civil subordinate to the military. But can his majesty thus put down all law under his feet? Can he erect a power superior to that which erected himself? He has done it indeed by force; but let him remember that force cannot give right.

That these are our grievances which we have thus laid before his majesty with that freedom of language and sentiment which becomes a free people, claiming their rights as derived from the laws of nature, and not as the gift of their chief magistrate. Let those flatter, who fear: it is not an American art. To give praise where it is not due, might be well from the venal, but would ill beseem those who are asserting the rights of human nature. They know, and will therefore say, that kings are the servants, not the proprietors of the people. Open your breast, Sire, to liberal and expanded thought. Let not the name of George the third be a blot in the page of history. You are surrounded by British counsellors, but remember that they are parties. You have no ministers for American affairs, because you have none taken from among us, nor amenable to the laws on which they are to give you advice. It behoves you therefore to think and to act for yourself and your people. The great principles of right and wrong are legible to every reader: to pursue them requires not the aid of many counsellors. The whole art of government consists in the art of being honest. Only aim to do your duty, and mankind will give you credit where you fail. No longer persevere in sacrificing the rights of one part of the empire to the inordinate desires of another: but deal out to all equal and impartial right. Let no act be passed by any one legislature which may infringe on the rights and liberties of another. This is the important post in which fortune has placed you, holding the balance of a great, if a well poised empire. This, Sire, is the advice of your great American council, on the observance of which may perhaps depend your felicity and future fame, and the preservation of that harmony which alone can continue both to Great Britain and America the reciprocal advantages of their connection. It is neither our wish nor our interest to separate from her. We are willing on our part to sacrifice every thing which reason can ask to the restoration of that tranquility for which all must wish. On their part let them be ready to establish union on a generous plan. Let them name their terms, but let them be just. Accept of every commercial preference it is in our power to give for such things as we can raise for their use, or they make for ours. But let them not think to exclude us from going to other markets, to dispose of those commodities which they cannot use, nor to supply those wants which they cannot supply. Still less let it be proposed that our properties within our own territories shall be taxed or regulated by any power on earth but our own. The god who gave us life, gave us liberty at the same time: the hand of force may destroy, but cannot disjoin them. This, Sire, is our last, our determined resolution: and that you will be pleased to interpose with that efficacy which your earnest endeavors may insure to procure redress of these our great grievances, to quiet the minds of your subjects in British America against any apprehensions of future incroachment, to establish fraternal love and harmony thro' the whole empire, and that that may continue to the latest ages of time, is the fervent prayer of all British America.

II

Notes on the
State of Virginia

ADVERTISEMENT.

THE following Notes were written in Virginia in the year 1781, and somewhat corrected and enlarged in the winter of 1782, in answer to Queries proposed to the Author, by a Foreigner of Distinction, then residing among us. The subjects are all treated imperfectly; some scarcely touched on. To apologize for this by developing the circumstances of the time and place of their composition, would be to open wounds which have already bled enough. To these circumstances some of their imperfections may with truth be ascribed; the great mass to the want of information and want of talents in the writer. He had a few copies printed, which he gave among his friends: and a translation of them has been lately published in France, but with such alterations as the laws of the press in that country rendered necessary. They are now offered to the public in their original form and language.

Feb. 27, 1787.

CONTENTS.

Notes on the
State of Virginia[1]

QUERY I.

Boundaries of Virginia

¶ *An exact description of the limits and boundaries
of the state of Virginia?*

VIRGINIA is bounded on the East by the Atlantic: on the North by a line of latitude, crossing the Eastern Shore through Watkins's Point, being about 37° . 57'. North latitude; from thence by a streight line

---

The footnotes in this section are Jefferson's own, unless indicated by [Ed.].

---

[1] Jefferson was Governor of Virginia when he received the request of François de Marbois, secretary of the French legation, for information on Virginia. Six months after his retirement, in December 1781, he returned his answers to Marbois's queries; and that might have been the end of it but for the interest Jefferson's report aroused among scientific men in Philadelphia. He continued his investigations, and enlarged and revised the entire work until in 1784 it had "swelled to nearly treble bulk." No longer able to provide manuscript copies, he decided to print it. A private edition of two hundred copies was printed in Paris in 1785. It contained no avowal of authorship, and Jefferson still hoped to confine his opinions to a small circle. But when a copy of the *Notes* fell into the hands of a Paris bookseller, Jefferson made the best arrangements he could for French

to Cinquac, near the mouth of Patowmac; thence by the Patowmac, which is common to Virginia and Maryland, to the first fountain of its northern branch; thence by a meridian line, passing through that fountain till it intersects a line running East and West, in latitude 39° . 43' . 42.4" which divides Maryland from Pennsylvania, and which was marked by Messrs. Mason and Dixon; thence by that line, and a continuation of it westwardly to the completion of five degrees of longitude from the eastern boundary of Pennsylvania, in the same latitude, and thence by a meridian line to the Ohio: on the West by the Ohio and Missisipi, to latitude 36° . 30' North: and on the South by the line of latitude last mentioned. By ad-measurements through nearly the whole of this last line, and supplying the unmeasured parts from good data, the Atlantic and Missisipi are found in this latitude to be 758 miles distant, equal to 13° . 38' of longitude, reckoning 55 miles and 3144 feet to the degree. This being our comprehension of longitude, that of our latitude, taken between this and Mason and Dixon's line, is 3° . 13' . 42.4" equal to 223.3 miles, supposing a degree of a great circle to be 69 m., 864 f., as computed by Cassini. These boundaries include an area somewhat triangular, of 121,525 square miles, whereof 79,650 lie westward of the Alleghaney mountains, and 57,034 westward of the meridian of the

---

translation and publication, which occurred early in 1787, and at the same time, overcoming his fears of hostile political opinion in Virginia, undertook publication of the work in England, submitting as well to acknowledgment of authorship. This authorized edition, by Stockdale in London, appeared in the summer of 1787. American newspapers at once began to publish the work piecemeal. The first American edition followed, in Philadelphia, in 1788. It is this edition, based on the Stockdale—the one known to American readers of the time—that is reprinted here, with the addition of chapter titles and subheadings where appropriate. (I am indebted to William Peden, whose modern annotated edition of the *Notes* follows the London, not the Philadelphia, version.) I have omitted three appendices (a commentary by Charles Thomson, a 1783 draft constitution for Virginia, and the Virginia Statute of Religious Freedom) which appeared in the 1787-1788 editions. [Ed.]

mouth of the Great Kanhaway. This state is therefore one third larger than the islands of Great-Britain and Ireland, which are reckoned at 88,357 square miles.

These limits result from, 1. The ancient charters from the crown of England. 2. The grant of Maryland to the Lord Baltimore, and the subsequent determinations of the British court as to the extent of that grant. 3. The grant of Pennsylvania to William Penn, and a compact between the general assemblies of the commonwealths of Virginia and Pennsylvania as to the extent of that grant. 4. The grant of Carolina, and actual location of its northern boundary, by consent of both parties. 5. The treaty of Paris of 1763. 6. The confirmation of the charters of the neighbouring states by the convention of Virginia at the time of constituting their commonwealth. 7. The cession made by Virginia to Congress of all the lands to which they had title on the North side of the Ohio.

QUERY II.

Rivers

¶ *A notice of its rivers, rivulets,
and how far they are navigable?*

AN INSPECTION of a map of Virginia, will give a better idea of the geography of its rivers, than any description in writing. Their navigation may be imperfectly noted.

Roanoke, so far as it lies within this state, is no where navigable, but for canoes, or light batteaux; and, even for these, in such detached parcels as to have prevented the inhabitants from availing themselves of it at all.

James River, and its waters, afford navigation as follows.

The whole of *Elizabeth River*, the lowest of those which run into James River, is a harbour, and would contain upwards of 300 ships. The channel is from 150 to 200 fathom wide, and at common flood tide, affords 18 feet water to Norfolk. The Strafford, a 60 gun ship, went there, lightening herself to cross the bar at Sowell's Point. The Fier Rodrigue, pierced for 64 guns, and carrying 50, went there without lightening. Craney island, at the mouth of this river, commands its channel tolerably well.

Nansemond River is navigable to Sleepy Hole, for vessels of 250 tons; to Suffolk, for those of 100 tons; and to Milner's, for those of 25.

Pagan Creek affords 8 to 10 feet water to Smithfeild, which admits vessels of 20 ton.

Chickahominy has at its mouth a bar, on which is only

12 feet water at common flood tide. Vessels passing that, may go 8 miles up the river; those of 10 feet draught may go four miles further, and those of six tons burthen, 20 miles further.

Appamattox may be navigated as far as Broadways, by any vessel which has crossed Harrison's bar in James River; it keeps 8 or 9 feet water a mile or two higher up to Fisher's bar, and 4 feet on that and upwards to Petersburgh, where all navigation ceases.

James River itself affords harbour for vessels of any size in Hampton Road, but not in safety through the whole winter; and there is navigable water for them as far as Mulberry island. A 40 gun ship goes to James town, and, lightening herself, may pass to Harrison's bar, on which there is only 15 feet water. Vessels of 250 tons may go to Warwick; those of 125 go to Rocket's, a mile below Richmond; from thence is about 7 feet water to Richmond; and about the centre of the town, four feet and a half, where the navigation is interrupted by falls, which in a course of six miles, descend about 80 feet perpendicular: above these it is resumed in canoes and batteaux, and is prosecuted safely and advantageously to within 10 miles of the Blue Ridge; and even through the Blue Ridge a ton weight has been brought; and the expence would not be great, when compared with its object, to open a tolerable navigation up Jackson's river and Carpenter's creek, to within 25 miles of Howard's creek of Green Briar, both of which have then water enough to float vessels into the Great Kanhaway. In some future state of population, I think it possible, that its navigation may also be made to interlock with that of the Patowmac, and through that to communicate by a short portage with the Ohio. It is to be noted, that this river is called in the maps *James River*, only to its confluence with the Rivanna; thence to the Blue Ridge it is called the Fluvanna; and thence to its source, Jackson's river. But in common speech, it is called James River to its source.

The *Rivanna*, a branch of James River, is navigable for

canoes and batteaux to its intersection with the South West mountains, which is about 22 miles; and may easily be opened to navigation through those mountains to its fork above Charlottesville.

York River, at York town, affords the best harbour in the state for vessels of the largest size. The river there narrows to the width of a mile, and is contained within very high banks, close under which the vessels may ride. It holds 4 fathom water at high tide for 25 miles above York to the mouth of Poropotank, where the river is a mile and a half wide, and the channel only 75 fathom, and passing under a high bank. At the confluence of *Pamunkey* and *Mattapony*, it is reduced to 3 fathom depth, which continues up Pamunkey to Cumberland, where the width is 100 yards, and up Mattapony to within two miles of Frazer's ferry, where it becomes 2½ fathom deep, and holds that about five miles. Pamunkey is then capable of navigation for loaded flats to Brockman's bridge, 50 miles above Hanover town, and Mattapony to Downer's bridge, 70 miles above its mouth.

Piankatank, the little rivers making out of *Mobjack bay* and those of the *Eastern shore*, receive only very small vessels, and these can but enter them.

Rappahanock affords 4 fathom water to Hobb's hole, and 2 fathom from thence to Fredericksburg.

Patowmac is 7½ miles wide at the mouth; 4½ at Nomony bay; 3 at Aquia; 1½ at Hallooing point; 1¼ at Alexandria. Its soundings are, 7 fathom at the mouth; 5 at St. George's island; 4½ at Lower Matchodic; 3 at Swan's point, and thence up to Alexandria; thence 10 feet water to the falls, which are 13 miles above Alexandria. These falls are 15 miles in length, and of very great descent, and the navigation above them for batteaux and canoes, is so much interrupted as to be little used. It is, however, used in a small degree up the Cohongoronta branch as far as Fort Cumberland, which was at the mouth of Wills's creek; and is capable, at no great expence, of being rendered very practicable. The Shenandoah branch interlocks with James river about the Blue Ridge, and may perhaps in future be opened.

The *Missisipi* will be one of the principal channels of future commerce for the country westward of the Alleghaney. From the mouth of this river to where it receives the Ohio, is 1000 miles by water, but only 500 by land, passing through the Chickasaw country. From the mouth of the Ohio to that of the Missouri, is 230 miles by water, and 140 by land. From thence to the mouth of the Illinois river, is about 25 miles. The Missisipi, below the mouth of the Missouri, is always muddy, and abounding with sand bars, which frequently change their places. However, it carries 15 feet water to the mouth of the Ohio, to which place it is from one and a half to two miles wide, and thence to Kaskaskia from one mile to a mile and a quarter wide. Its current is so rapid, that it never can be stemmed by the force of the wind alone, acting on sails. Any vessel, however, navigated with oars, may come up at any time, and receive much aid from the wind. A batteau passes from the mouth of Ohio to the mouth of Missisipi in three weeks, and is from two to three months getting up again. During its floods, which are periodical as those of the Nile, the largest vessels may pass down it, if their steerage can be insured. These floods begin in April, and the river returns into its banks early in August. The inundation extends further on the western than eastern side, covering the lands in some places for 50 miles from its banks. Above the mouth of the Missouri, it becomes much such a river as the Ohio, like it clear, and gentle in its current, not quite so wide, the period of its floods nearly the same, but not rising to so great a height. The streets of the village at Cohoes are not more than 10 feet above the ordinary level of the water, and yet were never overflowed. Its bed deepens every year. Cohoes, in the memory of many people now living, was insulated by every flood of the river. What was the eastern channel has now become a lake, 9 miles in length and one in width, into which the river at this day never flows. This river yields turtle of a peculiar kind, perch, trout, gar, pike, mullets, herrings, carp, spatula fish of 50 lb. weight, cat fish of 100 lb. weight, buffalo fish, and sturgeon. Aligators or crocodiles have been seen as high up as the Acansas. It also abounds in herons, cranes, ducks, brant, geese, and swans. Its passage is commanded by a fort established by this state, five miles below the mouth of Ohio, and ten miles above the Carolina boundary.

The Missouri, since the treaty of Paris, the Illinois and northern branches of the Ohio, since the cession to Congress, are no longer within our limits. Yet having been so heretofore, and still opening to us channels of extensive communication with the western and north-western country, they shall be noted in their order.

The *Missouri* is, in fact, the principal river, contributing more to the common stream than does the Missisipi, even after its junction with the Illinois. It is remarkably cold, muddy and rapid. Its overflowings are considerable. They happen during the months of June and July. Their commencement being so much later than those of the Missisipi, would induce a belief that the sources of the Missouri are northward of those of the Missisipi, unless we suppose that the cold increases again with the ascent of the land from the Missisipi westwardly. That this ascent is great, is proved by the rapidity of the river. Six miles above the mouth it is brought within the compass of a quarter of a mile's width: yet the Spanish merchants at Pancore, or St. Louis, say they go two thousand miles up it. It heads far westward of Rio Norte, or North River. There is, in the villages of Kaskaskia, Cohoes and St. Vincennes, no inconsiderable quantity of plate, said to have been plundered during the last war by the Indians from the churches and private houses of Santa Fé, on the North river, and brought to these villages for sale. From the mouth of the Ohio to Santa Fé are forty days journey, or about 1000 miles. What is the shortest distance between the navigable waters of the Missouri, and those of the North river, or how far this is navigable above Santa

Fé, I could never learn. From Santa Fé to its mouth in the Gulph of Mexico is about 1200 miles. The road from New Orleans to Mexico crosses this river at the post of Rio Norte, 800 miles below Santa Fé: and from this post to New Orleans is about 1200 miles; thus making 2000 miles between Santa Fé and New Orleans, passing down the North river, Red river, and Missisipi; whereas it is 2230 through the Missouri and Missisipi. From the same post of Rio Norte, passing near the mines of La Sierra and Laiguana, which are between the North river and the river Salina to Sartilla, is 375 miles; and from thence, passing the mines of Charcas, Zaccatecas and Potosi, to the city of Mexico, is 375 miles; in all, 1550 miles from Santa Fé to the city of Mexico. From New Orleans to the city of Mexico is about 1950 miles: the roads, after setting out from the Red river, near Natchitoches, keeping generally parallel with the coast, and about two hundred miles from it, till it enters the city of Mexico.

The *Illinois* is a fine river, clear, gentle, and without rapids; insomuch that it is navigable for batteaux to its source. From thence is a portage of two miles only to the Chickago, which affords a batteau navigation of 16 miles to its entrance into lake Michigan. The Illinois, about 10 miles above its mouth, is 300 yards wide.

The *Kaskaskia* is 100 yards wide at its entrance into the Missisipi, and preserves that breadth to the Buffalo plains, 70 miles above. So far also it is navigable for loaded batteaux, and perhaps much further. It is not rapid.

The *Ohio* is the most beautiful river on earth. Its current gentle, waters clear, and bosom smooth and unbroken by rocks and rapids, a single instance only excepted.

It is ¼ of a mile wide at Fort Pitt:

500 yards at the mouth of the Great Kanhaway:

1 mile and 25 poles at Louisville:

¼ of a mile on the rapids, three or four miles below Louisville:

½ a mile where the low country begins, which is 20 miles above Green river:

1¼ at the receipt of the Tanissee:
And a mile wide at the mouth.
Its length, as measured according to its meanders by
Capt. Hutchins,[1] is as follows:

From Fort Pitt

	Miles.		*Miles.*
To Log's town	18½	Little Miami	126¼
Big Beaver creek	10¾	Licking creek	8
Little Beaver creek	13½	Great Miami	26¾
Yellow creek	11¾	Big Bones	32½
Two creeks	21¾	Kentucky	44¼
Long reach	53¾	Rapids	77¼
End Long reach	16½	Low country	155¾
Muskingum	25½	Buffalo river	64½
Little Kanhaway	12¼	Wabash	97¼
Hockhocking	16	Big Cave	42¾
Great Kanhaway	82½	Shawanee river	52½
Guiandot	43¾	Cherokee river	13
Sandy creek	14½	Massac	11
Sioto	48¼	Missisipi	46
			———
			1188

In common winter and spring tides it affords 15 feet
water to Louisville, 10 feet to Le Tarte's rapids, 40 miles
above the mouth of the Great Kanhaway, and a sufficiency
at all times for light batteaux and canoes to Fort Pitt.
The rapids are in latitude 38° 8′. The inundations of this
river begin about the last of March, and subside in July.
During these a first rate man of war may be carried from
Louisville to New Orleans, if the sudden turns of the river
and the strength of its current will admit a safe steerage.
The rapids at Louisville descend about 30 feet in a length
of a mile and a half. The bed of the river there is a solid
rock, and is divided by an island into two branches, the
southern of which is about 200 yards wide, and is dry

[1] Thomas Hutchins (1730–1789), military officer and geographer, author of several journals and *A Topographical Description of Virginia, Pennsylvania, Maryland, and North Carolina*
(London, 1778). [Ed.]

four months in the year. The bed of the northern branch is worn into channels by the constant course of the water, and attrition of the pebble stones carried on with that, so as to be passable for batteaux through the greater part of the year. Yet it is thought that the southern arm may be the most easily opened for constant navigation. The rise of the waters in these rapids does not exceed 10 or 12 feet. A part of this island is so high as to have been never overflowed, and to command the settlement at Louisville, which is opposite to it. The fort, however, is situated at the head of the falls. The ground on the south side rises very gradually.

The *Tanissee*, Cherokee or Hogohege river is 600 yards wide at its mouth, ¼ of a mile at the mouth of Holston, and 200 yards at Chotee, which is 20 miles above Holston, and 300 miles above the mouth of the Tanissee. This river crosses the southern boundary of Virginia, 58 miles from the Missisipi. Its current is moderate. It is navigable for loaded boats of any burthen to the Muscle shoals, where the river passes through the Cumberland mountain. These shoals are 6 or 8 miles long, passable downwards for loaded canoes, but not upwards, unless there be a swell in the river. Above these the navigation for loaded canoes and batteaux continues to the Long island. This river has its inundations also. Above the Chickamogga towns is a whirlpool called the Sucking-pot, which takes in trunks of trees or boats, and throws them out again half a mile below. It is avoided by keeping very close to the bank, on the South side. There are but a few miles portage between a branch of this river and the navigable waters of the river Mobile, which runs into the Gulph of Mexico.

Cumberland, or Shawanee river, intersects the boundary between Virginia and North Carolina 67 miles from the Missisipi, and again 198 miles from the same river, a little above the entrance of Obey's river into the Cumberland. Its clear fork crosses the same boundary about 300 miles from the Missisipi. Cumberland is a very gentle stream, navigable for loaded batteaux 800 miles, without interruption; then intervene some rapids of 15 miles in length, after which it is again navigable 70 miles upwards, which brings you within 10 miles of the Cumberland mountains. It is about 120 yards wide through its whole course, from the head of its navigation to its mouth.

The *Wabash* is a very beautiful river, 400 yards wide at the mouth, and 300 at St. Vincennes, which is a post 100 miles above the mouth, in a direct line. Within this space there are two small rapids, which give very little obstruction to the navigation. It is 400 yards wide at the mouth, and navigable 30 leagues upwards for canoes and small boats. From the mouth of Maple river to that of Eel river is about 80 miles in a direct line, the river continuing navigable, and from one to two hundred yards in width. The Eel river is 150 yards wide, and affords at all times navigation for periaguas, to within 18 miles of the Miami of the Lake. The Wabash, from the mouth of Eel river to Little river, a distance of 50 miles direct, is interrupted with frequent rapids and shoals, which obstruct the navigation, except in a swell. Little river affords navigation during a swell to within 3 miles of the Miami, which thence affords a similar navigation into Lake Erié, 100 miles distant in a direct line. The Wabash overflows periodically in correspondence with the Ohio, and in some places two leagues from its banks.

Green River is navigable for loaded batteaux at all times 50 miles upwards; but it is then interrupted by impassable rapids, above which the navigation again commences, and continues good 30 or 40 miles to the mouth of Barren river.

Kentucky River is 90 yards wide at the mouth, and also at Boonsborough, 80 miles above. It affords a navigation for loaded batteaux 180 miles in a direct line, in the winter tides.

The *Great Miami* of the Ohio, is 200 yards wide at the mouth. At the Piccawee towns, 75 miles above, it is reduced to 30 yards; it is, nevertheless, navigable for loaded canoes 50 miles above these towns. The portage from its western branch into the Miami of Lake Erié, is 5 miles; that from its eastern branch into Sandusky river, is of 9 miles.

Salt River is at all times navigable for loaded batteaux 70 or 80 miles. It is 80 yards wide at its mouth, and keeps that width to its fork, 25 miles above.

The *Little Miami* of the Ohio, is 60 or 70 yards wide at its mouth, 60 miles to its source, and affords no navigation.

The *Sioto* is 250 yards wide at its mouth, which is in latitude 38° 22′ and at the Saltlick towns, 200 miles above the mouth, it is yet 100 yards wide. To these towns it is navigable for loaded batteaux, and its eastern branch affords navigation almost to its source.

Great Sandy River is about sixty yards wide, and navigable sixty miles for loaded batteaux.

Guiandot is about the width of the river last mentioned, but is more rapid. It may be navigated by canoes sixty miles.

The *Great Kanhaway* is a river of considerable note for the fertility of its lands, and still more, as leading towards the head waters of James river. Nevertheless, it is doubtful whether its great and numerous rapids will admit a navigation, but at an expence to which it will require ages to render its inhabitants equal. The great obstacles begin at what are called the Great Falls, 90 miles above the mouth, below which are only five or six rapids, and these passable, with some difficulty, even at low water. From the falls to the mouth of Greenbriar is 100 miles, and thence to the lead mines 120. It is 280 yards wide at its mouth.

Hockhocking is 80 yards wide at its mouth, and yields navigation for loaded batteaux to the Pressplace, 60 miles above its mouth.

The *Little Kanhaway* is 150 yards wide at the mouth. It yields a navigation of 10 miles only. Perhaps its northern branch, called Junius's creek, which interlocks with the western of Monongahela, may one day admit a shorter passage from the latter into the Ohio.

The *Muskingum* is 280 yards wide at its mouth, and 200 yards at the lower Indian towns, 150 miles upwards. It is navigable for small batteaux to within one mile of a navigable part of Cayahoga river, which runs into Lake Erié.

At Fort Pitt the river Ohio loses its name, branching into the Monongahela and Alleghaney.

The *Monongahela* is 400 yards wide at its mouth. From thence is 12 or 15 miles to the mouth of Yohoganey, where it is 300 yards wide. Thence to Redstone by water is 50 miles, by land 30. Then to the mouth of Cheat river by water 40 miles, by land 28, the width continuing at 300 yards, and the navigation good for boats. Thence the width is about 200 yards to the western fork, 50 miles higher, and the navigation frequently interrupted by rapids; which however with a swell of two or three feet become very passable for boats. It then admits light boats, except in dry seasons, 65 miles further to the head of Tygart's valley, presenting only some small rapids and falls of one or two feet perpendicular, and lessening in its width to 20 yards. The *Western fork* is navigable in the winter 10 or 15 miles towards the northern of the Little Kanhaway, and will admit a good waggon road to it. The *Yohoganey* is the principal branch of this river. It passes through the Laurel mountain, about 30 miles from its mouth; is so far from 300 to 150 yards wide, and the navigation much obstructed in dry weather by rapids and shoals. In its passage through the mountain it makes very great falls, admitting no navigation for ten miles to the Turkey Foot. Thence to the Great Crossing, about 20 miles, it is again navigable, except in dry seasons, and at this place is 200 yards wide. The sources of this river are divided from those of the Patowmac by the Alleghaney mountain. From the falls, where it intersects the Laurel mountain, to Fort Cumberland, the head of the navigation on the Patowmac, is 40 miles of very mountainous road. Wills's creek, at the mouth of which was Fort Cumberland, is 30 or 40 yards wide, but affords no navigation as yet. *Cheat* river, another considerable branch of the Monongahela, is 200 yards wide at its mouth, and 100 yards at the Dunkards' settlement, 50 miles higher. It is navigable for boats, except in dry seasons. The boundary between Virginia and Pennsylvania crosses it about three or four miles above its mouth.

The *Alleghaney* river, with a slight swell, affords navigation for light batteaux to Venango, at the mouth of French creek, where it is 200 yards wide; and it is practised even to Le Bœuf, from whence there is a portage of 15 miles to Presque Isle on Lake Erié.

The country watered by the Missisipi and its eastern branches, constitutes five-eighths of the United States, two of which five-eighths are occupied by the Ohio and its waters: the residuary streams which run into the Gulph of Mexico, the Atlantic, and the St. Laurence water, the remaining three-eighths.

Before we quit the subject of the western waters, we will take a view of their principal connexions with the Atlantic. These are three; the Hudson's river, the Patowmac, and the Missisipi itself. Down the last will pass all heavy commodities. But the navigation through the Gulph of Mexico is so dangerous, and that up the Missisipi so difficult and tedious, that it is thought probable that European merchandize will not return through that channel. It is most likely that flour, timber, and other heavy articles will be floated on rafts, which will themselves be an article for sale as well as their loading, the navigators returning by land or in light batteaux. There will therefore be a competition between the Hudson and Patowmac rivers for the residue of the commerce of all the country westward of Lake Erié, on the waters of the lakes, of the Ohio, and upper parts of the Missisipi. To go to New-York, that part of the trade which comes from the lakes or their waters must first be brought into Lake Erié. Between Lake Superior and its waters and Huron are the rapids of St. Mary, which will permit boats to pass, but not larger vessels. Lakes Huron and Michigan afford communication with Lake Erié by vessels of 8 feet draught. That part of the trade which comes from the waters of the Missisipi must pass from them through some portage into the waters of the lakes. The portage from the Illinois river into a water of Michigan is of one mile only. From the Wabash, Miami, Muskingum, or Alleghaney, are portages into the waters of Lake Erié, of from one to fifteen miles. When the commodities are brought into, and have passed through Lake Erié, there is between that and Ontario an interruption by the falls of Niagara, where the portage is of 8 miles; and between Ontario and the Hudson's river are portages at the falls of Onondago, a little above Oswego, of a quarter of a mile; from Wood creek to the Mohawks river two miles; at the little falls of the Mohawks river half a mile, and from Schenectady to Albany 16 miles. Besides the increase of expence occasioned by frequent change of carriage, there is an increased risk of pillage produced by committing merchandize to a greater number of hands successively. The Patowmac offers itself under the following circumstances. For the trade of the lakes and their waters westward of Lake Erié, when it shall have entered that lake, it must coast along its southern shore, on account of the number and excellence of its harbours, the northern, though shortest, having few harbours, and these unsafe. Having reached Cayahoga, to proceed on to New-York it will have 825 miles and five portages: whereas it is but 425 miles to Alexandria, its emporium on the Patowmac, if it turns into the Cayahoga, and passes through that, Bigbeaver, Ohio, Yohoganey, (or Monongala and Cheat) and Patowmac, and there are but two portages; the first of which between Cayahoga and Beaver may be removed by uniting the sources of these waters, which are lakes in the neighbourhood of each other, and in a champaign country; the other from the waters of Ohio to Patowmac will be from 15 to 40 miles, according to the trouble which shall be taken to approach the two navigations. For the trade of the Ohio, or that which shall come into it from its own waters or the Missisipi, it is nearer through the Patowmac to Alexandria than to New-York by 580 miles, and it is interrupted by one portage only. There is another circumstance of difference too. The lakes themselves never freeze, but the communications between them freeze, and the Hudson's river is itself shut up by the ice three months in the year; whereas the channel to the Chesapeak leads directly into a warmer climate. The southern parts of it very rarely freeze at all, and whenever the northern do, it is so near the sources of the rivers, that the frequent floods to which they are there liable break up the ice immediately, so that vessels may pass through the whole winter, subject only to accidental and short delays. Add to all this, that in case of a war with our neighbours the Anglo-Americans or the Indians, the route to New-York becomes a frontier through almost its whole length, and all commerce through it ceases from that moment.—But the channel to New-York is already known to practice; whereas the upper waters of the Ohio and the Patowmac, and the great falls of the latter, are yet to be cleared of their fixed obstructions.

QUERY III.

Sea-Ports

¶ *A notice of the best sea-ports of the state, and how big are the vessels they can receive?*

HAVING no ports but our rivers and creeks, this Query has been answered under the preceding one.

Mountains

¶ A notice of its Mountains?

FOR THE particular geography of our mountains I must refer to Fry and Jefferson's map of Virginia; and to Evans's analysis of his map of America[1] for a more philosophical view of them than is to be found in any other work. It is worthy notice, that our mountains are not solitary and scattered confusedly over the face of the country; but that they commence at about 150 miles from the sea-coast, are disposed in ridges one behind another, running nearly parallel with the sea-coast, though rather approaching it as they advance north-eastwardly. To the south-west, as the tract of country between the sea-coast and the Mississippi becomes narrower, the mountains converge into a single ridge, which, as it approaches the Gulph of Mexico, subsides into plain country, and gives rise to some of the waters of that Gulph, and particularly to a river called the Apalachicola, probably from the Apalachies, an Indian nation formerly residing on it. Hence the mountains giving rise to that river, and seen from its various parts, were called the Apalachian mountains, being in fact the end or termination only of the great ridges passing through the continent. European geographers however extended the name northwardly as far

[1] Joshua Fry and Peter Jefferson (Jefferson's father), *A Map of the Inhabited Part of Virginia* (London, 1753 or 1754); Lewis Evans, *Geographical, Historical, Political, Philosophical and Mechanical Essays: The First, Containing an Analysis of a General Map of the Middle British Colonies of America* (Philadelphia, 1755). [Ed.]

as the mountains extended; some giving it, after their separation into different ridges, to the Blue ridge, others to the North mountain, others to the Alleghaney, others to the Laurel ridge, as may be seen in their different maps. But the fact I believe is, that none of these ridges were ever known by that name to the inhabitants, either native or emigrant, but as they saw them so called in European maps. In the same direction generally are the veins of lime-stone, coal and other minerals hitherto discovered: and so range the falls of our great rivers. But the courses of the great rivers are at right angles with these. James and Patowmac penetrate through all the ridges of mountains eastward of the Alleghaney, that is broken by no water course. It is in fact the spine of the country between the Atlantic on one side, and the Missisipi and St. Laurence on the other. The passage of the Patowmac through the Blue ridge[2] is perhaps one of the most stupendous scenes in nature. You stand on a very high point of land. On your right comes up the Shenandoah, having ranged along the foot of the mountain an hundred miles to seek a vent. On your left approaches the Patowmac, in quest of a passage also. In the moment of their junction they rush together against the mountain, rend it asunder, and pass off to the sea. The first glance of this scene hurries our senses into the opinion, that this earth has been created in time, that the mountains were formed first, that the rivers began to flow afterwards, that in this place particularly they have been dammed up by the Blue ridge of mountains, and have formed an ocean which filled the whole valley; that continuing to rise they have at length broken over at this spot, and have torn the mountain down from its summit to its base. The piles of rock on each hand, but particularly on the Shenandoah, the evident marks of their disrupture and avulsion from their beds by the most powerful agents of nature, corroborate the impression. But the distant finishing which nature has given

[2] At Harpers Ferry, West Virginia. [Ed.]

to the picture is of a very different character. It is a true contrast to the fore-ground. It is as placid and delightful, as that is wild and tremendous. For the mountain being cloven asunder, she presents to your eye, through the cleft, a small catch of smooth blue horizon, at an infinite distance in the plain country, inviting you, as it were, from the riot and tumult roaring around, to pass through the breach and participate of the calm below. Here the eye ultimately composes itself; and that way too the road happens actually to lead. You cross the Patowmac above the junction, pass along its side through the base of the mountain for three miles, its terrible precipices hanging in fragments over you, and within about 20 miles reach Frederick town and the fine country round that. This scene is worth a voyage across the Atlantic. Yet here, as in the neighbourhood of the natural bridge, are people who have passed their lives within half a dozen miles, and have never been to survey these monuments of a war between rivers and mountains, which must have shaken the earth itself to its center.—The height of our mountains has not yet been estimated with any degree of exactness. The Alleghaney being the great ridge which divides the waters of the Atlantic from those of the Missisipi, its summit is doubtless more elevated above the ocean than that of any other mountain. But its relative height, compared with the base on which it stands, is not so great as that of some others, the country rising behind the successive ridges like the steps of stairs. The mountains of the Blue ridge, and of these the Peaks of Otter, are thought to be of a greater height, measured from their base, than any others in our country, and perhaps in North America. From data, which may found a tolerable conjecture, we suppose the highest peak to be about 4000 feet perpendicular, which is not a fifth part of the height of the mountains of South America, nor one third of the height which would be necessary in our latitude to preserve ice in the open air unmelted through the year. The ridge of mountains next beyond the Blue ridge, called by us the North mountain, is of the greatest extent; for which reason they were named by the Indians the Endless mountains.

A substance supposed to be pumice, found floating on the Missisipi, has induced a conjecture, that there is a volcano on some of its waters: and as these are mostly known to their sources, except the Missouri, our expectations of verifying the conjecture would of course be led to the mountains which divide the waters of the Mexican Gulph from those of the South Sea; but no volcano having ever yet been known at such a distance from the sea, we must rather suppose that this floating substance has been erroneously deemed pumice.

QUERY V.

Cascades

¶ Its Cascades and Caverns?

THE ONLY remarkable cascade in this country, is that of the Falling Spring in Augusta. It is a water of James river, where it is called Jackson's river, rising in the Warm Spring mountains about twenty miles South West of the Warm spring, and flowing into that valley. About three-quarters of a mile from its source, it falls over a rock 200 feet into the valley below. The sheet of water is broken in its breadth by the rock in two or three places, but not at all in its height. Between the sheet and rock, at the bottom, you may walk across dry. This cataract will bear no comparison with that of Niagara, as to the quantity of water composing it; the sheet being only 12 or 15 feet wide above, and somewhat more spread below; but it is half as high again, the latter being only 156 feet, according to the mensuration made by order of M. Vaudreuil, Governor of Canada, and 130 according to a more recent account.

In the lime-stone country, there are many caverns of very considerable extent. The most noted is called Madison's Cave, and is on the North side of the Blue ridge, near the intersection of the Rockingham and Augusta line with the South fork of the southern river of Shenandoah. It is in a hill of about 200 feet perpendicular height, the ascent of which, on one side, is so steep, that you may pitch a biscuit from its summit into the river which washes its base. The entrance of the cave is, in this side, about two-thirds of the way up. It extends into the earth about

300 feet, branching into subordinate caverns, sometimes ascending a little, but more generally descending, and at length terminates, in two different places, at basons of water of unknown extent, and which I should judge to be nearly on a level with the water of the river; however, I do not think they are formed by refluent water from that, because they are never turbid; because they do not rise and fall in correspondence with that in times of flood, or of drought; and because the water is always cool. It is probably one of the many reservoirs with which the interior parts of the earth are supposed to abound, and which yield supplies to the fountains of water, distin-

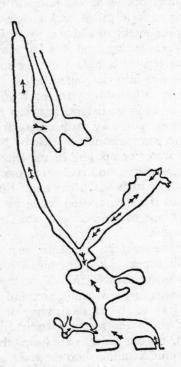

An Eye-draught of Madison's Cave, on a scale of 50 feet to the inch. The arrows shew where it descends or ascends.

guished from others only by its being accessible. The vault of this cave is of solid lime-stone, from 20 to 40 or 50 feet high, through which water is continually percolating. This, trickling down the sides of the cave, has incrusted them over in the form of elegant drapery; and dripping from the top of the vault generates on that, and on the base below, stalactites of a conical form, some of which have met and formed massive columns.

Another of these caves is near the North mountain, in the county of Frederick, on the lands of Mr. Zane. The entrance into this is on the top of an extensive ridge. You descend 30 or 40 feet, as into a well, from whence the cave then extends, nearly horizontally, 400 feet into the earth, preserving a breadth of from 20 to 50 feet, and a height of from 5 to 12 feet. After entering this cave a few feet, the mercury, which in the open air was at 50° rose to 57° of Farenheit's thermometer, answering to 11° of Reaumur's, and it continued at that to the remotest parts of the cave. The uniform temperature of the cellars of the observatory of Paris, which are 90 feet deep, and of all subterranean cavities of any depth, where no chymical agents may be supposed to produce a factitious heat, has been found to be 10° of Reaumur, equal to 54½° of Farenheit. The temperature of the cave above mentioned so nearly corresponds with this, that the difference may be ascribed to a difference of instruments.

At the Panther gap, in the ridge which divides the waters of the Cow and the Calf pasture, is what is called the *Blowing cave.* It is in the side of a hill, is of about 100 feet diameter, and emits constantly a current of air of such force, as to keep the weeds prostrate to the distance of twenty yards before it. This current is strongest in dry frosty weather, and in long spells of rain weakest. Regular inspirations and expirations of air, by caverns and fissures, have been probably enough accounted for, by supposing them combined with intermitting fountains; as they must of course inhale air while their reservoirs are emptying themselves, and again emit it while they are filling. But a

constant issue of air, only varying in its force as the
weather is drier or damper, will require a new hypothesis.
There is another blowing cave in the Cumberland mountain, about a mile from where it crosses the Carolina line.
All we know of this is, that it is not constant, and that a
fountain of water issues from it.

The *Natural bridge*,[1] the most sublime of nature's works,
though not comprehended under the present head, must
not be pretermitted. It is on the ascent of a hill, which
seems to have been cloven through its length by some
great convulsion. The fissure, just at the bridge, is, by
some admeasurements, 270 feet deep, by others only 205.
It is about 45 feet wide at the bottom, and 90 feet at the
top; this of course determines the length of the bridge,
and its height from the water. Its breadth in the middle,
is about 60 feet, but more at the ends, and the thickness
of the mass at the summit of the arch, about 40 feet. A
part of this thickness is constituted by a coat of earth,
which gives growth to many large trees. The residue, with
the hill on both sides, is one solid rock of lime-stone. The
arch approaches the semi-elliptical form; but the larger
axis of the ellipsis, which would be the cord of the arch,
is many times longer than the transverse. Though the
sides of this bridge are provided in some parts with a
parapet of fixed rocks, yet few men have resolution to
walk to them and look over into the abyss. You involuntarily fall on your hands and feet, creep to the parapet
and peep over it. Looking down from this height about a
minute, gave me a violent head ach. If the view from the
top be painful and intolerable, that from below is delightful in an equal extreme. It is impossible for the emotions
arising from the sublime, to be felt beyond what they are
here; so beautiful an arch, so elevated, so light: and springing as it were up to heaven, the rapture of the spectator
is really indescribable! The fissure continuing narrow,
deep, and streight for a considerable distance above and
below the bridge, opens a short but very pleasing view of

[1] On Jefferson's property in Rockbridge County. [Ed.]

the North mountain on one side, and Blue ridge on the other, at the distance each of them of about five miles. This bridge is in the county of Rockbridge, to which it has given name, and affords a public and commodious passage over a valley, which cannot be crossed elsewhere for a considerable distance. The stream passing under it is called Cedar creek. It is a water of James river, and sufficient in the driest seasons to turn a grist-mill, though its fountain is not more than two miles above.[2]

[2] Don Ulloa [Antonio de Ulloa (1716–1785), Spanish explorer of South America. Jefferson is referring to his *Noticias Americanas* (Madrid, 1772). The quoted passage, in Spanish in the text, has been translated into English.—Ed.] mentions a break, similar to this, in the province of Angaraez, in South America. It is from 16 to 22 feet wide, 111 feet deep, and of 1.3 miles continuance, English measures. Its breadth at top is not sensibly greater than at bottom. But the following fact is remarkable, and will furnish some light for conjecturing the probable origin of our natural bridge. "This cave, or passage, is cut out of the live rock with such precision that the recesses on one side correspond with the projections on the other, as if that mountain had parted on purpose, with its turns and windings, to make a passage for the waters between the two lofty walls on both sides; they being so like each other that if they were joined together they would cover each other without leaving any cavity between them." Not. Amer. II. §. 10. Don Ulloa inclines to the opinion, that this channel has been effected by the wearing of the water which runs through it, rather than that the mountain should have been broken open by any convulsion of nature. But if it had been worn by the running of water, would not the rocks which form the sides, have been worn plane? or if, meeting in some parts with veins of harder stone, the water had left prominences on the one side, would not the same cause have sometimes, or perhaps generally, occasioned prominences on the other side also? Yet Don Ulloa tells us, that on the other side there are always corresponding cavities, and that these tally with the prominences so perfectly, that, were the two sides to come together, they would fit in all their indentures, without leaving any void. I think that this does not resemble the effect of running water, but looks rather as if the two sides had parted asunder. The sides of the break, over which is the Natural bridge of Virginia, consisting of a veiny rock which yields to time, the correspondence between the salient and re-entering inequalities, if it existed at all, has now disappeared. This break has the advantage of the one described by Don Ulloa in its finest circumstance; no portion in that instance having held together, during the separation of the other parts, so as to form a bridge over the abyss.

Productions Mineral, Vegetable and Animal

¶ *A notice of the mines and other subterraneous riches;
its trees, plants, fruits, &c.*

MINERALS

Gold. I knew a single instance of gold found in this state. It was interspersed in small specks through a lump of ore, of about four pounds weight, which yielded seventeen pennyweight of gold, of extraordinary ductility. This ore was found on the North side of Rappahanock, about four miles below the falls. I never heard of any other indication of gold in its neighbourhood.

Lead. On the Great Kanhaway, opposite to the mouth of Cripple creek, and about twenty five miles from our southern boundary, in the county of Montgomery, are mines of lead. The metal is mixed, sometimes with earth, and sometimes with rock, which requires the force of gunpowder to open it; and is accompanied with a portion of silver, too small to be worth separation under any process hitherto attempted there. The proportion yielded is from 50 to 80 lb. of pure metal from 100 lb. of washed ore. The most common is that of 60 to the 100 lb. The veins are at sometimes most flattering; at others they disappear suddenly and totally. They enter the side of the hill, and proceed horizontally. Two of them are wrought at present by the public, the best of which is 100 yards under the hill. These would employ about 50 labourers to advantage. We have not, however, more than 30 generally, and these cultivate their own corn. They have produced 60 tons of lead in the year; but the general quantity is from 20 to 25 tons. The present furnace is a mile from the ore-bank, and on the opposite side of the river. The ore is first waggoned to the river, a quarter of a mile, then laden on board of canoes and carried across the river, which is there about 200 yards wide, and then again taken into waggons and carried to the furnace. This mode was originally adopted, that they might avail themselves of a good situation on a creek, for a pounding mill: but it would be easy to have the furnace and pounding mill on the same side of the river, which would yield water, without any dam, by a canal of about half a mile in length. From the furnace the lead is transported 130 miles along a good road, leading through the Peaks of Otter to Lynch's ferry, or Winston's, on James river, from whence it is carried by water about the same distance to Westham. This land carriage may be greatly shortened, by delivering the lead on James river, above the Blue ridge, from whence a ton weight has been brought on two canoes. The Great Kanhaway has considerable falls in the neighbourhood of the mines. About seven miles below are three falls, of three or four feet perpendicular each; and three miles above is a rapid of three miles continuance, which has been compared in its descent to the great fall of James river. Yet it is the opinion, that they may be laid open for useful navigation, so as to reduce very much the portage between the Kanhaway and James river.

A valuable lead mine is said to have been lately discovered in Cumberland, below the mouth of Red river. The greatest, however, known in the western country, are on the Missisipi, extending from the mouth of Rock river 150 miles upwards. These are not wrought, the lead used in that country being from the banks on the Spanish side of the Missisipi, opposite to Kaskaskia.

Copper. A mine of copper was once opened in the county of Amherst, on the North side of James river, and another in the opposite country, on the South side. However, either from bad management or the poverty of the veins, they were discontinued. We are told of a rich mine of native copper on the Ouabache, below the upper Wiaw.

Iron. The mines of iron worked at present are Callaway's, Ross's, and Ballendine's, on the South side of James river; Old's on the North side, in Albemarle; Millar's in Augusta, and Zane's in Frederick. These two last are in the valley between the Blue ridge and North mountain. Callaway's, Ross's, Millar's, and Zane's, make about 150 tons of bar iron each, in the year. Ross's makes also about 1600 tons of pig iron annually; Ballendine's 1000; Callaway's, Millar's, and Zane's, about 600 each. Besides these, a forge of Mr. Hunter's, at Fredericksburgh, makes about 300 tons a year of bar iron, from pigs imported from Maryland; and Taylor's forge on Neapsco of Patowmac, works in the same way, but to what extent I am not informed. The indications of iron in other places are numerous, and dispersed through all the middle country. The toughness of the cast iron of Ross's and Zane's furnaces is very remarkable. Pots and other utensils, cast thinner than usual, of this iron, may be safely thrown into, or out of the waggons in which they are transported. Salt-pans made of the same, and no longer wanted for that purpose, cannot be broken up, in order to be melted again, unless previously drilled in many parts.

In the western country, we are told of iron mines between the Muskingum and Ohio; of others on Kentucky, between the Cumberland and Barren rivers, between Cumberland and Tannissee, on Reedy creek, near the Long island, and on Chesnut creek, a branch of the Great Kanhaway, near where it crosses the Carolina line. What are called the iron banks, on the Missisipi, are believed, by a good judge, to have no iron in them. In general, from what is hitherto known of that country, it seems to want iron.

Black lead. Considerable quantities of black lead are taken occasionally for use from Winterham, in the county

of Amelia. I am not able, however, to give a particular
state of the mine. There is no work established at it, those
who want, going and procuring it for themselves.

Pit coal. The country on James river, from 15 to 20
miles above Richmond, and for several miles northward
and southward, is replete with mineral coal of a very excellent quality. Being in the hands of many proprietors,
pits have been opened, and before the interruption of our
commerce were worked to an extent equal to the demand.

In the western country coal is known to be in so many
places, as to have induced an opinion, that the whole tract
between the Laurel mountain, Missisipi, and Ohio, yields
coal. It is also known in many places on the North side
of the Ohio. The coal at Pittsburg is of very superior
quality. A bed of it at that place has been a-fire since the
year 1765. Another coal-hill on the Pike-run of Monongahela has been a-fire ten years; yet it has burnt away
about twenty yards only.

Precious stones. I have known one instance of an em-
erald found in this country. Amethysts have been frequent, and chrystals common; yet not in such numbers
any of them as to be worth seeking.

Marble. There is very good marble, and in very great
abundance, on James river, at the mouth of Rockfish. The
samples I have seen, were some of them of a white as pure
as one might expect to find on the surface of the earth:
but most of them were variegated with red, blue, and
purple. None of it has been ever worked. It forms a very
large precipice, which hangs over a navigable part of the
river. It is said there is marble at Kentucky.

Limestone. But one vein of lime-stone is known below
the Blue ridge. Its first appearance, in our country, is in
Prince William, two miles below the Pignut ridge of
mountains; thence it passes on nearly parallel with that,
and crosses the Rivanna about five miles below it, where
it is called the south-west ridge. It then crosses Hardware,
above the mouth of Hudson's creek, James river at the
mouth of Rockfish, at the marble quarry before spoken

of, probably runs up that river to where it appears again at Ross's iron-works, and so passes off south-westwardly by Flat creek of Otter river. It is never more than one hundred yards wide. From the Blue ridge westwardly the whole country seems to be founded on a rock of lime-stone, besides infinite quantities on the surface, both loose and fixed. This is cut into beds, which range, as the mountains and sea-coast do, from south-west to north-east, the lamina of each bed declining from the horizon towards a parallelism with the axis of the earth. Being struck with this observation, I made, with a quadrant, a great number of trials on the angles of their declination, and found them to vary from 22° to 60° but averaging all my trials, the result was within one-third of a degree of the elevation of the pole or latitude of the place, and much the greatest part of them taken separately were little different from that: by which it appears, that these lamina are, in the main, parallel with the axis of the earth. In some instances, indeed, I found them perpendicular, and even reclining the other way: but these were extremely rare, and always attended with signs of convulsion, or other circumstances of singularity, which admitted a possibility of removal from their original position. These trials were made between Madison's cave and the Patowmac. We hear of lime-stone on the Missisipi and Ohio, and in all the mountainous country between the eastern and western waters, not on the mountains themselves, but occupying the vallies between them.

Near the eastern foot of the North mountain are immense bodies of *Schist*, containing impressions of shells in a variety of forms. I have received petrified shells of very different kinds from the first sources of the Kentucky, which bear no resemblance to any I have ever seen on the tide-waters. It is said that shells are found in the Andes, in South-America, fifteen thousand feet above the level of the ocean. This is considered by many, both of the learned and unlearned, as a proof of an universal deluge. To the many considerations opposing this opinion, the following may be added. The atmosphere, and all its contents, whether of water, air, or other matters, gravitate to the earth; that is to say, they have weight. Experience tells us, that the weight of all these together never exceeds that of a column of mercury of 31 inches height, which is equal to one of rainwater of 35 feet high. If the whole contents of the atmosphere then were water, instead of what they are, it would cover the globe but 35 feet deep; but as these waters, as they fell, would run into the seas, the superficial measure of which is to that of the dry parts of the globe as two to one, the seas would be raised only 52½ feet above their present level, and of course would overflow the lands to that height only. In Virginia this would be a very small proportion even of the champaign country, the banks of our tide-waters being frequently, if not generally, of a greater height. Deluges beyond this extent then, as for instance, to the North mountain or to Kentucky, seem out of the laws of nature. But within it they may have taken place to a greater or less degree, in proportion to the combination of natural causes which may be supposed to have produced them. History renders probable some instances of a partial deluge in the country lying round the Mediterranean sea. It has been often supposed,[1] and is not unlikely, that that sea was once a lake. While such, let us admit an extraordinary collection of the waters of the atmosphere from the other parts of the globe to have been discharged over that and the countries whose waters run into it. Or without supposing it a lake, admit such an extraordinary collection of the waters of the atmosphere, and an influx of waters from the Atlantic ocean, forced by long continued western winds. That lake, or that sea, may thus have been so raised as to overflow the low lands adjacent to it, as those of Egypt and Armenia, which, according to a tradition of the Egyptians and Hebrews, were overflowed about 2300 years before the Christian æra;

[1] Buffon Epoques, 96. (That is, Buffon's *Époques de la Nature*, vol. II, p. 96. This was a part of Buffon's *Histoire Naturelle*, 44 vols. Paris, 1749–1804. [Ed.])

those of Attica, said to have been overflowed in the time of Ogyges, about 500 years later; and those of Thessaly, in the time of Deucalion, still 300 years posterior. But such deluges as these will not account for the shells found in the higher lands. A second opinion has been entertained, which is, that, in times anterior to the records either of history or tradition, the bed of the ocean, the principal residence of the shelled tribe, has, by some great convulsion of nature, been heaved to the heights at which we now find shells and other remains of marine animals. The favourers of this opinion do well to suppose the great events on which it rests to have taken place beyond all the æras of history; for within these, certainly none such are to be found: and we may venture to say further, that no fact has taken place, either in our own days, or in the thousands of years recorded in history, which proves the existence of any natural agents, within or without the bowels of the earth, of force sufficient to heave, to the height of 15,000 feet, such masses as the Andes. The difference between the power necessary to produce such an effect, and that which shuffled together the different parts of Calabria in our days, is so immense, that, from the existence of the latter we are not authorised to infer that of the former.

M. de Voltaire has suggested a third solution of this difficulty (Quest. encycl. Coquilles).[2] He cites an instance in Touraine, where, in the space of 80 years, a particular spot of earth had been twice metamorphosed into soft stone, which had become hard when employed in building. In this stone shells of various kinds were produced, discoverable at first only with the microscope, but afterwards growing with the stone. From this fact, I suppose he would have us infer, that, besides the usual process for generating shells by the elaboration of earth and water in animal vessels, nature may have provided an equivalent

[2] That is, the section on shells in Voltaire's *Questions sur l'Encyclopédie*, which is included in his collected works. [Ed.]

operation, by passing the same materials through the pores of calcareous earths and stones: as we see calcareous drop-stones generating every day by the percolation of water through lime-stone, and new marble forming in the quarries from which the old has been taken out; and it might be asked, whether it is more difficult for nature to shoot the calcareous juice into the form of a shell, than other juices into the forms of chrystals, plants, animals, according to the construction of the vessels through which they pass? There is a wonder somewhere. Is it greatest on this branch of the dilemma; on that which supposes the existence of a power, of which we have no evidence in any other case; or on the first, which requires us to believe the creation of a body of water, and its subsequent annihilation? The establishment of the instance, cited by M. de Voltaire, of the growth of shells unattached to animal bodies, would have been that of his theory. But he has not established it. He has not even left it on ground so respectable as to have rendered it an object of enquiry to the literati of his own country. Abandoning this fact, therefore, the three hypotheses are equally unsatisfactory; and we must be contented to acknowledge, that this great phænomenon is as yet unsolved. Ignorance is preferable to error; and he is less remote from the truth who believes nothing, than he who believes what is wrong.

Stone. There is great abundance (more especially when you approach the mountains) of stone, white, blue, brown, &c. fit for the chissel, good mill-stone, such also as stands the fire, and slate-stone. We are told of flint, fit for gun-flints, on the Meherrin in Brunswic, on the Missisipi between the mouth of Ohio and Kaskaskia, and on others of the western waters. Isinglass or mica is in several places; loadstone also, and an Asbestos of a ligneous texture, is sometimes to be met with.

Earths. Marle abounds generally. A clay, of which, like the Sturbridge in England, bricks are made, which will resist long the violent action of fire, has been found on

Tuckahoe creek of James river, and no doubt will be found in other places. Chalk is said to be in Botetourt and Bedford. In the latter county is some earth, believed to be Gypseous. Ochres are found in various parts.

Nitre. In the lime-stone country are many caves, the earthy floors of which are impregnated with nitre. On Rich creek, a branch of the Great Kanhaway, about 60 miles below the lead mines, is a very large one, about 20 yards wide, and entering a hill a quarter or half a mile. The vault is of rock, from 9 to 15 or 20 feet above the floor. A Mr. Lynch, who gives me this account, undertook to extract the nitre. Besides a coat of the salt which had formed on the vault and floor, he found the earth highly impregnated to the depth of seven feet in some places, and generally of three, every bushel yielding on an average three pounds of nitre. Mr. Lynch having made about 1000 lb. of the salt from it, consigned it to some others, who have since made 10,000 lb. They have done this by pursuing the cave into the hill, never trying a second time the earth they have once exhausted, to see how far or soon it receives another impregnation. At least fifty of these caves are worked on the Greenbriar. There are many of them known on Cumberland river.

Salt. The country westward of the Alleghaney abounds with springs of common salt. The most remarkable we have heard of are at Bullet's lick, the Big bones, the Blue licks, and on the North fork of Holston. The area of Bullet's lick is of many acres. Digging the earth to the depth of three feet, the water begins to boil up, and the deeper you go, and the drier the weather, the stronger is the brine. A thousand gallons of water yield from a bushel to a bushel and a half of salt, which is about 80 lb. of water to one lb. of salt; but of sea-water 25 lb. yield 1 lb. of salt. So that sea-water is more than three times as strong as that of these springs. A salt spring has been lately discovered at the Turkey foot on Yohogany, by which river it is overflowed, except at very low water. Its merit is not yet known. Duning's lick is also as yet untried, but it is supposed to be the best on this side the Ohio. The salt springs on the margin of the Onondago lake are said to give a saline taste to the waters of the lake.

Medicinal springs. There are several medicinal springs, some of which are indubitably efficacious, while others seem to owe their reputation as much to fancy, and change of air and regimen, as to their real virtues. None of them having undergone a chemical analysis in skilful hands, nor been so far the subject of observations as to have produced a reduction into classes of the disorders which they relieve, it is in my power to give little more than an enumeration of them.

The most effiacious of these are two springs in Augusta, near the first sources of James river, where it is called Jackson's river. They rise near the foot of the ridge of mountains, generally called the Warm Spring mountain, but in the maps Jackson's mountains. The one is distinguished by the name of the Warm spring, and the other of the Hot spring. The Warm spring issues with a very bold stream, sufficient to work a grist-mill, and to keep the waters of its bason, which is 30 feet in diameter, at the vital warmth, viz. 96° of Farenheit's thermometer. The matter with which these waters is allied is very volatile; its smell indicates it to be sulphureous, as also does the circumstance of its turning silver black. They relieve rheumatisms. Other complaints also of very different natures have been removed or lessened by them. It rains here four or five days in every week.

The *Hot Spring* is about six miles from the Warm, is much smaller, and has been so hot as to have boiled an egg. Some believe its degree of heat to be lessened. It raises the mercury in Farenheit's thermometer to 112 degrees, which is fever heat. It sometimes relieves where the Warm spring fails. A fountain of common water, issuing within a few inches of its margin, gives it a singular appearance. Comparing the temperature of these with that of the Hot springs of Kamschatka, of which Krachininni-kow gives an account,[3] the difference is very great, the latter raising the mercury to 200° which is within 12° of boiling water. These springs are very much resorted to in spite of a total want of accommodation for the sick. Their waters are strongest in the hottest months, which occasions their being visited in July and August principally.

The Sweet springs are in the county of Botetourt, at the eastern foot of the Alleghaney, about 42 miles from the Warm springs. They are still less known. Having been found to relieve cases in which the others had been ineffectually tried, it is probable their composition is different. They are different also in their temperature, being as cold as common water: which is not mentioned, however, as a proof of a distinct impregnation. This is among the first sources of James river.

On Patowmac river, in Berkeley county, above the North mountain, are medicinal springs, much more frequented than those of Augusta. Their powers, however, are less, the waters weakly mineralized, and scarcely warm. They are more visited, because situated in a fertile, plentiful, and populous country, better provided with accommodations, always safe from the Indians, and nearest to the more populous states.

In Louisa county, on the head waters of the South Anna branch of York river, are springs of some medicinal virtue. They are not much used however. There is a weak chalybeate at Richmond; and many others in various parts of the country, which are of too little worth, or too little note, to be enumerated after those before-mentioned.

We are told of a Sulphur spring on Howard's creek of Greenbriar, and another at Boonsborough on Kentucky.

Burning spring. In the low grounds of the Great Kanhaway, seven miles above the mouth of Elk river, and 67 above that of Kanhaway itself, is a hole in the earth of

[3] Etienne Petrovitch Kracheninnikov, *Histoire de Kamtchatka et de Contrées Voisines* (Lyon, 1767). [Ed.]

the capacity of 30 or 40 gallons, from which issues constantly a bituminous vapour in so strong a current, as to give to the sand about its orifice the motion which it has in a boiling spring. On presenting a lighted candle or torch within 18 inches of the hole, it flames up in a column of 18 inches diameter, and four or five feet height, which sometimes burns out within 20 minutes, and at other times has been known to continue three days, and then has been left still burning. The flame is unsteady, of the density of that of burning spirits, and smells like burning pit-coal. Water sometimes collects in the bason, which is remarkably cold, and is kept in ebullition by the vapour issuing through it. If the vapour be fired in that state, the water soon becomes so warm that the hand cannot bear it, and evaporates wholly in a short time. This, with the circumjacent lands, is the property of his Excellency General Washington and of General Lewis.

There is a similar one on Sandy river, the flame of which is a column of about 12 inches diameter, and three feet high. General Clarke,[4] who informs me of it, kindled the vapour, staid about an hour, and left it burning.

Syphon fountains. The mention of uncommon springs leads me to that of Syphon fountains. There is one of these near the intersection of the Lord Fairfax's boundary with the North mountain, not far from Brock's gap, on the stream of which is a grist-mill, which grinds two bushel of grain at every flood of the spring. Another, near the Cow-pasture river, a mile and a half below its confluence with the Bull-pasture river, and 16 or 17 miles from the Hot springs, which intermits once in every twelve hours. One also near the mouth of the North Holston.

After these may be mentioned the *Natural Well*, on the lands of a Mr. Lewis in Frederick county. It is somewhat larger than a common well: the water rises in it as near the surface of the earth as in the neighbouring artificial wells, and is of a depth as yet unknown. It is said there

[4] George Rogers Clark (1752–1818), "Conqueror of the Northwest" during the Revolutionary War. [Ed.]

is a current in it tending sensibly downwards. If this be
true, it probably feeds some fountain, of which it is the
natural reservoir, distinguished from others, like that of
Madison's cave, by being accessible. It is used with a
bucket and windlass as an ordinary well.

VEGETABLES

A complete catalogue of the trees, plants, fruits, &c. is
probably not desired. I will sketch out those which would
principally attract notice, as being 1. Medicinal, 2. Esculent, 3. Ornamental, or 4. Useful for fabrication; adding
the Linnæan to the popular names, as the latter might not
convey precise information to a foreigner. I shall confine
myself too to native plants.

1. Senna. Cassia ligustrina.
Arsmart. Polygonum Sagittatum.
Clivers, or goose-grass. Galium spurium.
Lobelia of several species.
Palma Christi. Ricinus.
James-town weed. Datura Stramonium.
Mallow. Malva rotundifolia.
Syrian mallow. Hibiscus moschentos.
      Hibiscus virginicus.
Indian mallow. Sida rhombifolia.
     Sida abutilon.
Virginia Marshmallow. Napæa hermaphrodita.
      Napæa dioica.
Indian physic. Spiræa trifoliata.
Euphorbia Ipecacuanhæ.
Pleurisy root. Asclepias decumbens.
Virginia snake-root. Aristolochia serpentaria.
Black snake-root. Actæa racemosa.
Seneca rattlesnake-root. Polygala Senega.
Valerian. Valeriana locusta radiata.
Gentiana, Saponaria, Villosa & Centaurium.
Ginseng. Panax quinquefolium.
Angelica. Angelica sylvestris.
Cassava. Jatropha urens.

2. Tuckahoe. Lycoperdon tuber.

Jerusalem artichoke. Helianthus tuberosus.

Long potatoes. Convolvulas batatas.

Granadadillas. Maycocks. Maracocks. Passiflora incarnata.

Panic. Panicum of many species.

Indian millet. Holcus laxus.
                    Holcus striosus.

Wild oat. Zizania aquatica.

Wild pea. Dolichos of Clayton.

Lupine. Lupinus perennis.

Wild hop. Humulus lupulus.

Wild cherry. Prunus Virginiana.

Cherokee plumb. Prunus sylvestris fructu
    majori. ⎫
            ⎬ Clayton.[5]
Wild plumb. Prunus sylvestris fructu minori. ⎭

Wild crab-apple. Pyrus coronaria.

Red mulberry. Morus rubra.

Persimmon. Diospyros Virginiana.

Sugar maple. Acer saccharinum.

Scaly bark hiccory. Juglans alba cortice squamoso.
    Clayton.

Common hiccory. Juglans alba, fructu minore rancido.
    Clayton.

Paccan, or Illinois nut. Not described by Linnæus, Millar,[6] or Clayton. Were I to venture to describe this, speaking of the fruit from memory, and of the leaf from plants of two years growth, I should specify it as the Juglans alba, foliolis lanceolatis, acuminatis, serratis, tomentosis, fructu minore, ovato, compresso, vix insculpto, dulci, putamine, tenerrimo. It grows on the Illinois, Wabash, Ohio, and Missisipi. It is spoken of by Don Ulloa under the name of Pacanos, in his Noticias Americanas. Entret. 6.

Black walnut. Juglans nigra.

[5] John Clayton, *Flora Virginica* (Leyden, 1739–1743). Jefferson later refers to the second revised edition, 1762. [Ed.]

[6] Philip Miller, *The Gardener's and Florist's Dictionary*, 2 vols. (London, 1724). [Ed.]

White walnut. Juglans alba.
Chesnut. Fagus castanea.
Chinquapin. Fagus pumila.
Hazlenut. Corylus avellana.
Grapes. Vitis. Various kinds, though only three described by Clayton.
Scarlet Strawberries. Fragaria Virginiana of Millar.
Whortleberries. Vaccinium uliginosum.
Wild gooseberries. Ribes grossularia.
Cranberries. Vaccinium oxycoccos.
Black raspberries. Rubus occidentalis.
Blackberries. Rubus fruticosus.
Dewberries. Rubus cæsius.
Cloudberries. Rubus chamæmorus.

3. Plane-tree. Platanus occidentalis.
Poplar. Liriodendron tulipifera.
        Populus heterophylla.
Black poplar. Populus nigra.
Aspen. Populus tremula.
Linden, or lime. Tilia Americana.
Red flowering maple. Acer rubrum.
Horse-chesnut, or Buck's-eye. Æsculus pavia.
Catalpa. Bignonia catalpa.
Umbrella. Magnolia tripetala.
Swamp laurel. Magnolia glauca.
Cucumber-tree. Magnolia acuminata.
Portugal bay. Laurus indica.
Red bay. Laurus borbonia.
Dwarf-rose bay. Rhododendron maximum.
Laurel of the western country. Qu. species?
Wild pimento. Laurus benzoin.
Sassafras. Laurus sassafras.
Locust. Robinia pseudo-acacia.
Honey-locust. Gleditsia. 1.
Dogwood. Cornus florida.
Fringe or snow-drop tree. Chionanthus Virginica.
Barberry. Berberis vulgaris.
Redbud, or Judas-tree. Cercis Canadensis.

Holly. Ilex aquifolium.
Cockspur hawthorn. Cratægus coccinea.
Spindle-tree. Euonymus Europæus.
Evergreen spindle-tree. Euonymus Americanus.
Itea Virginica.
Elder. Sambucus nigra.
Papaw. Annona triloba.
Candleberry myrtle. Myrica cerifera.
Dwarf-laurel. Kalmia angustifolia.⎫ called ivy
          Kalmia latifolia. ⎬ with us.
Ivy. Hedera quinquefolia.
Trumpet honeysuckle. Lonicera sempervirens.
Upright honeysuckle. Azalea nudiflora.
Yellow jasmine. Bignonia sempervirens.
Calycanthus floridus.
American aloe. Agave Virginica.
Sumach. Rhus. Qu. species?
Poke. Phytolacca decandra.
Long moss. Tillandsia Usneoides.

4. Reed. Arundo phragmitis.
Virginia hemp. Acnida cannabina.
Flax. Linum Virginianum.
Black, or pitch-pine. Pinus tæda.
White pine. Pinus strobus.
Yellow pine. Pinus Virginica.
Spruce pine. Pinus foliis singularibus. Clayton.
Hemlock spruce fir. Pinus Canadensis.
Arbor vitæ. Thuya occidentalis.
Juniper. Juniperus Virginica (called cedar with us).
Cypress. Cupressus disticha.
White cedar. Cupressus Thyoides.
Black oak. Quercus nigra.
White oak. Quercus alba.
Red oak. Quercus rubra.
Willow oak. Quercus phellos.
Chesnut oak. Quercus prinus.
Black jack oak. Quercus aquatica. Clayton. Query?
Ground oak. Quercus pumila. Clayton.

Live oak. Quercus Virginiana. Millar.
Black birch. Betula nigra.
White birch. Betula alba.
Beach. Fagus sylvatica.
Ash. Fraxinus Americana.
      Fraxinus Novæ Angliæ. Millar.
Elm. Ulmus Americana.
Willow. Salix. Query species?
Sweet Gum. Liquidambar styraciflua.

The following were found in Virginia when first visited by the English; but it is not said whether of spontaneous growth, or by cultivation only. Most probably they were natives of more southern climates, and handed along the continent from one nation to another of the savages.

Tobacco. Nicotiana.
Maize. Zea mays.
Round potatoes. Solanum tuberosum.
Pumkins. Cucurbita pepo.
Cymlings. Cucurbita verrucosa.
Squashes. Cucurbita melopepo.

There is an infinitude of other plants and flowers, for an enumeration and scientific description of which I must refer to the Flora Virginica of our great botanist Dr. Clayton, published by Gronovius at Leyden, in 1762. This accurate observer was a native and resident of this state, passed a long life in exploring and describing its plants, and is supposed to have enlarged the botanical catalogue as much as almost any man who has lived.

Besides these plants, which are native, our *farms* produce wheat, rye, barley, oats, buck wheat, broom corn, and Indian corn. The climate suits rice well enough wherever the lands do. Tobacco, hemp, flax, and cotton, are staple commodities. Indico yields two cuttings. The silkworm is a native, and the mulberry, proper for its food, grows kindly.

We cultivate also potatoes, both the long and the round, turnips, carrots, parsneps, pumkins, and ground nuts (Arachis.) Our grasses are lucerne, st. foin, burnet, timothy, ray and orchard grass; red, white, and yellow clover; greenswerd, blue grass, and crab grass.

The *gardens* yield musk-melons, water-melons, tomatas, okra, pomegranates, figs, and the esculent plants of Europe.

The *orchards* produce apples, pears, cherries, quinces, peaches, nectarines, apricots, almonds, and plumbs.

ANIMALS

Our quadrupeds have been mostly described by Linnæus and Mons. de Buffon. Of these the Mammoth, or big buffalo, as called by the Indians, must certainly have been the largest. Their tradition is, that he was carnivorous, and still exists in the northern parts of America. A delegation of warriors from the Delaware tribe having visited the governor of Virginia, during the present revolution, on matters of business, after these had been discussed and settled in council, the governor asked them some questions relative to their country, and, among others, what they knew or had heard of the animal whose bones were found at the Saltlicks, on the Ohio. Their chief speaker immediately put himself into an attitude of oratory, and with a pomp suited to what he conceived the elevation of his subject, informed him that it was a tradition handed down from their fathers, "That in ancient times a herd of these tremendous animals came to the Bigbone licks, and began an universal destruction of the bear, deer, elks, buffaloes, and other animals, which had been created for the use of the Indians: that the Great Man above, looking down and seeing this, was so enraged that he seized his lightning, descended on the earth, seated himself on a neighbouring mountain, on a rock, of which his seat and the print of his feet are still to be seen, and hurled his bolts among them till the whole were slaughtered, except the big bull, who presenting his forehead to the shafts, shook them off as they fell; but missing one at length, it wounded him in the side; whereon, springing round, he bounded over the Ohio, over the Wabash, the Illinois, and finally over the great lakes, where he is living at this day." It is well known that on the Ohio, and in many parts of America further north, tusks, grinders, and skeletons of unparalleled magnitude, are found in great numbers, some lying on the surface of the earth, and some a little below it. A Mr. Stanley, taken prisoner by the Indians near the mouth of the Tanissee, relates, that, after being transferred through several tribes, from one to another, he was at length carried over the mountains West of the Missouri to a river which runs westwardly; that these bones abounded there; and that the natives described to him the animal to which they belonged as still existing in the northern parts of their country; from which description he judged it to be an elephant. Bones of the same kind have been lately found, some feet below the surface of the earth, in salines opened on the North Holston, a branch of the Tanissee, about the latitude of 36½° North. From the accounts published in Europe, I suppose it to be decided, that these are of the same kind with those found in Siberia. Instances are mentioned of like animal remains found in the more southern climates of both hemispheres; but they are either so loosely mentioned as to leave a doubt of the fact, so inaccurately described as not to authorize the classing them with the great northern bones, or so rare as to found a suspicion that they have been carried thither as curiosities from more northern regions. So that on the whole there seem to be no certain vestiges of the existence of this animal further South than the salines last mentioned. It is remarkable that the tusks and skeletons have been ascribed by the naturalists of Europe to the elephant, while the grinders have been given to the hippopotamus, or riverhorse. Yet it is acknowledged, that the tusks and skeletons are much larger than those of the elephant, and the grinders many times greater than those of the hippopotamus, and essentially different in form. Wherever these grinders are found, there also we find the tusks and skeleton; but no skeleton of the hippopotamus nor grinders of the elephant. It will not be said that the hippopotamus and elephant came always to the same spot, the former to deposit his grinders, and the latter his tusks and skeleton. For what became of the parts not deposited there? We must agree then that these remains belong to each other, that they are of one and the same animal, that this was not a hippopotamus, because the hippopotamus had no tusks nor such a frame, and because the grinders differ in their size as well as in the number and form of their points. That it was not an elephant, I think ascertained by proofs equally decisive. I will not avail myself of the authority of the celebrated anatomist,[7] who, from an examination of the form and structure of the tusks, has declared they were essentially different from those of the elephant; because another anatomist,[8] equally celebrated, has declared, on a like examination, that they are precisely the same. Between two such authorities I will suppose this circumstance equivocal. But, 1. The skeleton of the mammoth (for so the incognitum has been called) bespeaks an animal of five or six times the cubic volume of the elephant, as Mons. de Buffon has admitted. 2. The grinders are five times as large, are square, and the grinding surface studded with four or five rows of blunt points: whereas those of the elephant are broad and thin, and their grinding surface flat. 3. I have never heard an instance, and suppose there has been none, of the grinder of an elephant being found in America. 4. From the known temperature and constitution of the elephant he could never have existed in those regions where the remains of the mammoth have been found. The elephant is a native only of the torrid zone and its vicinities: if, with the assistance of

[7] Hunter. (John Hunter, "Observations on the Bones Commonly Supposed to Be Elephant Bones, Which Have Been Found Near River Ohio, in America," *Royal Society Philosophical Transactions*, vol. 58, 1768. [Ed.])

[8] D'Aubenton. (Louis Jean Marie Daubenton, 1716–1799, French nautralist and collaborator with Buffon. [Ed.])

warm apartments and warm clothing, he has been preserved in life in the temperate climates of Europe, it has only been for a small portion of what would have been his natural period, and no instance of his multiplication in them has ever been known. But no bones of the mammoth, as I have before observed, have been ever found further south than the salines of the Holston, and they have been found as far north as the Arctic circle. Those, therefore, who are of opinion that the elephant and mammoth are the same, must believe, 1. That the elephant known to us can exist and multiply in the frozen zone; or, 2. That an internal fire may once have warmed those regions, and since abandoned them, of which, however, the globe exhibits no unequivocal indications; or, 3. That the obliquity of the ecliptic, when these elephants lived, was so great as to include within the tropics all those regions in which the bones are found; the tropics being, as is before observed, the natural limits of habitation for the elephant. But if it be admitted that this obliquity has really decreased, and we adopt the highest rate of decrease yet pretended, that is, of one minute in a century, to transfer the northern tropic to the Arctic circle, would carry the existence of these supposed elephants 250,000 years back; a period far beyond our conception of the duration of animal bones left exposed to the open air, as these are in many instances. Besides, though these regions would then be supposed within the tropics, yet their winters would have been too severe for the sensibility of the elephant. They would have had too but one day and one night in the year, a circumstance to which we have no reason to suppose the nature of the elephant fitted. However, it has been demonstrated, that, if a variation of obliquity in the ecliptic takes place at all, it is vibratory, and never exceeds the limits of 9 degrees, which is not sufficient to bring these bones within the tropics. One of these hypotheses, or some other equally voluntary and inadmissible to cautious philosophy, must be adopted to support the opinion that these are the bones of the elephant. For my own part, I find it easier to believe that an animal may have existed, resembling the elephant in his tusks, and general anatomy, while his nature was in other respects extremely different. From the 30th degree of South latitude to the 30th of North, are nearly the limits which nature has fixed for the existence and multiplication of the elephant known to us. Proceeding thence northwardly to 36½ degrees, we enter those assigned to the mammoth. The further we advance North, the more their vestiges multiply as far as the earth has been explored in that direction; and it is as probable as otherwise, that this progression continues to the pole itself, if land extends so far. The center of the frozen zone then may be the achmé of their vigour, as that of the torrid is of the elephant. Thus nature seems to have drawn a belt of separation between these two tremendous animals, whose breadth indeed is not precisely known, though at present we may suppose it about 6½ degrees of latitude; to have assigned to the elephant the regions South of these confines, and those North to the mammoth, founding the constitution of the one in her extreme of heat, and that of the other in the extreme of cold. When the Creator has therefore separated their nature as far as the extent of the scale of animal life allowed to this planet would permit, it seems perverse to declare it the same, from a partial resemblance of their tusks and bones. But to whatever animal we ascribe these remains, it is certain such a one has existed in America, and that it has been the largest of all terrestrial beings. It should have sufficed to have rescued the earth it inhabited, and the atmosphere it breathed, from the imputation of impotence in the conception and nourishment of animal life on a large scale: to have stifled, in its birth, the opinion of a writer, the most learned too of all others in the science of animal history, that in the new world, "La nature vivante est beaucoup moins agissante, beaucoup moins forte";[9] that nature is less active, less energetic on one side of the globe than she is on the other. As if both sides were not warmed by the same

9 Buffon, XVII, 122 edit. Paris, 1764.

genial sun; as if a soil of the same chemical composition, was less capable of elaboration into animal nutriment; as if the fruits and grains from that soil and sun, yielded a less rich chyle, gave less extension to the solids and fluids of the body, or produced sooner in the cartilages, membranes, and fibres, that rigidity which restrains all further extension, and terminates animal growth. The truth is, that a Pigmy and a Patagonian, a Mouse and a Mammoth, derive their dimensions from the same nutritive juices. The difference of increment depends on circumstances unsearchable to beings with our capacities. Every race of animals seems to have received from their Maker certain laws of extension at the time of their formation. Their elaborative organs were formed to produce this, while proper obstacles were opposed to its further progress. Below these limits they cannot fall, nor rise above them. What intermediate station they shall take may depend on soil, on climate, on food, on a careful choice of breeders. But all the manna of heaven would never raise the mouse to the bulk of the mammoth.

The opinion advanced by the Count de Buffon,[10] is 1. That the animals common both to the old and new world, are smaller in the latter. 2. That those peculiar to the new are on a smaller scale. 3. That those which have been domesticated in both, have degenerated in America: and 4. That on the whole it exhibits fewer species. And the reason he thinks is, that the heats of America are less; that more waters are spread over its surface by nature, and fewer of these drained off by the hand of man. In other words, that *heat* is friendly, and *moisture* adverse to the production and development of large quadrupeds. I will not meet this hypothesis on its first doubtful ground, whether the climate of America be comparatively more humid? Because we are not furnished with observations sufficient to decide this question. And though, till it be decided, we are as free to deny, as others are to affirm the fact, yet for a moment let it be supposed. The hypothesis,

[10] XVIII, 100–156.

after this supposition, proceeds to another; that *moisture* is unfriendly to animal growth. The truth of this is inscrutable to us by reasonings a priori. Nature has hidden from us her modus agendi. Our only appeal on such questions is to experience; and I think that experience is against the supposition. It is by the assistance of *heat* and *moisture* that vegetables are elaborated from the elements of earth, air, water, and fire. We accordingly see the more humid climates produce the greater quantity of vegetables. Vegetables are mediately or immediately the food of every animal: and in proportion to the quantity of food, we see animals not only multiplied in their numbers, but improved in their bulk, as far as the laws of their nature will admit. Of this opinion is the Count de Buffon himself in another part of his work:[11] "*en general il parois ques les pays un peu* froids *conviennent mieux à nos boeufs que es pays chauds, et qu'ils sont d'autant plus gros et plus grande que le climat est plus* humide *et plus abondans en paturages. Les boeufs de Danemarck, de la Podolie, de l'Ukraine et de la Tartarie qu'habitent des Calmouques sont le[s] plus grands de tous.*"[12] Here then a race of animals, and one of the largest too, has been increased in its dimensions by *cold* and *moisture,* in direct opposition to the hypothesis, which supposes that these two circumstances diminish animal bulk, and that it is their contraries *heat* and *dryness* which enlarge it. But when we appeal to experience, we are not to rest satisfied with a single fact. Let us therefore try our question on more general ground. Let us take two portions of the earth, Europe and America for instance, sufficiently extensive to give operation to general causes; let us consider the circumstances peculiar to each, and observe their effect on animal na-

[11] VIII, 134.

[12] "In general it appears that colder countries are better adapted to our oxen than hot countries, and they are weightier and larger in proportion to the humidity of the climate and abundance of pastures. The oxen of Denmark, of Podalie, of the Ukraine, and of Tartary which is inhabited by the Calmoques, are the largest of all." [Ed.]

ture. America, running through the torrid as well as the temperate zone, has more *heat*, collectively taken, than Europe. But Europe, according to our hypothesis, is the *dryest*. They are equally adapted then to animal productions; each being endowed with one of those causes which befriend animal growth, and with one which opposes it. If it be thought unequal to compare Europe with America, which is so much larger, I answer, not more so than to compare America with the whole world. Besides, the purpose of the comparison is to try an hypothesis, which makes the size of animals depend on the *heat* and *moisture* of climate. If therefore we take a region, so extensive as to comprehend a sensible distinction of climate, and so extensive too as that local accidents, or the intercourse of animals on its borders, may not materially affect the size of those in its interior parts, we shall comply with those conditions which the hypothesis may reasonably demand. The objection would be the weaker in the present case, because any intercourse of animals which may take place on the confines of Europe and Asia, is to the advantage of the former, Asia producing certainly larger animals than Europe. Let us then take a comparative view of the quadrupeds of Europe and America, presenting them to the eye in three different tables, in one of which shall be enumerated those found in both countries; in a second those found in one only; in a third those which have been domesticated in both. To facilitate the comparison, let those of each table be arranged in gradation according to their sizes, from the greatest to the smallest, so far as their sizes can be conjectured. The weights of the large animals shall be expressed in the English avoirdupoise pound and its decimals: those of the smaller in the ounce and its decimals. Those which are marked thus *, are actual weights of particular subjects, deemed among the largest of their species. Those marked thus †, are furnished by judicious persons, well acquainted with the species, and saying, from conjecture only, what the largest individual they had seen would probably have weighed. The other weights are taken from Messrs. Buffon and D'Aubenton, and are of such subjects as came casually to their hands for dissection. This circumstance must be remembered where their weights and mine stand opposed: the latter being stated, not to produce a conclusion in favour of the American species, but to justify a suspension of opinion until we are better informed, and a suspicion in the mean time that there is no uniform difference in favour of either; which is all I pretend.

I have not inserted in the first table the Phoca[13] nor leather-winged bat, because the one living half the year in the water, and the other being a winged animal, the individuals of each species may visit both continents.

Of the animals in the 1st table Mons. de Buffon himself informs us, [XXVII. 130. XXX. 213.] that the beaver, the otter, and shrew mouse, though of the same species, are larger in America than Europe. This should therefore have corrected the generality of his expressions XVIII. 145. and elsewhere, that the animals common to the two countries are considerably less in America than in Europe, "& cela sans ancune exception." He tells us too [Quadrup. VIII. 334. edit. Paris, 1777] that on examining a bear from America, he remarked no difference "dans le *forme* de cet ours d'Amerique comparé a celui d'Europe." But adds from Bartram's journal, that an American bear weighed 400 lb. English, equal to 367 lb. French: whereas we find the European bear examined by Mons. D'Aubenton [XVII. 82] weighed but 141 lb. French. That the palmated elk is larger in America than Europe we are informed by Kalm,[14] a naturalist who visited the former by public ap-

---

[13] It is said, that this animal is seldom seen above 30 miles from shore, or beyond the 56th degree of latitude. The interjacent islands between Asia and America admit his passage from one continent to the other without exceeding these bounds. And in fact, travellers tell us that these islands are places of principal resort for them, and specially in the season of bringing forth their young.

[14] I, 233. Lon. 1772. (Peter Kalm, *Travels into North America*, 3 vols., London, 1770–1771. [Ed.])

A COMPARATIVE VIEW OF THE QUADRUPEDS OF EUROPE AND OF AMERICA.

I. ABORIGINALS OF BOTH.

	Europe.	*America.*
	lb.	lb.
Mammoth		
Buffalo. Bison		*1800
White bear. Ours blanc		
Caribou. Renne		
Bear. Ours	153.7	*410
Elk. Elan. Original, palmated		
Red deer. Cerf	288.8	*273
Fallow deer. Daim	167.8	
Wolf. Loup	69.8	
Roe. Chevreuil	56.7	
Glutton. Glouton. Carcajou		
Wild cat. Chat sauvage		†30
Lynx. Loup cervier	25.	
Beaver. Castor	18.5	*45
Badger. Blaireau	13.6	
Red fox. Renard	13.5	
Grey fox. Isatis		
Otter. Loutre	8.9	†12
Monax. Marmotte	6.5	
Vison. Fouine	2.8	
Hedgehog. Herisson	2.2	
Martin. Marte	1.9	†6
	oz.	
Water rat. Rat d'eau	7.5	
Wesel. Belette	2.2	oz.
Flying squirrel. Polatouche	2.2	†4
Shrew mouse. Musaraigne	1.	

pointment for the express purpose of examining the subjects of natural history. In this fact Pennant concurs with him. [Barrington's Miscellanies.] The same Kalm tells us[15] that the black moose, or renne of America, is as high as

[15] Ib. 233.

II. ABORIGINALS OF ONE ONLY.

Europe.		America.	
	lb.		*lb.*
Sanglier. Wild boar	280.	Tapir	534.
Mouflon. Wild sheep	56.	Elk, round horned	†450.
Bouquetin. Wild goat		Puma	
Lievre. Hare	7.6	Jaguar	218.
Lapin. Rabbit	3.4	Cabiai	109.
Putois. Polecat	3.3	Tamanoir	109.
Genette	3.1	Tamandua	65.4
Desman. Muskrat	*oz.*	Cougar of N. Amer.	75.
Ecureuil. Squirrel	12.	Cougar of S. Amer.	59.4
Hermine. Ermin	8.2	Ocelot	
Rat. Rat	7.5	Pecari	46.3
Loirs	3.1	Jaguaret	43.6
Lerot. Dormouse	1.8	Alco	
Taupe. Mole	1.2	Lama	
Hamster	.9	Paco	
Zisel		Paca	32.7
Leming		Serval	
Souris. Mouse	.6	Sloth. Unau	27¼
		Saricovienne	
		Kincajou	
		Tatou Kabassou	21.8
		Urson. Urchin	
		Raccoon. Raton	16.5
		Coati	
		Coendou	16.3
		Sloth. Aï	13.
		Sapajou Ouarini	
		Sapajou Coaita	9.8
		Tatou Encubert	
		Tatou Apar	
		Tatou Cachica	7.
		Little Coendou	6.5
		Opossum. Sarigue	
		Tapeti	
		Margay	
		Crabier	
		Agouti	4.2
		Sapajou Saï	3.5
		Tatou Cirquinçon	

II. TABLE *continued.*

Europe.	America.	
		lb.
	Tatou Tatouate	3.3
	Mouffette Squash	
	Mouffette Chinche	
	Mouffette Conepate. Scunk	
	Mouffette. Zorilla	
	Whabus. Hare. Rabbit	
	Aperea	
	Akouchi	
	Ondatra. Muskrat	
	Pilori	
	Great grey squirrel	†2.7
	Fox squirrel of Virginia	†2.625
	Surikate	2.
	Mink	†2.
	Sapajou. Sajou	1.8
	Indian pig. Cochon d'Inde	1.6
	Sapajou. Saïmiri	1.5
	Phalanger	
	Coquallin	
	Lesser grey squirrel	†1.5
	Black squirrel	†1.5
	Red squirrel	10 *oz.*
	Sagoin Saki	
	Sagoin Pinche	
	Sagoin Tamarin	*oz.*
	Sagoin Ouistiti	4.4
	Sagoin Marikine	
	Sagoin Mico	
	Cayopollin	
	Fourmillier	
	Marmose	
	Sarigue of Cayenne	
	Tucan	
	Red mole	*oz.*
	Ground squirrel	4.

III. DOMESTICATED IN BOTH.

	Europe.	America.
	lb.	*lb.*
Cow	763.	*2500
Horse		*1366
Ass		
Hog		*1200
Sheep		*125
Goat		*80
Dog	67.6	
Cat	7.	

a tall horse; and Catesby,[16] that it is about the bigness of a middle sized ox. The same account of their size has been given me by many who have seen them. But Mons. D'Aubenton says[17] that the renne of Europe is about the size of a red deer. The wesel is larger in America than in Europe, as may be seen by comparing its dimensions as reported by Mons. D'Aubenton[18] and Kalm. The latter tells us,[19] that the lynx, badger, red fox, and flying squirrel, are the *same* in America as in Europe: by which expression I understand, they are the same in all material circumstances, in size as well as others: for if they were smaller, they would differ from the European. Our grey fox is, by Catesby's account[20] little different in size and shape from the European fox. I presume he means the red fox of Europe, as does Kalm, where he says,[21] that in size "they do not quite come up to our foxes." For proceeding next to the red fox of America, he says "they are entirely

[16] I, xxvii. (Mark Catesby, *The Natural History of the Carolinas, Florida, and the Bahama Islands*, 2 vols., London, 1731–1743. [Ed.])

[17] XXIV. 162.

[18] XV. 42.

[19] I. 359. I. 43, 221, 251. II. 52.

[20] II. 78.

[21] I. 220.

the same with the European sort." Which shews he had in view one European sort only, which was the red. So that the result of their testimony is, that the American grey fox is somewhat less than the European red; which is equally true of the grey fox of Europe, as may be seen by comparing the measures of the Count de Buffon and Mons. D'Aubenton.[22] The white bear of America is as large as that of Europe. The bones of the mammoth which have been found in America, are as large as those found in the old world. It may be asked, why I insert the mammoth, as if it still existed? I ask in return, why I should omit it, as if it did not exist? Such is the œconomy of nature, that no instance can be produced of her having permitted any one race of her animals to become extinct; of her having formed any link in her great work so weak as to be broken. To add to this, the traditionary testimony of the Indians, that this animal still exists in the northern and western parts of America, would be adding the light of a taper to that of the meridian sun. Those parts still remain in their aboriginal state, unexplored and undisturbed by us, or by others for us. He may as well exist there now, as he did formerly where we find his bones. If he be a carnivorous animal, as some anatomists have conjectured, and the Indians affirm, his early retirement may be accounted for from the general destruction of the wild game by the Indians, which commences in the first instant of their connection with us, for the purpose of purchasing matchcoats, hatchets, and fire locks, with their skins. There remain then the buffalo, red deer, fallow deer, wolf, roe, glutton, wild cat, monax, vison, hedgehog, martin, and water rat, of the comparative sizes of which we have not sufficient testimony. It does not appear that Messrs. de Buffon and D'Aubenton have measured, weighed, or seen those of America. It is said of some of them, by some travellers, that they are smaller than the European. But who were these travellers? Have they not

22 XXVII. 63. XIV. 119. Harris, II. 387. Buffon. Quad. IX. 1.

been men of a very different description from those who have laid open to us the other three quarters of the world? Was natural history the object of their travels? Did they measure or weigh the animals they speak of? or did they not judge of them by sight, or perhaps even from report only? Were they acquainted with the animals of their own country, with which they undertake to compare them? Have they not been so ignorant as often to mistake the species? A true answer to these questions would probably lighten their authority, so as to render it insufficient for the foundation of an hypothesis. How unripe we yet are, for an accurate comparison of the animals of the two countries, will appear from the work of Mons. de Buffon. The ideas we should have formed of the sizes of some animals, from the information he had received at his first publications concerning them, are very different from what his subsequent communications give us. And indeed his candour in this can never be too much praised. One sentence of his book must do him immortal honour. *"J'aime autant une personne qui me releve d'une erreur, qu'une autre qui m'apprend une verité, parce qu'en effet une erreur corrigée est une verité."* [23] He seems to have thought the cabiai he first examined wanted little of its full growth. *"Il n'était pas encore tout à fait adulte."* [24] Yet he weighed but 46½ lb. and[25] he found afterward,[26] that these animals, when full grown, weigh 100 lb. He had supposed, from the examination of a jaguar,[27] said to be two years old, which weighed but 16 lb. 12 oz. that, when he should have acquired his full growth, he would not be larger than a middle sized dog. But a subsequent account[28]

[23] Quad. IX. 158. ("I love as much a person who corrects me of an error, as another one who teaches me a truth, for an error corrected is a truth." [Ed.])

[24] "It was not yet fully grown." [Ed.]

[25] XXV. 184.

[26] Quad. IX. 132.

[27] XIX. 2.

[28] Quad. IX. 41.

raises his weight to 200 lb. Further information will, doubtless, produce further corrections. The wonder is, not that there is yet something in this great work to correct, but that there is so little. The result of this view then is, that of 26 quadrupeds common to both countries, 7 are said to be larger in America, 7 of equal size, and 12 not sufficiently examined. So that the first table impeaches the first member of the assertion, that of the animals common to both countries, the American are smallest, "*et cela sans aucune exception.*" It shews it not just, in all the latitude in which its author has advanced it, and probably not to such a degree as to found a distinction between the two countries.

Proceeding to the second table, which arranges the animals found in one of the two countries only, Mons. de Buffon observes, that the tapir, the elephant of America, is but of the size of a small cow. To preserve our comparison, I will add that the wild boar, the elephant of Europe, is little more than half that size. I have made an elk with round or cylindrical horns, an animal of America, and peculiar to it; because I have seen many of them myself, and more of their horns; and because I can say, from the best information, that, in Virginia, this kind of elk has abounded much, and still exists in smaller numbers; and I could never learn that the palmated kind had been seen here at all. I suppose this confined to the more northern latitudes.[29] I have made our hare or rabbit peculiar, be-

[29] The descriptions of Theodat, Denys and La Hontan, cited by Mons. de Buffon under the article Elan, authorise the supposition, that the flat-horned elk is found in the northern parts of America. It has not however extended to our latitudes. On the other hand, I could never learn that the round-horned elk has been further North than the Hudson's river. This agrees with the former elk in its general character, being, like that, when compared with a deer, very much larger, its ears longer, broader, and thicker in proportion, its hair much longer, neck and tail shorter, having a dewlap before the breast (caruncula gutturalia Linnaei) a white spot often, if not always, a foot diameter, on the hinder part of the buttocks round the tail; its gait a trot, and attended with a rattling of the hoofs; but distinguished from that decisively by its horns, which are not

lieving it to be different from both the European animals
of those denominations, and calling it therefore by its
Algonquin name Whabus, to keep it distinct from these.
Kalm is of the same opinion.[30] I have enumerated the
squirrels according to our own knowledge, derived from
daily sight of them, because I am not able to reconcile
with that the European appellations and descriptions. I
have heard of other species, but they have never come
within my own notice. These, I think, are the only instances in which I have departed from the authority of
Mons. de Buffon in the construction of this table. I take

---

palmated, but round and pointed. This is the animal described
by Catesby as the Cervus major Americanus, the stag of
America, le cerf de l'Amérique. But it differs from the Cervus
as totally, as does the palmated elk from the dama. And in fact
it seems to stand in the same relations to the palmated elk, as the
red deer does to the fallow. It has abounded in Virginia, has
been seen, within my knowledge, on the eastern side of the
Blue ridge since the year 1765, is now common beyond those
mountains, has been often brought to us and tamed, and their
horns are in the hands of many. I should designate it as the
"Alces Americanus cornibus terretibus." It were to be wished,
that naturalists, who are acquainted with the renne and elk of
Europe, and who may hereafter visit the northern parts of
America, would examine well the animals called there by the
names of grey and black moose, caribou, original, and elk.
Mons. de Buffon has done what could be done from the
materials in his hands, towards clearing up the confusion introduced by the loose application of these names among the animals
they are meant to designate. He reduces the whole to the renne
and flat-horned elk. From all the information I have been able
to collect, I strongly suspect they will be found to cover three,
if not four distinct species of animals. I have seen skins of a
moose, and of the caribou: they differ more from each other,
and from that of the round-horned elk, than I ever saw two
skins differ which belonged to different individuals of any wild
species. These differences are in the colour, length, and
coarseness of the hair, and in the size, texture, and marks of the
skin. Perhaps it will be found that there is, 1. The moose, black
and grey, the former being said to be the male, and the latter
the female. 2. The caribou or renne. 3. The flat-horned elk, or
original. 4. The round-horned elk. Should this last, though possessing to nearly the characters of the elk, be found to be the
same with the Cerf d'Ardennes or Brandhirtz of Germany, still
there will remain the three species first enumerated.

[30] Kalm II. 340 I. 82.

him for my ground work, because I think him the best informed of any naturalist who has ever written. The result is, that there are 18 quadrupeds peculiar to Europe; more than four times as many, to wit 74, peculiar to America; that the first of these 74 weighs more than the whole column of Europeans;[31] and consequently this second table disproves the second member of the assertion, that the animals peculiar to the new world are on a smaller scale, so far as that assertion relied on European animals for support: and it is in full opposition to the theory which makes the animal volume to depend on the circumstances of *heat* and *moisture*.

The IIId. table comprehends those quadrupeds only which are domestic in both countries. That some of these, in some parts of America, have become less than their original stock, is doubtless true; and the reason is very obvious. In a thinly peopled country, the spontaneous productions of the forests and waste fields are sufficient to support indifferently the domestic animals of the farmer, with a very little aid from him in the severest and scarcest season. He therefore finds it more convenient to receive them from the hand of nature in that indifferent state, than to keep up their size by a care and nourishment which would cost him much labour. If, on this low fare, these animals dwindle, it is no more than they do in those parts of Europe where the poverty of the soil, or poverty of the owner, reduces them to the same scanty subsistance. It is the uniform effect of one and the same cause, whether acting on this or that side of the globe. It would

[31] The Tapir is the largest of the animals peculiar to America. I collect his weight thus. Mons. de Buffon says, XXIII. 274. that he is of the size of a Zebu, or a small cow. He gives us the measures of a Zebu, lb. 94, as taken by himself, viz. 5 feet 7 inches from the muzzle to the root of the tail, and 5 feet 1 inch circumference behind the fore legs. A bull, measuring in the same way 6 feet 9 inches and 5 feet 2 inches, weighed 600 lb. VIII. 153. The Zebu then, and of course the Tapir, would weigh about 500 lb. But one individual of every species of European peculiars would probably weigh less than 400 lb. These are French measures and weights.

be erring therefore against that rule of philosophy, which teaches us to ascribe like effects to like causes, should we impute this diminution of size in America to any imbecility or want of uniformity in the operations of nature. It may be affirmed with truth that, in those countries, and with those individuals of America, where necessity or curiosity has produced equal attention as in Europe to the nourishment of animals, the horses, cattle, sheep, and hogs of the one continent are as large as those of the other. There are particular instances, well attested, where individuals of this country have imported good breeders from England, and have improved their size by care in the course of some years. To make a fair comparison between the two countries, it will not answer to bring together animals of what might be deemed the middle or ordinary size of their species; because an error in judging of that middle or ordinary size would vary the result of the comparison. Thus Monsieur D'Aubenton[32] considers a horse of 4 feet 5 inches high and 400 lb. weight French, equal to 4 feet 8.6 inches and 436 lb. English, as a middle sized horse. Such a one is deemed a small horse in America. The extremes must therefore be resorted to. The same anatomist[33] dissected a horse of 5 feet 9 inches height, French measure, equal to 6 feet 1.7 English. This is near 6 inches higher than any horse I have seen: and could it be supposed that I had seen the largest horses in America, the conclusion would be, that ours have diminished, or that we have bred from a smaller stock. In Connecticut and Rhode-Island, where the climate is favourable to the production of grass, bullocks have been slaughtered which weighed 2500, 2200, and 2100 lb. nett; and those of 1800 lb. have been frequent. I have seen a hog weigh 1050 lb. after the blood, bowels, and hair had been taken from him.[34] Before he was killed an attempt was made to weigh him with a pair of steel-yards, graduated to 1200 lb. but

[32] VII. 432.
[33] VII. 474.
[34] In Williamsburg, April, 1769.

he weighed more. Yet this hog was probably not within fifty generations of the European stock. I am well informed of another which weighed 1100 lb. gross. Asses have been still more neglected than any other domestic animal in America. They are neither fed nor housed in the most rigorous season of the year. Yet they are larger than those measured by Mons. D'Aubenton,[35] of 3 feet 7¼ inches, 3 feet 4 inches, and 3 feet 2½ inches, the latter weighing only 215.8 lb. These sizes, I suppose, have been produced by the same negligence in Europe, which has produced a like diminution here. Where care has been taken of them on that side of the water, they have been raised to a size bordering on that of the horse; not by the *heat* and *dryness* of the climate, but by good food and shelter. Goats have been also much neglected in America. Yet they are very prolific here, bearing twice or three times a year, and from one to five kids at a birth. Mons. de Buffon has been sensible of a difference in this circumstance in favour of America.[36] But what are their greatest weights I cannot say. A large sheep here weights 100 lb. I observe Mons. D'Aubenton calls a ram of 62 lb. one of the middle size.[37] But to say what are the extremes of growth in these and the other domestic animals of America, would require information of which no one individual is possessed. The weights actually known and stated in the third table preceding will suffice to shew, that we may conclude, on probable grounds, that, with equal food and care, the climate of America will preserve the races of domestic animals as large as the European stock from which they are derived; and consequently that the third member of Mons. de Buffon's assertion, that the domestic animals are subject to degeneration from the climate of America, is as probably wrong as the first and second were certainly so.

That the last part of it is erroneous, which affirms that

[35] VIII. 48. 55. 66.
[36] XVIII. 96.
[37] IX. 41.

the species of American quadrupeds are comparatively few, is evident from the tables taken altogether. By these it appears that there are an hundred species aboriginal of America. Mons. de Buffon supposes about double that number existing on the whole earth.[38] Of these Europe, Asia, and Africa, furnish suppose 126; that is, the 26 common to Europe and America, and about 100 which are not in America at all. The American species then are to those of the rest of the earth, as 100 to 126, or 4 to 5. But the residue of the earth being double the extent of America, the exact proportion would have been but as 4 to 8.

Hitherto I have considered this hypothesis as applied to brute animals only, and not in its extension to the man of America, whether aboriginal or transplanted. It is the opinion of Mons. de Buffon that the former furnishes no exception to it:[39] "Although the savage of the new world is about the same height as man in our world, this does not suffice for him to constitute an exception to the general fact that all living nature has become smaller on that continent. The savage is feeble, and has small organs of generation; he has neither hair nor beard, and no ardor whatever for his female; although swifter than the European because he is better accustomed to running, he is, on the other hand, less strong in body; he is also less sensitive, and yet more timid and cowardly; he has no vivacity, no activity of mind; the activity of his body is less an exercise, a voluntary motion, than a necessary action caused by want; relieve him of hunger and thirst, and you deprive him of the active principle of all his movements; he will rest stupidly upon his legs or lying down entire days. There is no need for seeking further the cause of the isolated mode of life of these savages and their repugnance for society: the most precious spark of the fire of nature has been refused to them; they lack ardor for their females, and consequently have no love for their fellow

[38] XXX. 219.
[39] XVII. 146. (The passage has been translated from French to English. [Ed.])

men: not knowing this strongest and most tender of all affections, their other feelings are also cold and languid; they love their parents and children but little; the most intimate of all ties, the family connection, binds them therefore but loosely together; between family and family there is no tie at all; hence they have no communion, no commonwealth, no state of society. Physical love constitutes their only morality; their heart is icy, their society cold, and their rule harsh. They look upon their wives only as servants for all work, or as beasts of burden, which they load without consideration with the burden of their hunting, and which they compel without mercy, without gratitude, to perform tasks which are often beyond their strength. They have only few children, and they take little care of them. Everywhere the original defect appears: they are indifferent because they have little sexual capacity, and this indifference to the other sex is the fundamental defect which weakens their nature, prevents its development, and—destroying the very germs of life—uproots society at the same time. Man is here no exception to the general rule. Nature, by refusing him the power of love, has treated him worse and lowered him deeper than any animal." An afflicting picture indeed, which, for the honor of human nature, I am glad to believe has no original. Of the Indian of South America I know nothing; for I would not honor with the appellation of knowledge, what I derive from the fables published of them. These I believe to be just as true as the fables of Æsop. This belief is founded on what I have seen of man, white, red, and black, and what has been written of him by authors, enlightened themselves, and writing amidst an enlightened people. The Indian of North America being more within our reach, I can speak of him somewhat from my own knowledge, but more from the information of others better acquainted with him, and on whose truth and judgment I can rely. From these sources I am able to say, in contradiction to this representation, that he is neither more defective in ardor, nor more impotent with his female, than the white reduced to the same diet and exercise: that he is brave, when an enterprise depends on bravery; education with him making the point of honor consist in the destruction of an enemy by strategem, and in the preservation of his own person free from injury; or perhaps this is nature; while it is education which teaches us to honor force more than finesse;[40] that he will defend himself against an host of enemies, always chusing to be killed, rather than to surrender,[41] though it be to the whites, who he knows will

[40] *Sol Rodomonte sprexxa di venire*
Se non, dove la via meno è sicura. Ariosto, 14, 117.
(Rodomont scorns any way
To wend, except what is most secure. Ludovico Ariosto, *Orlando Furioso*. [Ed.])

[41] In so judicious an author as Don Ulloa, and one to whom we are indebted for the most precise information we have of South America, I did not expect to find such assertions as the following. "The conquered Indians are the most cowardly and pusillanimous that can be seen: they blame themselves, humble themselves to contempt, apologize for their inconsiderate temerity, and by supplication and prayer give the best proof of their want of courage. Either the accounts given in the histories of the Conquest of their great exploits are a mere figure of speech, or the character of these people is not now as it was then; but this is beyond doubt, that the nations of the North enjoy the same liberty they have always had, without ever having been subject to foreign princes, and they live all their lives according to their rules and customs, without any compulsion to change their character; and herein they appear the same as those of Peru and of South America, now enslaved or never subjugated." Noticias Americanas. Entretenimiento XVIII. §1. Don Ulloa here admits, that the authors who have described the Indians of South America, before they were enslaved, had represented them as a brave people, and therefore seems to have suspected that the cowardice which he had observed in those of the present race might be the effect of subjugation. But, supposing the Indians of North America to be cowards also, he concludes the ancestors of those of South America to have been so too, and therefore that those authors have given fiction for truths. He was probably not acquainted himself with the Indians of North America, and had formed his opinion of them from hearsay. Great numbers of French, of English, and of Americans, are perfectly acquainted with these people. Had he had an opportunity of enquiring of any of these, they would have told him, that there never was an instance known of an Indian begging his life when in the power of his enemies: on the contrary, that he courts death by every

treat him well: that in other situations also he meets death with more deliberation, and endures tortures with a firmness unknown almost to religious enthusiasm with us: that he is affectionate to his children, careful of them, and indulgent in the extreme: that his affections comprehend his other connections, weakening, as with us, from circle to circle, as they recede from the center: that his friendships are strong and faithful to the uttermost extremity:[42] that his sensibility is keen, even the warriors weeping most bitterly on the loss of their children, though in general they endeavour to appear superior to human events: that his vivacity and activity of mind is equal to ours in the same situation; hence his eagerness for hunting, and for games of chance. The women are submitted to unjust drudgery. This I believe is the case with every barbarous people. With such, force is law. The stronger sex therefore imposes on the weaker. It is civilization alone which replaces women in the enjoyment of their natural equality. That

---

possible insult and provocation. His reasoning then would have been reversed thus. "Since the present Indian of North America is brave, and authors tell us, that the ancestors of those of South America were brave also; it must follow, that the cowardice of their descendants is the effect of subjugation and ill treatment." For he observes, ib. §27. that "hard labor destroys them on account of the inhumanity with which they have been treated." (Spanish passages translated into English. [Ed.])

[42] A remarkable instance of this appeared in the case of the late Col. Byrd, who was sent to the Cherokee nation to transact some business with them. It happened that some of our disorderly people had just killed one or two of that nation. It was therefore proposed in the council of the Cherokees that Col. Byrd should be put to death, in revenge for the loss of their countrymen. Among them was a chief called Silòuee, who, on some former occasion, had contracted an acquaintance and friendship with Col. Byrd. He came to him every night in his tent, and told him not to be afraid, they should not kill him. After many days deliberation, however, the determination was, contrary to Silòuee's expectation, that Byrd should be put to death, and some warriors were dispatched as executioners. Silòuee attended them, and when they entered the tent, he threw himself between them and Byrd, and said to the warriors, "this man is my friend: before you get at him, you must kill me." On which they returned, and the council respected the principle so much as to recede from their determination.

first teaches us to subdue the selfish passions, and to respect those rights in others which we value in ourselves. Were we in equal barbarism, our females would be equal drudges. The man with them is less strong than with us, but their woman stronger than ours; and both for the same obvious reason; because our man and their woman is habituated to labour, and formed by it. With both races the sex which is indulged with ease is least athletic. An Indian man is small in the hand and wrist for the same reason for which a sailor is large and strong in the arms and shoulders, and a porter in the legs and thighs.—They raise fewer children than we do. The causes of this are to be found, not in a difference of nature, but of circumstance. The women very frequently attending the men in their parties of war and of hunting, child-bearing becomes extremely inconvenient to them. It is said, therefore, that they have learnt the practice of procuring abortion by the use of some vegetable; and that it even extends to prevent conception for a considerable time after. During these parties they are exposed to numerous hazards, to excessive exertions, to the greatest extremities of hunger. Even at their homes the nation depends for food, through a certain part of every year, on the gleanings of the forest: that is, they experience a famine once in every year. With all animals, if the female be badly fed, or not fed at all, her young perish: and if both male and female be reduced to like want, generation becomes less active, less productive. To the obstacles then of want and hazard, which nature has opposed to the multiplication of wild animals, for the purpose of restraining their numbers within certain bounds, those of labour and of voluntary abortion are added with the Indian. No wonder then if they multiply less than we do. Where food is regularly supplied, a single farm will shew more of cattle, than a whole country of forests can of buffaloes. The same Indian women, when married to white traders, who feed them and their children plentifully and regularly, who exempt them from excessive drudgery, who keep them stationary and unexposed to accident, produce and raise as many children as the white women. Instances are known, under these circumstances, of their rearing a dozen children. An inhuman practice once prevailed in this country of making slaves of the Indians. It is a fact well known with us, that the Indian women so enslaved produced and raised as numerous families as either the whites or blacks among whom they lived.—It has been said, that Indians have less hair than the whites, except on the head. But this is a fact of which fair proof can scarcely be had. With them it is disgraceful to be hairy on the body. They say it likens them to hogs. They therefore pluck the hair as fast as it appears. But the traders who marry their women, and prevail on them to discontinue this practice, say, that nature is the same with them as with the whites. Nor, if the fact be true, is the consequence necessary which has been drawn from it. Negroes have notoriously less hair than the whites; yet they are more ardent. But if cold and moisture be the agents of nature for diminishing the races of animals, how comes she all at once to suspend their operation as to the physical man of the new world, whom the Count acknowledges to be "*à peu près de même stature que l'homme de notre monde,*" [43] and to let loose their influence on his moral faculties? How has this "combination of the elements and other physical causes, so contrary to the enlargement of animal nature in this new world, these obstacles to the development and formation of great germs," [44] been arrested and suspended, so as to permit the human body to acquire its just dimensions, and by what inconceivable process has their action been directed on his mind alone? To judge of the truth of this, to form a just estimate of their genius and mental powers, more facts are wanting, and great allowance to be made for those circumstances of their situation which call for a display of particular talents only. This done, we shall probably find that they are formed in mind as well as in body,

[43] "About the same size as the man of our hemisphere." [Ed.]
[44] XVIII. 145.

on the same module with the "Homo sapiens Europæus." [45]
The principles of their society forbidding all compulsion,
they are to be led to duty and to enterprise by personal
influence and persuasion. Hence eloquence in council,
bravery and address in war, become the foundations of all
consequence with them. To these acquirements all their
faculties are directed. Of their bravery and address in war
we have multiplied proofs, because we have been the subjects on which they were exercised. Of their eminence in
oratory we have fewer examples, because it is displayed
chiefly in their own councils. Some, however, we have of
very superior lustre. I may challenge the whole orations
of Demosthenes and Cicero, and of any more eminent
orator, if Europe has furnished more eminent, to produce
a single passage, superior to the speech of Logan, a Mingo
chief, to Lord Dunmore, when governor of this state. And,
as a testimony of their talents in this line, I beg leave to
introduce it, first stating the incidents necessary for understanding it. In the spring of the year 1774, a robbery and
murder were committed on an inhabitant of the frontiers
of Virginia, by two Indians of the Shawanee tribe. The
neighbouring whites, according to their custom, undertook to punish this outrage in a summary way. Col. Cresap,
a man infamous for the many murders he had committed on those much-injured people, collected a party,
and proceeded down the Kanhaway in quest of vengeance.
Unfortunately a canoe of women and children, with one
man only, was seen coming from the opposite shore, un-
armed and unsuspecting an hostile attack from the whites.
Cresap and his party concealed themselves on the bank of
the river, and the moment the canoe reached the shore,
singled out their objects, and, at one fire, killed every
person in it. This happened to be the family of Logan,
who had long been distinguished as a friend of the whites.
This unworthy return provoked his vengeance. He accordingly signalized himself in the war which ensued. In

[45] Linn[aeus], *Syst[ema Naturae]* Definition of a Man.

the autumn of the same year a decisive battle was fought at the mouth of the Great Kanhaway, between the collected forces of the Shawanese, Mingoes, and Delawares, and a detachment of the Virginia militia. The Indians were defeated, and sued for peace. Logan, however, disdained to be seen among the suppliants. But, lest the sincerity of a treaty should be distrusted, from which so distinguished a chief absented himself, he sent by a messenger the following speech to be delivered to Lord Dunmore.

"I appeal to any white man to say, if ever he entered Logan's cabin hungry, and he gave him not meat; if ever he came cold and naked, and he clothed him not. During the course of the last long and bloody war, Logan remained idle in his cabin, an advocate for peace. Such was my love for the whites, that my countrymen pointed as they passed, and said, 'Logan is the friend of white men.' I had even thought to have lived with you, but for the injuries of one man. Col. Cresap, the last spring, in cold blood, and unprovoked, murdered all the relations of Logan, not sparing even my women and children. There runs not a drop of my blood in the veins of any living creature. This called on me for revenge. I have sought it: I have killed many: I have fully glutted my vengeance. For my country, I rejoice at the beams of peace. But do not harbour a thought that mine is the joy of fear. Logan never felt fear. He will not turn on his heel to save his life. Who is there to mourn for Logan?—Not one."

Before we condemn the Indians of this continent as wanting genius, we must consider that letters have not yet been introduced among them. Were we to compare them in their present state with the Europeans North of the Alps, when the Roman arms and arts first crossed those mountains, the comparison would be unequal, because, at that time, those parts of Europe were swarming with numbers; because numbers produce emulation, and multiply the chances of improvement, and one improvement begets another. Yet I may safely ask, how many good poets, how many able mathematicians, how many great inventors in arts or sciences, had Europe North of the Alps then produced? And it was sixteen centuries after this before a Newton could be formed. I do not mean to deny, that there are varieties in the race of man, distinguished by their powers both of body and mind. I believe there are, as I see to be the case in the races of other animals. I only mean to suggest a doubt, whether the bulk and faculties of animals depend on the side of the Atlantic on which their food happens to grow, or which furnishes the elements of which they are compounded? Whether nature has enlisted herself as a Cis or Trans-Atlantic partisan? I am induced to suspect, there has been more eloquence than sound reasoning displayed in support of this theory; that it is one of those cases where the judgment has been seduced by a glowing pen: and whilst I render every tribute of honor and esteem to the celebrated zoologist, who has added, and is still adding, so many precious things to the treasures of science, I must doubt whether in this instance he has not cherished error also, by lending her for a moment his vivid imagination and bewitching language.

So far the Count de Buffon has carried this new theory of the tendency of nature to belittle her productions on this side of the Atlantic. Its application to the race of whites, transplanted from Europe, remained for the Abbé Raynal.[46] "*On doit être étonné que l'Amérique n'ait pas encore produit un bon poète, un habile mathématicien, un homme de génie dans un seul art, ou une seule science.*"[47] 7. Hist. Philos. p. 92. ed. Maestricht. 1774. "America has not yet produced one good poet." When we shall have existed as a people as long as the Greeks did before they produced a Homer, the Romans a Virgil, the French a Racine and Voltaire, the English a Shakespeare and Milton, should this reproach be still true, we will inquire from

[46] Guillaume Thomas François Raynal, *Histoire Philosophique et Politique des Éstablissement et du Commerce des Européens dans les deux Indes*, 4 vols. (Amsterdam, 1770). [Ed.]

[47] "One must be astonished that America has not yet produced one good poet, one able mathematician, one man of genius in a single art or a single science." [Ed.]

what unfriendly causes it has proceeded, that the other countries of Europe and quarters of the earth shall not have inscribed any name in the roll of poets.[48] But neither has America produced "one able mathematician, one man of genius in a single art or a single science." In war we have produced a Washington, whose memory will be adored while liberty shall have votaries, whose name will triumph over time, and will in future ages assume its just station among the most celebrated worthies of the world, when that wretched philosophy shall be forgotten which would have arranged him among the degeneracies of nature. In physics we have produced a Franklin, than whom no one of the present age has made more important discoveries, nor has enriched philosophy with more, or more ingenious solutions of the phænomena of nature. We have supposed Mr. Rittenhouse second to no astronomer living: that in genius he must be the first, because he is self-taught. As an artist he has exhibited as great a proof of mechanical genius as the world has ever produced. He has not indeed made a world; but he has by imitation approached nearer its Maker than any man who has lived from the creation to this day.[49] As in philosophy and war, so in government, in oratory, in painting, in the plastic art, we might shew that America, though but a child of yesterday, has already given hopeful proofs of genius, as well of the nobler kinds, which arouse the best feelings of man, which call him into action, which substantiate his freedom, and conduct him to happiness, as of the subordi-

[48] Has the world as yet produced more than two poets, acknowledged to be such by all nations? An Englishman, only, reads Milton with delight, an Italian Tasso, a Frenchman the Henriade, a Portuguese Camouens: but Homer and Virgil have been the rapture of every age and nation: they are read with enthusiasm in their originals by those who can read the originals, and in translations by those who cannot.

[49] There are various ways of keeping truth out of sight. Mr. Rittenhouse's model of the planetary system has the plagiary appellation of an orrery; and the quadrant invented by Godfrey, an American also, and with the aid of which the European nations traverse the globe, is called Hadley's quadrant.

nate, which serve to amuse him only. We therefore suppose, that this reproach is as unjust as it is unkind; and that, of the geniuses which adorn the present age, America contributes its full share. For comparing it with those countries, where genius is most cultivated, where are the most excellent models for art, and scaffoldings for the attainment of science, as France and England for instance, we calculate thus. The United States contain three millions of inhabitants; France twenty millions; and the British islands ten. We produce a Washington, a Franklin, a Rittenhouse. France then should have half a dozen in each of these lines, and Great-Britain half that number, equally eminent. It may be true, that France has: we are but just becoming acquainted with her, and our acquaintance so far gives us high ideas of the genius of her inhabitants. It would be injuring too many of them to name particularly a Voltaire, a Buffon, the constellation of Encyclopedists, the Abbé Raynal himself, &c. &c. We therefore have reason to believe she can produce her full quota of genius. The present war having so long cut off all communication with Great-Britain, we are not able to make a fair estimate of the state of science in that country. The spirit in which she wages war is the only sample before our eyes, and that does not seem the legitimate offspring either of science or of civilization. The sun of her glory is fast descending to the horizon. Her philosophy has crossed the channel, her freedom the Atlantic, and herself seems passing to that awful dissolution, whose issue is not given human foresight to scan.[50]

[50] In a later edition of the Abbé Raynal's work, he has withdrawn his censure from that part of the new world inhabited by the Federo-Americans; but has left it still on the other parts. North America has always been more accessible to strangers than South. If he was mistaken then as to the former, he may be so as to the latter. The glimmerings which reach us from South America enable us only to see that its inhabitants are held under the accumulated pressure of slavery, superstition, and ignorance. Whenever they shall be able to rise under this weight, and to shew themselves to the rest of the world, they will probably shew they are like the rest of the

Having given a sketch of our minerals, vegetables, and quadrupeds, and being led by a proud theory to make a comparison of the latter with those of Europe, and to extend it to the Man of America, both aboriginal and emigrant, I will proceed to the remaining articles comprehended under the present query.

Between ninety and an hundred of our birds have been described by Catesby. His drawings are better as to form and attitude, than colouring, which is generally too high. They are the following [see pages 106–110].

To this catalogue of our indigenous animals, I will add a short account of an anomaly of nature, taking place sometimes in the race of negroes brought from Africa, who, though black themselves, have in rare instances, white children, called Albinos. I have known four of these myself, and have faithful accounts of three others. The circumstances in which all the individuals agree are these. They are of a pallid cadaverous white, untinged with red, without any coloured spots or seams; their hair of the same kind of white, short, coarse, and curled as is that of the negro; all of them well formed, strong, healthy, perfect in their senses, except that of sight, and born of parents who had no mixture of white blood. Three of these Albinos were sisters, having two other full sisters, who were black. The youngest of the three was killed by lightning, at twelve years of age. The eldest died at about 27

---

world. We have not yet sufficient evidence that there are more *lakes* and *fogs* in South America than in other parts of the earth. As little do we know what would be their operation on the mind of man. That country has been visited by Spaniards and Portuguese chiefly, and almost exclusively. These, going from a country of the old world remarkably dry in its soil and climate, fancied there were more lakes and fogs in South America than in Europe. An inhabitant of Ireland, Sweden, or Finland, would have formed the contrary opinion. Had South America then been discovered and seated by a people from a fenny country, it would probably have been represented as much drier than the old world. A patient pursuit of facts, and cautious combination and comparison of them, is the drudgery to which man is subjected by his Maker, if he wishes to attain sure knowledge.

years of age, in child-bed, with her second child. The middle one is now alive in health, and has issue, as the eldest had, by a black man, which issue was black. They are uncommonly shrewd, quick in their apprehensions and in reply. Their eyes are in a perpetual tremulous vibration, very weak, and much affected by the sun: but they see better in the night than we do. They are of the property of Col. Skipwith, of Cumberland. The fourth is a negro woman, whose parents came from Guinea, and had three other children, who were of their own colour. She is freckled, her eye-sight so weak that she is obliged to wear a bonnet in the summer; but it is better in the night than day. She had an Albino child by a black man. It died at the age of a few weeks. These were the property of Col. Carter, of Albemarle. A sixth instance is a woman of the property of a Mr. Butler, near Petersburgh. She is stout and robust, has issue a daughter, jet black, by a black man. I am not informed as to her eye-sight. The seventh instance is of a male belonging to a Mr. Lee, of Cumberland. His eyes are tremulous and weak. He is tall of stature, and now advanced in years. He is the only male of the Albinos which have come within my information. Whatever be the cause of the disease in the skin, or in its colouring matter, which produces this change, it seems more incident to the female than male sex. To these I may add the mention of a negro man within my own knowledge, born black, and of black parents; on whose chin, when a boy, a white spot appeared. This continued to increase till he became a man, by which time it had extended over his chin, lips, one cheek, the under jaw and neck on that side. It is of the Albino white, without any mixture of red, and has for several years been stationary. He is robust and healthy, and the change of colour was not accompanied with any sensible disease, either general or topical.

Of our fish and insects there has been nothing like a full description or collection. More of them are described in

BIRDS OF VIRGINIA.

Linnaean designation.	Catesby's designation.	Popular names.		Buffon oiseaux.
Lanius tyrannus	Muscicapa coronâ rubrâ	Tyrant. Field martin	1.55	8.398
Vultur Aura	Buteo specie Gallo-pavonis	Turkey buzzard	1.6	1.246
Falco leucocephalus	Aquila capite albo	Bald Eagle	1.1	1.138
Falco sparverius	Accipiter minor	Little hawk. Sparrow hawk	1.5	
Falco columbarius	Accipiter palumbarius	Pigeon hawk	1.3	1.338
Falco furcatus	Accipiter caudâ furcatâ	Forked tail hawk	1.4	1.286,312
	Accipiter piscatorius	Fishing hawk	1.2	1.199
Strix asio	Noctua aurita minor	Little owl	1.7	1.141
Psittacus Caroliniensis	Psitticus Caroliniensis	Parrot of Carolina. Perroquet	1.11	11.383
Corvus cristatus	Pica glandaria, cærulea, cristata	Blue jay	1.15	5.164
Oriolus Baltimore	Icterus ex aureo nigroque varius	Baltimore bird	1.48	5.318
Oriolus spurius	Icterus minor	Bastard Baltimore	1.49	5.321
Gracula quiscula	Monedula purpurea	Purple jackdaw. Crow blackbird	1.12	5.134
Cuculus Americanus	Cuculus Caroliniensis	Carolina cuckow	1.9	12.62
Picus principalis	Picus maximus rostro albo	White bill woodpecker	1.16	13.69
Picus pileatus	Picus niger maximus, capite rubro	Larger red-crested woodpecker	1.17	13.72
Picus erythrocephalus	Picus capite toto rubro	Red-headed woodpecker	1.20	13.83
Picus auratus	Picus major alis aureis	Gold winged woodpecker. Yucker	1.18	13.59
Picus Carolinus	Picus ventre rubro	Red bellied woodpecker	1.19	13.105
Picus pubescens	Picus varius minimus	Smallest spotted woodpecker	1.21	13.113
Picus villosus	Picus medius quasi-villosus	Hairy woodpecker. Speck. woodpec.	1.19	13.111
Picus varius	Picus varius minor ventre luteo	Yellow bellied woodpecker	1.21	13.115

Latin name	Synonym		English name	
Sitta Europaea	{ Sitta capite nigro	1.22	Nuthatch	10.213
	{ Sitta capite fusco	1.22	Small Nuthatch	10.214
Alcedo alcyon	Ispida	1.69	Kingfisher	13.310
Certhia pinus	Parus Americanus lutescens	1.61	Pinecreeper	9.433
Trochilus colubris	Mellivora avis Caroliniensis	1.65	Humming bird	11.16
Anas Canadensis	Anser Canadensis	1.92	Wild goose	17.122
Anas bucephala	Anas minor purpureo capite	1.95	Buffel's head duck	17.356
Anas rustica	Anas minor ex albo & fusco vario	1.98	Little brown duck	17.413
Anas discors	Querquedula Americana variegata	1.100	White face teal	17.403
Anas discors. β	Querquedula Americana fusca	1.99	Blue wing teal	17.405
Anas sponsa	Anas Americanus cristatus elegans	1.97	Summer duck	17.351
	Anas Americanus lato rostro	1.96	Blue wing shoveler	17.275
Mergus cucullatus	Anas cristatus	1.94	Round crested duck	15.437
Colymbus podiceps	Prodicipes minor rostro vario	1.91	Pied bill dopchick	15.383
Ardea Herodias	Ardea cristata maxima Americana	3.10	Largest crested heron	14.113
Ardea violacea	Ardea stellaris cristata Americana	1.79	Crested bittern	14.134
Ardea caerulea	Ardea caerulea	1.76	Blue heron. Crane	14.131
Ardea virescens	Ardea stellaris minima	1.80	Small bittern	14.142
Ardea aequinoctialis	Ardea alba minor Caroliniensis	1.77	Little white heron	14.136
	Ardea stellaris Americana	1.78	Brown bittern. Indian hen	14.175
Tantalus loculator	Pelicanus Americanus	1.81	Wood pelican	13.403
Tantalus alber	Numenius albus	1.82	White curlew	15.62
Tantalus fuscus	Numenius fuscus	1.83	Brown curlew	15.64
Charadrius vociferus	Pluvialis vociferus	1.71	Chattering plover. Kildee	15.151
Haematopus ostralegus	Haematopus	1.85	Oyster Catcher	15.185
Rallus Virginianus	Gallinula Americana	1.70	Soree. Ral-bird	15.256
Meleagris Gallopavo	Gallopavo Sylvestris	xliv.	Wild turkey	3.187.229
Tetrao Virginianus	Perdix Sylvestris Virginiana	3.12	American partridge. American quail	4.237

BIRDS OF VIRGINIA—*Continued.*

Linnaean designation.	Catesby's designation.		Popular names.	Buffon oiseaux.
	Urogallus minor, or a kind of Lagopus	3.1	Pheasant. Mountain partridge	3.409
Columba passerina	Turtur minimus guttatus	1.26	Ground dove	4.404
Columba migratoria	Palumbus migratorius	1.23	Pigeon of passage. Wild pigeon	4.351
Columba Caroliniensis	Turtur Caroliniensis	1.24	Turtle. Turtle dove	4.401
Alauda alpestris	Alauda gutture flavo	1.32	Lark. Sky lark	9.79
Alauda magna	Alauda magna	1.33	Field lark. Large lark	6.59
	Sturnus niger alis superné rubentibus	1.13	Red winged starling. Marsh blackbird	5.293
Turdus migratorius	Turdus pilaris migratorius	1.29	Fieldfare of Carolina. Robin redbreast	{ 5.426 9.257
Turdus rufus	Turdus ruffus	1.28	Fox coloured thrush. Thrush	5.449
Turdus polyglottos	Turdus minor cinereo albus non maculatus	1.27	Mocking bird	5.451
	Turdus minimus	1.31	Little thrush	5.400
Ampelis garrulus. β	Garrulus Caroliniensis	1.46	Chatterer	6.162
Loxia Cardinalis	Coccothraustes rubra	1.38	Red bird. Virginia nightingale	6.185
Loxia Caerulea	Coccothraustes caerulea	1.39	Blue gross beak	8.125
Emberiza hyemalis	Passer nivalis	1.36	Snow bird	8.47
Emberiza Oryzivora	Hortulanus Caroliniensis	1.14	Rice bird	8.49
Emberiza Ciris	Fringilla tricolor	1.44	Painted finch	7.247
Tanagra cyanea	Linaria caerulea	1.45	Blue linnet	7.122
	Passer culus	1.35	Little sparrow	7.120

	Passer fuscus	1.34	Cowpen bird	7.196
Fringilla erythrophthalma	Passer niger oculis rubris	1.34	Towhe bird	7.201
Fringilla tristis	Carduelis Americanus	1.43	American goldfinch. Lettuce bird	7.297
	Fringilla purpurea	1.41	Purple finch	8.129
Muscicapa crinita	Muscicapa cristata ventre luteo	1.52	Crested flycatcher	8.379
Muscicapa rubra	Muscicapa rubra	1.56	Summer red bird	8.410
Muscicapa ruticilla	Ruticilla Americana	1.67	Red start	8.349 / 9.259
Muscicapa Caroliniensis	Muscicapa vertice nigro	1.66	Cat bird	8.372
	Muscicapa nigrescens	1.53	Black-cap flycatcher	8.341
	Muscicapa fusca	1.54	Little brown flycatcher	8.344
	Muscicapa oculis rubris	1.54	Red-eyed flycatcher	8.337
Motacilla Sialis	Rubicula Americana cærulea	1.47	Blue bird	9.308
Motacilla regulus	Regulus cristatus	3.13	Wren	10.58
Motacilla trochilus. β	Oenanthe Americana pectore luteo	1.50	Yellow-breasted chat	6.96
Parus bicolor	Parus cristatus	1.57	Crested titmouse	10.181
Parus Americanus	Parus fringillaris	1.64	Finch creeper	9.442
Parus Virginianus	Parus uropygeo luteo	1.58	Yellow rump	10.184
	Parus cuculio nigro	1.60	Hooded titmouse	10.183
	Parus Americanus gutture luteo	1.62	Yellow-throated creeper	
	Parus Caroliniensis	1.63	Yellow titmouse	
Hirundo Pelasgia	Hirundo cauda aculeata Americana	3.8	American swallow	9.431
Hirundo purpurea	Hirundo purpurea	1.51	Purple martin. House martin	12.478 / 12.445
Caprimulgus Europæus. α	Caprimulgus	1.8	Goatsucker. Great bat	12.243
Caprimulgus Europæus. β	Caprimulgus minor Americanus	3.16	Whip-poor Will	12.246

Besides these, we have

The Royston crow. Corvus
  cornix.
  Crane. Ardea Canadensis.
  House swallow. Hirundo
  rustica.
  Ground swallow. Hi-
  rundo riparia.
  Greatest grey eagle.
  Smaller turkey buzzard,
  with a feathered head.
  Greatest owl, or night
  hawk.
  Wet hawk, which feeds
  flying.
  Raven.
  Water pelican of the
  Missisipi, whose
  pouch holds a peck.
  Swan.
  Loon.
  Cormorant.

The Duck and Mallard.
  Widgeon.
  Sheldrach, or Canvas
  back.
  Black head.
  Ballcoot.
  Sprigtail.
  Didapper, or Dopchick.
  Spoon billed duck.
  Water-witch.
  Water-pheasant.
  Mow-bird.
  Blue peter.
  Water wagtail.
  Yellow-legged snipe.
  Squatting snipe.
  Small plover.
  Whistling plover.
  Woodcock.
  Red bird, with black
  head, wings and tail.

And doubtless many others which have not yet been
described and classed.

Catesby than in any other work. Many also are to be
found in Sir Hans Sloane's Jamaica,[51] as being common
to that and this country. The honey-bee is not a native of
our continent. Marcgrave indeed mentions a species of
honey-bee in Brasil.[52] But this has no sting, and is therefore different from the one we have, which resembles per-

[51] Sir Hans Sloane, *A Voyage to the Islands of Madera,
Barbadoes, Nieves, St. Christopher's, and Jamaica,* 2 vols.
(London, 1707–1725). [Ed.]
[52] Georg Margraf and William Piso, *Historia Naturalis
Brasiliae* (Leyden, 1648). [Ed.]

fectly that of Europe. The Indians concur with us in the tradition that it was brought from Europe; but when, and by whom, we know not. The bees have generally extended themselves into the country, a little in advance of the white settlers. The Indians therefore call them the white man's fly, and consider their approach as indicating the approach of the settlements of the whites. A question here occurs, How far northwardly have these insects been found? That they are unknown in Lapland, I infer from Scheffer's information, that the Laplanders eat the pine bark, prepared in a certain way, instead of those things sweetened with sugar. "*Hoc comedunt pro rebus saccharo conditis.*" Scheff. Lapp. c. 18.[53] Certainly if they had honey, it would be a better substitute for sugar than any preparation of the pine bark. Kalm tells us[54] the honey-bee cannot live through the winter in Canada. They furnish then an additional proof of the remarkable fact first observed by the Count de Buffon, and which has thrown such a blaze of light on the field of natural history, that no animals are found in both continents, but those which are able to bear the cold of those regions where they probably join.

[53] "They eat this in place of things made with sugar." John Scheffer, *History of Lapland* (London, 1751). [Ed.]

[54] I. 126.

QUERY VII.

Climate

¶ *A notice of all that can increase the progress of human knowledge?*

UNDER the latitude of this query, I will presume it not improper nor unacceptable to furnish some data for estimating the climate of Virginia. Journals of observations on the quantity of rain, and degree of heat, being lengthy, confused, and too minute to produce general and distinct ideas, I have taken five years' observations, to wit, from 1772 to 1777, made in Williamsburgh and its neighbourhood, have reduced them to an average for every month in the year, and stated those averages in the following table, adding an analytical view of the winds during the same period [see page 113].

The rains of every month, (as of January for instance) through the whole period of years, were added separately, and an average drawn from them. The coolest and warmest point of the same day in each year of the period were added separately, and an average of the greatest cold and greatest heat of that day, was formed. From the averages of every day in the month, a general average for the whole month was formed. The point from which the wind blew was observed two or three times in every day. These observations, in the month of January for instance, through the whole period amounted to 337. At 73 of these, the wind was from the North; at 47, from the North-east, &c. So that it will be easy to see in what proportion each wind usually prevails in each month: or, taking the whole year, the total of observations through the whole period

	Fall of rain, &c. in inches.	Least & greatest daily heat by Farenheit's thermometer.		WINDS								
		8.A.M.	4.P.M.	N.	N.E.	E.	S.E.	S.	S.W.	W.	N.W.	Total.
Jan.	3.192	38½	to 44	73	47	32	10	11	78	40	46	337
Feb.	2.049	41	47½	61	52	24	11	4	63	30	31	276
Mar.	3.95	48	54½	49	44	38	28	14	83	29	33	318
April	3.68	56	62½	35	44	54	19	9	58	18	20	257
May	2.871	63	70½	27	36	62	23	7	74	32	20	281
June	3.751	71½	78¼	22	34	43	24	13	81	25	25	267
July	4.497	77	82½	41	44	75	15	7	95	32	19	328
Aug.	9.153	76¼	81	43	52	40	30	9	103	27	30	334
Sept.	4.761	69½	74¼	70	60	51	18	10	81	18	37	345
Oct.	3.633	61¼	66½	52	77	64	15	6	56	23	34	327
Nov.	2.617	47¾	53½	74	21	20	14	9	63	35	58	294
Dec.	2.877	43	48¾	64	37	18	16	10	91	42	56	334
Total.	47.038	8.A.M.	4.P.M.	611	548	521	223	109	926	351	409	3698

having been 3698, it will be observed that 611 of them were from the North, 558 from the North-east, &c.

Though by this table it appears we have on an average 47 inches of rain annually, which is considerably more than usually falls in Europe, yet from the information I have collected, I suppose we have a much greater proportion of sunshine here than there. Perhaps it will be found there are twice as many cloudy days in the middle parts of Europe, as in the United States of America. I mention the middle parts of Europe, because my information does not extend to its northern or southern parts.

In an extensive country, it will of course be expected that the climate is not the same in all its parts. It is remarkable that, proceeding on the same parallel of latitude westwardly, the climate becomes colder in like manner as when you proceed northwardly. This continues to be the case till you attain the summit of the Alleghaney, which is the highest land between the ocean and the Missisipi. From thence, descending in the same latitude to the Missisipi, the change reverses; and, if we may believe travellers, it becomes warmer there than it is in the same latitude on the sea side. Their testimony is strengthened by the vegetables and animals which subsist and multiply there naturally, and do not on our sea coast. Thus Catalpas grow spontaneously on the Missisipi, as far as the latitude of 37° and reeds as far as 38°. Perroquets even winter on the Sioto, in the 39th degree of latitude. In the summer of 1779, when the thermometer was at 90° at Monticello, and 96 at Williamsburgh, it was 110° at Kaskaskia. Perhaps the mountain, which overhangs this village on the North side, may, by its reflexion, have contributed somewhat to produce this heat. The difference of temperature of the air at the sea coast, or on Chesapeak bay, and at the Alleghaney, has not been ascertained; but cotemporary observations, made at Williamsburgh, or in its neighbourhood, and at Monticello, which is on the most eastern ridge of mountains, called the South West, where they are intersected by the Rivanna, have furnished a ratio by which that difference may in some degree be conjectured. These observations make the difference between Williamsburgh and the nearest mountains, at the position before mentioned, to be on an average 6⅛ degrees of Farenheit's thermometer. Some allowance however is to be made for the difference of latitude between these two places, the latter being 38° 8' 17" which is 52' 22" North of the former. By cotemporary observations of between five and six weeks, the averaged and almost unvaried difference of the height of mercury in the barometer, at those two places, was .784 of an inch, the atmosphere at Monticello being so much the lightest, that is to say, about one-thirty-seventh of its whole weight. It should be observed, however, that the hill of Monticello is of 500 feet perpendicular height above the river which washes its base. This position being nearly central between our northern and southern boundaries, and between the bay and Alleghaney, may be considered as furnishing the best average of the temperature of our climate. Williamsburgh is much too near the South-eastern corner to give a fair idea of our general temperature.

But a more remarkable difference is in the winds which prevail in the different parts of the country. The following table exhibits a comparative view of the winds prevailing at Williamsburgh, and at Monticello. It is formed by reducing nine months observations at Monticello to four principal points, to wit, the North-east, South-east, South-west, and North-west; these points being perpendicular to, or parallel with our coast, mountains and rivers: and by reducing, in like manner, an equal number of observations, to wit, 421 from the preceding table of winds at Williamsburgh, taking them proportionably from every point.

	N. E.	S. E.	S. W.	N. W.	Total.
Williamsburgh	127	61	132	101	421
Monticello	32	91	126	172	421

By this it may be seen that the South-west wind prevails equally at both places; that the North-east is, next
to this, the principal wind towards the sea coast, and the
North-west is the predominant wind at the mountains.
The difference between these two winds to sensation, and
in fact, is very great. The North-east is loaded with
vapour, insomuch, that the salt-makers have found that
their crystals would not shoot while that blows; it brings
a distressing chill, is heavy and oppressive to the spirits:
the North-west is dry, cooling, elastic and animating. The
Eastern and South-eastern breezes come on generally in
the afternoon. They have advanced into the country very
sensibly within the memory of people now living. They
formerly did not penetrate far above Williamsburgh.
They are now frequent at Richmond, and every now and
then reach the mountains. They deposit most of their
moisture however before they get that far. As the lands
become more cleared, it is probable they will extend still
further westward.

Going out into the open air, in the temperate, and in
the warm months of the year, we often meet with bodies
of warm air, which, passing by us in two or three seconds, do not afford time to the most sensible thermometer
to seize their temperature. Judging from my feelings only,
I think they approach the ordinary heat of the human
body. Some of them perhaps go a little beyond it. They
are of about 20 or 30 feet diameter horizontally. Of their
height we have no experience, but probably they are
globular volumes wafted or rolled along with the wind.
But whence taken, where found, or how generated? They
are not to be ascribed to volcanos, because we have none.
They do not happen in the winter when the farmers
kindle large fires in clearing up their grounds. They are
not confined to the spring season, when we have fires
which traverse whole counties, consuming the leaves
which have fallen from the trees. And they are too frequent and general to be ascribed to accidental fires. I am
persuaded their cause must be sought for in the atmos-

phere itself, to aid us in which I know but of these constant circumstances; a dry air; a temperature as warm at least as that of the spring or autumn; and a moderate current of wind. They are most frequent about sun-set; rare in the middle parts of the day; and I do not recollect having ever met with them in the morning.

The variation in the weight of our atmosphere, as indicated by the barometer, is not equal to two inches of mercury. During twelve months observation at Williamsburgh, the extremes were 29, and 30.86 inches, the difference being 1.86 of an inch: and in nine months, during which the height of the mercury was noted at Monticello, the extremes were 28.48 and 29.69 inches, the variation being 1.21 of an inch. A gentleman, who has observed his barometer many years, assures me it has never varied two inches. Cotemporary observations, made at Monticello and Williamsburgh, proved the variations in the weight of air to be simultaneous and corresponding in these two places.

Our changes from heat to cold, and cold to heat, are very sudden and great. The mercury in Farenheit's thermometer has been known to descend from 92° to 47° in thirteen hours.

It is taken for granted, that the preceding table of averaged heat will not give a false idea on this subject, as it proposes to state only the ordinary heat and cold of each month, and not those which are extraordinary. At Williamsburgh in August 1766, the mercury in Farenheit's thermometer was at 98° corresponding with 29⅓ of Reaumur. At the same place in January 1780, it was at 6° corresponding with 11½ below 0. of Reaumur. I believe these may be considered to be nearly the extremes of heat and cold in that part of the country.[1] The latter may most certainly, as, at that time, York river, at York town,

[1] At Paris, in 1753, the mercury in Reaumur's thermometer was at 30½ above 0, and in 1776, it was at 16 below 0. The extremities of heat and cold therefore at Paris, are greater than at Williamsburgh, which is in the hottest part of Virginia.

was frozen over, so that people walked across it; a circumstance which proves it to have been colder than the winter of 1740, 1741, usually called the cold winter, when York river did not freeze over at that place. In the same season of 1780, Chesapeak bay was solid, from its head to the mouth of Patowmac. At Annapolis, where it is 5¼ miles over between the nearest points of land, the ice was from 5 to 7 inches thick quite across, so that loaded carriages went over on it. Those, our extremes of heat and cold, of 6° and 98° were indeed very distressing to us, and were thought to put the extent of the human constitution to considerable trial. Yet a Siberian would have considered them as scarcely a sensible variation. At Jenniseitz in that country, in latitude 58° 27' we are told, that the cold in 1735 sunk the mercury by Farenheit's scale to 126° below nothing; and the inhabitants of the same country use stove rooms two or three times a week, in which they stay two hours at a time, the atmosphere of which raises the mercury to 135° above nothing. Late experiments shew that the human body will exist in rooms heated to 140° of Reaumur, equal to 347° of Farenheit, and 135° above boiling water. The hottest point of the 24 hours is about four o'clock, P.M. and the dawn of day the coldest.

The access of frost in autumn, and its recess in the spring, do not seem to depend merely on the degree of cold; much less on the air's being at the freezing point. White frosts are frequent when the thermometer is at 47°, have killed young plants of Indian corn at 48°, and have been known at 54°. Black frost, and even ice, have been produced at 38½° which is 6½ degrees above the freezing point. That other circumstances must be combined with the cold to produce frost, is evident from this also, that on the higher parts of mountains, where it is absolutely colder than in the plains on which they stand, frosts do not appear so early by a considerable space of time in autumn, and go off sooner in the spring, than in the plains. I have known frosts so severe as to kill the hiccory trees round about Monticello, and yet not injure the tender fruit blossoms then in bloom on the top and higher parts of the mountain; and in the course of 40 years, during which it has been settled, there have been but two instances of a general loss of fruit on it: while, in the circumjacent country, the fruit has escaped but twice in the last seven years. The plants of tobacco, which grow from the roots of those which have been cut off in the summer, are frequently green here at Christmas. This privilege against the frost is undoubtedly combined with the want of dew on the mountains. That the dew is very rare on their higher parts, I may say with certainty, from 12 years observations, having scarcely ever, during that time, seen an unequivocal proof of its existence on them at all during summer. Severe frosts in the depth of winter prove that the region of dews extends higher in that season than the tops of the mountains: but certainly, in the summer season, the vapours, by the time they attain that height, are become so attenuated as not to subside and form a dew when the sun retires.

The weavil has not yet ascended the high mountains.

A more satisfactory estimate of our climate to some, may perhaps be formed, by noting the plants which grow here, subject however to be killed by our severest colds. These are the fig, pomegranate, artichoke, and European walnut. In mild winters, lettuce and endive require no shelter; but generally they need a slight covering. I do not know that the want of long moss, reed, myrtle, swamp laurel, holly and cypress, in the upper country, proceeds from a greater degree of cold, nor that they were ever killed with any degree of cold in the lower country. The aloe lived in Williamsburgh in the open air through the severe winter of 1779, 1780.

A change in our climate however is taking place very sensibly. Both heats and colds are become much more moderate within the memory even of the middle-aged. Snows are less frequent and less deep. They do not often lie, below the mountains, more than one, two, or three days, and very rarely a week. They are remembered to have been formerly frequent, deep, and of long continuance. The elderly inform me the earth used to be covered with snow about three months in every year. The rivers, which then seldom failed to freeze over in the course of the winter, scarcely ever do so now. This change has produced an unfortunate fluctuation between heat and cold, in the spring of the year, which is very fatal to fruits. From the year 1741 to 1769, an interval of twenty-eight years, there was no instance of fruit killed by the frost in the neighbourhood of Monticello. An intense cold, produced by constant snows, kept the buds locked up till the sun could obtain, in the spring of the year, so fixed an ascendency as to dissolve those snows, and protect the buds, during their development, from every danger of returning cold. The accumulated snows of the winter remaining to be dissolved all together in the spring, produced those overflowings of our rivers, so frequent then, and so rare now.

Having had occasion to mention the particular situation of Monticello for other purposes, I will just take notice that its elevation affords an opportunity of seeing a phænomenon which is rare at land, though frequent at sea. The seamen call it *looming*. Philosophy is as yet in the rear of the seamen, for so far from having accounted for it, she has not given it a name. Its principal effect is to make distant objects appear larger, in opposition to the general law of vision, by which they are diminished. I knew an instance, at York-town, from whence the water prospect eastwardly is without termination, wherein a canoe with three men, at a great distance, was taken for a ship with its three masts. I am little acquainted with the phænomenon as it shews itself at sea; but at Monticello it is familiar. There is a solitary mountain about 40 miles off, in the South, whose natural shape, as presented to view there, is a regular cone; but, by the effect of looming, it sometimes subsides almost totally into the horizon; sometimes it rises more acute and more elevated;

sometimes it is hemispherical; and sometimes its sides are perpendicular, its top flat, and as broad as its base. In short it assumes at times the most whimsical shapes, and all these perhaps successively in the same morning. The Blue ridge of mountains comes into view, in the Northeast, at about 100 miles distance, and, approaching in a direct line, passes by within 20 miles, and goes off to the South-west. This phænomenon begins to shew itself on these mountains, at about 50 miles distance, and continues beyond that as far as they are seen. I remark no particular state, either in the weight, moisture, or heat of the atmosphere, necessary to produce this. The only constant circumstances are, its appearance in the morning only, and on objects at least 40 or 50 miles distant. In this latter circumstance, if not in both, it differs from the looming on the water. Refraction will not account for this metamorphosis. That only changes the proportions of length and breadth, base and altitude, preserving the general outlines. Thus it may make a circle appear elliptical, raise or depress a cone, but by none of its laws, as yet developed, will it make a circle appear a square, or a cone a sphere.

QUERY VIII.

Population

¶ *The number of its inhabitants?*

THE FOLLOWING table shews the number of persons imported for the establishment of our colony in its infant state, and the census of inhabitants at different periods, extracted from our historians and public records, as particularly as I have had opportunities and leisure to examine them. Successive lines in the same year shew successive periods of time in that year. I have stated the census in two different columns, the whole inhabitants having been sometimes numbered, and sometimes the *tythes* only. This term, with us, includes the free males above 16 years of age, and slaves above that age of both sexes. A further examination of our records would render this history of our population much more satisfactory and perfect, by furnishing a greater number of intermediate terms. Those however which are here stated will enable us to calculate, with a considerable degree of precision, the rate at which we have increased. During the infancy of the colony, while numbers were small, wars, importations, and other accidental circumstances render the progression fluctuating and irregular. By the year 1654, however, it becomes tolerably uniform, importations having in a great measure ceased from the dissolution of the company, and the inhabitants become too numerous to be sensibly affected by Indian wars. Beginning at that period, therefore, we find that from thence to the year 1772, our tythes had increased from 7209 to 153,000. The whole term being of 118 years, yields a duplication once in every

Years	Settlers imported.	Census of inhabitants.	Census of tythes.	Years	Settlers imported.	Census of inhabitants.	Census of tythes.
1607	100			1619	1216		
		40		1621	1300		
	120			1622		3800	
1608		130				2500	
	70			1628		3000	
1609		490		1632			2000
	16			1644			4822
		60		1645			5000
1610	150			1652			7000
		200		1654			7209
1611	3 ship loads			1700			22,000
	300			1748			82,100
1612	80			1759			105,000
1617		400		1772			153,000
1618	200			1782		567,614	
	40						
		600					

27¼ years. The intermediate enumerations taken in 1700, 1748, and 1759, furnish proofs of the uniformity of this progression. Should this rate of increase continue, we shall have between six and seven millions of inhabitants within 95 years. If we suppose our country to be bounded, at some future day, by the meridian of the mouth of the Great Kanhaway, (within which it has been before conjectured, are 64,491 square miles) there will then be 100 inhabitants for every square mile, which is nearly the state of population in the British islands.

Here I will beg leave to propose a doubt. The present desire of America is to produce rapid population by as great importations of foreigners as possible. But is this founded in good policy? The advantage proposed is the multiplication of numbers. Now let us suppose (for ex-

ample only) that, in this state, we could double our
numbers in one year by the importation of foreigners;
and this is a greater accession than the most sanguine advocate for emigration has a right to expect. Then I say,
beginning with a double stock, we shall attain any given
degree of population only 27 years and 3 months sooner
than if we proceed on our single stock. If we propose
four millions and a half as a competent population for this
state, we should be 54½ years attaining it, could we at
once double our numbers; and 81¾ years, if we rely on
natural propagation, as may be seen by the following table.

	Proceeding on our present stock.	Proceeding on a double stock.
1781	567,614	1,135,228
1808¼	1,135,228	2,270,456
1835½	2,270,456	4,540,912
1862¾	4,540,912	

In the first column are stated periods of 27¼ years; in
the second are our numbers, at each period, as they will
be if we proceed on our actual stock; and in the third are
what they would be, at the same periods, were we to set
out from the double of our present stock. I have taken
the term of four millions and a half of inhabitants for example's sake only. Yet I am persuaded it is a greater number than the country spoken of, considering how much
inarable land it contains, can clothe and feed, without a
material change in the quality of their diet. But are there
no inconveniences to be thrown into the scale against the
advantage expected from a multiplication of numbers by
the importation of foreigners? It is for the happiness of
those united in society to harmonize as much as possible
in matters which they must of necessity transact together.
Civil government being the sole object of forming societies, its administration must be conducted by common
consent. Every species of government has its specific
principles. Ours perhaps are more peculiar than those of
any other in the universe. It is a composition of the freest

principles of the English constitution, with others derived from natural right and natural reason. To these nothing can be more opposed than the maxims of absolute monarchies. Yet, from such, we are to expect the greatest number of emigrants. They will bring with them the principles of the governments they leave, imbibed in their early youth; or, if able to throw them off, it will be in exchange for an unbounded licentiousness, passing, as is usual, from one extreme to another. It would be a miracle were they to stop precisely at the point of temperate liberty. These principles, with their language, they will transmit to their children. In proportion to their numbers, they will share with us the legislation. They will infuse into it their spirit, warp and bias its direction, and render it a heterogeneous, incoherent, distracted mass. I may appeal to experience, during the present contest, for a verification of these conjectures. But, if they be not certain in event, are they not possible, are they not probable? Is it not safer to wait with patience 27 years and three months longer, for the attainment of any degree of population desired, or expected? May not our government be more homogeneous, more peaceable, more durable? Suppose 20 millions of republican Americans thrown all of a sudden into France, what would be the condition of that kingdom? If it would be more turbulent, less happy, less strong, we may believe that the addition of half a million of foreigners to our present numbers would produce a similar effect here. If they come of themselves, they are entitled to all the rights of citizenship: but I doubt the expediency of inviting them by extraordinary encouragements. I mean not that these doubts should be extended to the importation of useful artificers. The policy of that measure depends on very different considerations. Spare no expence in obtaining them. They will after a while go to the plough and the hoe; but, in the mean time, they will teach us something we do not know. It is not so in agriculture. The indifferent state of that among us does not proceed from a want of knowledge merely; it is from our having such quantities of land to waste as we please. In Europe the object is to make the most of their land, labour being abundant: here it is to make the most of our labour, land being abundant.

It will be proper to explain how the numbers for the year 1782 have been obtained; as it was not from a perfect census of the inhabitants. It will at the same time develope the proportion between the free inhabitants and slaves. The following return of taxable articles for that year was given in.

    53,289 free males above 21 years of age.
   211,698 slaves of all ages and sexes.
    23,766 not distinguished in the returns, but said to be
           titheable slaves.
   195,439 horses.
   609,734 cattle.
     5,126 wheels of riding-carriages.
       191 taverns.

There were no returns from the 8 counties of Lincoln, Jefferson, Fayette, Monongalia, Yohogania, Ohio, Northampton, and York. To find the number of slaves which should have been returned instead of the 23,766 titheables, we must mention that some observations on a former census had given reason to believe that the numbers above and below 16 years of age were equal. The double of this number, therefore, to wit, 47,532 must be added to 211,698, which will give us 259,230 slaves of all ages and sexes. To find the number of free inhabitants, we must repeat the observation, that those above and below 16 are nearly equal. But as the number 53,289 omits the males between 16 and 21, we must supply them from conjecture. On a former experiment it had appeared that about one-third of our militia, that is, of the males between 16 and 50, were unmarried. Knowing how early marriage takes place here, we shall not be far wrong in supposing that the unmarried part of our militia are those between 16 and 21. If there be young men who do not marry till after 21, there are as many who marry before that age. But as the men above 50 were not included in the militia, we will suppose the unmarried, or those between 16 and 21, to be one-fourth of the whole number above 16, then we have the following calculation:

53,289 free males above 21 years of age.
17,763 free males between 16 and 21.
71,052 free males under 16.
142,104 free females of all ages.
284,208 free inhabitants of all ages.
259,230 slaves of all ages.

543,438 inhabitants, exclusive of the 8 counties from which were no returns. In these 8 counties in the years 1779 and 1780 were 3,161 milita. Say then,

3,161 free males above the age of 16.
3,161 ditto under 16.
6,322 free females.
12,644 free inhabitants in these 8 counties.

To find the number of slaves, say, as 284,208 to 259,230, so is 12,644 to 11,532. Adding the third of these numbers to the first, and the fourth to the second, we have,

296,852 free inhabitants.
270,762 slaves.
567,614 inhabitants of every age, sex, and condition.

But 296,852, the number of free inhabitants, are to 270,762, the number of slaves, nearly as 11 to 10. Under the mild treatment our slaves experience, and their wholesome, though coarse, food, this blot in our country increases as fast, or faster, than the whites. During the regal government, we had at one time obtained a law, which imposed such a duty on the importation of slaves, as amounted nearly to a prohibition, when one inconsiderate assembly, placed under a peculiarity of circumstance, repealed the law. This repeal met a joyful sanction from the then sovereign, and no devices, no expedients, which could ever after be attempted by subsequent assemblies, and they seldom met without attempting them, could succeed in getting the royal assent to a renewal of the duty. In the very first session held under the republican government, the assembly passed a law for the perpetual prohibition of the importation of slaves. This will in some measure stop the increase of this great political and moral evil, while the minds of our citizens may be ripening for a complete emancipation of human nature.

QUERY IX.

Military Force

*¶ The number and condition of the militia
and regular troops, and their pay?*

THE FOLLOWING [see page 130] is a state of
the militia, taken from returns of 1780 and 1781, except in
those counties marked with an asterisk, the returns from
which are somewhat older.

Every able-bodied freeman, between the ages of 16 and
50, is enrolled in the militia. Those of every county are
formed into companies, and these again into one or more
battalions, according to the numbers in the county. They
are commanded by colonels, and other subordinate officers,
as in the regular service. In every county is a county-
lieutenant, who commands the whole militia of his county,
but ranks only as a colonel in the field. We have no general
officers always existing. These are appointed occasionally,
when an invasion or insurrection happens, and their commission determines with the occasion. The governor is head
of the military, as well as civil power. The law requires
every militia-man to provide himself with the arms usual in
the regular service. But this injunction was always indifferently complied with, and the arms they had have been so
frequently called for to arm the regulars, that in the lower
parts of the country they are entirely disarmed. In the
middle country a fourth or fifth part of them may have
such firelocks as they had provided to destroy the noxious
animals which infest their farms; and on the western side of
the Blue ridge they are generally armed with rifles. The
pay of our militia, as well as of our regulars, is that of the

Counties.	Militia.	Counties.	Militia.
Westward of the Allegany. 4458.		*On the Tide Waters and in that Parallel.* 19,012.	
Lincoln	600	*Between James River and Carolina.* 6959.	
Jefferson	300	Greenesville	500
Fayette	156	Dinwiddie	*750
Ohio		Chesterfield	655
Monongalia	*1000	Prince George	382
Washington	*829	Surry	380
Montgomery	1071	Sussex	*700
Green-briar	502	Southampton	874
		Isle of Wight	*600
Between the Allegany and Blue Ridge. 7673.		Nansemond	*644
		Norfolk	*880
		Princess Anne	*594
Hampshire	930	*Between James and York Rivers.* 3009.	
Berkeley	*1100		
Frederick	1143	Henrico	619
Shenando	*925	Hanover	796
Rockingham	875	New Kent	*418
Augusta	1375	Charles City	286
Rockbridge	*625	James City	235
Botetourt	*700	Williamsburg	129
		York	*244
Between the Blue Ridge and Tide Waters. 18,828.		Warwick	*100
		Elizabeth City	182
Loudoun	1746	*Between York and Rappahanock.* 3269.	
Fauquier	1078	Caroline	805
Culpeper	1513	King William	436
Spotsylvania	480	King & Queen	500
Orange	*600	Essex	468
Louisa	603	Middlesex	*210
Goochland	*550	Gloucester	850
Fluvanna	*296	*Between Rappahanock & Patowmac.* 4137.	
Albemarle	873		
Amherst	896	Fairfax	652
Buckingham	*625	Prince William	614
Bedford	1300	Stafford	*500
Henry	1004	King George	483
Pittsylvania	*725	Richmond	412
Halifax	*1139	Westmoreland	544
Charlotte	612	Northumberl.	630
Prince Edward	589	Lancaster	302
Cumberland	408		
Powhatan	330	*East. Shore.* 1638.	
Amelia	*1125		
Lunenburg	677	Accomac	*1208
Mecklenburg	1100	Northampton	*430
Brunswic	559		
		Whole Militia of the State	49,971

continental regulars. The condition of our regulars, of whom we have none but continentals, and part of a battalion of state troops, is so constantly on the change, that a state of it at this day would not be its state a month hence. It is much the same with the condition of the other continental troops, which is well enough known.

QUERY X.

Marine Force

¶ The marine?

BEFORE the present invasion of this state by the British, under the command of General Phillips,[1] we had three vessels of 16 guns, one of 14, five small gallies, and two or three armed boats. They were generally so badly manned as seldom to be in condition for service. Since the perfect possession of our rivers assumed by the enemy, I believe we are left with a single armed boat only.

[1] General William Phillips (c. 1731–1781), whose invasion on April 18, 1781, was in advance of Cornwallis's southern army. [Ed.]

Aborigines

¶ A description of the Indians established in that state?

WHEN the first effectual settlement of our colony was made, which was in 1607, the country from the sea-coast to the mountains, and from Patowmac to the most southern waters of James river, was occupied by upwards of forty different tribes of Indians. Of these the *Powhatans*, the *Mannahoacs*, and *Monacans*, were the most powerful. Those between the sea-coast and falls of the rivers, were in amity with one another, and attached to the *Powhatans* as their link of union. Those between the falls of the rivers and the mountains, were divided into two confederacies; the tribes inhabiting the head waters of Patowmac and Rappahanoc being attached to the *Mannahoacs*; and those on the upper parts of James river to the *Monacans*. But the *Monacans* and their friends were in amity with the *Mannahoacs* and their friends, and waged joint and perpetual war against the *Powhatans*. We are told that the *Powhatans*, *Mannahoacs*, and *Monacans*, spoke languages so radically different, that interpreters were necessary when they transacted business. Hence we may conjecture, that this was not the case between all the tribes, and probably that each spoke the language of the nation to which it was attached; which we know to have been the case in many particular instances. Very possibly there may have been anciently three different stocks, each of which multiplying in a long course of time, had separated into so many little societies. This practice results from the circumstance of their having never submitted themselves to any laws, any coercive power, any shadow of government. Their only controuls are their manners, and that moral sense of right and wrong, which, like the sense of tasting and feeling, in every man makes a part of his nature. An offence against these is punished by contempt, by exclusion from society, or, where the case is serious, as that of murder, by the individuals whom it concerns. Imperfect as this species of coercion may seem, crimes are very rare among them: insomuch that were it made a question, whether no law, as among the savage Americans, or too much law, as among the civilized Europeans, submits man to the greatest evil, one who has seen both conditions of existence would pronounce it to be the last: and that the sheep are happier of themselves, than under care of the wolves. It will be said, that great societies cannot exist without government. The savages therefore break them into small ones.

The territories of the *Powhatan* confederacy, south of the Patowmac, comprehended about 8000 square miles, 30 tribes, and 2400 warriors. Capt. Smith tells us,[1] that within 60 miles of James town were 5000 people, of whom 1500 were warriors. From this we find the proportion of their warriors to their whole inhabitants, was as 3 to 10. The *Powhatan* confederacy then would consist of about 8000 inhabitants, which was one for every square mile; being about the twentieth part of our present population in the same territory, and the hundredth of that of the British islands.

Besides these, were the *Nottoways*, living on Nottoway river, the *Meherrins* and *Tuteloes* on Meherrin river, who were connected with the Indians of Carolina, probably with the Chowanocs.

The following table [pages 136–37] contains a state of these several tribes, according to their confederacies and geographical situation, with their numbers when we first became acquainted with them, where these numbers are

[1] John Smith, *The General History of Virginia, New England, and the Summer Isles* (London, 1624). [Ed.]

known. The numbers of some of them are again stated as they were in the year 1669, when an attempt was made by the assembly to enumerate them. Probably the enumeration is imperfect, and in some measure conjectural, and that a further search into the records would furnish many more particulars. What would be the melancholy sequel of their history, may however be augured from the census of 1669; by which we discover that the tribes therein enumerated were, in the space of 62 years, reduced to about one-third of their former numbers. Spirituous liquors, the small-pox, war, and an abridgment of territory, to a people who lived principally on the spontaneous productions of nature, had committed terrible havock among them, which generation, under the obstacles opposed to it among them, was not likely to make good. That the lands of this country were taken from them by conquest, is not so general a truth as is supposed. I find in our historians and records, repeated proofs of purchase, which cover a considerable part of the lower country; and many more would doubtless be found on further search. The upper country we know has been acquired altogether by purchases made in the most unexceptionable form.

Westward of all these tribes, beyond the mountains, and extending to the great lakes, were the *Massawomecs,* a most powerful confederacy, who harassed unremittingly the *Powhatans* and *Manahoacs.* These were probably the ancestors of the tribes known at present by the name of the *Six Nations.*

Very little can now be discovered of the subsequent history of these tribes severally. The *Chickahominies* removed, about the year 1661, to Mattapony river. Their chief, with one from each of the tribes of the Pamunkies and Mattaponies, attended the treaty of Albany in 1685. This seems to have been the last chapter in their history. They retained however their separate name so late as 1705, and were at length blended with the Pamunkies and Mattaponies, and exist at present only under their names. There remain of the *Mattaponies* three or four men only,

NORTH.

				MANNAHOACS.			
	Tribes.	Country.	Chief town.	Warriors. 1607	1669		Tribes.
BETWEEN PATOWMAC AND RAPPAHANOC.	Whonkenties	Fauquier					Tauxenents
							Patówomekes
	Tegninaties	Culpeper					Cuttatawomans
							Pissasecs
	Ontponies	Orange					Onaumanìents
							Rappahànocs
	Tauxitanians	Fauquier					Moràughtacunds
							Secacaonies
	Hassinungaes	Culpeper					Wighcocòmicoes
							Cuttatawomans
BETWEEN RAPPAHANOC AND YORK.	Stegarakies	Orange					Nantaughtacunds
	Shackakonies	Spotsylvania					Màttapomènts
	Mannahoacs	Stafford					Pamùnkies
		Spotsylvania					Wèrowocòmicos
							Payànkatanks
			MONACANS.				Youghtanunds
							Chickahòminies
							Powhatàns
BETWEEN YORK AND JAMES.	Monacans	James R. above the falls	Fork of James R.		30		Arrowhàtocs
							Wèanocs
							Paspahèghes
	Monasiccapanoes	Louisa. Fluvanna					Chìskiacs
							Kecoughtáns
BETWEEN JAMES AND CAROLINA.	Monahassanoes	Bedford. Buckingham					Appamàttocs
							Quiocohànocs
	Massinacacs	Cumberland					Wàrrasqeaks
	Mohemenchoes	Powhatan					Nansamònds
							Chèsapeaks
EASTERN SHORE.							Accohanocs
							Accomàcks

SOUTH.

and they have more negro than Indian blood in them. They have lost their language, have reduced themselves, by voluntary sales, to about fifty acres of land, which lie on the river of their own name, and have, from time to time, been joining the Pamunkies, from whom they are distant but 10 miles. The *Pamunkies* are reduced to about 10 or 12 men, tolerably pure from mixture with other

POWHATANS.

Country.	Chief town.	Warriors. 1607	1669	
Fairfax	About General Washington's	40		
Stafford. King George	Patowmac creek	200		By the name of Matchotics. U. Matchodic. Nanzaticos. Nanzatico. Appamatox. Matox.
King George	About Lamb creek	20	60	
King Geo. Richmond	Above Leeds town	—		
Westmoreland	Nomony river	100		
Richmond county	Rappahanoc creek	100	30	
Lancaster. Richmond	Moratico river	80	40	by the name of Totuskeys.
Northumberland	Coan river	30		
Northumberland	Wicocomico river	130	70	
Lancaster	Corotoman	30		
Essex. Caroline	Port tobacco creek	150	60	
Mattapony river	- - - -	30	20	
King William	Romuncock	300	50	
Gloucester	About Rosewell	40		
Piankatank river	Turk's Ferry Grimesby	55		
Pamunkey river	- - - -	60		
Chickahominy river	Orapaks	250	60	
Henrico	Powhatan. Mayo's	40	10	
Henrico	Arrohatocs	30		
Charles city	Weynoke	100	15	
Charles city. James city	Sandy point	40		
York	Chiskiac	45	15	
Elizabeth city	Roscows	20		
Chesterfield	Bermuda hundred	60	50	1669
Surry	About Upper Chipoak	25	3 Pohics	Nottoways
Isle of Wight	Warrasqueac			Meherrics 90
Nansamond	About the mouth of West. branch	200	45	Tuteloes 50
Princess Anne	About Lynhaven river	100		
Accom. Northampton	Accohanoc river	40		
Northampton	About Cheriton's	80		

colours. The older ones among them preserve their language in a small degree, which are the last vestiges on earth, as far as we know, of the Powhatan language. They have about 300 acres of very fertile land, on Pamunkey river, so encompassed by water that a gate shuts in the whole. Of the *Nottoways*, not a male is left. A few women constitute the remains of that tribe. They are seated on

Nottoway river, in Southampton county, on very fertile lands. At a very early period, certain lands were marked out and appropriated to these tribes, and were kept from encroachment by the authority of the laws. They have usually had trustees appointed, whose duty was to watch over their interests, and guard them from insult and injury.

The *Monacans* and their friends, better known latterly by the name of *Tuscaroras*, were probably connected with the Massawomecs, or Five Nations. For though we are told their languages were so different that the intervention of interpreters was necessary between them,[2] yet do we also learn that the Erigas, a nation formerly inhabiting on the Ohio, were of the same original stock with the Five Nations, and that they partook also of the Tuscarora language.[3] Their dialects might, by long separation, have become so unlike as to be unintelligible to one another. We know that in 1712, the Five Nations received the Tuscaroras into their confederacy, and made them the Sixth Nation. They received the Meherrins and Tuteloes also into their protection: and it is most probable, that the remains of many other of the tribes, of whom we find no particular account, retired westwardly in like manner, and were incorporated with one or other of the western tribes.

I know of no such thing existing as an Indian monument: for I would not honour with that name arrow points, stone hatchets, stone pipes, and half-shapen images. Of labour on the large scale, I think there is no remain as respectable as would be a common ditch for the draining of lands: unless indeed it be the Barrows, of which many are to be found all over this country. These are of different sizes, some of them constructed of earth, and some of loose stones. That they were repositories of the dead, has been obvious to all: but on what particular occasion constructed, was matter of doubt. Some have thought they

[2] Smith.

[3] Evans (Lewis Evans, map previously cited. See footnote, page 47. [Ed.])

covered the bones of those who have fallen in battles fought on the spot of interment. Some ascribed them to the custom, said to prevail among the Indians, of collecting, at certain periods, the bones of all their dead, wheresoever deposited at the time of death. Others again supposed them the general sepulchres for towns, conjectured to have been on or near these grounds; and this opinion was supported by the quality of the lands in which they are found, (those constructed of earth being generally in the softest and most fertile meadow-grounds on river sides) and by a tradition, said to be handed down from the aboriginal Indians, that, when they settled in a town, the first person who died was placed erect, and earth put about him, so as to cover and support him; that, when another died, a narrow passage was dug to the first, the second reclined against him, and the cover of earth replaced, and so on. There being one of these in my neighbourhood, I wished to satisfy myself whether any, and which of these opinions were just. For this purpose I determined to open and examine it thoroughly. It was situated on the low grounds of the Rivanna, about two miles above its principal fork, and opposite to some hills, on which had been an Indian town. It was of a spheroidical form, of about 40 feet diameter at the base, and had been of about twelve feet altitude, though now reduced by the plough to seven and a half, having been under cultivation about a dozen years. Before this it was covered with trees of 12 inches diameter, and round the base was an excavation of five feet depth and width, from whence the earth had been taken of which the hillock was formed. I first dug superficially in several parts of it, and came to collections of human bones, at different depths, from six inches to three feet below the surface. These were lying in the utmost confusion, some vertical, some oblique, some horizontal, and directed to every point of the compass, entangled, and held together in clusters by the earth. Bones of the most distant parts were found together, as, for instance, the small bones of the foot in the hollow of a scull, many sculls would sometimes be in contact, lying on the face, on the side, on the back, top or bottom, so as, on the whole, to give the idea of bones emptied promiscuously from a bag or basket, and covered over with earth, without any attention to their order. The bones of which the greatest numbers remained, were sculls, jaw-bones, teeth, the bones of the arms, thighs, legs, feet, and hands. A few ribs remained, some vertebræ of the neck and spine, without their processes, and one instance only of the bone[4] which serves as a base to the vertebral column. The sculls were so tender, that they generally fell to pieces on being touched. The other bones were stronger. There were some teeth which were judged to be smaller than those of an adult; a scull, which, on a slight view, appeared to be that of an infant, but it fell to pieces on being taken out, so as to prevent satisfactory examination; a rib, and a fragment of the under-jaw of a person about half grown; another rib of an infant; and part of the jaw of a child, which had not yet cut its teeth. This last furnishing the most decisive proof of the burial of children here, I was particular in my attention to it. It was part of the right-half of the under-jaw. The processes, by which it was articulated to the temporal bones, were entire; and the bone itself firm to where it had been broken off, which, as nearly as I could judge, was about the place of the eyetooth. Its upper edge, wherein would have been the sockets of the teeth, was perfectly smooth. Measuring it with that of an adult, by placing their hinder processes together, its broken end extended to the penultimate grinder of the adult. This bone was white, all the others of a sand colour. The bones of infants being soft, they probably decay sooner, which might be the cause so few were found here. I proceeded then to make a perpendicular cut through the body of the barrow, that I might examine its internal structure. This passed about three feet from its center, was opened to the former surface of the earth, and was wide enough for a man to walk through and examine its sides. At the bottom, that is, on the level of the circum-

4 The os sacrum.

jacent plain, I found bones; above these a few stones, brought from a cliff a quarter of a mile off, and from the river one-eighth of a mile off; then a large interval of earth, then a stratum of bones, and so on. At one end of the section were four strata of bones plainly distinguishable; at the other, three; the strata in one part not ranging with those in another. The bones nearest the surface were least decayed. No holes were discovered in any of them, as if made with bullets, arrows, or other weapons. I conjectured that in this barrow might have been a thousand skeletons. Every one will readily seize the circumstances above related, which militate against the opinion, that it covered the bones only of persons fallen in battle; and against the tradition also, which would make it the common sepulchre of a town, in which the bodies were placed upright, and touching each other. Appearances certainly indicate that it has derived both origin and growth from the accustomary collection of bones, and deposition of them together; that the first collection had been deposited on the common surface of the earth, a few stones put over it, and then a covering of earth, that the second had been laid on this, had covered more or less of it in proportion to the number of bones, and was then also covered with earth; and so on. The following are the particular circumstances which give it this aspect. 1. The number of bones. 2. Their confused position. 3. Their being in different strata. 4. The strata in one part having no correspondence with those in another. 5. The different states of decay in these strata, which seem to indicate a difference in the time of inhumation. 6. The existence of infant bones among them.

But on whatever occasion they may have been made, they are of considerable notoriety among the Indians: for a party passing, about thirty years ago, through the part of the country where this barrow is, went through the woods directly to it, without any instructions or enquiry, and having staid about it some time, with expressions which were construed to be those of sorrow, they returned to the high road, which they had left about half a dozen miles to pay this visit, and pursued their journey. There is another barrow, much resembling this in the low grounds of the South branch of Shenandoah, where it is crossed by the road leading from the Rock-fish gap to Staunton. Both of these have, within these dozen years, been cleared of their trees and put under cultivation, are much reduced in their height, and spread in width, by the plough, and will probably disappear in time. There is another on a hill in the Blue ridge of mountains, a few miles North of Wood's gap, which is made up of small stones thrown together. This has been opened and found to contain human bones, as the others do. There are also many others in other parts of the country.

Great question has arisen from whence came those aboriginal inhabitants of America? Discoveries, long ago made, were sufficient to shew that a passage from Europe to America was always practicable, even to the imperfect navigation of ancient times. In going from Norway to Iceland, from Iceland to Groenland, from Groenland to Labrador, the first traject is the widest: and this having been practised from the earliest times of which we have any account of that part of the earth, it is not difficult to suppose that the subsequent trajects may have been sometimes passed. Again, the late discoveries of Captain Cook, coasting from Kamschatka to California, have proved that, if the two continents of Asia and America be separated at all, it is only by a narrow streight. So that from this side also, inhabitants may have passed into America: and the resemblance between the Indians of America and the Eastern inhabitants of Asia, would induce us to conjecture, that the former are the descendants of the latter, or the latter of the former: excepting indeed the Eskimaux, who, from the same circumstance of resemblance, and from identity of language, must be derived from the Groenlanders, and these probably from some of the northern parts of the old continent. A knowledge of their several languages would be the most certain evidence of their derivation which could be produced. In fact, it is the best proof of the affinity of nations which ever can be referred to. How many ages have elapsed since the English, the Dutch, the Germans, the Swiss, the Norwegians, Danes and Swedes have separated from their common stock? Yet how many more must elapse before the proofs of their common origin, which exist in their several languages, will disappear? It is to be lamented then, very much to be lamented, that we have suffered so many of the Indian tribes already to extinguish, without our having previously collected and deposited in the records of literature, the general rudiments at least of the languages they spoke. Were vocabularies formed of all the languages spoken in North and South America, preserving their appellations of the most common objects in nature, of those which must be present to every nation barbarous or civilised, with the inflections of their nouns and verbs, their principles of regimen and concord, and these deposited in all the public libraries, it would furnish opportunities to those skilled in the languages of the old world to compare them with these, now, or at any future time, and hence to construct the best evidence of the derivation of this part of the human race.

But imperfect as is our knowledge of the tongues spoken in America, it suffices to discover the following remarkable fact. Arranging them under the radical ones to which they may be palpably traced, and doing the same by those of the red men of Asia, there will be found probably twenty in America for one in Asia, of those radical languages, so called because, if they were ever the same, they have lost all resemblance to one another. A separation into dialects may be the work of a few ages only, but for two dialects to recede from one another till they have lost all vestiges of their common origin, must require an immense course of time; perhaps not less than many people give to the age of the earth. A greater number of those radical changes of language having taken place among the red men of America, proves them of greater antiquity than those of Asia.

I will now proceed to state the nations and numbers of the Aborigines which still exist in a respectable and independant form. And as their undefined boundaries would render it difficult to specify those only which may be within any certain limits, and it may not be unacceptable to present a more general view of them, I will reduce within the form of a Catalogue all those within, and circumjacent to, the United States, whose names and numbers have come to my notice. These are taken from four different lists, the first of which was given in the year 1759 to General Stanwix by George Croghan, deputy agent for Indian affairs under Sir William Johnson; the second was drawn up by a French trader of considerable note, resident among the Indians many years, and annexed to Colonel Bouquet's printed account of his expedition in 1764. The third was made out by Captain Hutchins, who visited most of the tribes, by order, for the purpose of learning their numbers in 1768. And the fourth by John Dodge, an Indian trader, in 1779, except the numbers marked *, which are from other information.

But, apprehending these might be different appellations for some of the tribes already enumerated, I have not inserted them in the table, but state them separately [on page 150] as worthy of further inquiry. The variations observable in numbering the same tribe may sometimes be ascribed to imperfect information, and sometimes to a greater or less comprehension of settlements under the same name.

Tribes Northward and Westward of the United States.	Croghan. 1759.	Bouquet. 1764.	Hutchins. 1768.	Where they reside.
Oswegatchies	—	—	100	At Swagatchy, on the river St. Laurence
Connasedagoes	—	—	300	Near Montreal
Cohunnewagoes	—	200	—	
Orondocs	—	—	100	Near Trois Rivieres
Abenakies	—	350	150	Near Trois Rivieres
Little Algonkins	—	—	100	Near Trois Rivieres
Michmacs	—	700	—	River St. Laurence
Amelistes	—	550	—	River St. Laurence
Chalas	—	130	—	River St. Laurence
Nipissins	—	400	—	Towards the heads of the Ottawas river
Algonquins	—	300	—	Towards the heads of the Ottawas river
Round heads	—	2500	—	Riviere aux Tetes boules on the East side of Lake Superior
Messasagues	—	2000	—	Lakes Huron and Superior
Christinaux, Kris	—	3000	—	Lake Christinaux
Assinaboes	—	1500	—	Lake Assinaboes
Blancs, or Barbus	—	1500	—	
Sioux of the Meadows	—	2500	—	On the heads of the Missisipi and Westward of that river
Sioux of the Woods	10,000	1800	10,000	
Sioux	—	1100	—	
Ajoues	—	—	—	North of the Padoucas
Panis. White	—	2000	—	South of the Missouri

Tribes Northward and Westward of the United States.	Croghan. 1759.	Bouquet. 1764.	Hutchins. 1768.	Where they reside.
Panis. Freckled	—	1700	—	South of the Missouri
Padoucas	—	500	—	South of the Missouri
Grandes eaux	—	1000	—	
Canses	—	1600	—	South of the Missouri
Osages	—	600	—	South of the Missouri
Missouris	400	3000	—	On the river Missouri
Arkanzas	—	2000	—	On the river Arkanzas
Caouitas	—	700	—	East of the Alibamous

Tribes Within the Limits of the United States.	Croghan. 1759.	Bouquet. 1764.	Hutchins. 1768.	Dodge. 1779.	Where they reside.
Mohocks	—	—	160	100	Mohocks river.
Onéidas	—	—	300	400	E. side of Oneida L. and head branches of Susquehanna.
Tuscaròras	—	—	200		Between the Oneidas and Onondagoes.
Onondàgoes	—	1550	260	230	Near Onondago L.
Cayùgas	—		200	220	On the Cayuga L. near the N. branch of Susquehanna.
Sénecas	—	—	1000	650	On the waters of Susquehanna, of Ontario, and the heads of the Ohio.
Aughquàgahs	—	—	150	-	East branch of Susquehanna, and on Aughquagah.
Nànticocs	—	—	100	—	Utsanango, Chaghtnet, and Owegy, on the East branch of Susquehanna.
Mohìccons	—	—	100	—	In the same parts.
Condies	—	—	30	—	In the same parts.
Sapòonies	—	—	30	—	At Diahago and other villages up the N. branch of Susquehanna.
Mùnsies	—	—	150	*150	At Diahago and other villages up the N. branch of Susquehanna.
Delawares, or Linnelinopies	—	—	150	—	At Diahago and other villages up the N. branch of Susquehanna.
Delawares, or Linnelinopies	600	600	600	*500	Between Ohio and L. Erie and the branches of Beaver creek, Cayahoga and Muskingham.
Shàwanees	400	500	300	300	Sioto and the branches of Muskingham.
Mingoes	—	—	—	60	On a branch of Sioto.

Tribes Within the Limits of the United States.	Croghan. 1759.	Bouquet. 1764.	Hutchins. 1768.	Dodge. 1779.	Where they reside.
Mohiccons	—	—	—	*60	Near Sandusky.
Cohunnewagos	—	—	—	—	
Wyandots	300	—	300	—	Near Fort St. Joseph's and Detroit.
Wyandots	—	300	250	180	Miami river near Fort Miami.
Twightwees	300	—	250	—	Miami river, about Fort St. Joseph.
Miamis	—	350	300	300	On the banks of the Wabash, near Fort Ouiatonon.
Ouiàtonons	200	400	300	*300	On the banks of the Wabash, near Fort Ouiatonon.
Piànkishas	300	250	200	*400	On the banks of the Wabash, near Fort Ouiatonon.
Shàkies	—	—	300	—	
Kaskaskias	400	600	300	—	Near Kaskaskia.
Illinois	—	—	—	—	Near Cahokia. Qu. If not the same with the Mitchigamis?
Piorias	—	800	—	—	On the Illinois R. called Pianrias, but supposed to mean Piorias.
Pouteòtamies	—	350	300	450	Near St. Joseph's and Fort Detroit.
Ottàwas	—	—	550	*300	Near St. Joseph's and Fort Detroit.
Chippawas	—	—	200	—	On Saguinam bay of Lake Huron.
Ottawas	—	—	400	—	On Saguinam bay of Lake Huron.
Chippawas	2000	5900	250	5450	Near Michillimakinac.
Ottawas	—	—	400	—	Near Michillimakinac.
Chippawas	—	—	—	—	Near Fort St. Mary's on Lake Superior.
Chippawas	—	—	—	—	Several other villages along the banks of Lake Superior. Numbers unknown.
Chippawas	200	400	550	—	Near Puans bay, on Lake Michigan.
Shakies	—	—	—	—	Near Puans bay, on Lake Michigan.
Mynonàmies	—	—	—	—	Near Puans bay, on Lake Michigan.

Tribes Within the Limits of the United States.	Croghan. 1759.	Bouquet. 1764.	Hutchins. 1768.	Dodge. 1779.	Where they reside.
Ouisconsings	—	—	—	—	Ouisconsing River.
Kickapous	600	550	—	250	
Otogamies. Foxes	—	300	—	—	On Lake Michigan, and between that and the Missisipi.
Mascoutens	—	500	4000	—	
Miscothins	—	—	—	—	
Outimacs	—	—	—	—	
Musquakies	200	250	—	250	
Sioux. Eastern	—	—	—	500	On the Eastern heads of Missisipi, and the islands of Lake Superior.
			Galphin. 1768.		
Cherokees	1500	2500	3000	—	Western parts of North Carolina.
Chickasaws	—	750	500	—	Western parts of Georgia.
Catawbas	—	150	—	—	On the Catawba R, in S. Carolina.
Chacktaws	2000	4500	6000	—	Western parts of Georgia.
Upper Creeks	—	1180	3000	—	Western parts of Georgia.
Lower Creeks	—		—	—	Western parts of Georgia.
Natchez	—	150	—	—	
Alibamous	—	600	—	—	Alibama R. in the Western parts of Georgia.

The following tribes are also mentioned:

Croghan's catalo.			
	Lezar	400	From the mouth of Ohio to the mouth of Wabash.
	Webings	200	On the Missisipi below the Shakies.
	Ousasoys. Grand Tuc.	4000	On White creek, a branch of the Missisipi.
	Linways	1000	On the Missisipi.

Bouquet's.			
	Les Puans	700	Near Puans bay.
	Folle avoine	350	Near Puans bay.
	Ouanakina	300	
	Chiakanessou	350	Conjectured to be tribes of the Creeks.
	Machecous	800	
	Souikilas	200	

Dodge's.			
	Mineamis	2000	North-west of lake Michigan, to the heads of Missisipi, and up to lake Superior.
	Piankishas Mascoutins Vermillions	800	On and near the Wabash, towards the Illinois.

QUERY XII.

Counties and Towns

¶ *A notice of the counties, cities, townships, and villages?*

THE COUNTIES have been enumerated under Query IX. They are 74 in number, of very unequal size and population. Of these 35 are on the tide waters, or in that parallel; 23 are in the midlands, between the tide waters and Blue ridge of mountains; 8 between the Blue ridge and Alleghaney; and 8 westward of the Alleghaney.

The state, by another division, is formed into parishes, many of which are commensurate with the counties: but sometimes a county comprehends more than one parish, and sometimes a parish more than one county. This division had relation to the religion of the state, a Parson of the Anglican church, with a fixed salary, having been heretofore established in each parish. The care of the poor was another object of the parochial division.

We have no townships. Our country being much intersected with navigable waters, and trade brought generally to our doors, instead of our being obliged to go in quest of it, has probably been one of the causes why we have no towns of any consequence. Williamsburgh, which, till the year 1780, was the seat of our government, never contained above 1800 inhabitants; and Norfolk, the most populous town we ever had, contained but 6000. Our towns, but more properly our villages or hamlets, are as follows.

On *James river* and its waters, Norfolk, Portsmouth, Hampton, Suffolk, Smithfield, Williamsburgh, Petersburg,

Richmond the seat of our government, Manchester, Charlottesville, New London.

On *York river* and its waters, York, Newcastle, Hanover.

On *Rappahannoc*, Urbanna, Portroyal, Fredericksburg, Falmouth.

On *Patowmac* and its waters, Dumfries, Colchester, Alexandria, Winchester, Staunton.

On *Ohio*, Louisville.

There are other places at which, like some of the foregoing, the *laws* have said there shall be towns; but *Nature* has said there shall not, and they remain unworthy of enumeration. *Norfolk* will probably be the emporium for all the trade of the Chesapeak bay and its waters; and a canal of 8 or 10 miles will bring to it all that of Albermarle sound and its waters. Secondary to this place, are the towns at the head of the tidewaters, to wit, Petersburgh on Appamattox, Richmond on James river, Newcastle on York river, Alexandria on Patowmac, and Baltimore on the Patapsco. From these the distribution will be to subordinate situations in the country. Accidental circumstances however may controul the indications of nature, and in no instances do they do it more frequently than in the rise and fall of towns.

Constitution

¶ The constitution of the state, and its several charters?

QUEEN ELIZABETH by her letters-patent, bearing date March 25, 1584, licensed Sir Walter Raleigh to search for remote heathen lands, not inhabited by Christian people, and granted to him, in fee simple, all the soil within 200 leagues of the places where his people should, within 6 years, make their dwellings or abidings; reserving only, to herself and her successors, their allegiance and one-fifth part of all the gold and silver ore they should obtain. Sir Walter immediately sent out two ships which visited Wococon island in North Carolina, and the next year dispatched seven with 107 men, who settled in Roanoke island, about latitude 35° 50'. Here Okisko, king of the Weopomeiocs, in a full council of his people, is said to have acknowledged himself the homager of the Queen of England, and, after her, of Sir Walter Raleigh. A supply of 50 men were sent in 1586, and 150 in 1587. With these last, Sir Walter sent a governor, appointed him twelve assistants, gave them a charter of incorporation, and instructed them to settle on Chesapeak bay. They landed however at Hatorask. In 1588, when a fleet was ready to sail with a new supply of colonists and necessaries, they were detained by the Queen to assist against the Spanish Armada. Sir Walter having now expended 40,000 l. in these enterprises, obstructed occasionally by the crown, without a shilling of aid from it, was under a necessity of engaging others to adventure their money. He therefore, by deed bearing date the 7th of March 1589, by the name of Sir Walter Raleigh,

Chief Governor of Assamàcomòc, (probably Acomàc), alias Wingadacoia, alias Virginia, granted to Thomas Smith and others, in consideration of their adventuring certain sums of money, liberty of trade to his new country, free from all customs and taxes for seven years, excepting the fifth part of the gold and silver ore to be obtained; and stipulated with them, and the other assistants, then in Virginia, that he would confirm the deed of incorporation which he had given in 1587, with all the prerogatives, jurisdictions, royalties and privileges granted to him by the Queen. Sir Walter, at different times, sent five other adventures hither, the last of which was in 1602: for in 1603 he was attainted, and put into close imprisonment, which put an end to his cares over his infant colony. What was the particular fate of the colonists he had before sent and seated, has never been known: whether they were murdered, or incorporated with the savages.

Some gentlemen and merchants, supposing that by the attainder of Sir Walter Raleigh the grant to him was forfeited, not enquiring over-carefully whether the sentence of an English court could affect lands not within the jurisdiction of that court, petitioned king James for a new grant of Virginia to them. He accordingly executed a grant to Sir Thomas Gates and others, bearing date the 9th of March 1607, under which, in the same year a settlement was effected at James-town and ever after maintained. Of this grant however no particular notice need be taken, as it was superseded by letters-patent of the same king, of May 23, 1609, to the Earl of Salisbury and others, incorporating them by the name of "the Treasurer and Company of adventurers and planters of the City of London for the first colony in Virginia," granting to them and their successors all the lands in Virginia from Point Comfort along the sea coast to the northward 200 miles, and from the same point along the sea coast to the southward 200 miles, and all the space from this precinct on the sea coast up into the land, West and North-west, from sea to sea, and the islands within one hundred miles of it, with all the commodities, jurisdictions, royalties, privileges, franchises and pre-eminences within the same, and thereto and thereabouts, by sea and land, appertaining, in as ample manner as had before been granted to any adventurer: to be held of the king and his successors, in common soccage, yielding one fifth part of the gold and silver ore to be therein found, for all manner of services; establishing a council in England for the direction of the enterprise, the members of which were to be chosen and displaced by the voice of the majority of the company and adventurers, and were to have the nomination and revocation of governors, officers, and ministers, which by them should be thought needful for the colony, the power of establishing laws and forms of government and magistracy, obligatory not only within the colony, but also on the seas in going and coming to and from it; authorising them to carry thither any persons who should consent to go, freeing them for ever from all taxes and impositions on any goods or merchandise on importation into the colony, or exportation out of it, except the five per cent. due for custom on all goods imported into the British dominions, according to the ancient trade of merchants; which five per cent. only being paid, they might, within 13 months, re-export the same goods into foreign parts, without any custom, tax, or other duty, to the king or any his officers or deputies: with powers of waging war against those who should annoy them: giving to the inhabitants of the colony all the rights of natural subjects, as if born and abiding in England; and declaring that these letters should be construed, in all doubtful parts, in such manner as should be most for the benefit of the grantees.

Afterwards, on the 12th of March 1612, by other letters-patent, the king added to his former grants, all islands in any part of the ocean between the 30th and 41st degrees of latitude, and within 300 leagues of any of the parts before granted to the treasurer and company, not being possessed or inhabited by any other christian prince or state, nor within the limits of the northern colony.

In pursuance of the authorities given to the company by

these charters, and more especially of that part in the charter of 1609, which authorised them to establish a form of
government, they on the 24th of July 1621, by charter under their common seal, declared that from thenceforward
there should be two supreme councils in Virginia, the
one to be called the council of state, to be placed and displaced by the treasurer, council in England, and company,
from time to time, whose office was to be that of assisting
and advising the governor; the other to be called the general assembly, to be convened by the governor once yearly
or oftener, which was to consist of the council of state, and
two burgesses out of every town, hundred, or plantation,
to be respectively chosen by the inhabitants. In this all matters were to be decided by the greater part of the votes
present; reserving to the governor a negative voice; and
they were to have power to treat, consult, and conclude all
emergent occasions concerning the public weal, and to
make laws for the behoof and government of the colony,
imitating and following the laws and policy of England as
nearly as might be: providing that these laws should have
no force till ratified in a general quarter court of the company in England, and returned under their common seal,
and declaring that, after the government of the colony
should be well framed and settled, no orders of the council in England should bind the colony unless ratified in the
said general assembly. The king and company quarrelled,
and, by a mixture of law and force, the latter were ousted
of all their rights, without retribution, after having expended 100,000 l. in establishing the colony, without the
smallest aid from government. King James suspended their
powers by proclamation of July 15, 1624, and Charles I.
took the government into his own hands. Both sides had
their partisans in the colony: but in truth the people of the
colony in general thought themselves little concerned in
the dispute. There being three parties interested in these
several charters, what passed between the first and second
it was thought could not affect the third. If the king seized
on the powers of the company, they only passed into other

hands, without increase or diminution, while the rights of the people remained as they were. But they did not remain so long. The northern parts of their country were granted away to the Lords Baltimore and Fairfax, the first of these obtaining also the rights of separate jurisdiction and government. And in 1650 the parliament, considering itself as standing in the place of their deposed king, and as having succeeded to all his powers, without as well as within the realm, began to assume a right over the colonies, passing an act for inhibiting their trade with foreign nations. This succession to the exercise of the kingly authority gave the first colour for parliamentary interference with the colonies, and produced that fatal precedent which they continued to follow after they had retired, in other respects, within their proper functions. When this colony, therefore, which still maintained its opposition to Cromwell and the parliament, was induced in 1651 to lay down their arms, they previously secured their most essential rights, by a solemn convention, which having never seen in print, I will here insert literally from the records.

"ARTICLES agreed on & concluded at James Cittie in Virginia for the surrendering and settling of that plantation under the obedience & government of the common wealth of England by the Commissioners of the Councill of state by authoritie of the parliamt. of England & by the Grand assembly of the Governour, Councill & Burgesses of that countrey.

"First it is agreed and consted that the plantation of Virginia, and all the inhabitants thereof shall be and remaine in due obedience and subjection to the Comon wealth of England, according to the lawes there established, and that this submission and subscription bee acknowledged a voluntary act not forced nor constrained by a conquest upon the countrey, and that they shall have & enjoy such freedomes and priviledges as belong to the free borne people of England, and that the former government by the Comissions and Instructions be void and null.

"2ly, Secondly that the Grand assembly as formerly

shall convene & transact the affairs of Virginia wherein nothing is to be acted or done contrarie to the government of the Comon wealth of England & the lawes there established.

"3ly, That there shall be a full & totall remission and indempnitie of all acts, words, or writeings done or spoken against the parliament of England in relation to the same.

"4ly, That Virginia shall have & enjoy the antient bounds and Lymitts granted by the charters of the former kings, and that we shall seek a new charter from the parliament to that purpose against any that have intrencht upon the rights thereof.

"5ly, That all the pattents of land granted under the collony seale by any of the precedent governours shall be & remaine in their full force & strength.

"6ly, That the priviledge of haveing ffiftie acres of land for every person transported in that collonie shall continue as formerly granted.

"7ly, That the people of Virginia have free trade as the people of England do enjoy to all places and with all nations according to the lawes of that common wealth, and that Virginia shall enjoy all priviledges equall with any English plantations in America.

"8ly, That Virginia shall be free from all taxes, customs & impositions whatsoever, & none to be imposed on them without consent of the Grand assembly, And soe that neither ffortes nor castles bee erected or garrisons maintained without their consent.

"9ly, That noe charge shall be required from this country in respect of this present ffleet.

"10ly, That for the future settlement of the countrey in their due obedience, the Engagement shall be tendred to all the inhabitants according to act of parliament made to that purpose, that all persons who shall refuse to subscribe the said engagement, shall have a yeare's time if they please to remove themselves & their estates out of Virginia, and in the mean time during the said yeare to have equall justice as formerly.

"11ly, That the use of the booke of common prayer shall be permitted for one yeare ensueinge with referrence to the consent of the major part of the parishes, provided that those things which relate to kingshipp or that government be not used publiquely, and the continuance of ministers in their places, they not misdemeaning themselves, and the payment of their accustomed dues and agreements made with them respectively shall be left as they now stand dureing this ensueing yeare.

"12ly, That no man's cattell shall be questioned as the companies unless such as have been entrusted with them or have disposed of them without order.

"13ly, That all ammunition, powder & armes, other then for private use, shall be delivered up, securitie being given to make satisfaction for it.

"14ly, That all goods allreadie brought hither by the Dutch or others which are now on shoar shall be free from surprizall.

"15ly, That the quittrents granted unto us by the late kinge for seaven yeares bee confirmed.

"16ly, That the commissioners for the parliament subscribeing these articles engage themselves & the honour of the parliament for the full performance thereof: and that the present governour & the councill & the burgesses do likewise subscribe & engage the whole collony on their parts.

RICH. BENNETT. ——Seale.
WM. CLAIBORNE. ——Seale.
EDMOND CURTIS. ——Seale.

"Theise articles were signed & sealed by the Commissioners of the Councill of state for the Commonwealth of England the twelveth day of March 1651."

Then follow the articles stipulated by the governor and council, which relate merely to their own persons and property, and then the ensuing instrument:

"An act of indempnitie made att the surrender of the countrey.

"Whereas by the authoritie of the parliament of England wee the commissioners appointed by the councill of state authorized thereto having brought a fleete & force before James cittie in Virginia to reduce that collonie under the obedience of the commonwealth of England, & findeing force raised by the Governour & countrey to make opposition against the said ffleet whereby assured danger appearinge of the ruine & destruction of the plantation, for prevention whereof the Burgesses of all the severall plantations being called to advise & assist therein, uppon long & serious debate, and in sad contemplation of the greate miseries & certaine destruction which were soe neerely hovering over the whole countrey; Wee the said Comissioners have thought fitt & condescended and granted to signe & confirme under our hands, seales, & by our oath, Articles bearinge date with theise presents, and do further declare that by the authoritie of the parliament & commonwealth of England derived unto us theire comissioners, that according to the articles in generall wee have granted an act of indempnitie and oblivion to all the inhabitants of this coloney from all words, actions, or writings that have been spoken acted or writt against the parliament or commonwealth of England or any other person from the beginning of the world to this daye. And this wee have done that all the inhabitants of the collonie may live quietly & securely under the comonwealth of England. And wee do promise that the parliament and commonwealth of England shall confirme & make good all those transactions of ours. Wittnes our hands & seales this 12th of March 1651. Richard Bennett—Seale. Wm. Claiborne—Seale. Edm. Curtis—Seale."

The colony supposed, that, by this solemn convention, entered into with arms in their hands, they had secured the ancient limits[1] of their country, its free trade,[2] its exemption from taxation[3] but by their own assembly, and

[1] Art. 4.
[2] Art. 7.
[3] Art. 8.

exclusion of military force[4] from among them. Yet in every of these points was this convention violated by subsequent kings and parliaments, and other infractions of their constitution, equally dangerous, committed. Their general assembly, which was composed of the council of state and burgesses, sitting together and deciding by plurality of voices, was split into two houses, by which the council obtained a separate negative on their laws. Appeals from their supreme court, which had been fixed by law in their general assembly, were arbitrarily revoked to England, to be there heard before the king and council. Instead of four hundred miles on the sea coast, they were reduced, in the space of thirty years, to about one hundred miles. Their trade with foreigners was totally suppressed, and, when carried to Great-Britain, was there loaded with imposts. It is unnecessary, however, to glean up the several instances of injury, as scattered through American and British history, and the more especially as, by passing on to the accession of the present king, we shall find specimens of them all, aggravated, multiplied and crouded within a small compass of time, so as to evince a fixed design of considering our rights natural, conventional and chartered as mere nullities. The following is an epitome of the first fifteen years of his reign. The colonies were taxed internally and externally; their essential interests sacrificed to individuals in Great-Britain; their legislatures suspended; charters annulled; trials by juries taken away; their persons subjected to transportation across the Atlantic, and to trial before foreign judicatories; their supplications for redress thought beneath answer; themselves published as cowards in the councils of their mother country and courts of Europe; armed troops sent among them to enforce submission to these violences; and actual hostilities commenced against them. No alternative was presented but resistance, or unconditional submission. Between these could be no hesitation. They closed in the appeal to arms.

[4]Art. 8.

They declared themselves independent States. They confederated together into one great republic; thus securing to every state the benefit of an union of their whole force. In each state separately a new form of government was established. Of ours particularly the following are the outlines. The executive powers are lodged in the hands of a governor, chosen annually, and incapable of acting more than three years in seven. He is assisted by a council of eight members. The judiciary powers are divided among several courts, as will be hereafter explained. Legislation is exercised by two houses of assembly, the one called the house of Delegates, composed of two members from each county, chosen annually by the citizens possessing an estate for life in 100 acres of uninhabited land, or 25 acres with a house on it, or in a house or lot in some town: the other called the Senate, consisting of 24 members, chosen quadrennially by the same electors, who for this purpose are distributed into 24 districts. The concurrence of both houses is necessary to the passage of a law. They have the appointment of the governor and council, the judges of the superior courts, auditors, attorney-general, treasurer, register of the land office, and delegates to congress. As the dismemberment of the state had never had its confirmation, but, on the contrary, had always been the subject of protestation and complaint, that it might never be in our own power to raise scruples on that subject, or to disturb the harmony of our new confederacy, the grants to Maryland, Pennsylvania, and the two Carolinas, were ratified.

This constitution was formed when we were new and inexperienced in the science of government. It was the first too which was formed in the whole United States. No wonder then that time and trial have discovered very capital defects in it.

1. The majority of the men in the state, who pay and fight for its support, are unrepresented in the legislature, the roll of freeholders entitled to vote, not including generally the half of those on the roll of the militia, or of the tax-gatherers.

2. Among those who share the representation, the shares are very unequal. Thus the county of Warwick, with only 100 fighting men, has an equal representation with the county of Loudon, which has 1746. So that every man in Warwick has as much influence in the government as 17 men in Loudon. But lest it should be thought that an equal interspersion of small among large counties, through the whole state, may prevent any danger of injury to particular parts of it, we will divide it into districts, and shew the proportions of land, of fighting men, and of representation in each.

	Square miles.	Fighting men.	Dele-gates.	Sena-tors.
Between the sea-coast and falls of the rivers	11,205[5]	19,012	71	12
Between the falls of the rivers and the Blue ridge of mountains	18,759	18,828	46	8
Between the Blue ridge and the Alleghaney	11,911	7,673	16	2
Between the Alleghaney and Ohio	79,650[6]	4,458	16	2
Total	121,525	49,971	149	24

An inspection of this table will supply the place of commentaries on it. It will appear at once that 19,000 men, living below the falls of the rivers, possess half the senate, and want four members only of possessing a majority of the house of delegates; a want more than supplied by the vicinity of their situation to the seat of government, and of course the greater degree of convenience and punctuality with which their members may and will attend in the legislature. These 19,000, therefore, living in one part of

[5] Of these, 542 are on the Eastern shore.
[6] Of these, 22,616 are eastward of the meridian of the mouth of the Great Kanhaway.

the country, give law to upwards of 30,000, living in another, and appoint all their chief officers executive and judiciary. From the difference of their situation and circumstances, their interests will often be very different.

3. The senate is, by its constitution, too homogeneous with the house of delegates. Being chosen by the same electors, at the same time, and out of the same subjects, the choice falls of course on men of the same description. The purpose of establishing different houses of legislation is to introduce the influence of different interests or different principles. Thus in Great-Britain it is said their constitution relies on the house of commons for honesty, and the lords for wisdom; which would be a rational reliance if honesty were to be bought with money, and if wisdom were hereditary. In some of the American states the delegates and senators are so chosen, as that the first represent the persons, and the second the property of the state. But with us, wealth and wisdom have equal chance for admission into both houses. We do not therefore derive from the separation of our legislature into two houses, those benefits which a proper complication of principles is capable of producing, and those which alone can compensate the evils which may be produced by their dissensions.

4. All the powers of government, legislative, executive, and judiciary, result to the legislative body. The concentrating these in the same hands is precisely the definition of despotic government. It will be no alleviation that these powers will be exercised by a plurality of hands, and not by a single one. 173 despots would surely be as oppressive as one. Let those who doubt it turn their eyes on the republic of Venice. As little will it avail us that they are chosen by ourselves. An *elective despotism* was not the government we fought for; but one which should not only be founded on free principles, but in which the powers of government should be so divided and balanced among several bodies of magistracy, as that no one could transcend their legal limits, without being effectually checked and restrained by the others. For this reason that convention,

which passed the ordinance of government, laid its foundation on this basis, that the legislative, executive and judiciary departments should be separate and distinct, so that no person should exercise the powers of more than one of them at the same time. But no barrier was provided between these several powers. The judiciary and executive members were left dependant on the legislative, for their subsistence in office, and some of them for their continuance in it. If therefore the legislature assumes executive and judiciary powers, no opposition is likely to be made; nor, if made, can it be effectual; because in that case they may put their proceedings into the form of an act of assembly, which will render them obligatory on the other branches. They have accordingly, in many instances, decided rights which should have been left to judiciary controversy: and the direction of the executive, during the whole time of their session, is becoming habitual and familiar. And this is done with no ill intention. The views of the present members are perfectly upright. When they are led out of their regular province, it is by art in others, and inadvertence in themselves. And this will probably be the case for some time to come. But it will not be a very long time. Mankind soon learn to make interested uses of every right and power which they possess, or may assume. The public money and public liberty, intended to have been deposited with three branches of magistracy, but found inadvertently to be in the hands of one only, will soon be discovered to be sources of wealth and dominion to those who hold them; distinguished too by this tempting circumstance, that they are the instrument, as well as the object of acquisition. With money we will get men, said Cæsar, and with men we will get money. Nor should our assembly be deluded by the integrity of their own purposes, and conclude that these unlimited powers will never be abused, because themselves are not disposed to abuse them. They should look forward to a time, and that not a distant one, when corruption in this, as in the country from which we derive our origin, will have seized the heads of government, and be spread by them through the body of the people; when they will purchase the voices of the people, and make them pay the price. Human nature is the same on every side of the Atlantic, and will be alike influenced by the same causes. The time to guard against corruption and tyranny, is before they shall have gotten hold on us. It is better to keep the wolf out of the fold, than to trust to drawing his teeth and talons after he shall have entered. To render these considerations the more cogent, we must observe in addition,

5. That the ordinary legislature may alter the constitution itself. On the discontinuance of assemblies, it became necessary to substitute in their place some other body, competent to the ordinary business of government, and to the calling forth the powers of the state for the maintenance of our opposition to Great-Britain. Conventions were therefore introduced, consisting of two delegates from each county, meeting together and forming one house, on the plan of the former house of burgesses, to whose places they succeeded. These were at first chosen anew for every particular session. But in March 1775, they recommended to the people to chuse a convention, which should continue in office a year. This was done accordingly in April 1775, and in the July following that convention passed an ordinance for the election of delegates in the month of April annually. It is well known, that in July 1775, a separation from Great-Britain and establishment of republican government had never yet entered into any person's mind. A convention therefore, chosen under that ordinance, cannot be said to have been chosen for purposes which certainly did not exist in the minds of those who passed it. Under this ordinance, at the annual election in April 1776, a convention for the year was chosen. Independance, and the establishment of a new form of government, were not even yet the objects of the people at large. One extract from the pamphlet called Common Sense had appeared in the Virginia papers in February, and copies of the pamphlet itself had got into a few hands. But the idea

had not been opened to the mass of the people in April, much less can it be said that they had made up their minds in its favour. So that the electors of April 1776, no more than the legislators of July 1775, not thinking of independance and a permanent republic, could not mean to vest in these delegates powers of establishing them, or any authorities other than those of the ordinary legislature. So far as a temporary organization of government was necessary to render our opposition energetic, so far their organization was valid. But they received in their creation no powers but what were given to every legislature before and since. They could not therefore pass an act transcendant to the powers of other legislatures. If the present assembly pass any act, and declare it shall be irrevocable by subsequent assemblies, the declaration is merely void, and the act repealable, as other acts are. So far, and no farther authorized, they organized the government by the ordinance entitled a Constitution or Form of government. It pretends to no higher authority than the other ordinances of the same session; it does not say, that it shall be perpetual; that it shall be unalterable by other legislatures; that it shall be transcendant above the powers of those, who they knew would have equal power with themselves. Not only the silence of the instrument is a proof they thought it would be alterable, but their own practice also: for this very convention, meeting as a house of delegates in general assembly with the new senate in the autumn of that year, passed acts of assembly in contradiction to their ordinance of government; and every assembly from that time to this has done the same. I am safe therefore in the position, that the constitution itself is alterable by the ordinary legislature. Though this opinion seems founded on the first elements of common sense, yet is the contrary maintained by some persons. 1. Because, say they, the conventions were vested with every power necessary to make effectual opposition to Great-Britain. But to complete this argument, they must go on, and say further, that effectual opposition could not be made to Great-Britain, without establishing a form of government perpetual and unalterable by the legislature; which is not true. An opposition which at some time or other was to come to an end, could not need a perpetual institution to carry it on: and a government, amendable as its defects should be discovered, was as likely to make effectual resistance, as one which should be unalterably wrong. Besides, the assemblies were as much vested with all powers requisite for resistance as the conventions were. If therefore these powers included that of modelling the form of government in the one case, they did so in the other. The assemblies then as well as the conventions may model the government; that is, they may alter the ordinance of government. 2. They urge, that if the convention had meant that this instrument should be alterable, as their other ordinances were, they would have called it an ordinance: but they have called it a *constitution*, which *ex vi termini* means "an act above the power of the ordinary legislature." I answer, that *constitutio, constitutum, statutum, lex*, are convertible terms. "*Constitutio dicitur jus quod a principe conditur.*" "*Constitutum, quod ab imperatoribus rescriptum statutumve est.*" "*Statutum, idem quod lex.*" Calvini *Lexicon Juridicum.*[7] *Constitution* and *statute* were originally terms of the civil law,[8] and from thence introduced by ecclesiastics into the English law. Thus in the statute 25. Hen. 8. c. 19. §1. "*Constitutions* and *ordinances*" are used as synonimous. The term *constitution* has many other significations in physics and in politics; but in jurisprudence, whenever it is applied to any act of the legislature, it invariably means a statute, law, or ordinance, which is the present case. No inference then of a different meaning can be drawn from the adoption of this title: on the contrary, we might conclude, that,

---

[7] "A *constitution* is called that which is made by the ruler." "An *ordinance*, that which emperors rewrite or ordain." "A *statute*, that which is the same as law." Johanus Calvinus, *Lexicon Juridicum*. [Ed.]

[8] To *bid*, to *set*. Ll. [laws] Hlothari & Eadrici. Ll. Inae. Ll. Eadwerdi. Ll. Aethelstani. (That is, legal codes of Saxon kings. [Ed.])

by their affixing to it a term synonimous with ordinance, or statute. But of what consequence is their meaning, where their power is denied? If they meant to do more than they had power to do, did this give them power? It is not the name, but the authority which renders an act obligatory. Lord Coke says, "an article of the statute 11 R. 2. c. 5. that no person should attempt to revoke any ordinance then made, is repealed, for that such restraint is against the jurisdiction and power of the parliament." 4. Inst. 42. and again, though divers parliaments have attempted to restrain subsequent parliaments, yet could they never effect it; for the latter parliament hath ever power to abrogate, suspend, qualify, explain, or make void the former in the whole or in any part thereof, notwithstanding any words of restraint, prohibition, or penalty, in the former: for it is a maxim in the laws of the parliament, "*quod leges posteriores priores contrarias abrogant.*" [9] 4. Inst. 43.—To get rid of the magic supposed to be in the word *constitution*, let us translate it into its definition as given by those who think it above the power of the law; and let us suppose the convention instead of saying, "We, the ordinary legislature, establish a *constitution*," had said, "We, the ordinary legislature, establish an act *above the power of the ordinary legislature.*" Does not this expose the absurdity of the attempt? 3. But, say they, the people have acquiesced, and this has given it an authority superior to the laws. It is true, that the people did not rebel against it: and was that a time for the people to rise in rebellion? Should a prudent acquiescence, at a critical time, be construed into a confirmation of every illegal thing done during that period? Besides, why should they rebel? At an annual election, they had chosen delegates for the year, to exercise the ordinary powers of legislation, and to manage the great contest in which they were engaged. These delegates thought the contest would be best managed by an organized government. They therefore, among others,

[9] "because subsequent laws nullify earlier laws which are contrary."

passed an ordinance of government. They did not presume to call it perpetual and unalterable. They well knew they had no power to make it so; that our choice of them had been for no such purpose, and at a time when we could have no such purpose in contemplation. Had an unalterable form of government been meditated, perhaps we should have chosen a different set of people. There was no cause then for the people to rise in rebellion. But to what dangerous lengths will this argument lead? Did the acquiescence of the colonies under the various acts of power exercised by Great-Britain in our infant state, confirm these acts, and so far invest them with the authority of the people as to render them unalterable, and our present resistance wrong? On every unauthoritative exercise of power by the legislature, must the people rise in rebellion, or their silence be construed into a surrender of that power to them? If so, how many rebellions should we have had already? One certainly for every session of assembly. The other states in the Union have been of opinion, that to render a form of government unalterable by ordinary acts of assembly, the people must delegate persons with special powers. They have accordingly chosen special conventions to form and fix their governments. The individuals then who maintain the contrary opinion in this country, should have the modesty to suppose it possible that they may be wrong and the rest of America right. But if there be only a possibility of their being wrong, if only a plausible doubt remains of the validity of the ordinance of government, is it not better to remove that doubt, by placing it on a bottom which none will dispute? If they be right, we shall only have the unnecessary trouble of meeting once in convention. If they be wrong, they expose us to the hazard of having no fundamental rights at all. True it is, this is no time for deliberating on forms of government. While an enemy is within our bowels, the first object is to expel him. But when this shall be done, when peace shall be established, and leisure given us for intrenching within good forms, the rights for which we have bled, let no man be found indolent enough to decline a little more trouble for placing them beyond the reach of question. If any thing more be requisite to produce a conviction of the expediency of calling a convention, at a proper season, to fix our form of government, let it be the reflection,

6. That the assembly exercises a power of determining the quorum of their own body which may legislate for us. After the establishment of the new form they adhered to the *Lex majoris partis*[10] founded in common law as well as common right.[11] It is the natural law of every assembly of men, whose numbers are not fixed by any other law.[12] They continued for some time to require the presence of a majority of their whole number, to pass an act. But the British parliament fixes its own quorum: our former assemblies fixed their own quorum: and one precedent in favour of power is stronger than an hundred against it. The house of delegates therefore have lately voted[13] that, during the present dangerous invasion, forty members shall be a house to proceed to business. They have been moved to this by the fear of not being able to collect a house. But this danger could not authorise them to call that a house which was none: and if they may fix it at one number, they may at another, till it loses its fundamental character of being a representative body. As this vote expires with the present invasion, it is probable the former rule will be permitted to revive: because at present no ill is meant. The power however of fixing their own quorum has been avowed, and a precedent set. From forty it may be reduced to four, and from four to one: from a house to a committee, from a committee to

[10] Law of the majority. [Ed.]

[11] Bro. abr. Corporations. 31. 34. Hakewell, 93. (Sir Robert Brooke, *Le Graunde Abridgement*. London, 1586. William Hakewell, *Modus Tenedi Parliamentum*. London, 1671. [Ed.])

[12] Puff. Off. hom. I. 2. c. 6. §12. (Samuel von Puffendorf, *De Officio Hominis* (London, 1673. [Ed.])

[13] June 4, 1781.

a chairman or speaker, and thus an oligarchy or monarchy be substituted under forms supposed to be regular. *"Omnia mala exempla ex bonis orta sunt: sed ubi imperium ad ignaros aut minus bonos pervenit, novum illud exemplum ab dignis et idoneis ad indignos et non idoneos fertur."* [14] When therefore it is considered, that there is no legal obstacle to the assumption by the assembly of all the powers legislative, executive, and judiciary, and that these may come to the hands of the smallest rag of delegation, surely the people will say, and their representatives, while yet they have honest representatives, will advise them to say, that they will not acknowledge as laws any acts not considered and assented to by the major part of their delegates.

In enumerating the defects of the constitution, it would be wrong to count among them what is only the error of particular persons. In December 1776, our circumstances being much distressed, it was proposed in the house of delegates to create a *dictator*, invested with every power legislative, executive and judiciary, civil and military, of life and of death, over our persons and over our properties: and in June 1781, again under calamity, the same proposition was repeated, and wanted a few votes only of being passed.—One who entered into this contest from a pure love of liberty, and a sense of injured rights, who determined to make every sacrifice, and to meet every danger, for the re-establishment of those rights on a firm basis; who did not mean to expend his blood and substance for the wretched purpose of changing this master for that, but to place the powers of governing him in a plurality of hands of his own choice, so that the corrupt will of no one man might in future oppress him, must stand confounded and dismayed when he is told, that a considerable portion of that plurality had meditated the surrender of them into a

[14] "All the bad examples are taken from good ones: but when power passes to the ignorant or less good, the new example is transferred from the worthy and fit to the unworthy and unfit." [Ed.]

single hand, and, in lieu of a limited monarch, to deliver him over to a despotic one! How must we find his efforts and sacrifices abused and baffled, if he may still by a single vote be laid prostrate at the feet of one man! In God's name, from whence have they derived this power? Is it from our ancient laws? None such can be produced. Is it from any principle in our new constitution, expressed or implied? Every lineament of that expressed or implied, is in full opposition to it. Its fundamental principle is, that the state shall be governed as a commonwealth. It provides a republican organization, proscribes under the name of *prerogative* the exercise of all powers undefined by the laws; places on this basis the whole system of our laws; and, by consolidating them together, chuses that they shall be left to stand or fall together, never providing for any circumstances, nor admitting that such could arise, wherein either should be suspended, no, not for a moment. Our ancient laws expressly declare, that those who are but delegates themselves shall not delegate to others powers which require judgment and integrity in their exercise.— Or was this proposition moved on a supposed right in the movers of abandoning their posts in a moment of distress? The same laws forbid the abandonment of that post, even on ordinary occasions; and much more a transfer of their powers into other hands and other forms, without consulting the people. They never admit the idea that these, like sheep or cattle, may be given from hand to hand without an appeal to their own will.—Was it from the necessity of the case? Necessities which dissolve a government, do not convey its authority to an oligarchy or a monarchy. They throw back, into the hands of the people, the powers they had delegated, and leave them as individuals to shift for themselves. A leader may offer, but not impose himself, nor be imposed on them. Much less can their necks be submitted to his sword, their breath be held at his will or caprice. The necessity which should operate these tremendous effects should at least be palpable and irresistible. Yet in both instances, where it was feared, or pretended with us, it was belied by the event. It was belied too by the preceding experience of our sister states, several of whom had grappled through greater difficulties without abandoning their forms of government. When the proposition was first made, Massachusets had found even the government of committees sufficient to carry them through an invasion. But we at the time of that proposition were under no invasion. When the second was made, there had been added to this example those of Rhode-Island, New-York, New-Jersey, and Pennsylvania, in all of which the republican form had been found equal to the task of carrying them through the severest trials. In this state alone did there exist so little virtue, that fear was to be fixed in the hearts of the people, and to become the motive of their exertions and the principle of their government? The very thought alone was treason against the people; was treason against mankind in general; as rivetting for ever the chains which bow down their necks, by giving to their oppressors a proof, which they would have trumpeted through the universe, of the imbecility of republican government, in times of pressing danger, to shield them from harm. Those who assume the right of giving away the reins of government in any case, must be sure that the herd, whom they hand on to the rods and hatchet of the dictator, will lay their necks on the block when he shall nod to them. But if our assemblies supposed such a resignation in the people, I hope they mistook their character. I am of opinion, that the government, instead of being braced and invigorated for greater exertions under their difficulties, would have been thrown back upon the bungling machinery of county committees for administration, till a convention could have been called, and its wheels again set into regular motion. What a cruel moment was this for creating such an embarrassment, for putting to the proof the attachment of our countrymen to republican government! Those who meant well, of the advocates for this measure, (and most of them meant well, for I know them personally, had been their fellow-labourers in the common cause, and had often proved the purity of their principles), had been seduced in their judgment by the example of an ancient republic, whose constitution and circumstances were fundamentally different. They had sought this precedent in the history of Rome, where alone it was to be found, and where at length too it had proved fatal. They had taken it from a republic, rent by the most bitter factions and tumults, where the government was of a heavy-handed unfeeling aristocracy, over a people ferocious, and rendered desperate by poverty and wretchedness; tumults which could not be allayed under the most trying circumstances, but by the omnipotent hand of a single despot. Their constitution therefore allowed a temporary tyrant to be erected, under the name of a Dictator; and that temporary tyrant, after a few examples, became perpetual. They misapplied this precedent to a people, mild in their dispositions, patient under their trial, united for the public liberty, and affectionate to their leaders. But if from the constitution of the Roman government there resulted to their senate a power of submitting all their rights to the will of one man, does it follow, that the assembly of Virginia have the same authority? What clause in our constitution has substituted that of Rome, by way of residuary provision, for all cases not otherwise provided for? Or if they may step *ad libitum* into any other form of government for precedents to rule us by, for what oppression may not a precedent be found in this world of the *bellum omnia in omnia?* Searching for the foundations of this proposition, I can find none which may pretend a colour of right or reason, but the defect before developed, that there being no barrier between the legislative, executive, and judiciary departments, the legislature may seize the whole: that having seized it, and possessing a right to fix their own quorum, they may reduce that quorum to one, whom they may call a chairman, speaker, dictator, or by any other name they please.—Our situation is indeed perilous, and I hope my countrymen will be sensible of it, and will apply, at a proper season, the proper remedy; which is a convention to fix the constitution, to amend its defects, to bind up the several branches of government by certain laws, which when they transgress their acts shall become nullities; to render unnecessary an appeal to the people, or in other words a rebellion, on every infraction of their rights, on the peril that their acquiescence shall be construed into an intention to surrender those rights.

QUERY XIV.

Laws

¶ *The administration of justice and description of the laws?*

THE STATE is divided into counties. In every county are appointed magistrates, called justices of the peace, usually from eight to thirty or forty in number, in proportion to the size of the county, of the most discreet and honest inhabitants. They are nominated by their fellows, but commissioned by the governor, and act without reward. These magistrates have jurisdiction both criminal and civil. If the question before them be a question of law only, they decide on it themselves; but if it be of fact, or of fact and law combined, it must be referred to a jury. In the latter case, of a combination of law and fact, it is usual for the jurors to decide the fact, and to refer the law arising on it to the decision of the judges. But this division of the subject lies with their discretion only. And if the question relate to any point of public liberty, or if it be one of those in which the judges may be suspected of bias, the jury undertake to decide both law and fact. If they be mistaken, a decision against right, which is casual only, is less dangerous to the state, and less afflicting to the loser, than one which makes part of a regular and uniform system. In truth, it is better to toss up cross and pile in a cause, than to refer it to a judge whose mind is warped by any motive whatever, in that particular case. But the common sense of twelve honest men gives still a better chance of just decision, than the hazard of cross and pile. These judges execute their process by the sheriff or coroner of the county, or by constables of their own appointment. If any free person commit an offence against the commonwealth, if it be below the degree of felony, he is bound by a justice to appear before their court, to answer it on indictment or information. If it amount to felony, he is committed to jail, a court of these justices is called; if they on examination think him guilty, they send him to the jail of the general court, before which court he is to be tried first by a grand jury of 24, of whom 13 must concur in opinion: if they find him guilty, he is then tried by a jury of 12 men of the county where the offence was committed, and by their verdict, which must be unanimous, he is acquitted or condemned without appeal. If the criminal be a slave the trial by the county court is final. In every case however, except that of high treason, there resides in the governor a power of pardon. In high treason, the pardon can only flow from the general assembly. In civil matters these justices have jurisdiction in all cases of whatever value, not appertaining to the department of the admiralty. This jurisdiction is twofold. If the matter in dispute be of less value than four dollars and one-sixth, a single member may try it at any time and place within his county, and may award execution on the goods of the party cast. If it be of that or greater value, it is determinable before the county court, which consists of four at the least of those justices, and assembles at the court-house of the county on a certain day in every month. From their determination, if the matter be of the value of ten pounds sterling, or concern the title or bounds of lands, an appeal lies to one of the superior courts.

There are three superior courts, to wit, the high-court of chancery, the general court, and court of admiralty. The first and second of these receive appeals from the county courts, and also have original jurisdiction where the subject of controversy is of the value of ten pounds sterling, or where it concerns the title or bounds of land. The jurisdiction of the admiralty is original altogether. The high-court of chancery is composed of three judges, the general court of five, and the court of admiralty of three. The two first hold their sessions at Richmond at stated times, the chancery twice in the year, and the general court twice for business civil and criminal, and twice more for criminal only. The court of admiralty sits at Williamsburgh whenever a controversy arises.

There is one supreme court, called the court of appeals, composed of the judges of the three superior courts, assembling twice a year at stated times at Richmond. This court receives appeals in all civil cases from each of the superior courts, and determines them finally. But it has no original jurisdiction.

If a controversy arise between two foreigners of a nation in alliance with the United States, it is decided by the Consul for their state, or, if both parties chuse it, by the ordinary courts of justice. If one of the parties only be such a foreigner, it is triable before the courts of justice of the country. But if it shall have been instituted in a county court, the foreigner may remove it into the general court, or court of chancery, who are to determine it at their first sessions, as they must also do if it be originally commenced before them. In cases of life and death, such foreigners have a right to be tried by a jury, the one half foreigners, the other natives.

All public accounts are settled with a board of auditors, consisting of three members, appointed by the general assembly, any two of whom may act. But an individual, dissatisfied with the determination of that board, may carry his case into the proper superior court.

A description of the laws.

The general assembly was constituted, as has been already shewn, by letters-patent of March the 9th, 1607, in the 4th year of the reign of James the First. The laws of England seem to have been adopted by consent of the settlers, which might easily enough be done whilst they were few and living all together. Of such adoption however we have no other proof than their practice, till the year 1661, when they were expressly adopted by an act of the assembly, except so far as "a difference of condition" rendered them inapplicable. Under this adoption, the rule, in our courts of judicature was, that the common law of England, and the general statutes previous to the 4th of James, were in force here; but that no subsequent statutes were, *unless we were named in them,* said the judges and other partisans of the crown, but *named or not named,* said those who reflected freely. It will be unnecessary to attempt a description of the laws of England, as that may be found in English publications. To those which were established here, by the adoption of the legislature, have been since added a number of acts of assembly passed during the monarchy, and ordinances of convention and acts of assembly enacted since the establishment of the republic. The following variations from the British model are perhaps worthy of being specified.

Debtors unable to pay their debts, and making faithful delivery of their whole effects, are released from confinement, and their persons for ever discharged from restraint for such previous debts: but any property they may afterwards acquire will be subject to their creditors.

The poor, unable to support themselves, are maintained by an assessment on the tytheable persons in their parish. This assessment is levied and administered by twelve persons in each parish, called vestrymen, originally chosen by the housekeepers of the parish, but afterwards filling vacancies in their own body by their own choice. These are usually the most discreet farmers, so distributed through their parish, that every part of it may be under the immediate eye of some one of them. They are well acquainted with the details and œconomy of private life, and they find sufficient inducements to execute their charge well, in their philanthropy, in the approbation of their neighbours, and the distinction which that gives them. The poor who have neither property, friends, nor strength to labour, are boarded in the houses of good farmers, to whom a stipulated sum is annually paid. To those who are able to help themselves a little, or have friends from whom they derive some succours, inadequate however to their full maintenance, supplementary aids are given, which enable them to live comfortably in their own houses, or in the houses of their friends. Vagabonds, without visible property or vocation, are placed in workhouses, where they are well cloathed, fed, lodged, and made to labour. Nearly the same method of providing for the poor prevails through all our states; and from Savannah to Portsmouth you will seldom meet a beggar. In the larger towns indeed they sometimes present themselves. These are usually foreigners, who have never obtained a settlement in any parish. I never yet saw a native American begging in the streets or highways. A subsistence is easily gained here: and if, by misfortunes, they are thrown on the charities of the world, those provided by their own country are so comfortable and so certain, that they never think of relinquishing them to become strolling beggars. Their situation too, when sick, in the family of a good farmer, where every member is emulous to do them kind offices, where they are visited by all the neighbours, who bring them the little rarities which their sickly appetites may crave, and who take by rotation the nightly watch over them, when their condition requires it, is without comparison better than in a general hospital, where the sick, the dying, and the dead are crammed together, in the same rooms, and often in the same beds. The disadvantages, inseparable from general hospitals, are such as can never be counterpoised by all the regularities of medicine and regimen. Nature and kind nursing save a much greater proportion in our plain way, at a smaller expence, and with less abuse. One branch only of hospital institution is wanting with us; that is, a general establishment for those labouring under difficult cases of chirurgery. The aids of this art are not equivocal. But an able chirurgeon cannot be had in every parish. Such a receptacle should therefore be provided for those patients: but no others should be admitted.

Marriages must be solemnized either on special licence, granted by the first magistrate of the county, on proof of the consent of the parent or guardian of either party under age, or after solemn publication, on three several Sundays, at some place of religious worship, in the parishes where the parties reside. The act of solemnization may be by the minister of any society of Christians, who shall have been previously licensed for this purpose by the court of the county. Quakers and Menonists however are exempted from all these conditions, and marriage among them is to be solemnized by the society itself.

A foreigner of any nation, not in open war with us, becomes naturalized by removing to the state to reside, and taking an oath of fidelity: and thereupon acquires every right of a native citizen: and citizens may divest themselves of that character, by declaring, by solemn deed, or in open court, that they mean to expatriate themselves, and no longer to be citizens of this state.

Conveyances of land must be registered in the court of the county wherein they lie, or in the general court, or they are void, as to creditors, and subsequent purchasers.

Slaves pass by descent and dower as lands do. Where the descent is from a parent, the heir is bound to pay an equal share of their value in money to each of his brothers and sisters.

Slaves, as well as lands, were entailable during the monarchy: but, by an act of the first republican assembly, all donees in tail, present and future, were vested with the absolute dominion of the entailed subject.

Bills of exchange, being protested, carry 10 per cent. interest from their date.

No person is allowed, in any other case, to take more than five per cent. per annum simple interest, for the loan of monies.

Gaming debts are made void, and monies actually paid to discharge such debts (if they exceeded 40 shillings) may be recovered by the payer within three months, or by any other person afterwards.

Tobacco, flour, beef, pork, tar, pitch, and turpentine, must be inspected by persons publicly appointed, before they can be exported.

The erecting iron-works and mills is encouraged by many privileges; with necessary cautions however to prevent their dams from obstructing the navigation of the watercourses. The general assembly have on several occasions shewn a great desire to encourage the opening the great falls of James and Patowmac rivers. As yet, however, neither of these have been effected.

The laws have also descended to the preservation and improvement of the races of useful animals, such as horses, cattle, deer; to the extirpation of those which are noxious, as wolves, squirrels, crows, blackbirds; and to the guarding our citizens against infectious disorders, by obliging suspected vessels coming into the state, to perform quarantine, and by regulating the conduct of persons having such disorders within the state.

The mode of acquiring lands, in the earliest times of our settlement, was by petition to the general assembly. If the lands prayed for were already cleared of the Indian title, and the assembly thought the prayer reasonable, they passed the property by their vote to the petitioner. But if they had not yet been ceded by the Indians, it was necessary that the petitioner should previously purchase their right. This purchase the assembly verified, by inquiries of the Indian proprietors; and being satisfied of its reality and fairness, proceeded further to examine the reasonableness of the petition, and its consistence with policy; and, according to the result, either granted or rejected the petition. The company also sometimes, though very rarely, granted lands, independently of the general assembly. As the colony increased, and individual applications for land multiplied, it was found to give too much occupation to the general assembly to inquire into and execute the grant in every special case. They therefore thought it better to establish general rules, according to which all grants should be made, and to leave to the governor the execution of them, under these rules. This they did by what have been usually called the land laws, amending them from time to time, as their defects were developed. According to these laws, when an individual wished a portion of unappropriated land, he was to locate and survey it by a public officer, appointed for that purpose: its breadth was to bear a certain proportion to its length: the grant was to be executed by the governor: and the lands were to be improved in a certain manner, within a given time. From these regulations there resulted to the state a sole and exclusive power of taking conveyances of the Indian right of soil: since, according to them, an Indian conveyance alone could give no right to an individual, which the laws would acknowledge. The state, or the crown, thereafter, made general purchases of the Indians from time to time, and the governor parcelled them out by special grants, conformed to the rules before described, which it was not in his power, or in that of the crown, to dispense with. Grants, unaccompanied by their proper legal circumstances, were set aside regularly by *scire facias,* or by bill in chancery. Since the establishment of our new government, this order of things is but little changed. An individual, wishing to appropriate to himself lands still unappropriated by any other, pays to the public treasurer a sum of money proportioned to the quantity he wants. He carries the treasurer's receipt to the auditors of public accompts, who thereupon debit the treasurer with the sum, and order the register of the land-office to give the party a warrant for his land. With this warrant from the register, he goes to the surveyor of the county where the land lies on which he has cast his eye. The surveyor lays it off for him, gives him its exact description, in the form of a certificate, which certificate he returns to the land-office, where a grant is made out, and is signed by the governor. This vests in him a perfect dominion in his lands, transmissible to whom he pleases by deed or will, or by descent to his heirs if he die intestate.

Many of the laws which were in force during the monarchy being relative merely to that form of government, or inculcating principles inconsistent with republicanism, the first assembly which met after the establishment of the commonwealth appointed a committee to revise the whole code, to reduce it into proper form and volume, and report it to the assembly. This work has been executed by three gentlemen, and reported;[1] but probably will not be taken up till a restoration of peace shall leave to the legislature leisure to go through such a work.

The plan of the revisal was this. The common law of England, by which is meant, that part of the English law which was anterior to the date of the oldest statutes extant, is made the basis of the work. It was thought dangerous to attempt to reduce it to a text: it was therefore left to be collected from the usual monuments of it. Necessary alterations in that, and so much of the whole body of the British statutes, and of acts of assembly, as were thought proper to be retained, were digested into 126 new acts, in which simplicity of style was aimed at, as far as was safe. The following are the most remarkable alterations proposed:

To change the rules of descent, so as that the lands of any person dying interstate shall be divisible equally among all his children, or other representatives, in equal degree.

To make slaves distributable among the next of kin, as other moveables.

To have all public expences, whether of the general treasury, or of a parish or county, (as for the maintenance of the poor, building bridges, court-house, &c.) supplied by assessments on the citizens, in proportion to their property.

To hire undertakers for keeping the public roads in repair, and indemnify individuals through whose lands new roads shall be opened.

To define with precision the rules whereby aliens should become citizens, and citizens make themselves aliens.

To establish religious freedom on the broadest bottom.

To emancipate all slaves born after passing the act. The

---

[1] Jefferson, George Wythe, and Edmund Pendleton, whose Report of the Committee of the Revisors was submitted to the General Assembly in June, 1779, and later printed. [Ed.]

bill reported by the revisors does not itself contain this proposition; but an amendment containing it was prepared, to be offered to the legislature whenever the bill should be taken up, and further directing, that they should continue with their parents to a certain age, then be brought up, at the public expence, to tillage, arts or sciences, according to their geniusses, till the females should be eighteen, and the males twenty-one years of age, when they should be colonized to such place as the circumstances of the time should render most proper, sending them out with arms, implements of household and of the handicraft arts, seeds, pairs of the useful domestic animals, &c. to declare them a free and independant people, and extend to them our alliance and protection, till they have acquired strength; and to send vessels at the same time to other parts of the world for an equal number of white inhabitants; to induce whom to migrate hither, proper encouragements were to be proposed. It will probably be asked, Why not retain and incorporate the blacks into the state, and thus save the expence of supplying, by importation of white settlers, the vacancies they will leave? Deep rooted prejudices entertained by the whites; ten thousand recollections, by the blacks, of the injuries they have sustained; new provocations; the real distinctions which nature has made; and many other circumstances, will divide us into parties, and produce convulsions which will probably never end but in the extermination of the one or the other race.—To these objections, which are political, may be added others, which are physical and moral. The first difference which strikes us is that of colour. Whether the black of the negro resides in the reticular membrane between the skin and scarf-skin, or in the scarf-skin itself; whether it proceeds from the colour of the blood, the colour of the bile, or from that of some other secretion, the difference is fixed in nature, and is as real as if its seat and cause were better known to us. And is this difference of no importance? Is it not the foundation of a greater or less share of beauty in the two races? Are not the fine mixtures of red and white, the expressions of every passion by greater or less suffusions of colour in the one, preferable to that eternal monotony, which reigns in the countenances, that immoveable veil of black which covers all the emotions of the other race? Add to these, flowing hair, a more elegant symmetry of form, their own judgment in favour of the whites, declared by their preference of them, as uniformly as is the preference of the Oranootan for the black women over those of his own species. The circumstance of superior beauty, is thought worthy attention in the propagation of our horses, dogs, and other domestic animals; why not in that of man? Besides those of colour, figure, and hair, there are other physical distinctions proving a difference of race. They have less hair on the face and body. They secrete less by the kidnies, and more by the glands of the skin, which gives them a very strong and disagreeable odour. This greater degree of transpiration renders them more tolerant of heat, and less so of cold, than the whites. Perhaps too a difference of structure in the pulmonary apparatus, which a late ingenious experimentalist[2] has discovered to be the principal regulator of animal heat, may have disabled them from extricating, in the act of inspiration, so much of that fluid from the outer air, or obliged them in expiration, to part with more of it. They seem to require less sleep. A black, after hard labour through the day, will be induced by the slightest amusements to sit up till midnight, or later, though knowing he must be out with the first dawn of the morning. They are at least as brave, and more adventuresome. But this may perhaps proceed from a want of fore-thought, which prevents their seeing a danger till it be present. When present, they do not go through it with more coolness or steadiness than the whites. They are more ardent after their female: but love seems with them to be more an eager desire, than a tender delicate mixture of sentiment and sensation. Their griefs are transient. Those numberless afflictions, which

[2] Crawford. (Adair Crawford, *Experiments and Observations on Animal Heat.* London, 1779. [Ed.])

render it doubtful whether heaven has given life to us in mercy or in wrath, are less felt, and sooner forgotten with them. In general, their existence appears to participate more of sensation than reflection. To this must be ascribed their disposition to sleep when abstracted from their diversions, and unemployed in labour. An animal whose body is at rest, and who does not reflect, must be disposed to sleep of course. Comparing them by their faculties of memory, reason, and imagination, it appears to me, that in memory they are equal to the whites; in reason much inferior, as I think one could scarcely be found capable of tracing and comprehending the investigations of Euclid; and that in imagination they are dull, tasteless, and anomalous. It would be unfair to follow them to Africa for this investigation. We will consider them here, on the same stage with the whites, and where the facts are not apocryphal on which a judgment is to be formed. It will be right to make great allowances for the difference of condition, of education, of conversation, of the sphere in which they move. Many millions of them have been brought to, and born in America. Most of them indeed have been confined to tillage, to their own homes, and their own society: yet many have been so situated, that they might have availed themselves of the conversation of their masters; many have been brought up to the handicraft arts, from that circumstance have always been associated with the whites. Some have been liberally educated, and all have lived in countries where the arts and sciences are cultivated to a considerable degree, and have had before their eyes samples of the best works from abroad. The Indians, with no advantages of this kind, will often carve figures on their pipes not destitute of design and merit. They will crayon out an animal, a plant, or a country, so as to prove the existence of a germ in their minds which only wants cultivation. They astonish you with strokes of the most sublime oratory; such as prove their reason and sentiment strong, their imagination glowing and elevated. But never yet could I find that a black had uttered a thought above the level of plain narration; never see even an elementary trait of painting or sculpture. In music they are more generally gifted than the whites with accurate ears for tune and time, and they have been found capable of imagining a small catch.[3] Whether they will be equal to the composition of a more extensive run of melody, or of complicated harmony, is yet to be proved. Misery is often the parent of the most affecting touches in poetry.—Among the blacks is misery enough, God knows, but no poetry. Love is the peculiar cestrum of the poet. Their love is ardent, but it kindles the senses only, not the imagination. Religion indeed has produced a Phyllis Whately;[4] but it could not produce a poet. The compositions published under her name are below the dignity of criticism. The heroes of the Dunciad are to her, as Hercules to the author of that poem. Ignatius Sancho has approached nearer to merit in composition;[5] yet his letters do more honour to the heart than the head. They breathe the purest effusions of friendship and general philanthropy, and shew how great a degree of the latter may be compounded with strong religious zeal. He is often happy in the turn of his compliments, and his style is easy and familiar, except when he affects a Shandean fabrication of words. But his imagination is wild and extravagant, escapes incessantly from every restraint of reason and taste, and, in the course of its vagaries, leaves a tract of thought as incoherent and eccentric, as is the course of a meteor through the sky. His subjects should often have led him to a process of sober reasoning: yet we find him always substituting sentiment for demonstration. Upon the whole, though we admit him to the first place among those of his own colour who have presented themselves to the public judgment, yet when we compare him with the

[3] The instrument proper to them is the Banjar, which they brought hither from Africa, and which is the original of the guitar, its chords being the four lower chords of the guitar.

[4] Phyllis Wheatley, *Poems on Various Subjects, Religious and Moral* (London, 1773). [Ed.]

[5] Ignatius Sancho's *Letters* were published in London in 1782. [Ed.]

writers of the race among whom he lived, and particularly with the epistolary class, in which he has taken his own stand, we are compelled to enroll him at the bottom of the column. This criticism supposes the letters published under his name to be genuine, and to have received amendment from no other hand; points which would not be of easy investigation. The improvement of the blacks in body and mind, in the first instance of their mixture with the whites, has been observed by every one, and proves that their inferiority is not the effect merely of their condition of life. We know that among the Romans, about the Augustan age especially, the condition of their slaves was much more deplorable than that of the blacks on the continent of America. The two sexes were confined in separate apartments, because to raise a child cost the master more than to buy one. Cato, for a very restricted indulgence to his slaves in this particular, took from them a certain price.[6] But in this country the slaves multiply as fast as the free inhabitants. Their situation and manners place the commerce between the two sexes almost without restraint. —The same Cato, on a principle of œconomy, always sold his sick and superannuated slaves. He gives it as a standing precept to a master visiting his farm, to sell his old oxen, old waggons, old tools, old and diseased servants, and every thing else become useless. "*Vendat boves vetulos, plaustrum vetus, ferramenta vetera, servum senem, servum morbosum, & si quid aliud supersit vendat.*" Cato de re rustica. c. 2. The American slaves cannot enumerate this among the injuries and insults they receive. It was the common practice to expose in the island of Æsculapius, in the Tyber, diseased slaves, whose cure was like to become tedious.[7] The Emperor Claudius, by an edict, gave freedom to such of them as should recover, and first de-

---

[6] *Tous doulous etaxen örismenou nomesmatos homilein tais therapainisin.* Plutarch. Cato. (He allowed the male slaves intercourse with the female at a set price. [Ed.])

[7] Suet. Claud. 25. (Gaius Suetonius Tranquillus, *Lives of the Caesars.* [Ed.])

clared, that if any person chose to kill rather than to expose them, it should be deemed homicide. The exposing them is a crime of which no instance has existed with us; and were it to be followed by death, it would be punished capitally. We are told of a certain Vedius Pollio, who, in the presence of Augustus, would have given a slave as food to his fish, for having broken a glass. With the Romans, the regular method of taking the evidence of their slaves was under torture. Here it has been thought better never to resort to their evidence. When a master was murdered, all his slaves, in the same house, or within hearing, were condemned to death. Here punishment falls on the guilty only, and as precise proof is required against him as against a freeman. Yet notwithstanding these and other discouraging circumstances among the Romans, their slaves were often their rarest artists. They excelled too in science, insomuch as to be usually employed as tutors to their master's children. Epictetus, Terence, and Phædrus, were slaves. But they were of the race of whites. It is not their condition then, but nature, which has produced the distinction.— Whether further observation will or will not verify the conjecture, that nature has been less bountiful to them in the endowments of the head, I believe that in those of the heart she will be found to have done them justice. That disposition to theft with which they have been branded, must be ascribed to their situation, and not to any depravity of the moral sense. The man, in whose favour no laws of property exist, probably feels himself less bound to respect those made in favour of others. When arguing for ourselves, we lay it down as a fundamental, that laws, to be just, must give a reciprocation of right: that, without this, they are mere arbitrary rules of conduct, founded in force, and not in conscience: and it is a problem which I give to the master to solve, whether the religious precepts against the violation of property were not framed for him as well as his slave? And whether the slave may not as justifiably take a little from one, who has taken all from him, as he may slay one who would slay him? That a change in the relations in which a man is placed should change his ideas of moral right and wrong, is neither new, nor peculiar to the colour of the blacks. Homer tells us it was so 2600 years ago.

> *Emisu, gar t'aretes apoainutai europa Zeus*
> *Haneros, eut' an min kata doulion ema elesin.*
> Od. 17.323.

> Jove fix'd it certain, that whatever day
> Makes man a slave, takes half his worth away.

But the slaves of which Homer speaks were whites. Notwithstanding these considerations which must weaken their respect for the laws of property, we find among them numerous instances of the most rigid integrity, and as many as among their better instructed masters, of benevolence, gratitude, and unshaken fidelity.—The opinion, that they are inferior in the faculties of reason and imagination, must be hazarded with great diffidence. To justify a general conclusion, requires many observations, even where the subject may be submitted to the anatomical knife, to optical glasses, to analysis by fire, or by solvents. How much more then where it is a faculty, not a substance, we are examining; where it eludes the research of all the senses; where the conditions of its existence are various and variously combined; where the effects of those which are present or absent bid defiance to calculation; let me add too, as a circumstance of great tenderness, where our conclusion would degrade a whole race of men from the rank in the scale of beings which their Creator may perhaps have given them. To our reproach it must be said, that though for a century and a half we have had under our eyes the races of black and of red men, they have never yet been viewed by us as subjects of natural history. I advance it therefore as a suspicion only, that the blacks, whether originally a distinct race, or made distinct by time and circumstances, are inferior to the whites in the endowments both of body and mind. It is not against experience to suppose, that different species of the same genus, or varieties of the same species, may possess different qualifications. Will not a lover of natural history then, one who views the gradations in all the races of animals with the eye of philosophy, excuse an effort to keep those in the department of man as distinct as nature has formed them? This unfortunate difference of colour, and perhaps of faculty, is a powerful obstacle to the emancipation of these people. Many of their advocates, while they wish to vindicate the liberty of human nature, are anxious also to preserve its dignity and beauty. Some of these, embarrassed by the question "What further is to be done with them?" join themselves in opposition with those who are actuated by sordid avarice only. Among the Romans emancipation required but one effort. The slave, when made free, might mix with, without staining the blood of his master. But with us a second is necessary, unknown to history. When freed, he is to be removed beyond the reach of mixture.

The revised code further proposes to proportion crimes and punishments. This is attempted on the following scale [pages 194–95].

Pardon and privilege of clergy are proposed to be abolished; but if the verdict be against the defendant, the court in their discretion, may allow a new trial. No attainder to cause a corruption of blood, or forfeiture of dower. Slaves guilty of offences punishable in others by labour, to be transported to Africa, or elsewhere, as the circumstance of the time admit, there to be continued in slavery. A rigorous regimen proposed for those condemned to labour.

Another object of the revisal is, to diffuse knowledge more generally through the mass of the people. This bill proposes to lay off every county into small districts of five or six miles square, called hundreds, and in each of them to establish a school for teaching reading, writing, and arithmetic. The tutor to be supported by the hundred, and

I. Crimes whose punishment extends to *Life.*

1. High treason. Death by hanging.
  Forfeiture of lands and goods to the commonwealth.

2. Petty treason. Death by hanging. Dissection.
  Forfeiture of half the lands and goods to the representatives of the party slain.

3. Murder.
 1. by poison. Death by poison.
  Forfeiture of one-half as before.
 2. in Duel. Death by hanging. Gibbeting, if the challenger.
  Forfeiture of one-half as before, unless it be the party challenged, then the forfeiture is to the commonwealth.
 3. in any other way. Death by hanging.
  Forfeiture of one-half as before.

4. Manslaughter. The second offence is murder.

II. Crimes whose punishment goes to *Limb.*

1. Rape,
2. Sodomy, Dismemberment.
3. Maiming, Retaliation, and the forfeiture of half the lands and goods to the sufferer.
4. Disfiguring,

III. Crimes punishable by *Labour*.

Crime	Punishment	Reparation/Forfeiture
1. Manslaughter, 1st offence.	Labour VII. years for the public.	Forfeiture of half as in murder
2. Counterfeiting money.	Labour VI. years.	Forfeiture of lands and goods to the commonwealth.
3. Arson	Labour V. years.	Reparation threefold.
4. Asportation of vessels.		
5. Robbery.	Labour IV. years.	Reparation double.
6. Burglary.		
7. Housebreaking.	Labour III. years.	Reparation.
8. Horse-stealing.		
9. Grand Larceny.	Labour II. years.	Reparation. — Pillory.
10. Petty Larceny.	Labour I. year.	Reparation. — Pillory.
11. Pretensions to witchcraft, &c.	Ducking.	Stripes.
12. Excusable homicide.		
13. Suicide.	to be pitied, not punished.	
14. Apostacy. Heresy.		

every person in it entitled to send their children three years gratis, and as much longer as they please, paying for it. These schools to be under a visitor, who is annually to chuse the boy, of best genius in the school, of those whose parents are too poor to give them further education, and to send him forward to one of the grammar schools, of which twenty are proposed to be erected in different parts of the country, for teaching Greek, Latin, geography, and the higher branches of numerical arithmetic. Of the boys thus sent in any one year, trial is to be made at the grammar schools one or two years, and the best genius of the whole selected, and continued six years, and the residue dismissed. By this means twenty of the best geniusses will be raked from the rubbish annually, and be instructed, at the public expence, so far as the grammar schools go. At the end of six years instruction, one half are to be discontinued (from among whom the grammar schools will probably be supplied with future masters); and the other half, who are to be chosen for the superiority of their parts and disposition, are to be sent and continued three years in the study of such sciences as they shall chuse, at William and Mary college, the plan of which is proposed to be enlarged, as will be hereafter explained, and extended to all the useful sciences. The ultimate result of the whole scheme of education would be the teaching all the children of the state reading, writing, and common arithmetic: turning out ten annually of superior genius, well taught in Greek, Latin, geography, and the higher branches of arithmetic: turning out ten others annually, of still superior parts, who, to those branches of learning, shall have added such of the sciences as their genius shall have led them to: the furnishing to the wealthier part of the people convenient schools, at which their children may be educated, at their own expence.—The general objects of this law are to provide an education adapted to the years, to the capacity, and the condition of every one, and directed to their freedom and happiness. Specific details were not proper for the law. These must be the business of the visitors entrusted with its execution. The first stage of this education being the schools of the hundreds, wherein the great mass of the people will receive their instruction, the principal foundations of future order will be laid here. Instead therefore of putting the Bible and Testament into the hands of the children, at an age when their judgments are not sufficiently matured for religious inquiries, their memories may here be stored with the most useful facts from Grecian, Roman, European and American history. The first elements of morality too may be instilled into their minds; such as, when further developed as their judgments advance in strength, may teach them how to work out their own greatest happiness, by shewing them that it does not depend on the condition of life in which chance has placed them, but is always the result of a good conscience, good health, occupation, and freedom in all just pursuits.— Those whom either the wealth of their parents or the adoption of the state shall destine to higher degrees of learning, will go on to the grammar schools, which constitute the next stage, there to be instructed in the languages. The learning Greek and Latin, I am told, is going into disuse in Europe. I know not what their manners and occupations may call for: but it would be very ill-judged in us to follow their example in this instance. There is a certain period of life, say from eight to fifteen or sixteen years of age, when the mind, like the body, is not yet firm enough for laborious and close operations. If applied to such, it falls an early victim to premature exertion; exhibiting indeed at first, in these young and tender subjects, the flattering appearance of their being men while they are yet children, but ending in reducing them to be children when they should be men. The memory is then most susceptible and tenacious of impressions; and the learning of languages being chiefly a work of memory, it seems precisely fitted to the powers of this period, which is long enough too for acquiring the most useful languages ancient and modern. I do not pretend that language is science. It is only an instrument for the attainment of science.

But that time is not lost which is employed in providing tools for future operation: more especially as in this case the books put into the hands of the youth for this purpose may be such as will at the same time impress their minds with useful facts and good principles. If this period be suffered to pass in idleness, the mind becomes lethargic and impotent, as would the body it inhabits if unexercised during the same time. The sympathy between body and mind during their rise, progress and decline, is too strict and obvious to endanger our being misled while we reason from the one to the other.—As soon as they are of sufficient age, it is supposed they will be sent on from the grammar schools to the university, which constitutes our third and last stage, there to study those sciences which may be adapted to their views.—By that part of our plan which prescribes the selection of the youths of genius from among the classes of the poor, we hope to avail the state of those talents which nature has sown as liberally among the poor as the rich, but which perish without use, if not sought for and cultivated.—But of all the views of this law none is more important, none more legitimate, than that of rendering the people the safe, as they are the ultimate, guardians of their own liberty. For this purpose the reading in the first stage, where *they* will receive their whole education, is proposed, as has been said, to be chiefly historical. History by apprising them of the past will enable them to judge of the future; it will avail them of the experience of other times and other nations; it will qualify them as judges of the actions and designs of men; it will enable them to know ambition under every disguise it may assume; and knowing it, to defeat its views. In every government on earth is some trace of human weakness, some germ of corruption and degeneracy, which cunning will discover, and wickedness insensibly open, cultivate, and improve. Every government degenerates when trusted to the rulers of the people alone. The people themselves therefore are its only safe depositories. And to render even them safe their minds must be improved to a certain degree. This indeed is not all that is necessary, though it be essentially necessary. An amendment of our constitution must here come in aid of the public education. The influence over government must be shared among all the people. If every individual which composes their mass participates of the ultimate authority, the government will be safe; because the corrupting the whole mass will exceed any private resources of wealth: and public ones cannot be provided but by levies on the people. In this case every man would have to pay his own price. The government of Great-Britain has been corrupted, because but one man in ten has a right to vote for members of parliament. The sellers of the government therefore get nine-tenths of their price clear. It has been thought that corruption is restrained by confining the right of suffrage to a few of the wealthier of the people: but it would be more effectually restrained by an extension of that right to such numbers as would bid defiance to the means of corruption.

Lastly, it is proposed, by a bill in this revival, to begin a public library and gallery, by laying out a certain sum annually in books, paintings, and statues.

Colleges, Buildings, and Roads

¶ *The colleges and public establishments,
the roads, buildings, &c.?*

THE COLLEGE of William and Mary is the only public seminary of learning in this state. It was founded in the time of king William and queen Mary, who granted to it 20,000 acres of land, and a penny a pound duty on certain tobaccoes exported from Virginia and Maryland, which had been levied by the statute of 25 Car. II. The assembly also gave it, by temporary laws, a duty on liquors imported, and skins and furs exported. From these resources it received upwards of 3000£ communibus annis. The buildings are of brick, sufficient for an indifferent accommodation of perhaps an hundred students. By its charter it was to be under the government of twenty visitors, who were to be its legislators, and to have a president and six professors, who were incorporated. It was allowed a representative in the general assembly. Under this charter, a professorship of the Greek and Latin languages, a professorship of mathematics, one of moral philosophy, and two of divinity, were established. To these were annexed, for a sixth professorship, a considerable donation by Mr. Boyle of England,[1] for the instruction of the Indians, and their conversion to Christianity. This was called the professorship of Brafferton, from an estate of that name in England, purchased with the monies given. The admission of the learners of Latin and Greek filled the college

[1] Robert Boyle (1627–1691), the English scientist. [Ed.]

with children. This rendering it disagreeable and degrading to young gentlemen already prepared for entering on the sciences, they were discouraged from resorting to it, and thus the schools for mathematics and moral philosophy, which might have been of some service, became of very little. The revenues too were exhausted in accommodating those who came only to acquire the rudiments of science. After the present revolution, the visitors, having no power to change those circumstances in the constitution of the college which were fixed by the charter, and being therefore confined in the number of professorships, undertook to change the objects of the professorships. They excluded the two schools for divinity, and that for the Greek and Latin languages, and substituted others; so that at present they stand thus:

A Professorship for Law and Police:
   Anatomy and Medicine:
   Natural Philosophy and Mathematics:
   Moral Philosophy, the Law of Nature and Nations, the Fine Arts:
   Modern Languages:
   For the Brafferton.

And it is proposed, so soon as the legislature shall have leisure to take up this subject, to desire authority from them to increase the number of professorships, as well for the purpose of subdividing those already instituted, as of adding others for other branches of science. To the professorships usually established in the universities of Europe, it would seem proper to add one for the ancient languages and literature of the North, on account of their connexion with our own language, laws, customs, and history. The purposes of the Brafferton institution would be better answered by maintaining a perpetual mission among the Indian tribes, the object of which, besides instructing them in the principles of Christianity, as the founder requires, should be to collect their traditions, laws, customs, languages, and other circumstances which might lead to a discovery of their relation with one another, or descent from other nations. When these objects are accomplished with one tribe, the missionary might pass on to another.

The roads are under the government of the county courts, subject to be controuled by the general court. They order new roads to be opened wherever they think them necessary. The inhabitants of the county are by them laid off into precincts, to each of which they allot a convenient portion of the public roads to be kept in repair. Such bridges as may be built without the assistance of artificers, they are to build. If the stream be such as to require a bridge of regular workmanship, the court employs workmen to build it, at the expence of the whole county. If it be too great for the county, application is made to the general assembly, who authorize individuals to build it, and to take a fixed toll from all passengers, or give sanction to such other proposition as to them appears reasonable.

Ferries are admitted only at such places as are particularly pointed out by law, and the rates of ferriage are fixed.

Taverns are licensed by the courts, who fix their rates from time to time.

The private buildings are very rarely constructed of stone or brick; much the greatest proportion being of scantling and boards, plaistered with lime. It is impossible to devise things more ugly, uncomfortable, and happily more perishable. There are two or three plans, on one of which, according to its size, most of the houses in the state are built. The poorest people build huts of logs, laid horizontally in pens, stopping the interstices with mud. These are warmer in winter, and cooler in summer, than the more expensive constructions of scantling and plank. The wealthy are attentive to the raising of vegetables, but very little so to fruits. The poorer people attend to neither, living principally on milk and animal diet. This is the more inexcusable, as the climate requires indispensably a free use of vegetable food, for health as well as comfort,

and is very friendly to the raising of fruits.—The only public buildings worthy [of] mention are the Capitol, the Palace, the College, and the Hospital for Lunatics, all of them
in Williamsburg, heretofore the seat of our government.
The Capitol is a light and airy structure, with a portico in
front of two orders, the lower of which, being Doric, is
tolerably just in its proportions and ornaments, save only
that the intercolonnations are too large. The upper is Ionic,
much too small for that on which it is mounted, its ornaments not proper to the order, nor proportioned within
themselves. It is crowned with a pediment, which is too
high for its span. Yet, on the whole, it is the most pleasing
piece of architecture we have. The Palace is not handsome
without: but it is spacious and commodious within, is
prettily situated, and with the grounds annexed to it, is
capable of being made an elegant seat. The College and
Hospital are rude, mis-shapen piles, which, but that they
have roofs, would be taken for brick-kilns. There are no
other public buildings but churches and court-houses in
which no attempts are made at elegance. Indeed it would
not be easy to execute such an attempt, as a workman
could scarcely be found here capable of drawing an order.
The genius of architecture seems to have shed its maledic-
tions over this land. Buildings are often erected, by individuals, of considerable expence. To give these symmetry
and taste would not increase their cost. It would only
change the arrangement of the materials, the form and
combination of the members. This would often cost less
than the burthen of barbarous ornaments with which these
buildings are sometimes charged. But the first principles of
the art are unknown, and there exists scarcely a model
among us sufficiently chaste to give an idea of them. Architecture being one of the fine arts, and as such within the
department of a professor of the college, according to the
new arrangement, perhaps a spark may fall on some young
subjects of natural taste, kindle up their genius, and produce a reformation in this elegant and useful art. But all
we shall do in this way will produce no permanent im-

provement to our country, while the unhappy prejudice prevails that houses of brick or stone are less wholesome than those of wood. A dew is often observed on the walls of the former in rainy weather, and the most obvious solution is, that the rain has penetrated through these walls. The following facts however are sufficient to prove the error of this solution. 1. This dew on the walls appears when there is no rain, if the state of the atmosphere be moist. 2. It appears on the partition as well as the exterior walls. 3. So also on pavements of brick or stone. 4. It is more copious in proportion as the walls are thicker; the reverse of which ought to be the case, if this hypothesis were just. If cold water be poured into a vessel of stone, or glass, a dew forms instantly on the outside: but if it be poured into a vessel of wood, there is no such appearance. It is not supposed, in the first case, that the water has exuded through the glass, but that it is precipitated from the circumambient air; as the humid particles of vapour, passing from the boiler of an alembic through its refrigerant, are precipitated from the air, in which they were suspended, on the internal surface of the refrigerant. Walls of brick or stone act as the refrigerant in this instance. They are sufficiently cold to condense and precipitate the moisture suspended in the air of the room, when it is heavily charged therewith. But walls of wood are not so. The question then is, whether air in which this moisture is left floating, or that which is deprived of it, be most wholesome? In both cases the remedy is easy. A little fire kindled in the room, whenever the air is damp, prevents the precipitation on the walls: and this practice, found healthy in the warmest as well as coldest seasons, is as necessary in a wooden as in a stone or a brick house. I do not mean to say, that the rain never penetrates through walls of brick. On the contrary I have seen instances of it. But with us it is only through the northern and eastern walls of the house, after a north-easterly storm, these being the only ones which continue long enough to force through the walls. This however happens too rarely to give a just character of unwholesomeness to such houses. In a house the walls of which are of well-burnt brick and good mortar, I have seen the rain penetrate through but twice in a dozen or fifteen years. The inhabitants of Europe, who dwell chiefly in houses of stone or brick, are surely as healthy as those of Virginia. These houses have the advantage too of being warmer in winter and cooler in summer than those of wood; of being cheaper in their first construction, where lime is convenient, and infinitely more durable. The latter consideration renders it of great importance to eradicate this prejudice from the minds of our countrymen. A country whose buildings are of wood, can never increase in its improvements to any considerable degree. Their duration is highly estimated at 50 years. Every half century then our country becomes a tabula rasa, whereon we have to set out anew, as in the first moment of seating it. Whereas when buildings are of durable materials, every new edifice is an actual and permanent acquisition to the state, adding to its value as well as to its ornament.

QUERY XVI.

Proceedings as to Tories

*¶ The measures taken with regard to the estates
and possessions of the rebels, commonly called tories?*

A TORY has been properly defined to be a traitor in
thought but not in deed. The only description, by which
the laws have endeavoured to come at them, was that of
non-jurors, or persons refusing to take the oath of fidelity
to the state. Persons of this description were at one time
subjected to double taxation, at another to treble, and
lastly were allowed retribution, and placed on a level
with good citizens. It may be mentioned as a proof both
of the lenity of our government, and unanimity of its
inhabitants, that though this war has now raged near
seven years, not a single execution for treason has taken
place.

Under this query I will state the measures which have
been adopted as to British property, the owners of which
stand on a much fairer footing than the tories. By our
laws, the same as the English in this respect, no alien can
hold lands, nor alien enemy maintain an action for money,
or other moveable thing. Lands acquired or held by
aliens become forfeited to the state; and, on an action by
an alien enemy to recover money, or other moveable
property, the defendant may plead that he is an alien
enemy. This extinguishes his right in the hands of the
debtor or holder of his moveable property. By our separation from Great-Britain, British subjects became aliens, and
being at war, they were alien enemies. Their lands were of
course forfeited, and their debts irrecoverable. The as-

sembly however passed laws, at various times, for saving their property. They first sequestered their lands, slaves, and other property on their farms, in the hands of commissioners, who were mostly the confidential friends or agents of the owners, and directed their clear profits to be paid into the treasury: and they gave leave to all persons owing debts to British subjects to pay them also into the treasury. The monies so to be brought in were declared to remain the property of the British subject, and, if used by the state, were to be repaid, unless an improper conduct in Great-Britain should render a detention of it reasonable. Depreciation had at that time, though unacknowledged and unperceived by the whigs, begun in some small degree. Great sums of money were paid in by debtors. At a later period, the assembly, adhering to the political principles which forbid an alien to hold lands in the state, ordered all British property to be sold: and, become sensible of the real progress of depreciation, and of the losses which would thence occur, if not guarded against, they ordered that the proceeds of the sales should be converted into their then worth in tobacco, subject to the future direction of the legislature. This act has left the question of retribution more problematical. In May 1780 another act took away the permission to pay into the public treasury debts due to British subjects.

Religion

¶ The different religions received into that state?

THE FIRST SETTLERS in this country were emigrants from England, of the English church, just at a point of time when it was flushed with complete victory over the religious of all other persuasions. Possessed, as they became, of the powers of making, administering, and executing the laws, they shewed equal intolerance in this country with their Presbyterian brethren, who had emigrated to the northern government. The poor Quakers were flying from persecution in England. They cast their eyes on these new countries as asylums of civil and religious freedom; but they found them free only for the reigning sect. Several acts of the Virginia assembly of 1659, 1662, and 1693, had made it penal in parents to refuse to have their children baptized; had prohibited the unlawful assembling of Quakers; had made it penal for any master of a vessel to bring a Quaker into the state; had ordered those already here, and such as should come thereafter, to be imprisoned till they should abjure the country; provided a milder punishment for their first and second return, but death for their third; had inhibited all persons from suffering their meetings in or near their houses, entertaining them individually, or disposing of books which supported their tenets. If no capital execution took place here, as did in New-England, it was not owing to the moderation of the church, or spirit of the legislature, as may be inferred from the law itself; but to historical circumstances which have not been handed down to us. The

Anglicans retained full possession of the country about a century. Other opinions began then to creep in, and the great care of the government to support their own church, having begotten an equal degree of indolence in its clergy, two-thirds of the people had become dissenters at the commencement of the present revolution. The laws indeed were still oppressive on them, but the spirit of the one party had subsided into moderation, and of the other had risen to a degree of determination which commanded respect.

The present state of our laws on the subject of religion is this. The convention of May 1776, in their declaration of rights, declared it to be a truth, and a natural right, that the exercise of religion should be free; but when they proceeded to form on that declaration the ordinance of government, instead of taking up every principle declared in the bill of rights, and guarding it by legislative sanction, they passed over that which asserted our religious rights, leaving them as they found them. The same convention, however, when they met as a member of the general assembly in October 1776, repealed all *acts of parliament* which had rendered criminal the maintaining any opinions in matters of religion, the forbearing to repair to church, and the exercising any mode of worship; and suspended the laws giving salaries to the clergy, which suspension was made perpetual in October 1779. Statutory oppressions in religion being thus wiped away, we remain at present under those only imposed by the common law, or by our own acts of assembly. At the common law, *heresy* was a capital offence, punishable by burning. Its definition was left to the ecclesiastical judges, before whom the conviction was, till the statute of the 1 El. c. 1. circumscribed it, by declaring, that nothing should be deemed heresy, but what had been so determined by authority of the canonical scriptures, or by one of the four first general councils, or by some other council having for the grounds of their declaration the express and plain words of the scriptures. Heresy, thus circumscribed,

being an offence at the common law, our act of assembly
of October 1777, c. 17. gives cognizance of it to the general court, by declaring, that the jurisdiction of that court
shall be general in all matters at the common law. The
execution is by the writ *de hæretico comburendo*. By our
own act of assembly of 1705, c. 30, if a person brought
up in the Christian religion denies the being of a God, or
the Trinity, or asserts there are more gods than one, or
denies the Christian religion to be true, or the scriptures
to be of divine authority, he is punishable on the first offence by incapacity to hold any office or employment ecclesiastical, civil, or military; on the second by disability
to sue, to take any gift or legacy, to be guardian, executor,
or administrator, and by three years imprisonment, without bail. A father's right to the custody of his own children being founded in law on his right of guardianship,
this being taken away, they may of course be severed
from him, and put, by the authority of a court, into more
orthodox hands. This is a summary view of that religious
slavery, under which a people have been willing to remain, who have lavished their lives and fortunes for the
establishment of their civil freedom.

The error seems not sufficiently eradicated, that the
operations of the mind, as well as the acts of the body,
are subject to the coercion of the laws.[1] But our rulers
can have authority over such natural rights only as we
have submitted to them. The rights of conscience we never
submitted, we could not submit. We are answerable for
them to our God. The legitimate powers of government
extend to such acts only as are injurious to others. But
it does me no injury for my neighbour to say there are
twenty gods, or no god. It neither picks my pocket nor
breaks my leg. If it be said, his testimony in a court of
justice cannot be relied on, reject it then, and be the
stigma on him. Constraint may make him worse by mak-

[1] Furneaux passim. (Philip Furneaux, *Letters to the Honorable
Mr. Justice Blackstone, Concerning His Exposition of the Act
of Toleration* . . . . London, 1770. [Ed.])

ing him a hypocrite, but it will never make him a truer man. It may fix him obstinately in his errors, but will not cure them. Reason and free inquiry are the only effectual agents against error. Give a loose to them, they will support the true religion, by bringing every false one to their tribunal, to the test of their investigation. They are the natural enemies of error, and of error only. Had not the Roman government permitted free inquiry, Christianity could never have been introduced. Had not free inquiry been indulged, at the æra of the reformation, the corruptions of Christianity could not have been purged away. If it be restrained now, the present corruptions will be protected, and new ones encouraged. Was the government to prescribe to us our medicine and diet, our bodies would be in such keeping as our souls are now. Thus in France the emetic was once forbidden as a medicine, and the potatoe as an article of food. Government is just as infallible too when it fixes systems in physics. Galileo was sent to the inquisition for affirming that the earth was a sphere: the government had declared it to be as flat as a trencher, and Galileo was obliged to abjure his error. This error however at length prevailed, the earth became a globe, and Descartes declared it was whirled round its axis by a vortex. The government in which he lived was wise enough to see that this was no question of civil jurisdiction, or we should all have been involved by authority in vortices. In fact, the vortices have been exploded, and the Newtonian principle of gravitation is now more firmly established, on the basis of reason, than it would be were the government to step in, and to make it an article of necessary faith. Reason and experiment have been indulged, and error has fled before them. It is error alone which needs the support of government. Truth can stand by itself. Subject opinion to coercion: whom will you make your inquisitors? Fallible men; men governed by bad passions, by private as well as public reasons. And why subject it to coercion? To produce uniformity. But is uniformity of opinion desireable? No more than of face and stature. Introduce the bed of Procrustes then, and as there is danger that the large men may beat the small, make us all of a size, by lopping the former and stretching the latter. Difference of opinion is advantageous in religion. The several sects perform the office of a Censor morum over each other. Is uniformity attainable? Millions of innocent men, women, and children, since the introduction of Christianity, have been burnt, tortured, fined, imprisoned; yet we have not advanced one inch towards uniformity. What has been the effect of coercion? To make one half the world fools, and the other half hypocrites. To support roguery and error all over the earth. Let us reflect that it is inhabited by a thousand millions of people. That these profess probably a thousand different systems of religion. That ours is but one of that thousand. That if there be but one right, and ours that one, we should wish to see the 999 wandering sects gathered into the fold of truth. But against such a majority we cannot effect this by force. Reason and persuasion are the only practicable instruments. To make way for these, free inquiry must be indulged; and how can we wish others to indulge it while we refuse it ourselves. But every state, says an inquisitor, has established some religion. No two, say I, have established the same. Is this a proof of the infallibility of establishments? Our sister states of Pennsylvania and New York, however, have long subsisted without any establishment at all. The experiment was new and doubtful when they made it. It has answered beyond conception. They flourish infinitely. Religion is well supported; of various kinds, indeed, but all good enough; all sufficient to preserve peace and order: or if a sect arises, whose tenets would subvert morals, good sense has fair play, and reasons and laughs it out of doors, without suffering the state to be troubled with it. They do not hang more malefactors than we do. They are not more disturbed with religious dissensions. On the contrary, their harmony is unparalleled, and can be ascribed to nothing but their unbounded tolerance, because there is no other circumstance in which they differ from every nation on earth. They have made the happy discovery, that the way to silence religious disputes, is to take no notice of them. Let us too give this experiment fair play, and get rid, while we may, of those tyrannical laws. It is true, we are as yet secured against them by the spirit of the times. I doubt whether the people of this country would suffer an execution for heresy, or a three years imprisonment for not comprehending the mysteries of the Trinity. But is the spirit of the people an infallible, a permanent reliance? Is it government? Is this the kind of protection we receive in return for the rights we give up? Besides, the spirit of the times may alter, will alter. Our rulers will become corrupt, our people careless. A single zealot may commence persecutor, and better men be his victims. It can never be too often repeated, that the time for fixing every essential right on a legal basis is while our rulers are honest, and ourselves united. From the conclusion of this war we shall be going down hill. It will not then be necessary to resort every moment to the people for support. They will be forgotten, therefore, and their rights disregarded. They will forget themselves, but in the sole faculty of making money, and will never think of uniting to effect a due respect for their rights. The shackles, therefore, which shall not be knocked off at the conclusion of this war, will remain on us long, will be made heavier and heavier, till our rights shall revive or expire in a convulsion.

Manners

¶ *The particular customs and manners that may happen to be received in that state?*

IT IS DIFFICULT to determine on the standard by which the manners of a nation may be tried, whether *catholic*, or *particular*. It is more difficult for a native to bring to that standard the manners of his own nation, familiarized to him by habit. There must doubtless be an unhappy influence on the manners of our people produced by the existence of slavery among us. The whole commerce between master and slave is a perpetual exercise of the most boisterous passions, the most unremitting despotism on the one part, and degrading submissions on the other. Our children see this, and learn to imitate it; for man is an imitative animal. This quality is the germ of all education in him. From his cradle to his grave he is learning to do what he sees others do. If a parent could find no motive either in his philanthropy or his self-love, for restraining the intemperance of passion towards his slave, it should always be a sufficient one that his child is present. But generally it is not sufficient. The parent storms, the child looks on, catches the lineaments of wrath, puts on the same airs in the circle of smaller slaves, gives a loose to his worst of passions, and thus nursed, educated, and daily exercised in tyranny, cannot but be stamped by it with odious peculiarities. The man must be a prodigy who can retain his manners and morals undepraved by such circumstances. And with what execration should the statesman be loaded, who permitting one half the citizens thus to trample on the rights of the other, transforms those into despots; and these into enemies, destroys the morals of the one part, and the amor patriæ of the other. For if a slave can have a country in this world, it must be any other in preference to that in which he is born to live and labour for another: in which he must lock up the faculties of his nature, contribute as far as depends on his individual endeavours to the evanishment of the human race, or entail his own miserable condition on the endless generations proceeding from him. With the morals of the people, their industry also is destroyed. For in a warm climate, no man will labour for himself who can make another labour for him. This is so true, that of the proprietors of slaves a very small proportion indeed are ever seen to labour. And can the liberties of a nation be thought secure when we have removed their only firm basis, a conviction in the minds of the people that these liberties are of the gift of God? That they are not to be violated but with his wrath? Indeed I tremble for my country when I reflect that God is just: that his justice cannot sleep for ever: that considering numbers, nature and natural means only, a revolution of the wheel of fortune, an exchange of situation, is among possible events: that it may become probable by supernatural interference! The Almighty has no attribute which can take side with us in such a contest.—But it is impossible to be temperate and to pursue this subject through the various considerations of policy, of morals, of history natural and civil. We must be contented to hope they will force their way into every one's mind. I think a change already perceptible, since the origin of the present revolution. The spirit of the master is abating, that of the slave rising from the dust, his condition mollifying, the way I hope preparing, under the auspices of heaven, for a total emancipation, and that this is disposed, in the order of events, to be with the consent of the masters, rather than by their extirpation.

Manufactures

¶ *The present state of manufactures, commerce, interior and exterior trade?*

WE NEVER had an interior trade of any importance. Our exterior commerce has suffered very much from the beginning of the present contest. During this time we have manufactured within our families the most necessary articles of cloathing. Those of cotton will bear some comparison with the same kinds of manufacture in Europe; but those of wool, flax and hemp are very coarse, unsightly, and unpleasant: and such is our attachment to agriculture, and such our preference for foreign manufactures, that be it wise or unwise, our people will certainly return as soon as they can, to the raising raw materials, and exchanging them for finer manufactures than they are able to execute themselves.

The political œconomists of Europe have established it as a principle that every state should endeavour to manufacture for itself: and this principle, like many others, we transfer to America, without calculating the difference of circumstance which should often produce a difference of result. In Europe the lands are either cultivated, or locked up against the cultivator. Manufacture must therefore be resorted to of necessity not of choice, to support the surplus of their people. But we have an immensity of land courting the industry of the husbandman. Is it best then that all our citizens should be employed in its improvement, or that one half should be called off from that to exercise manufactures and handicraft arts for the other?

Those who labour in the earth are the chosen people of God, if ever he had a chosen people, whose breasts he has made his peculiar deposit for substantial and genuine virtue. It is the focus in which he keeps alive that sacred fire, which otherwise might escape from the face of the earth. Corruption of morals in the mass of cultivators is a phænomenon of which no age nor nation has furnished an example. It is the mark set on those, who not looking up to heaven, to their own soil and industry, as does the husbandman, for their subsistance, depend for it on the casualties and caprice of customers. Dependance begets subservience and venality, suffocates the germ of virtue, and prepares fit tools for the designs of ambition. This, the natural progress and consequence of the arts, has sometimes perhaps been retarded by accidental circumstances: but, generally speaking, the proportion which the aggregate of the other classes of citizens bears in any state to that of its husbandmen, is the proportion of its unsound to its healthy parts, and is a good-enough barometer whereby to measure its degree of corruption. While we have land to labour then, let us never wish to see our citizens occupied at a work-bench, or twirling a distaff. Carpenters, masons, smiths, are wanting in husbandry: but, for the general operations of manufacture, let our workshops remain in Europe. It is better to carry provisions and materials to workmen there, than bring them to the provisions and materials, and with them their manners and principles. The loss by the transportation of commodities across the Atlantic will be made up in happiness and permanence of government. The mobs of great cities add just so much to the support of pure government, as sores do to the strength of the human body. It is the manners and spirit of a people which preserve a republic in vigour. A degeneracy in these is a canker which soon eats to the heart of its laws and constitution.

QUERY XX.

Subjects of Commerce

¶ *A notice of the commercial productions particular to
the state, and of those objects which the inhabitants are
obliged to get from Europe and from other parts
of the world?*

BEFORE the present war we exported, *communibus
annis*, according to the best information I can get, nearly
as follows:

In the year 1758 we exported seventy thousand hogsheads of tobacco, which was the greatest quantity ever
produced in this country in one year. But its culture was
fast declining at the commencement of this war and that
of wheat taking its place: and it must continue to decline
on the return of peace. I suspect that the change in the
temperature of our climate has become sensible to that
plant, which, to be good, requires an extraordinary degree
of heat. But it requires still more indispensably an uncommon fertility of soil: and the price which it commands at market will not enable the planter to produce
this by manure. Was the supply still to depend on Virginia and Maryland alone, as its culture becomes more
difficult, the price would rise, so as to enable the planter
to surmount those difficulties and to live. But the western
country on the Missisipi, and the midlands of Georgia,
having fresh and fertile lands in abundance, and a hotter
sun, will be able to undersell these two states, and will
oblige them to abandon the raising tobacco altogether.
And a happy obligation for them it will be. It is a culture productive of infinite wretchedness. Those employed

Articles.	Quantity.	Price in dollars.	Amount in dollars.
Tobacco	55,000 hhds. of 1000 lb.	at 30 d. per hhd.	1,650,000
Wheat	800,000 bushels	at ⅚ d. per bush.	666,666⅔
Indian corn	600,000 bushels	at ⅓ d. per bush.	200,000
Shipping	— — — —	— — —	100,000
Masts, planks, skantling, shingles, staves	— — — —	— — —	66,666⅔
Tar, pitch, turpentine	30,000 barrels	at 1⅓ d. per bar.	40,000
Peltry, viz. skins of deer, beavers, otters, muskrats, racoons, foxes	180 hhds. of 600 lb.	at 1/12 d. per lb.	42,000
Pork	4,000 barrels	at 10 d. per bar.	40,000
Flax-seed, hemp, cotton	— — — —	— — —	8,000
Pit-coal, pig-iron	— — — —	— — —	6,666⅔
Peas	5,000 bushels	at ⅔ d. per bush.	3,333⅓
Beef	1,000 barrels	at 3⅓ d. per bar.	3,333⅓
Sturgeon, white-shad, herring	— — — —	— — —	3,333⅓
Brandy from peaches and apples, and whiskey	— — — —	— — —	1,666⅔
Horses	— — — —	— — —	1,666⅔
			2,833,333⅓ D.[1]

[1] This sum is equal to 850,000 [£] Virginia money, 607,142 guineas.

in it are in a continued state of exertion beyond the powers of nature to support. Little food of any kind is raised by them; so that the men and animals on these farms are badly fed, and the earth is rapidly impoverished. The cultivation of wheat is the reverse in every circumstance. Besides cloathing the earth with herbage, and preserving its fertility, it feeds the labourers plentifully, requires from them only a moderate toil, except in the season of harvest, raises great numbers of animals for food and service, and diffuses plenty and happiness among the whole. We find it easier to make an hundred bushels of wheat than a thousand weight of tobacco, and they are worth more when made. The weavil indeed is a formidable obstacle to the cultivation of this grain with us. But principles are already known which must lead to a remedy. Thus a certain degree of heat, to wit, that of the common air in summer, is necessary to hatch the egg. If subterranean granaries, or others, therefore, can be contrived below that temperature, the evil will be cured by cold. A degree of heat beyond that which hatches the egg, we know will kill it. But in aiming at this we easily run into that which produces putrefaction. To produce putrefaction, however, three agents are requisite, heat, moisture, and the external air. If the absence of any one of these be secured, the other two may safely be admitted. Heat is the one we want. Moisture then, or external air, must be excluded. The former has been done by exposing the grain in kilns to the action of fire, which produces heat, and extracts moisture at the same time: the latter, by putting the grain into hogsheads, covering it with a coat of lime, and heading it up. In this situation its bulk produces a heat sufficient to kill the egg; the moisture is suffered to remain indeed, but the external air is excluded. A nicer operation yet has been attempted; that is, to produce an intermediate temperature of heat between that which kills the egg, and that which produces putrefaction. The threshing the grain as soon as it is cut, and laying it in its chaff in large heaps, has been found very nearly to hit this temperature, though not perfectly, nor always. The heap generates heat sufficient to kill most of the eggs, whilst the chaff commonly restrains it from rising into putrefaction. But all these methods abridge too much the quantity which the farmer can manage, and enable other countries to undersell him which are not infested with this insect. There is still a desideratum then to give with us decisive triumph to this branch of agriculture over that of tobacco.—The culture of wheat, by enlarging our pasture, will render the Arabian horse an article of very considerable profit. Experience has shewn that ours is the particular climate of America where he may be raised without degeneracy. Southwardly the heat of the sun occasions a deficiency of pasture, and northwardly the winters are too cold for the short and fine hair, the particular sensibility and constitution of that race. Animals transplanted into unfriendly climates, either change their nature and acquire new fences against the new difficulties in which they are placed, or they multiply poorly and become extinct. A good foundation is laid for their propagation here by our possessing already great numbers of horses of that blood, and by a decided taste and preference for them established among the people. Their patience of heat without injury, their superior wind, fit them better in this and the more southern climates even for the drudgeries of the plough and waggon. Northwardly they will become an object only to persons of taste and fortune, for the saddle and light carriages. To these, and for these uses, their fleetness and beauty will recommend them.—Besides these there will be other valuable substitutes when the cultivation of tobacco shall be discontinued, such as cotton in the eastern parts of the state, and hemp and flax in the western.

It is not easy to say what are the articles either of necessity, comfort, or luxury, which we cannot raise, and which we therefore shall be under a necessity of importing from abroad, as every thing hardier than the olive, and as hardy as the fig, may be raised here in the open air. Sugar, coffee and tea, indeed, are not between these limits; and habit having placed them among the necessaries of life with the wealthy part of our citizens, as long as these habits remain, we must go for them to those countries which are able to furnish them.

QUERY XXI.

Weights, Measures, and Money

¶ *The weights, measures, and the currency of the hard money? Some details relating to the exchange with Europe?*

OUR WEIGHTS and measures are the same which are fixed by acts of parliament in England.—How it has happened that in this as well as the other American states the nominal value of coin was made to differ from what it was in the country we had left, and to differ among ourselves too, I am not able to say with certainty. I find that in 1631 our house of burgesses desired of the privy council in England, a coin debased to twenty-five per cent: that in 1645 they forbid dealing by barter for tobacco, and established the Spanish piece of eight at six shillings, as the standard of their currency: that in 1655 they changed it to five shillings sterling. In 1680 they sent an address to the king, in consequence of which, by proclamation in 1683, he fixed the value of French crowns, rixdollars and pieces of eight at six shillings, and the coin of New-England at one shilling. That in 1710, 1714, 1727, and 1762, other regulations were made, which will be better presented to the eye stated in the form of a table as follows [see page 223].

The first symptom of the depreciation of our present paper-money, was that of silver dollars selling at six shillings, which had before been worth but five shillings and ninepence. The assembly thereupon raised them by law to six shillings. As the dollar is now likely to become the money-unit of America, as it passes at this rate in

	1710.	1714.	1727.	1762.
Guineas	— —	26s		
British gold coin not milled, coined gold of Spain and France, chequins, Arabian gold, moidores of Portugal	— —	5s the dwt.		
Coined gold of the empire	— —	5s the dwt.	— —	4s3 the dwt.
English milled silver money, in proportion to the crown, at	— —	5s10	6s3	
Pieces of eight of Mexico, Seville, and Pillar, ducatoons of Flanders, French ecus, or silver Louis, crusados of Portugal	3¾ d. the dwt.	— —	4 d. the dwt.	
Peru pieces, cross dollars, and old rixdollars of the empire	3½ d. the dwt.	— —	3¾ d. the dwt.	
Old British silver coin not milled	— —	3¾ d. the dwt.		

some of our sister states, and as it facilitates their computation in pounds and shillings, & *e converso*, this seems to be more convenient than it's former denomination. But as this particular coin now stands higher than any other in the proportion of 133⅓ to 125, or 16 to 15, it will be necessary to raise the others in the same proportion.

Public Revenue and Expences

¶ *The public income and expences?*

THE NOMINAL amount of these varying constantly and rapidly, with the constant and rapid depreciation of our paper money, it becomes impracticable to say what they are. We find ourselves cheated in every essay by the depreciation intervening between the declaration of the tax and its actual receipt. It will therefore be more satisfactory to consider what our income may be when we shall find means of collecting what the people may spare. I should estimate the whole taxable property of this state at an hundred millions of dollars, or thirty millions of pounds our money. One per cent on this, compared with any thing we ever yet paid, would be deemed a very heavy tax. Yet I think that those who manage well, and use reasonable œconomy, could pay one and a half per cent, and maintain their houshould comfortably in the mean time, without aliening any part of their principal, and that the people would submit to this willingly for the purpose of supporting their present contest. We may say then, that we could raise, and ought to raise, from one million to one million and a half of dollars annually, that is from three hundred to four hundred and fifty thousand pounds, Virginia money.

Of our expences it is equally difficult to give an exact state, and for the same reason. They are mostly stated in paper money, which varying continually, the legislature endeavours at every session, by new corrections, to adapt the nominal sums to the value it is wished they should bear. I will state them therefore in real coin, at the point at which they endeavour to keep them.

	Dollars.
The annual expences of the general assembly are about	20,000
The governor	3,333⅓
The council of state	10,666⅔
Their clerks	1,166⅔
Eleven judges	11,000
The clerk of the chancery	666⅔
The attorney general	1,000
Three auditors and a solicitor	5,333⅓
Their clerks	2,000
The treasurer	2,000
His clerks	2,000
The keeper of the public jail	1,000
The public printer	1,666⅔
Clerks of the inferior courts	43,333⅓
Public levy: this is chiefly for the expences of criminal justice	40,000
County levy, for bridges, court houses, prisons, &c.	40,000
Members of congress	7,000
Quota of the Federal civil list, supposed 1/6 of about 78,000 dollars	13,000
Expences of collection, 6 per cent. on the above	12,310
The clergy receive only voluntary contributions: suppose them on an average 1/8 of a dollar a tythe on 200,000 tythes	25,000
Contingencies, to make round numbers not far from truth	7,523⅓
	250,000

Dollars, or 53,571 guineas. This estimate is exclusive of the military expence. That varies with the force actually employed, and in time of peace will probably be little or nothing. It is exclusive also of the public debts, which are growing while I am writing, and cannot therefore be now fixed. So it is of the maintenance of the poor, which being merely a matter of charity, cannot be deemed expended in the administration of government. And if we strike out the 25,000 dollars for the services of the clergy, which neither makes part of that administration, more than what is paid to physicians or lawyers, and being voluntary, is either much or nothing as every one pleases, it leaves 225,000 dollars, equal to 48,208 guineas, the real cost of the apparatus of government with us. This, divided among the actual inhabitants of our country, comes to about two-fifths of a dollar, 21d sterling, or 42 sols, the price which each pays annually for the protection of the residue of his property, that of his person, and the other advantages of a free government. The public revenues of Great Britain divided in like manner on its inhabitants would be sixteen times greater. Deducting even the double of the expences of government, as before estimated, from the million and a half of dollars which we before supposed might be annually paid without distress, we may conclude that this state can contribute one million of dollars annually towards supporting the federal army, paying the federal debt, building a federal navy, or opening roads, clearing rivers, forming safe ports, and other useful works.

To this estimate of our abilities, let me add a word as to the application of them, if, when cleared of the present contest, and of the debts with which that will charge us, we come to measure force hereafter with any European power. Such events are devoutly to be deprecated. Young as we are, and with such a country before us to fill with people and with happiness, we should point in that direction the whole generative force of nature, wasting none of it in efforts of mutual destruction. It should be our endeavour to cultivate the peace and friendship of every nation, even of that which has injured us most, when we shall have carried our point against her. Our interest will be to throw open the doors of commerce, and to knock off all its shackles, giving perfect freedom to all persons for the vent of whatever they may chuse to bring into our ports, and asking the same in theirs. Never was so much false arithmetic employed on any subject, as that which has been employed to persuade nations that it is their interest to go to war. Were the money which it has cost to gain, at the close of a long war, a little town, or a little territory, the right to cut wood here, or to catch fish there, expended in improving what they already possess, in making roads, opening rivers, building ports, improving the arts, and finding employment for their idle poor, it would render them much stronger, much wealthier and happier. This I hope will be our wisdom. And, perhaps, to remove as much as possible the occasions of making war, it might be better for us to abandon the ocean altogether, that being the element whereon we shall be principally exposed to jostle with other nations: to leave to others to bring what we shall want, and to carry what we can spare. This would make us invulnerable to Europe, by offering none of our property to their prize, and would turn all our citizens to the cultivation of the earth; and, I repeat it again, cultivators of the earth are the most virtuous and independant citizens. It might be time enough to seek employment for them at sea, when the land no longer offers it. But the actual habits of our countrymen attach them to commerce. They will exercise it for themselves. Wars then must sometimes be our lot; and all the wise can do, will be to avoid that half of them which would be produced by our own follies, and our own acts of injustice; and to make for the other half the best preparations we can. Of what nature should these be? A land army would be useless for offence, and not the best nor safest instrument of defence. For either of these purposes, the sea is the field on which we should meet an European enemy. On that element it is necessary we should possess some power. To aim at such a navy as the greater nations of Europe possess, would be a foolish and wicked waste of the energies of our countrymen. It would be to pull on our own heads that load of military expence, which makes the European labourer go supperless to bed, and moistens his bread with the sweat of his brows. It will be enough if we enable ourselves to prevent insults from those nations of Europe which are weak on the sea, because circumstances exist, which render even the stronger ones weak as to us. Providence has placed their richest and most defenceless possessions at our door; has obliged their most precious commerce to pass as it were in review before us. To protect this, or to assail us, a small part only of their naval force will ever be risqued across the Atlantic. The dangers to which the elements expose them here are too well known, and the greater dangers to which they would be exposed at home, were any general calamity to involve their whole fleet. They can attack us by detachment only; and it will suffice to make ourselves equal to what they may detach. Even a smaller force than they may detach will be rendered equal or superior by the quickness with which any check may be repaired with us, while losses with them will be irreparable till too late. A small naval force then is sufficient for us, and a small one is necessary. What this should be, I will not undertake to say. I will only say, it should by no means be so great as we are able to make it. Suppose the million of dollars, or 300,000 pounds, which Virginia could annually spare without distress, to be applied to the creating a navy. A single year's contribution would build, equip, man, and send to sea a force which should carry 300 guns. The rest of the confederacy, exerting themselves in the same proportion, would equip in the same time 1500 guns more. So that one year's contributions would set up a navy of 1800 guns. The British ships of the line average 76 guns; their frigates 38. 1800 guns then would form a fleet of 30 ships, 18 of which might be of the line, and 12 frigates. Allowing 8 men, the British average, for every gun, their annual expence, including subsistence, cloathing, pay, and ordinary repairs, would be about 1,280 dollars for every gun, or 2,304,000 dollars for the whole. I staté this only as one year's possible exertion, without deciding whether more or less than a year's exertion should be thus applied.

The value of our lands and slaves, taken conjunctly, doubles in about twenty years. This arises from the multiplication of our slaves, from the extension of culture, and increased demand for lands. The amount of what may be raised will of course rise in the same proportion.

Histories, Memorials, and State-Papers

¶ *The histories of the state, the memorials published
in its name in the time of its being a colony,
and the pamphlets relating to its interior
or exterior affairs present or ancient?*

CAPTAIN SMITH, who next to Sir Walter Raleigh may be considered as the founder of our colony, has written its history, from the first adventures to it till the year 1624. He was a member of the council, and afterwards president of the colony; and to his efforts principally may be ascribed its support against the opposition of the natives. He was honest, sensible, and well informed; but his style is barbarous and uncouth. His history, however, is almost the only source from which we derive any knowledge of the infancy of our state.

The reverend William Stith, a native of Virginia, and president of its college, has also written the history of the same period, in a large octavo volume of small print.[1] He was a man of classical learning, and very exact, but of no taste in style. He is inelegant, therefore, and his details often too minute to be tolerable, even to a native of the country, whose history he writes.

Beverley, a native also, has run into the other extreme; he has comprised our history, from the first propositions of Sir Walter Raleigh to the year 1700, in the hundredth

---

[1] William Stith, *The History of the First Discovery and Settlement of Virginia* (Williamsburg, 1747). [Ed.]

part of the space which Stith employs for the fourth part of the period.[2]

Sir William Keith has taken it up at its earliest period, and continued it to the year 1725.[3] He is agreeable enough in style, and passes over events of little importance. Of course he is short, and would be preferred by a foreigner.

During the regal government, some contest arose on the exaction of an illegal fee by governor Dinwiddie, and doubtless there were others on other occasions not at present recollected. It is supposed, that these are not sufficiently interesting to a foreigner to merit a detail.

The petition of the council and burgesses of Virginia to the king, their memorial to the lords, and remonstrance to the commons in the year 1764, began the present contest: and these having proved ineffectual to prevent the passage of the stamp-act, the resolutions of the house of burgesses of 1765 were passed, declaring the independance of the people of Virginia on the parliament of Great-Britain, in matters of taxation. From that time till the declaration of independance by Congress in 1776, their journals are filled with assertions of the public rights.

The pamphlets published in this state on the controverted question were,

1766, An Inquiry into the Rights of the British Colonies, by Richard Bland.
1769, The Monitor's Letters, by Dr. Arthur Lee.
1774, A summary View of the Rights of British America.[4]
—— Considerations, &c. by Robert Carter Nicholas.

Since the declaration of independance this state has had no controversy with any other, except with that of Penn-

---

[2] Robert Beverley, *The History of the Present State of Virginia* (London, 1705). [Ed.]

[3] Sir William Keith, *The History of the British Plantations in America. Part I, History of Virginia* (London, 1738). [Ed.]

[4] By the author of these Notes.

sylvania, on their common boundary. Some papers on this subject passed between the executive and legislative bodies of the two states, the result of which was a happy accommodation of their rights.

To this account of our historians, memorials, and pamphlets, it may not be unuseful to add a chronological catalogue of American state-papers, as far as I have been able to collect their titles. It is far from being either complete or correct. Where the title alone, and not the paper itself, has come under my observation, I cannot answer for the exactness of the date. Sometimes I have not been able to find any date at all, and sometimes have not been satisfied that such a paper exists. An extensive collection of papers of this description has been for some time in a course of preparation by a gentleman fully equal to the task,[5] and from whom, therefore, we may hope ere long to receive it. In the mean time accept this as the result of my labours, and as closing the tedious detail which you have so undesignedly drawn upon yourself.[6]

[5] Mr. Hazard. (Ebenezer Hazard, of New York, eventually published two volumes of *Historical Collections*. Philadelphia, 1729–1794. [Ed.])

[6] The catalogue, containing approximately 250 items, has been omitted by the editor.

III

Public Papers and Addresses

The Declaration of Independence[1]

[*July 4, 1776*]

WHEN, IN THE COURSE OF HUMAN EVENTS, it becomes necessary for one people to dissolve the political bands which have connected them with another, and to assume among the powers of the earth the separate and equal station to which the laws of nature and of nature's God entitle them, a decent respect to the opinions of mankind requires that they should declare the causes which impel them to the separation.

We hold these truths to be self evident: that all men are created equal; that they are endowed by their Creator with CERTAIN [*inherent and*] inalienable rights; that among these are life, liberty, and the pursuit of happiness; that to secure these rights, governments are instituted among men, deriving their just powers from the consent of the governed; that whenever any form of government becomes destructive of these ends, it is the right of the people to alter or to abolish it, and to institute new government, laying its foundation on such principles, and organizing its powers in such form, as to them shall seem most likely to effect their safety and happiness. Prudence, indeed, will dictate that governments long established should not be changed for light and transient causes; and accordingly all experience hath shown that mankind are more

---

[1] The text is taken from Jefferson's Autobiography. The form of the Declaration as reported is printed in roman type, the parts stricken by Congress are bracketed in italics, while the parts substituted are in small capitals. [Ed.]

disposed to suffer while evils are sufferable, than to right themselves by abolishing the forms to which they are accustomed. But when a long train of abuses and usurpations, [*begun at a distinguished period and*] pursuing invariably the same object, evinces a design to reduce them under absolute despotism, it is their right, it is their duty to throw off such government, and to provide new guards for their future security. Such has been the patient sufferance of these colonies; and such is now the necessity which constrains them to ALTER [*expunge*] their former systems of government. The history of the present king of Great Britain is a history of REPEATED [*unremitting*] injuries and usurpations, ALL HAVING [*among which appears no solitary fact to contradict the uniform tenor of the rest, but all have*] in direct object the establishment of an absolute tyranny over these states. To prove this, let facts be submitted to a candid world [*for the truth of which we pledge a faith yet unsullied by falsehood*].

He has refused his assent to laws the most wholesome and necessary for the public good.

He has forbidden his governors to pass laws of immediate and pressing importance, unless suspended in their operation till his assent should be obtained; and, when so suspended, he has utterly neglected to attend to them.

He has refused to pass other laws for the accommodation of large districts of people, unless those people would relinquish the right of representation in the legislature, a right inestimable to them, and formidable to tyrants only.

He has called together legislative bodies at places unusual, uncomfortable, and distant from the depository of their public records, for the sole purpose of fatiguing them into compliance with his measures.

He has dissolved representative houses repeatedly [*and continually*] for opposing with manly firmness his invasions on the rights of the people.

He has refused for a long time after such dissolutions to cause others to be elected, whereby the legislative powers, incapable of annihilation, have returned to the people at large for their exercise, the state remaining, in the meantime, exposed to all the dangers of invasion from without and convulsions within.

He has endeavored to prevent the population of these states; for that purpose obstructing the laws for naturalization of foreigners, refusing to pass others to encourage their migrations hither, and raising the conditions of new appropriations of lands.

He has OBSTRUCTED [*suffered*] the administration of justice BY [*totally to cease in some of these states*] refusing his assent to laws for establishing judiciary powers.

He has made [*our*] judges dependent on his will alone for the tenure of their offices, and the amount and payment of their salaries.

He has erected a multitude of new offices, [*by a self-assumed power*] and sent hither swarms of new officers to harass our people and eat out their substance.

He has kept among us in times of peace standing armies [*and ships of war*] without the consent of our legislatures.

He has affected to render the military independent of, and superior to, the civil power.

He has combined with others to subject us to a jurisdiction foreign to our constitutions and unacknowledged by our laws, giving his assent to their acts of pretended legislation for quartering large bodies of armed troops among us; for protecting them by a mock trial from punishment for any murders which they should commit on the inhabitants of these states; for cutting off our trade with all parts of the world; for imposing taxes on us without our consent; for depriving us IN MANY CASES of the benefits of trial by jury; for transporting us beyond seas to be tried for pretended offences; for abolishing the free system of English laws in a neighboring province, establishing therein an arbitrary government, and enlarging its boundaries, so as to render it at once an example and fit instrument for introducing the same absolute rule into these COLONIES [*states*]; for taking away our charters, abolishing our most valuable laws, and altering fundamentally the forms of our governments; for suspending our own legislatures, and declaring themselves invested with power to legislate for us in all cases whatsoever.

He has abdicated government here BY DECLARING US OUT OF HIS PROTECTION, AND WAGING WAR AGAINST US [*withdrawing his governors, and declaring us out of his allegiance and protection*].

He has plundered our seas, ravaged our coasts, burnt our towns, and destroyed the lives of our people.

He is at this time transporting large armies of foreign mercenaries to complete the works of death, desolation and tyranny already begun with circumstances of cruelty and perfidy SCARCELY PARALLELED IN THE MOST BARBAROUS AGES, AND TOTALLY unworthy the head of a civilized nation.

He has constrained our fellow citizens taken captive on the high seas, to bear arms against their country, to become the executioners of their friends and brethren, or to fall themselves by their hands.

He has EXCITED DOMESTIC INSURRECTION AMONG US, AND HAS endeavored to bring on the inhabitants of our frontiers, the merciless Indian savages, whose known rule of warfare is an undistinguished destruction of all ages, sexes and conditions [*of existence*].

[*He has incited treasonable insurrections of our fellow citizens, with the allurements of forfeiture and confiscation of our property.*

He has waged cruel war against human nature itself, violating its most sacred rights of life and liberty in the persons of a distant people who never offended him, captivating and carrying them into slavery in another hemisphere, or to incur miserable death in their transportation hither. This piratical warfare, the opprobrium of INFIDEL powers, is the warfare of the CHRISTIAN king of Great Britain. Determined to keep open a market where MEN should be bought and sold, he has prostituted his negative for suppressing every legislative attempt to prohibit or to restrain this execrable commerce. And that this assemblage

of horrors might want no fact of distinguished die, he is
now exciting those very people to rise in arms among us,
and to purchase that liberty of which he has deprived
them, by murdering the people on whom he also obtruded
them: thus paying off former crimes committed against
the LIBERTIES of one people, with crimes which he
urges them to commit against the LIVES of another.]

In every stage of these oppressions we have petitioned
for redress in the most humble terms: our repeated peti-
tions have been answered only by repeated injuries.

A prince whose character is thus marked by every act
which may define a tyrant is unfit to be the ruler of a
FREE people [*who mean to be free. Future ages will scarcely*
believe that the hardiness of one man adventured, within
the short compass of twelve years only, to lay a founda-
tion so broad and so undisguised for tyranny over a people
fostered and fixed in principles of freedom.]

Nor have we been wanting in attentions to our British
brethren. We have warned them from time to time of attempts by their legislature to extend AN UNWARRANTABLE
[*a*] jurisdiction over US [*these our states*]. We have reminded them of the circumstances of our emigration and
settlement here, [*no one of which could warrant so strange*
a pretension: that these were effected at the expense of our
own blood and treasure, unassisted by the wealth or the
strength of Great Britain: that in constituting indeed our
several forms of government, we had adopted one com-
mon king, thereby laying a foundation for perpetual league
and amity with them: but that submission to their parlia-
ment was no part of our constitution, nor ever in idea,
if history may be credited: and,] we HAVE appealed to
their native justice and magnanimity AND WE HAVE CON-
JURED THEM BY [*as well as to*] the ties of our common
kindred to disavow these usurpations which WOULD IN-
EVITABLY [*were likely to*] interrupt our connection and
correspondence. They too have been deaf to the voice of
justice and of consanguinity. WE MUST THEREFORE [*and*

when occasions have been given them, by the regular course of their laws, of removing from their councils the disturbers of our harmony, they have, by their free election, re-established them in power. At this very time too, they are permitting their chief magistrate to send over not only soldiers of our common blood, but Scotch and foreign mercenaries to invade and destroy us. These facts have given the last stab to agonizing affection, and manly spirit bids us to renounce forever these unfeeling brethren. We must endeavor to forget our former love for them, and hold them as we hold the rest of mankind, enemies in war, in peace friends. We might have a free and a great people together; but a communication of grandeur and of freedom, it seems, is below their dignity. Be it so, since they will have it. The road to happiness and to glory is open to us, too. We will tread it apart from them, and] acquiesce in the necessity which denounces our [*eternal*] separation AND HOLD THEM AS WE HOLD THE REST OF MANKIND, ENEMIES IN WAR, IN PEACE FRIENDS!

We, therefore, the representatives of the United States of America in General Congress assembled, appealing to the supreme judge of the world for the rectitude of our intentions, do in the name, and by the authority of the good people of these COLONIES, SOLEMNLY PUBLISH AND DECLARE, THAT THESE UNITED COLONIES ARE, AND OF RIGHT OUGHT TO BE FREE AND INDEPENDENT STATES; THAT THEY ARE ABSOLVED FROM ALL ALLEGIANCE TO THE BRITISH CROWN, AND THAT ALL POLITICAL CONNECTION BETWEEN THEM AND THE STATE OF GREAT BRITAIN IS, AND OUGHT TO BE, TOTALLY DISSOLVED; [*states reject and renounce all allegiance and subjection to the kings of Great Britain and all others who may hereafter claim by, through or under them; we utterly dissolve all political connection which may heretofore have subsisted between us and the people or parliament of Great Britain: and finally we do assert and declare these colonies to be free and independent states,*] and that as free and independent states, they have full power to levy war, conclude peace, contract alliances, establish commerce, and to do all other acts and things which independent states may of right do.

And for the support of this declaration, with a firm reliance on the protection of divine providence, we mutually pledge to each other our lives, our fortunes, and our sacred honor.

Draft Constitution for Virginia[1]

[*Before June 13, 1776*]

A Bill for new-modelling the form of Government and for establishing the Fundamental principles thereof in future.

Whereas George. . . .

Be it therefore enacted by the authority of the people that the said George   Guelf be, and he hereby is deposed from the kingly office within this government and absolutely divested of all it's rights, power and prerogatives; and that he and his descendants and all persons claiming by or through him, and all other persons whatsoever shall be & for ever remain incapable of the same; and that the said office shall henceforth cease and never more either in name or substance be re-established within this colony.

[1] This was actually the third and final draft of the constitution Jefferson proposed for Virginia and forwarded to Williamsburg in June 1776. To it Jefferson appended this note: "It is proposed that this bill, after correction by the Convention, shall be referred by them to the people to be assembled in their respective counties and that the suffrages of two thirds of the counties shall be requisite to establish it." The preamble, omitted from the text above, was the original of Jefferson's indictment of George III in the Declaration of Independence and was added to the constitution adopted at Williamsburg. All brackets and italics are Jefferson's. The text was first published in 1806, though Jefferson himself published the constitution he had proposed in 1783 as an appendix to the *Notes on Virginia*. [Ed.]

And be it further enacted by the authority aforesaid that the following fundamental laws and principles of government shall henceforth be established.

The Legislative, Executive and Judiciary offices shall be kept for ever separate, & no person exercising the one shall be capable of appointment to the others, or to either of them.

I. LEGISLATIVE.

Legislation shall be exercised by two separate houses, to wit a house of Representatives and a house of Senators, which shall be called the General Assembly of Virginia.

The sd. house of Representatives shall be composed of persons chosen by the people annually on the [1'st day of October] and shall meet in General assembly on the [15'th day of November] following, and so from time to time on their own adjournments, or at any other time when summoned by the Administrator and shall continue sitting so long as they shall think the publick service requires.

Vacancies in the said house by death or disqualification shall be filled by the electors under a warrant from the Speaker of the said house.

All male persons of full age and sane mind having a freehold estate in [one fourth of an acre] of land in any town, or in [25] acres of land in the country, and all persons resident in the colony who shall have paid *scot* and *lot* to government the last [two years] shall have right to give their vote in the election of their respective representatives. And every person so qualified to elect shall be capable of being elected, provided he shall have given no bribe either directly or indirectly to any elector, and shall take an oath of fidelity to the state and of duty in his office, before he enters on the exercise thereof. during his continuance in the said office he shall hold no public pension nor post of profit, either himself, or by another for his use.

The number of representatives for each county or

borough shall be so proportioned to the number of it's qualified electors that the whole number of representatives shall not exceed [300] nor be less than [125.] For the present there shall be one representative for every [   ] qualified electors in each county or borough: but whenever this or any future proportion shall be likely to exceed or fall short of the limits beforementioned, it shall be again adjusted by the house of representatives.

The house of Representatives when met shall be free to act according to their own judgment and conscience.

The Senate shall consist of not less than [15] nor more than [50] members who shall be appointed by the house of Representatives. One third of them shall be removed out of office by lot at the end of the first [three] years and their places be supplied by a new appointment; one other third shall be removed by lot in like manner at the end of the second [three] years and their places be supplied by a new appointment; after which one third shall be removed annually at the end of every [three] years according to seniority. When once removed, they shall be for ever incapable of being re-appointed to that house. their qualifications shall be an oath of fidelity to the state, and of duty in their office, the being [31] years of age at the least, and the having given no bribe directly or indirectly to obtain their appointment. While in the Senatorial office they shall be incapable of holding any public pension or post of profit either themselves, or by others for their use.

The judges of the General court and of the High court of Chancery shall have session and deliberative voice, but not suffrage in the house of Senators.

The Senate and the house of representatives shall each of them have power to originate and amend bills; save only that bills for levying money shall be originated and amended by the representatives only: the assent of both houses shall be requisite to pass a law.

The General assembly shall have no power to pass any law inflicting death for any crime, excepting murder, & those offences in the military service for which they shall think punishment by death absolutely necessary: and all capital punishments in other cases are hereby abolished. nor shall they have power to prescribe torture in any case whatever: nor shall there be power any where to pardon crimes or to remit fines or punishments: nor shall any law for levying money be in force longer than [ten years.] from the time of it's commencement.

[Two thirds] of the members of either house shall be a *Quorum* to proceed to business.

II. EXECUTIVE.

The executive powers shall be exercised in manner following.

One person to be called the [Administrator] shall be annually appointed by the house of Representatives on the second day of their first session, who after having acted [one] year shall be incapable of being again appointed to that office until he shall have been out of the same [three] years.

Under him shall be appointed by the same house and at the same time a Deputy Administrator to assist his principal in the discharge of his office, and to succeed, in case of his death before the year shall have expired, to the whole powers thereof during the residue of the year.

The Administrator shall possess the powers formerly held by the king: save only that, he shall be bound by acts of legislature tho' not expressly named;

he shall have no negative on the bills of the Legislature;

he shall be liable to action, tho' not to personal restraint for private duties or wrongs;

he shall not possess the prerogatives

of dissolving, proroguing or adjourning either house of Assembly;

of declaring war or concluding peace;

of issuing letters of marque or reprisal;

of raising or introducing armed forces, building armed vessels, forts, or strong holds;

of coining monies or regulating their value;

of regulating weights and measures;

of erecting courts, offices, boroughs, corporations, fairs, markets, ports, beacons, lighthouses, seamarks,

of laying embargoes, or prohibiting the exportation of any commodity for a longer space than [40] days,

of retaining or recalling a member of the state but by legal process pro delicto vel contractu,

of making denizens;

of creating dignities or granting rights of precedence. But these powers shall be exercised by the legislature alone, and excepting also those powers which by these fundamentals are given to others, or abolished.

A Privy council shall be annually appointed by the house of representatives, whose duty it shall be to give advice to the Administrator when called on by him. With them the Deputy Administrator shall have session and suffrage.

Delegates to represent this colony in the American Congress shall be appointed when necessary by the house of Representatives. After serving [one] year in that office they shall not be capable of being re-appointed to the same during an interval of [one] year.

A Treasurer shall be appointed by the house of Representatives who shall issue no money but by authority of both houses.

An Attorney general shall be appointed by the house of Representatives.

High-sheriffs and Coroners of counties shall be annually elected by those qualified to vote for representatives: and no person who shall have served as highsheriff [one] year shall be capable of being re-elected to the said office in the same county till he shall have been out of office [five] years.

All other Officers civil and military shall be appointed by the Administrator; but such appointment shall be subject to the negative of the Privy council, saving however to the Legislature a power of transferring to any other persons the appointment of such officers or of any of them.

III. JUDICIARY.

The Judiciary powers shall be exercised

First by County courts and other inferior jurisdictions:

Secondly by a General court & a High court of Chancery:

Thirdly by a Court of Appeals.

The judges of the County courts and other inferior jurisdictions shall be appointed by the Administrator, subject to the negative of the privy council. they shall not be fewer than [five] in number. Their jurisdiction shall be defined from time to time by the legislature: and they shall be removeable for misbehavior by the court of Appeals.

The Judges of the General court and of the High court of Chancery shall be appointed by the Administrator and Privy council. If kept united they shall be [5] in number, if separate, there shall be [5] for the General court & [3] for the High court of Chancery. The appointment shall be made from the faculty of the law, and of such persons of that faculty as shall have actually exercised the same at the bar of some court or courts of record within this colony for [seven] years. They shall hold their commissions during good behavior, for breach of which they shall be removeable by the court of Appeals. Their jurisdiction shall be defined from time to time by the Legislature.

The Court of Appeals shall consist of not less than [7] nor more than [11] members, to be appointed by the house of Representatives: they shall hold their offices during good behavior, for breach of which they shall be removeable by an act of the legislature only. Their jurisdiction shall be to determine finally all causes removed before them from the General court or High court of Chancery on suggestion of error: to remove judges of the General court or High court of Chancery, or of the County courts or other inferior jurisdictions for misbehavior: [to try impeachments against high offenders lodged before them by the house of representatives for such crimes as shall hereafter be precisely defined by the Legislature, and for the punishment of which the said legislature shall have previously prescribed certain and determinate pains.] In this court the judges of the General court and High court of Chancery shall have session and deliberative voice, but no suffrage.

All facts in causes, whether of Chancery, Common, Ecclesiastical, or Marine law, shall be tried by a jury upon evidence given vivâ voce, in open court: but where witnesses are out of the colony or unable to attend through sickness or other invincible necessity, their depositions may be submitted to the credit of the jury.

All Fines and Amercements shall be assessed, & Terms of imprisonment for Contempts & Misdemeanors shall be fixed by the verdict of a jury.

All Process Original & Judicial shall run in the name of the court from which it issues.

Two thirds of the members of the General court, High court of Chancery, or Court of Appeals shall be a Quorum to proceed to business.

IV. RIGHTS PRIVATE AND PUBLIC.

Unappropriated or Forfeited lands shall be appropriated by the Administrator with the consent of the Privy council.

Every person of full age neither owning nor having owned [50] acres of land, shall be entitled to an appropriation of [50] acres or to so much as shall make up what he owns or has owned [50] acres in full and absolute dominion, and no other person shall be capable of taking an appropriation.

Lands heretofore holden of the crown in feesimple, and those hereafter to be appropriated shall be holden in full and absolute dominion, of no superior whatever.

No lands shall be appropriated until purchased of the Indian native proprietors; nor shall any purchases be made of them but on behalf of the public, by authority of acts of the General assembly to be passed for every purchase specially.

The territories contained within the charters erecting the colonies of Maryland, Pennsylvania, North and South Carolina, are hereby ceded, released, & for ever confirmed to the people of those colonies respectively, with all the rights of property, jurisdiction and government and all other rights whatsoever which might at any time heretofore have been claimed by this colony. The Western and Northern extent of this country shall in all other respects stand as fixed by the charter of

until by act of the Legislature one or more territories shall be laid off Westward of the Alleghaney mountains for new colonies, which colonies shall be established on the same fundamental laws contained in this instrument, and shall be free and independant of this colony and of all the world.

Descents shall go according to the laws of Gavelkind, save only that females shall have equal rights with males.

No person hereafter coming into this country shall be held within the same in slavery under any pretext whatever.

All persons who by their own oath or affirmation, or by other testimony shall give satisfactory proof to any court of record in this colony that they purpose to reside in the same [7] years at the least and who shall subscribe the fundamental laws, shall be considered as residents and entitled to all the rights of persons natural born.

All persons shall have full and free liberty of religious opinion; nor shall any be compelled to frequent or maintain any religious institution.

No freeman shall be debarred the use of arms [within his own lands or tenements].

There shall be no standing army but in time of actual war.

Printing presses shall be free, except so far as by commission of private injury cause may be given of private action.

All Forfeitures heretofore going to the king, shall go to the state; save only such as the legislature may hereafter abolish.

The royal claim to Wrecks, waifs, strays, treasure-trove, royal mines, royal fish, royal birds, are declared to have been usurpations on common right.

No Salaries or Perquisites shall be given to any officer but by some future act of the legislature. No salaries shall be given to the Administrator, members of the Legislative houses, judges of the court of Appeals, judges of the County courts, or other inferior jurisdictions, Privy counsellors, or Delegates to the American Congress: but the reasonable expences of the Administrator, members of the house of representatives, judges of the court of Appeals, Privy counsellors, & Delegates, for subsistence while acting in the duties of their office, may be borne by the public, if the Legislature shall so direct.

No person shall be capable of acting in any office, Civil, Military [or Ecclesiastical] who shall have given any bribe to obtain such office, or who shall not previously take an oath of fidelity to the state.

None of these fundamental laws and principles of government shall be repealed or altered, but by the personal consent of the people on summons to meet in their respective counties on one and the same day by an act of Legislature to be passed for every special occasion: and if in such county meetings the people of two thirds of the counties shall give their suffrage for any particular alteration or repeal referred to them by the said act, the same shall be accordingly repealed or altered, and such repeal or alteration shall take it's place among these fundamentals & stand on the same footing with them, in lieu of the article repealed or altered.

The laws heretofore in force in this colony shall remain in force, except so far as they are altered by the foregoing fundamental laws, or so far as they may be hereafter altered by acts of the Legislature.

A Bill for Establishing Religious Freedom[1]

[*1777*]

Well aware that the opinions and belief of men depend not on their own will, but follow involuntarily the evidence proposed to their minds; that Almighty God hath created the mind free, *and manifested his supreme will that free it shall remain by making it altogether insusceptible of restraint;* that all attempts to influence it by temporal punishments, or burthens, or by civil incapacitations, tend only to beget habits of hypocrisy and meanness, and are a departure from the plan of the holy author of our religion, who being lord both of body and mind, yet chose not to propagate it by coercions on either, as was in his Almighty power to do, *but to extend it by its influence on reason alone;* that the impious presumption of legislators and rulers, civil as well as ecclesiastical, who, being themselves but fallible and uninspired men, have assumed dominion over the faith of others, setting up their own opinions and modes of thinking as the only true and infallible, and as such endeavoring to impose them on oth-

[1] The text is taken from the 1784 *Report of the Committee of Revisors.* The bill was drafted by Jefferson sometime in 1777. It was debated, but not adopted, in the House of Delegates in June 1779, when it was also first printed. Brought forward by James Madison in October 1785, it was at length adopted on January 16, 1786. The parts of the bill deleted by amendment are in italics. The celebrated statute begins with the words "Whereas Almighty God." [Ed.]

ers, hath established and maintained false religions over the greatest part of the world and through all time: That to compel a man to furnish contributions of money for the propagation of opinions which he disbelieves *and abhors*, is sinful and tyrannical: that even the forcing him to support this or that teacher of his own religious persuasion, is depriving him of the comfortable liberty of giving his contributions to the particular pastor whose morals he would make his pattern, and whose powers he feels most persuasive to righteousness; and is withdrawing from the ministry those temporary rewards, which proceeding from an approbation of their personal conduct, are an additional incitement to earnest and unremitting labours for the instruction of mankind; that our civil rights have no dependance on our religious opinions, any more than our opinions in physics or geometry; that therefore the proscribing any citizen as unworthy the public confidence by laying upon him an incapacity of being called to offices of trust and emolument, unless he profess or renounce this or that religious opinion, is depriving him injuriously of those privileges and advantages to which, in common with his fellow citizens, he has a natural right; that it tends also to corrupt the principles of that *very* religion it is meant to encourage, by bribing, with a monopoly of worldly honours and emoluments, those who will externally profess and conform to it; that though indeed these are criminal who do not withstand such temptation, yet neither are those innocent who lay the bait in their way; *that the opinions of men are not the object of civil government, nor under its jurisdiction;* that to suffer the civil magistrate to intrude his powers into the field of opinion and to restrain the profession or propagation of principles on supposition of their ill tendency is a dangerous falacy, which at once destroys all religious liberty, because he being of course judge of that tendency will make his opinions the rule of judgment, and approve or condemn the sentiments of others only as they shall square with or differ from his own; that it is time enough for the rightful purposes of civil government for its officers to interfere when principles break out into overt acts against peace and good order; and finally, that truth is great and will prevail if left to herself; that she is the proper and sufficient antagonist to error, and has nothing to fear from the conflict unless by human interposition disarmed of her natural weapons, free argument and debate; errors ceasing to be dangerous when it is permitted freely to contradict them.

We the General Assembly of Virginia do enact that no man shall be compelled to frequent or support any religious worship, place, or ministry whatsoever, nor shall be enforced, restrained, molested, or burthened in his body or goods, nor shall otherwise suffer, on account of his religious opinions or belief; but that all men shall be free to profess, and by argument to maintain, their opinions in matters of religion, and that the same shall in no wise diminish, enlarge, or affect their civil capacities.

And though we well know that this assembly, elected by the people for the ordinary purposes of legislation only, have no power to restrain the acts of succeeding Assemblies, constituted with powers equal to our own, and that therefore to declare this act irrevocable would be of no effect in law; yet we are free to declare, and do declare, that the rights hereby asserted are of the natural rights of mankind, and that if any act shall be hereafter passed to repeal the present or to narrow its operation, such act will be an infringement of natural right.

Report of a Plan of Government for the Western Territory[1]

March 1, 1784

The Committee appointed to prepare a plan for the temporary government of the Western territory have agreed to the following resolutions.

Resolved, that the territory ceded or to be ceded by Individual states to the United states shall be formed into distinct states, bounded in the following manner as nearly as such cessions will admit, that is to say; Northwardly and Southwardly by parallels of latitude so that each state shall comprehend from South to North two degrees of latitude beginning to count from the completion of thirty one degrees North of the Equator: but any territory Northwardly of the 47th. degree shall make part of the state next below. And Eastwardly and Westwardly they shall be bounded, those on the Missisipi by that river on one side and the meridian of the lowest point of the rapids of Ohio on the other; and those adjoining on the East by the same meridian on their Western side, and on their Eastern by the meridian of the Western cape of the mouth of the Great Kanhaway. And the territory East-

[1] The text is from a manupscript in Jefferson's hand. Although considered by Congress, it was returned to the committee, of which Jefferson was chairman, and a revised report, also of his authorship, was presented on March 22 and adopted, after amendment, on April 23, 1784. The latter report differed from the former principally in the omission of the names Jefferson wished to give to the territories. [Ed.]

ward of this last meridian between the Ohio, Lake Erie, and Pennsylvania shall be one state.

That the settlers within any of the said states shall, either on their own petition, or on the order of Congress, receive authority from them, with appointments of time and place for their free males of full age to meet together for the purpose of establishing a temporary government,

A map showing the bounds of states proposed by the Report of March 1, 1784, with names assigned in territory already ceded.

to adopt the constitution and laws of any one of these states, so that such laws nevertheless shall be subject to alteration by their ordinary legislature, and to erect, subject to a like alteration, counties or townships for the election of members for their legislature.

That such temporary government shall only continue in force in any state until it shall have acquired 20.000. free inhabitants; when giving due proof thereof to Congress, they shall receive from them authority with appointments of time and place to call a Convention of representatives to establish a permanent constitution and government for themselves.

Provided that both the temporary and permanent governments be established on these principles as their basis. 1. That they shall for ever remain a part of the United states of America. 2. That in their persons, property and territory they shall be subject to the government of the United states in Congress assembled, and to the Articles of confederation in all those cases in which the original states shall be so subject. 3. That they shall be subject to pay a part of the federal debts contracted or to be contracted to be apportioned on them by Congress according to the same common rule and measure by which apportionments thereof shall be made on the other states. 4. That their respective governments shall be in republican forms, and shall admit no person to be a citizen who holds any hereditary title. 5. That after the year 1800 of the Christian æra, there shall be neither slavery nor involuntary servitude in any of the said states, otherwise than in punishment of crimes, whereof the party shall have been duly convicted to have been personally guilty.

That whensoever any of the said states shall have, of free inhabitants, as many as shall then be in any one the least numerous of the thirteen original states, such state shall be admitted by it's delegates into the Congress of the United states, on an equal footing with the said original states: after which the assent of two thirds of the United states in Congress assembled shall be requisite in all those cases, wherein by the Confederation, the assent of nine states is now required. Provided the consent of nine states to such admission may be obtained according to the eleventh of the articles of Confederation. Until such admission by their delegates into Congress, any of the said states, after the establishment of their temporary government, shall have authority to keep a sitting member in Congress, with a right of debating, but not of voting.

That the territory Northward of the 45th. degree that is to say, of the completion of 45°. from the Equator, and extending to the Lake of the Woods shall be called SYLVANIA:

That of the territory under the 45th and 44th degrees that which lies Westward of Lake Michigan shall be called MICHIGANIA, and that which is Eastward thereof within the peninsul formed by the lakes and waters of Michigan, Huron, St. Clair and Erie, shall be called CHERRONESUS, and shall include any part of the peninsul which may extend above the 45th. degree.

Of the territory under the 43d and 42d degrees, that to the Westward thro' which the Assenisipi or Rock river runs shall be called ASSENISIPIA, and that to the Eastward in which are the fountains of the Muskingum, the two Miamis of Ohio, the Wabash, the Illinois, the Miami of the lake and Sandusky rivers shall be called METROPOTAMIA.

Of the territory which lies under the 41st. and 40th. degrees, the Western, thro' which the river Illinois runs, shall be called ILLINOIA; that next adjoining to the Eastward SARATOGA, and that between this last and Pennsylvania and extending from the Ohio to Lake Erie, shall be called WASHINGTON.

Of the territory which lies under the 39th. and 38th. degrees to which shall be added so much of the point of land within the fork of the Ohio and Missisipi as lies under the 37th. degree, that to the Westward within and adjacent to which are the confluences of the rivers Wabash, Shawanee, Tanissee, Ohio, Illinois, Missisipi and Missouri, shall be called POLYPOTAMIA, and that to the

Eastward farther up the Ohio, otherwise called the Pelisipi shall be called PELISIPIA.

That the preceding articles shall be formed into a Charter of Compact, shall be duly executed by the President of the U.S. in Congress assembled under his hand and the seal of the United States, shall be promulgated, and shall stand as fundamental constitutions between the thirteen original states, and those now newly described, unalterable but by the joint consent of the U.S. in Congress assembled and of the particular state within which such alteration is proposed to be made.

Response to the Citizens of Albemarle[1]

February 12, 1790

GENTLEMEN

The testimony of esteem with which you are pleased to honour my return to my native county fills me with gratitude and pleasure. While it shews that my absence has not lost me your friendly recollection, it holds out the comfortable hope that when the hour of retirement shall come, I shall again find myself amidst those with whom I have long lived, with whom I wish to live, and whose affection is the source of my purest happiness. Their favor was the door thro' which I was ushered on the stage of public life; and while I have been led on thro' it's varying scenes, I could not be unmindful of those who assigned me my first part.

My feeble and obscure exertions in their service, and in the holy cause of freedom, have had no other merit than that they were my best. We have all the same. We have been fellow-labourers and fellow-sufferers, and heaven has rewarded us with a happy issue from our struggles. It rests now with ourselves alone to enjoy in peace and concord the blessings of self-government, so long denied to mankind: to shew by example the sufficiency of human

---

1 Jefferson delivered this brief address at Monticello to a group of local citizens who had earlier presented an address of welcome to him. The response put an end to more than two months of agonizing indecision on acceptance of the post of Secretary of State. The text is from a manuscript copy in Jefferson's papers. [Ed.]

reason for the care of human affairs and that the will of the majority, the Natural law of every society, is the only sure guardian of the rights of man. Perhaps even this may sometimes err. But it's errors are honest, solitary and short-lived.—Let us then, my dear friends, for ever bow down to the general reason of the society. We are safe with that, even in it's deviations, for it soon returns again to the right way. These are lessons we have learnt together. We have prospered in their practice, and the liberality with which you are pleased to approve my attachment to the general rights of mankind assures me we are still together in these it's kindred sentiments.

Wherever I may be stationed, by the will of my country, it will be my delight to see, in the general tide of happiness, that yours too flows on in just place and measure. That it may flow thro' all times, gathering strength as it goes, and spreading the happy influence of reason and liberty over the face of the earth, is my fervent prayer to heaven.

Opinion on the Constitutionality
of a National Bank[1]

February 15, 1791.

The bill for establishing a National Bank undertakes among other things:—

1. To form the subscribers into a corporation.

2. To enable them in their corporate capacities to receive grants of land; and so far is against the laws of *Mortmain.*[2]

3. To make alien subscribers capable of holding lands; and so far is against the laws of *Alienage.*

4. To transmit these lands, on the death of a proprietor, to a certain line of successors; and so far changes the course of *Descents.*

5. To put the lands out of the reach of forfeiture or escheat; and so far is against the laws of *Forfeiture and Escheat.*

[1] Jefferson wrote this opinion at President Washington's request. Upon receiving it, Washington submitted the opinion to Alexander Hamilton, author of the bank bill, for rebuttal. In arguing the case for constitutionality of a national bank, Hamilton advanced the .doctrine of *implied powers.* Convinced by Hamilton's reasoning, Washington signed the bill into law. Jefferson's opinion, being advisory only, was not published for many years. [Ed.]

[2] Though the Constitution controls the laws of Mortmain so far as to permit Congress itself to hold land for certain purposes, yet not so far as to permit them to communicate a similar right to other corporate bodies.

6. To transmit personal chattels to successors in a certain line; and so far is against the laws of *Distribution*.

7. To give them the sole and exclusive right of banking under the national authority; and so far is against the laws of Monopoly.

8. To communicate to them a power to make laws paramount to the laws of the States: for so they must be construed, to protect the institution from the control of the State legislatures; and so, probably, they will be construed.

I consider the foundation of the Constitution as laid on this ground: That "all powers not delegated to the United States, by the Constitution, nor prohibited by it to the States, are reserved to the States or to the people." [XIIth amendment.][3] To take a single step beyond the boundaries thus specially drawn around the powers of Congress, is to take possession of a boundless field of power, no longer susceptible of any definition.

The incorporation of a bank, and the powers assumed by this bill, have not, in my opinion, been delegated to the United States, by the Constitution.

I. They are not among the powers specially enumerated: for these are: 1st. A power to lay taxes for the purpose of paying the debts of the United States; but no debt is paid by this bill, nor any tax laid. Were it a bill to raise money, its origination in the Senate would condemn it by the Constitution.

2d. "To borrow money." But this bill neither borrows money nor ensures the borrowing it. The proprietors of the bank will be just as free as any other money holders, to lend or not to lend their money to the public. The operation proposed in the bill, first, to lend them two millions, and then to borrow them back again, cannot change the nature of the latter act, which will still be a payment, and not a loan, call it by what name you please.

3. To "regulate commerce with foreign nations, and

[3] The Xth as the several amendments were finally ratified in November 1791. [Ed.]

among the States, and with the Indian tribes." To erect a bank, and to regulate commerce, are very different acts. He who erects a bank, creates a subject of commerce in its bills; so does he who makes a bushel of wheat, or digs a dollar out of the mines; yet neither of these persons regulates commerce thereby. To make a thing which may be bought and sold, is not to prescribe regulations for buying and selling. Besides, if this was an exercise of the power of regulating commerce, it would be void, as extending as much to the internal commerce of every State, as to its external. For the power given to Congress by the Constitution does not extend to the internal regulation of the commerce of a State, (that is to say of the commerce between citizen and citizen,) which remain exclusively with its own legislature; but to its external commerce only, that is to say, its commerce with another State, or with foreign nations, or with the Indian tribes. Accordingly the bill does not propose the measure as a regulation of trade, but as "productive of considerable advantages to trade." Still less are these powers covered by any other of the special enumerations.

II. Nor are they within either of the general phrases, which are the two following:—

1. To lay taxes to provide for the general welfare of the United States, that is to say, "to lay taxes for *the purpose* of providing for the general welfare." For the laying of taxes is the *power*, and the general welfare the *purpose* for which the power is to be exercised. They are not to lay taxes *ad libitum for any purpose they please;* but only *to pay the debts or provide for the welfare of the Union.* In like manner, they are not *to do anything they please* to provide for the general welfare, but only to *lay taxes* for that purpose. To consider the latter phrase, not as describing the purpose of the first, but as giving a distinct and independent power to do any act they please, which might be for the good of the Union, would render all the preceding and subsequent enumerations of power completely useless.

It would reduce the whole instrument to a single phrase, that of instituting a Congress with power to do whatever would be for the good of the United States; and, as they would be the sole judges of the good or evil, it would be also a power to do whatever evil they please.

It is an established rule of construction where a phrase will bear either of two meanings, to give it that which will allow some meaning to the other parts of the instrument, and not that which would render all the others useless. Certainly no such universal power was meant to be given them. It was intended to lace them up straitly within the enumerated powers, and those without which, as means, these powers could not be carried into effect. It is known that the very power now proposed *as a means* was rejected as *an end* by the Convention which formed the Constitution. A proposition was made to them to authorize Congress to open canals, and an amendatory one to empower them to incorporate. But the whole was rejected, and one of the reasons for rejection urged in debate was, that then they would have a power to erect a bank, which would render the great cities, where there were prejudices and jealousies on the subject, adverse to the reception of the Constitution.

2. The second general phrase is, "to make all laws *necessary* and proper for carrying into execution the enumerated powers." But they can all be carried into execution without a bank. A bank therefore is not *necessary*, and consequently not authorized by this phrase.

It has been urged that a bank will give great facility or convenience in the collection of taxes. Suppose this were true: yet the Constitution allows only the means which are "*necessary*," not those which are merely "convenient" for effecting the enumerated powers. If such a latitude of construction be allowed to this phrase as to give any non-enumerated power, it will go to every one, for there is not one which ingenuity may not torture into a *convenience* in some instance *or other*, to *some one* of so long a list of enumerated powers. It would swallow up all the delegated powers, and reduce the whole to one power, as before observed. Therefore it was that the Constitution restrained them to the *necessary* means, that is to say, to those means without which the grant of power would be nugatory.

But let us examine this convenience and see what it is. The report on this subject, page 3, states the only *general* convenience to be, the preventing the transportation and re-transportation of money between the States and the treasury, (for I pass over the increase of circulating medium, ascribed to it as a want, and which, according to my ideas of paper money, is clearly a demerit.) Every State will have to pay a sum of tax money into the treasury; and the treasury will have to pay, in every State, a part of the interest on the public debt, and salaries to the officers of government resident in that State. In most of the States there will still be a surplus of tax money to come up to the seat of government for the officers residing there. The payments of interest and salary in each State may be made by treasury orders on the State collector. This will take up the greater part of the money he has collected in his State, and consequently prevent the great mass of it from being drawn out of the State. If there be a balance of commerce in favor of that State against the one in which the government resides, the surplus of taxes will be remitted by the bills of exchange drawn for that commercial balance. And so it must be if there was a bank. But if there be no balance of commerce, either direct or circuitous, all the banks in the world could not bring up the surplus of taxes but in the form of money. Treasury orders then, and bills of exchange may prevent the displacement of the main mass of the money collected, without the aid of any bank; and where these fail, it cannot be prevented even with that aid.

Perhaps, indeed, bank bills may be a more *convenient* vehicle than treasury orders. But a little *difference* in the degree of *convenience*, cannot constitute the necessity which the constitution makes the ground for assuming any non-enumerated power.

Besides; the existing banks will, without a doubt, enter into arrangements for lending their agency, and the more favorable, as there will be a competition among them for it; whereas the bill delivers us up bound to the national bank, who are free to refuse all arrangement, but on their own terms, and the public not free, on such refusal, to employ any other bank. That of Philadelphia, I believe, now does this business, by their post-notes, which, by an arrangement with the treasury, are paid by any State collector to whom they are presented. This expedient alone suffices to prevent the existence of that *necessity* which may justify the assumption of a non-enumerated power as a means for carrying into effect an enumerated one. The thing may be done, and has been done, and well done, without this assumption; therefore, it does not stand on that degree of *necessity* which can honestly justify it.

It may be said that a bank whose bills would have a currency all over the States, would be more convenient than one whose currency is limited to a single State. So it would be still more convenient that there should be a bank, whose bills should have a currency all over the world. But it does not follow from this superior conveniency, that there exists anywhere a power to establish such a bank; or that the world may not go on very well without it.

Can it be thought that the Constitution intended that for a shade or two of *convenience*, more or less, Congress should be authorised to break down the most ancient and fundamental laws of the several States; such as those against Mortmain, the laws of Alienage, the rules of descent, the acts of distribution, the laws of escheat and forfeiture, the laws of monopoly? Nothing but a necessity invincible by any other means, can justify such a prostitution of laws, which constitute the pillars of our whole system of jurisprudence. Will Congress be too straightlaced to carry the constitution into honest effect, unless they may pass over the foundation-laws of the State government for the slightest convenience of theirs?

The negative of the President is the shield provided by the constitution to protect against the invasions of the legislature: 1. The right of the Executive. 2. Of the Judiciary. 3. Of the States and State legislatures. The present is the case of a right remaining exclusively with the States, and consequently one of those intended by the Constitution to be placed under its protection.

It must be added, however, that unless the President's mind on a view of everything which is urged for and against this bill, is tolerably clear that it is unauthorised by the Constitution; if the pro and the con hang so even as to balance his judgment, a just respect for the wisdom of the legislature would naturally decide the balance in favor of their opinion. It is chiefly for cases where they are clearly misled by error, ambition, or interest, that the Constitution has placed a check in the negative of the President.

Opinion on the French Treaties[1]

I proceed, in compliance with the requisition of the President, to give an opinion in writing on the general Question, Whether the U S. have a right to renounce their treaties with France, or to hold them suspended till the government of that country shall be established?

In the Consultation at the President's on the 19th inst. the Secretary of the Treasury took the following positions & consequences. 'France was a monarchy when we entered into treaties with it: but it has now declared itself a Republic, & is preparing a Republican form of government. As it may issue in a Republic, or a Military despotism, or in something else which may possibly render our alliance with it dangerous to ourselves, we have a right of election to renounce the treaty altogether, or to declare it suspended till their government shall be settled in the form it is ultimately to take; and then we may judge whether we will call the treaties into operation again, or declare them forever null. Having that right of election

---

[1] This written opinion, given to President Washington, was the by-product of a heated discussion in the cabinet on the reception of Genêt, recognition of the Republic of France, and the validity of the treaties of 1778. The Treaty of Alliance contained a mutual "guarantee clause" under which the United States might be called upon to defend French possessions in the West Indies, while the Treaty of Amity and Commerce gave certain concessions to France as a belligerent. The text is taken from the original manuscript in Washington's papers. [Ed.]

now, if we receive their minister[2] without any qualifications, it will amount to an act of election to continue the
treaties; & if the change they are undergoing should issue
in a form which should bring danger on us, we shall not
be then free to renounce them. To elect to continue them
is equivalent to the making a new treaty at this time in the
same form, that is to say, with a clause of guarantee; but
to make a treaty with a clause of guarantee, during a war,
is a departure from neutrality, and would make us associates in the war. To renounce or suspend the treaties therefore is a necessary act of neutrality.'

If I do not subscribe to the soundness of this reasoning,
I do most fully to its ingenuity.—I shall now lay down
the principles which according to my understanding govern the case.

I consider the people who constitute a society or nation
as the source of all authority in that nation, as free to
transact their common concerns by any agents they think
proper, to change these agents individually, or the organisation of them in form or function whenever they please:
that all the acts done by those agents under the authority
of the nation, are the acts of the nation, are obligatory on
them, & enure to their use, & can in no wise be annulled
or affected by any change in the form of the government,
or of the persons administering it. Consequently the Treaties between the U S. and France, were not treaties between the U S. & Louis Capet, but between the two nations of America & France, and the nations remaining in
existance, tho' both of them have since changed their
forms of government, the treaties are not annulled by
these changes.

The Law of nations, by which this question is to be determined, is composed of three branches. 1. The Moral
law of our nature. 2. The Usages of nations. 3. Their
special Conventions. The first of these only, concerns this
question, that is to say the Moral law to which Man has

2 Edmond Genêt. [Ed.]

been subjected by his creator, & of which his feelings, or Conscience as it is sometimes called, are the evidence with which his creator has furnished him. The Moral duties which exist between individual and individual in a state of nature, accompany them into a state of society & the aggregate of the duties of all the individuals composing the society constitutes the duties of that society towards any other; so that between society & society the same moral duties exist as did between the individuals composing them while in an unassociated state, their maker not having released them from those duties on their forming themselves into a nation. Compacts then between nation & nation are obligatory on them by the same moral law which obliges individuals to observe their compacts. There are circumstances however which sometimes excuse the non-performance of contracts between man & man: so are there also between nation & nation. When performance, for instance, becomes *impossible*, non-performance is not immoral. So if performance becomes *self-destructive* to the party, the law of self-preservation overrules the laws of obligation to others. For the reality of these principles I appeal to the true fountains of evidence, the head & heart of every rational & honest man. It is there Nature has written her moral laws, & where every man may read them for himself. He will never read there the permission to annul his obligations for a time, or for ever, whenever they become 'dangerous, useless, or disagreeable.' Certainly not when merely *useless* or *disagreeable*, as seems to be said in an authority which has been quoted, Vattel. 2. 197, and tho he may under certain degrees of *danger*, yet the danger must be imminent, & the degree great. Of these, it is true, that nations are to be judges for themselves, since no one nation has a right to sit in judgment over another. But the tribunal of our consciences remains, & that also of the opinion of the world. These will revise the sentence we pass in our own case, & as we respect these, we must see that in judging ourselves we have honestly done the part of impartial & vigorous judges.

But Reason, which gives this right of self-liberation from a contract in certain cases, has subjected it to certain just limitations.

I. The danger which absolves us must be great, inevitable & imminent. Is such the character of that now apprehended from our treaties with France? What is that danger. 1. Is it that if their government issues in a military despotism, an alliance with them may taint us with despotic principles? But their government, when we allied ourselves to it, was a perfect despotism, civil & military. Yet the treaties were made in that very state of things, & therefore that danger can furnish no just cause. 2. Is it that their government may issue in a republic, and too much strengthen our republican principles? But this is the hope of the great mass of our constituents, & not their dread. They do not look with longing to the happy mean of a limited monarchy. 3. But says the doctrine I am combating, the change the French are undergoing may possibly end in something we know not what, and bring on us danger we know not whence. In short it may end in a Rawhead & bloody-bones in the dark. Very well. Let Rawhead & bloody bones come, & then we shall be justified in making our peace with him, by renouncing our antient friends & his enemies. For observe, it is not the *possibility of danger*, which absolves a party from his contract: for that possibility always exists, & in every case. It existed in the present one at the moment of making the contract. If *possibilities* would avoid contracts, there never could be a valid contract. For possibilities hang over everything. Obligation is not suspended, till the danger is become real, & the moment of it so imminent, that we can no longer avoid decision without forever losing the opportunity to do it. But can a danger which has not yet taken it's shape, which does not yet exist, & never may exist, which cannot therefore be defined, can such a danger I ask, be so imminent that if we fail to pronounce on it in this moment we can never have another opportunity of doing it?

4. The danger apprehended, is it that, the treaties remaining valid, the clause guarantying their West India islands will engage us in the war? But Does the Guarantee engage us to enter into the war in any event?

Are we to enter into it before we are called on by our allies? Have we been called on by them?—shall we ever be called on? Is it their interest to call on us?

Can they call on us before their islands are invaded, or imminently threatened?

If they can save them themselves, have they a right to call on us?

Are we obliged to go to war at once, without trying peaceable negociations with their enemy?

If all these questions be against us, there are still others behind.

Are we in a condition to go to war?

Can we be expected to begin before we are in condition?

Will the islands be lost if we do not save them? Have we the means of saving them?

If we cannot save them are we bound to go to war for a desperate object?

Will not a 10. years forbearance in us to call them into the guarantee of our posts, entitle us to some indulgence?

Many, if not most of these questions offer grounds of doubt whether the clause of guarantee will draw us into the war. Consequently if this be the danger apprehended, it is not yet certain enough to authorize us in sound morality to declare, at this moment, the treaties null.

5. Is the danger apprehended from the 17th article of the treaty of Commerce, which admits French ships of war & privateers to come and go freely, with prizes made on their enemies, while their enemies are not to have the same privilege with prizes made on the French? But Holland & Prussia have approved of this article in our treaty with France, by subscribing to an express Salvo of it in our treaties with them. [Dutch treaty 22. Convention 6. Prussian treaty 19.] And England in her last treaty with

France [art. 40] has entered into the same stipulation verbatim, & placed us in her ports on the same footing on which she is in ours, in case of a war of either of us with France. If we are engaged in such a war, England must receive prizes made on us by the French, & exclude those made on the French by us. Nay further, in this very article of her treaty with France, is a salvo of any similar article in any anterior treaty of either party. and ours with France being anterior, this salvo confirms it expressly. Neither of these three powers then have a right to complain of this article in our treaty.

6. Is the danger apprehended from the 22^d Art. of our treaty of commerce, which prohibits the enemies of France from fitting out privateers in our ports, or selling their prizes here. But we are free to refuse the same thing to France, there being no stipulation to the contrary, and we ought to refuse it on principles of fair neutrality.

7. But the reception of a Minister from the Republic of France, without qualifications, it is thought will bring us into danger: because this, it is said, will determine the continuance of the treaty, and take from us the right of self-liberation when at any time hereafter our safety would require us to use it. The reception of the Minister at all (in favor of which Col^o. Hamilton has given his opinion, tho reluctantly as he confessed) is an acknolegement of the legitimacy of their government: and if the qualifications meditated are to deny that legitimacy, it will be a curious compound which is to admit & deny the same thing. But I deny that the reception of a Minister has any thing to do with the treaties. There is not a word, in either of them, about sending ministers. This has been done between us under the common usage of nations, & can have no effect either to continue or annul the treaties.

But how can any act of election have the effect to continue a treaty which is acknowledged to be going on still? For it was not pretended the treaty was void, but only voidable if we chuse to declare it so. To make it void would require an act of election, but to let it go on requires only that we should do nothing, and doing nothing can hardly be an infraction of peace or neutrality.

But I go further & deny that the most explicit declaration made at this moment that we acknolege the obligation of the treatys could take from us the right of non-compliance at any future time when compliance would involve us in great & inevitable danger.

I conclude then that few of these sources threaten any danger at all; and from none of them is it inevitable: & consequently none of them give us the right at this moment of releasing ourselves from our treaties.

II. A second limitation on our right of releasing ourselves is that we are to do it from so much of the treaties only as is bringing great & inevitable danger on us, & not from the residue, allowing to the other party a right at the same time to determine whether on our non-compliance with that part they will declare the whole void. This right they would have, but we should not. Vattel. 2. 202. The only part of the treaties which can really lead us into danger is the clause of guarantee. That clause is all then we could suspend in any case, and the residue will remain or not at the will of the other party.

III. A third limitation is that where a party from necessity or danger withholds compliance with part of a treaty, it is bound to make compensation where the nature of the case admits & does not dispense with it. 2. Vattel 324. Wolf. 270. 443. If actual circumstances excuse us from entering into the war under the clause of guarantee, it will be a question whether they excuse us from compensation. Our weight in the war admits of an estimate; & that estimate would form the measure of compensation.

If in withholding a compliance with any part of the treaties, we do it without just cause or compensation, we give to France a cause of war, and so become associated in it on the other side. An injured friend is the bitterest of foes, & France had not discovered either timidity, or over-much forbearance on the late occasions. Is this the position we wish to take for our constituents? It is certainly not the one they would take for themselves.

I will proceed now to examine the principal authority which has been relied on for establishing the right of self liberation; because tho' just in part, it would lead us far beyond justice, if taken in all the latitude of which his expressions would admit. Questions of natural right are triable by their conformity with the moral sense & reason of man. Those who write treatises of natural law, can only declare what their own moral sense & reason dictate in the several cases they state. Such of them as happen to have feelings & a reason coincident with those of the wise & honest part of mankind, are respected & quoted as witnesses of what is morally right or wrong in particular cases. Grotius, Puffendorf, Wolf, & Vattel are of this number. Where they agree their authority is strong. But where they differ, & they often differ, we must appeal to our own feelings and reason to decide between them.

The passages in question shall be traced through all these writers, that we may see wherein they concur, & where that concurrence is wanting. It shall be quoted from them in the order in which they wrote, that is to say, from Grotius first, as being the earliest writer, Puffendorf next, then Wolf, & lastly Vattel as latest in time. . . .[8]

The doctrine then of Grotius, Puffendorf & Wolf is that 'treaties remain obligatory notwithstanding any change in the form of government, except in the single case where the preservation of that form was the object of the treaty.' There the treaty extinguishes, not by the election or declaration of the party remaining in statu quo; but independantly of that, by the evanishment of the object. Vattel lays down, in fact, the same doctrine, that treaties continue

[8] Jefferson's quotations from these authorities in four columns is omitted. Hugo Grotius, *Concerning the Law of War and Peace* (1631); Samuel von Pufendorf, *On the Law of Nature and Nations* (1672); Christian von Wolff, *Institutes of the Law of Nature and of Nations* (1748); Emerich de Vattel, *The Law of Nations* (1760). [Ed.]

obligatory, notwithstanding a change of government by the will of the other party, that to oppose that will would be a wrong, & that the ally remains an ally notwithstanding the change. So far he concurs with all the previous writers. But he then adds what they had not said, nor would say 'but if this change renders the alliance *useless*, dangerous, or *disagreeable* to it, it is free to renounce it.' It was unnecessary for him to have specified the exception of *danger* in this particular case, because that exception exists in all cases & it's extent has been considered. But when he adds that, because a contract is become merely *useless* or *diagreeable*, we are free to renounce it, he is in opposition to Grotius, Puffendorf, & Wolf, who admit no such license against the obligation of treaties, & he is in opposition to the morality of every honest man, to whom we may safely appeal to decide whether he feels himself free to renounce a contract the moment it becomes merely *useless* or *disagreeable*, to him? We may appeal too to Vattel himself, in those parts of his book where he cannot be misunderstood, & to his known character, as one of the most zealous & constant advocates for the preservation of good faith in all our dealings. Let us hear him on other occasions; & first where he shews what degree of danger or injury will authorize self-liberation from a treaty. 'If simple lezion' (lezion means the loss sustained by selling a thing for less than half value, which degree of loss rendered the sale void by the Roman law), 'if simple lezion, says he, or some degree of disadvantage in a treaty does not suffice to render it invalid, it is not so as to inconveniences which would go to the *ruin* of the nation. As every treaty ought to be made by a sufficient power, a treaty pernicious to the state is null, & not at all obligatory; no governor of a nation having power to engage things capable of *destroying* the state, for the safety of which the empire is trusted to him. The nation itself, bound necessarily to whatever it's preservation & safety require, cannot enter into engagements contrary to it's indispensable obligations.' Here then we find that the degree of injury or danger which he deems sufficient to liberate us from a treaty, is that which would go to the absolute *ruin* or *destruction* of the state; not simply the lezion of the Roman law, not merely the being disadvantageous, or dangerous. For as he says himself § 158. 'lezion cannot render a treaty invalid. It is his duty, who enters into engagements, to weigh well all things before he concludes. He may do with his property what he pleases, he may relinquish his rights, renounce his advantages, as he judges proper: the acceptant is not obliged to inform himself of his motives, nor to weigh their just value. If we could free ourselves from a compact because we find ourselves injured by it, there would be nothing firm in the contracts of nations. Civil laws set limits to lezion, & determine the degree capable of producing a nullity of the contract. But sovereigns acknolege no judge. How establish lezion among them? Who will determine the degree sufficient to invalidate a treaty? The happiness & peace of nations require manifestly that their treaties should not depend on a means of nullity so vague & so dangerous.'

Let us hear him again on the general subject of the observance of treaties § 163. 'It is demonstrated in natural law that he who promises another confers on him a perfect right to require the thing promised, & that, consequently, not to observe a perfect promise, is to violate the right of another; it is as manifest injustice as to plunder any one of their right. All the tranquillity, the happiness & security of mankind rest on justice, on the obligation to respect the rights of others. The respect of others for our rights of domain & property is the security of our actual possessions; the faith of promises is our security for the things which cannot be delivered or executed on the spot. No more security, no more commerce among men, if they think themselves not obliged to preserve faith, to keep their word. This obligation then is as necessary as it is natural & indubitable, among nations who live together in a state of nature, & who acknolege no superior on earth, to maintain order & peace in their society. Nations & their governors then ought to observe inviolably their promises & their treaties. This great truth, altho' too often neglected in practice, is generally acknoleged by all nations: the reproach of perfidy is a bitter affront among sovereigns: now he who does not observe a treaty is assuredly perfidious, since he violates his faith. On the contrary nothing is so glorious to a prince & his nation, as the reputation of inviolable fidelity to his word?' Again § 219. 'Who will doubt that treaties are of the things sacred among nations? They decide matters the most important. They impose rules on the pretensions of sovereigns: they cause the rights of nations to be acknoleged, they assure their most precious interests. Among political bodies, sovereigns, who acknolege no superior on earth, treaties are the only means of adjusting their different pretensions, of establishing a rule, to know on what to count, on what to depend. But treaties are but vain words if nations do not consider them as respectable engagements, as rules, inviolable for sovereigns, & sacred through the whole earth. § 220. The faith of treaties, that firm & sincere will, that invariable constancy in fulfilling engagements, of which a declaration is made in a treaty, is there holy & sacred, among nations, whose safety & repose it ensures; & if nations will not be wanting to themselves, they will load with infamy whoever violates his faith.'

After evidence so copious & explicit of the respect of this author for the sanctity of treaties, we should hardly have expected that his authority would have been resorted to for a wanton invalidation of them whenever they should become merely *useless* or *disagreeable*. We should hardly have expected that, rejecting all the rest of his book, this scrap would have been culled, & made the hook whereon to hang such a chain of immoral consequences. Had the passage accidentally met our eye, we should have imagined it had fallen from the author's pen under some momentary view, not sufficiently developed to found a conjecture what he meant: and we may certainly affirm that a fragment like this cannot weigh against the authority of all other writers, against the uniform & systematic doctrine of every work from which it is torn, against the moral feelings & the reason of all honest men. If the terms of the fragment are not misunderstood, they are in full contradiction to all the written & unwritten evidences of morality: if they are misunderstood, they are no longer a foundation for the doctrines which have been built on them.

But even had this doctrine been as true as it is manifestly false, it would have been asked, to whom is it that the treaties with France have become *disagreeable?* How will it be proved that they are *useless?*

The conclusion of the sentence suggests a reflection too strong to be suppressed 'for the party may say with truth that it would not have allied itself with this nation, if it had been under the present form of it's government.' The Republic of the U. S. allied itself with France when under a despotic government. She changes her government, declares it shall be a Republic, prepares a form of Republic extremely free, and in the mean time is governing herself as such, and it is proposed that America shall declare the treaties void because 'it may say with truth that it would not have allied itself with that nation, if it had been under the present form of it's government!' Who is the American who can say with truth that he would not have allied himself to France if she had been a republic? or that a Republic of any form would be as *disagreeable* as her antient despotism?

Upon the whole I conclude

That the treaties are still binding, notwithstanding the change of government in France: that no part of them, but the clause of guarantee, holds up *danger*, even at a distance.

And consequently that a liberation from no other part could be proposed in any case: that if that clause may ever bring *danger*, it is neither extreme, nor imminent, nor even probable: that the authority for renouncing a treaty, when *useless* or *disagreeable*, is either misunderstood, or in opposition to itself, to all their writers, & to every moral feeling: that were it not so, these treaties are in fact neither useless nor disagreeable.

That the receiving a Minister from France at this time is an act of no significance with respect to the treaties, amounting neither to an admission nor a denial of them, forasmuch as he comes not under any stipulation in them:

That were it an explicit admission, or were an express declaration of this obligation now to be made, it would not take from us that right which exists at all times of liberating ourselves when an adherence to the treaties would be *ruinous* or *destructive* to the society: and that the not renouncing the treaties now is so far from being a breach of neutrality, that the doing it would be the breach, by giving just cause of war to France.

The Kentucky Resolutions[1]

[*October 1798*]

1. *Resolved,* That the several States composing the United States of America; are not united on the principle of unlimited submission to their General Government; but that, by a compact under the style and title of a Constitution for the United States, and of amendments thereto, they constituted a General Government for special purposes,—delegated to that government certain definite powers, reserving, each State to itself, the residuary mass of right to their own self-government; and that whensoever the General Government assumes undelegated powers, its acts are unauthoritative, void, and of no force: that to this compact each State acceded as a State, and is an integral party, its co-States forming, as to itself, the other party: that the government created by this compact was not made the exclusive or final judge of the extent of the powers delegated to itself; since that would have made its discretion, and not the Constitution, the measure of its powers; but that, as in all other cases of compact among powers having no common judge, each party has an equal right to judge for itself, as well of infractions as of the mode and measure of redress.

[1] These resolutions in protest of the Alien and Sedition Laws were carried to Kentucky and adopted by its legislature, after minor amendment, in November 1798. Jefferson's authorship was a well-kept secret until 1821, when he disclosed the fact, and his original draft of the resolutions (the present text) was first published in 1832. [Ed.]

2. *Resolved,* That the Constitution of the United States, having delegated to Congress a power to punish treason, counterfeiting the securities and current coin of the United States, piracies, and felonies committed on the high seas, and offences against the law of nations, and no other crimes whatsoever; and it being true as a general principle, and one of the amendments to the Constitution having also declared, that "the powers not delegated to the United States by the Constitution, nor prohibited by it to the States, are reserved to the States respectively, or to the people," therefore the act of Congress, passed on the 14th day of July, 1798, and intituled "An Act in addition to the act intituled An Act for the punishment of certain crimes against the United States," as also the act passed by them on the — day of June, 1798, intituled "An Act to punish frauds committed on the bank of the United States," (and all their other acts which assume to create, define, or punish crimes, other than those so enumerated in the Constitution,) are altogether void, and of no force; and that the power to create, define, and punish such other crimes is reserved, and, of right, appertains solely and exclusively to the respective States, each within its own territory.

3. *Resolved,* That it is true as a general principle, and is also expressly declared by one of the amendments to the Constitution, that "the powers not delegated to the United States by the Constitution, nor prohibited by it to the States, are reserved to the States respectively, or to the people;" and that no power over the freedom of religion, freedom of speech, or freedom of the press being delegated to the United States by the Constitution, nor prohibited by it to the States, all lawful powers respecting the same did of right remain, and were reserved to the States or the people: that thus was manifested their determination to retain to themselves the right of judging how far the licentiousnes of speech and of the press may be abridged without lessening their useful freedom, and how far those

abuses which cannot be separated from their use should be tolerated, rather than the use be destroyed. And thus also they guarded against all abridgment by the United States of the freedom of religious opinions and exercises, and retained to themselves the right of protecting the same, as this State, by a law passed on the general demand of its citizens, had already protected them from all human restraint or interference. And that in addition to this general principle and express declaration, another and more special provision has been made by one of the amendments to the Constitution, which expressly declares, that "Congress shall make no law respecting an establishment of religion, or prohibiting the free exercise thereof, or abridging the freedom of speech or of the press:" thereby guarding in the same sentence, and under the same words, the freedom of religion, of speech, and of the press: insomuch, that whatever violated either, throws down the sanctuary which covers the others, and that libels, falsehood, and defamation, equally with heresy and false religion, are withheld from the cognizance of federal tribunals. That, therefore, the act of Congress of the United States, passed on the 14th day of July, 1798, intituled "An Act in addition to the act intituled An Act for the punishment of certain crimes against the United States," which does abridge the freedom of the press, is not law, but is altogether void, and of no force.

4. *Resolved,* That alien friends are under the jurisdiction and protection of the laws of the State wherein they are: that no power over them has been delegated to the United States, nor prohibited to the individual States, distinct from their power over citizens. And it being true as a general principle, and one of the amendments to the Constitution having also declared, that "the powers not delegated to the United States by the Constitution, nor prohibited by it to the States, are reserved to the States respectively, or to the people," the act of the Congress of the United States, passed on the — day of July, 1798, intituled

"An Act concerning aliens," which assumes powers over alien friends, not delegated by the Constitution, is not law, but is altogether void, and of no force.

5. *Resolved*, That in addition to the general principle, as well as the express declaration, that powers not delegated are reserved, another and more special provision, inserted in the Constitution from abundant caution, has declared that "the migration or importation of such persons as any of the States now existing shall think proper to admit, shall not be prohibited by the Congress prior to the year 1808;" that this commonwealth does admit the migration of alien friends, described as the subject of the said act concerning aliens: that a provision against prohibiting their migration, is a provision against all acts equivalent thereto, or it would be nugatory: that to remove them when migrated, is equivalent to a prohibition of their migration, and is, therefore, contrary to the said provision of the Constitution, and void.

6. *Resolved*, That the imprisonment of a person under the protection of the laws of this commonwealth, on his failure to obey the simple *order* of the President to depart out of the United States, as is undertaken by said act intituled "An Act concerning aliens," is contrary to the Constitution, one amendment to which has provided that "no person shall be deprived of liberty without due process of law;" and that another having provided that "in all criminal prosecutions the accused shall enjoy the right to public trial by an impartial jury, to be informed of the nature and cause of the accusation, to be confronted with the witnesses against him, to have compulsory process for obtaining witnesses in his favor, and to have the assistance of counsel for his defence," the same act, undertaking to authorize the President to remove a person out of the United States, who is under the protection of the law, on his own suspicion, without accusation, without jury, without public trial, without confrontation of the witnesses against him, without hearing witnesses in his favor, without defence, without counsel, is contrary to the

provision also of the Constitution, is therefore not law, but utterly void, and of no force: that transferring the power of judging any person, who is under the protection of the laws, from the courts to the President of the United States, as is undertaken by the same act concerning aliens, is against the article of the Constitution which provides that "the judicial power of the United States shall be vested in courts, the judges of which shall hold their offices during good behavior;" and that the said act is void for that reason also. And it is further to be noted, that this transfer of judiciary power is to that magistrate of the General Government who already possesses all the Executive, and a negative on all legislative powers.

7. *Resolved*, That the construction applied by the General Government (as is evidenced by sundry of their proceedings) to those parts of the Constitution of the United States which delegate to Congress a power "to lay and collect taxes, duties, imports, and excises, to pay the debts, and provide for the common defence and general welfare of the United States," and "to make all laws which shall be necessary and proper for carrying into execution the powers vested by the Constitution in the government of the United States, or in any department or officer thereof," goes to the destruction of all limits prescribed to their power by the Constitution: that words meant by the instrument to be subsidiary only to the execution of limited powers, ought not to be so construed as themselves to give unlimited powers, nor a part to be so taken as to destroy the whole residue of that instrument: that the proceedings of the General Government under color of these articles, will be a fit and necessary subject of revisal and correction, at a time of greater tranquillity, while those specified in the preceding resolutions call for immediate redress.

8th. *Resolved*, That a committee of conference and correspondence be appointed, who shall have in charge to communicate the preceding resolutions to the legislatures of the several States; to assure them that this commonwealth continues in the same esteem of their friendship and union which it has manifested from that moment at which a common danger first suggested a common union: that it considers union, for specified national purposes, and particularly to those specified in their late federal compact, to be friendly to the peace, happiness and prosperity of all the States: that faithful to that compact, according to the plain intent and meaning in which it was understood and acceded to by the several parties, it is sincerely anxious for its preservation: that it does also believe, that to take from the States all the powers of self-government and transfer them to a general and consolidated government, without regard to the special delegations and reservations solemnly agreed to in that compact, is not for the peace, happiness or prosperity of these States; and that therefore this commonwealth is determined, as it doubts not its co-States are, to submit to undelegated, and consequently unlimited powers in no man, or body of men on earth: that in cases of an abuse of the delegated powers, the members of the General government, being chosen by the people, a change by the people would be the constitutional remedy; but, where powers are assumed which have not been delegated, a nullification of the act is the rightful remedy: that every State has a natural right in cases not within the compact, (casus non fœderis,) to nullify of their own authority all assumptions of power by others within their limits: that without this right, they would be under the dominion, absolute and unlimited, of whosoever might exercise this right of judgment for them: that nevertheless, this commonwealth, from motives of regard and respect for its co-States, has wished to communicate with them on the subject: that with them alone it is proper to communicate, they alone being parties to the compact, and solely authorized to judge in the last resort of the powers exercised under it, Congress being not a party, but merely the creature of the compact, and subject as to its assumptions of power to the final judgment of those by whom, and for whose use itself and its powers were all created and modified: that if the acts before specified should stand, these conclusions would flow from them; that the General Government may place any act they think proper on the list of crimes, and punish it themselves whether enumerated or not enumerated by the Constitution as cognizable by them: that they may transfer its cognizance to the President, or any other person, who may himself be the accuser, counsel, judge and jury, whose *suspicions* may be the evidence, his *order* the sentence, his *officer* the executioner, and his breast the sole record of the transaction: that a very numerous and valuable description of the inhabitants of these States being, by this precedent, reduced, as outlaws, to the absolute dominion of one man, and the barrier of the Constitution thus swept away from us all, no rampart now remains against the passions and the powers of a majority in Congress to protect from a like exportation, or other more grievous punishment, the minority of the same body, the legislatures, judges, governors, and counsellors of the States, nor their other peaceable inhabitants, who may venture to reclaim the constitutional rights and liberties of the States and people, or who for other causes, good or bad, may be obnoxious to the views, or marked by the suspicions of the President, or be thought dangerous to his or their election, or other interests, public or personal: that the friendless alien has indeed been selected as the safest subject of a first experiment; but the citizen will soon follow, or rather, has already followed, for already has a sedition act marked him as its prey: that these and successive acts of the same character, unless arrested at the threshold, necessarily drive these States into revolution and blood, and will furnish new calumnies against republican government, and new pretexts for those who wish it to be believed that man cannot be governed but by a rod of iron: that it would be a dangerous delusion were a confidence in the men of our choice to silence our fears for the safety of our rights: that confidence is everywhere the parent of despotism—free government is founded in jealousy, and not in confidence;

it is jealousy and not confidence which prescribes limited constitutions, to bind down those whom we are obliged to trust with power: that our Constitution has accordingly fixed the limits to which, and no further, our confidence may go; and let the honest advocate of confidence read the alien and sedition acts, and say if the Constitution has not been wise in fixing limits to the government it created, and whether we should be wise in destroying those limits. Let him say what the government is, if it be not a tyranny, which the men of our choice have conferred on our President, and the President of our choice has assented to, and accepted over the friendly strangers to whom the mild spirit of our country and its laws have pledged hospitality and protection: that the men of our choice have more respected the bare *suspicions* of the President, than the solid right of innocence, the claims of justification, the sacred force of truth, and the forms and substance of law and justice. In questions of power, then, let no more be heard of confidence in man, but bind him down from mischief by the chains of the Constitution. That this commonwealth does therefore call on its co-States for an expression of their sentiments on the acts concerning aliens, and for the punishment of certain crimes herein before specified, plainly declaring whether these acts are or are not authorized by the federal compact. And it doubts not that their sense will be so announced as to prove their attachment unaltered to limited government, whether general or particular. And that the rights and liberties of their co-States will be exposed to no dangers by remaining embarked in a common bottom with their own. That they will concur with this commonwealth in considering the said acts as so palpably against the Constitution as to amount to an undisguised declaration that that compact is not meant to be the measure of the powers of the General Government, but that it will proceed in the exercise over these States, of all powers whatsoever: that they will view this as seizing the rights of the States, and consolidating them in the hands of the General Government, with a power assumed to bind the States, (not merely as the cases made federal, (casus fœderis,) but in all cases whatsoever, by laws made, not with their consent, but by others against their consent: that this would be to surrender the form of government we have chosen, and live under one deriving its powers from its own will, and not from our authority; and that the co-States, recurring to their natural right in cases not made federal, will concur in declaring these acts void, and of no force, and will each take measures of its own for providing that neither these acts, nor any others of the General Government not plainly and intentionally authorized by the Constitution, shall be exercised within their respective territories.

9th. *Resolved*, That the said committee be authorized to communicate by writing or personal conferences, at any times or places whatever, with any person or persons who may be appointed by any one or more co-States to correspond or confer with them; and that they lay their proceedings before the next session of Assembly.

First Inaugural Address[1]

March 4, 1801

Friends and Fellow Citizens:—

Called upon to undertake the duties of the first executive office of our country, I avail myself of the presence of that portion of my fellow citizens which is here assembled, to express my grateful thanks for the favor with which they have been pleased to look toward me, to declare a sincere consciousness that the task is above my talents, and that I approach it with those anxious and awful presentiments which the greatness of the charge and the weakness of my powers so justly inspire. A rising nation, spread over a wide and fruitful land, traversing all the seas with the rich productions of their industry, engaged in commerce with nations who feel power and forget right, advancing rapidly to destinies beyond the reach of mortal eye—when I contemplate these transcendent objects, and see the honor, the happiness, and the hopes of this beloved country committed to the issue and the auspices of this day, I shrink from the contemplation, and humble myself before the magnitude of the undertaking. Utterly indeed, should I despair, did not the presence of many whom I here see remind me, that in the other

[1] Jefferson wrote two earlier drafts of this address. He delivered the third and final one in the crowded Senate chamber of the Capitol, still uncompleted, and saw to its immediate publication in the *National Intelligencer*, in Washington, which was copied nationally. The text above follows this more or less official version. [Ed.]

high authorities provided by our constitution, I shall find resources of wisdom, of virtue, and of zeal, on which to rely under all difficulties. To you, then, gentlemen, who are charged with the sovereign functions of legislation, and to those associated with you, I look with encouragement for that guidance and support which may enable us to steer with safety the vessel in which we are all embarked amid the conflicting elements of a troubled world.

During the contest of opinion through which we have passed, the animation of discussion and of exertions has sometimes worn an aspect which might impose on strangers unused to think freely and to speak and to write what they think; but this being now decided by the voice of the nation, announced according to the rules of the constitution, all will, of course, arrange themselves under the will of the law, and unite in common efforts for the common good. All, too, will bear in mind this sacred principle, that though the will of the majority is in all cases to prevail, that will, to be rightful, must be reasonable; that the minority possess their equal rights, which equal laws must protect, and to violate which would be oppression. Let us, then, fellow citizens, unite with one heart and one mind. Let us restore to social intercourse that harmony and affection without which liberty and even life itself are but dreary things. And let us reflect that having banished from our land that religious intolerance under which mankind so long bled and suffered, we have yet gained little if we countenance a political intolerance as despotic, as wicked, and capable of as bitter and bloody persecutions. During the throes and convulsions of the ancient world, during the agonizing spasms of infuriated man, seeking through blood and slaughter his long-lost liberty, it was not wonderful that the agitation of the billows should reach even this distant and peaceful shore; that this should be more felt and feared by some and less by others; that this should divide opinions as to measures of safety. But every difference of opinion is not a difference of principle. We have called by different names brethren of the same principle. We are all republicans—we are all federalists. If there be any among us who would wish to dissolve this Union or to change its republican form, let them stand undisturbed as monuments of the safety with which error of opinion may be tolerated where reason is left free to combat it. I know, indeed, that some honest men fear that a republican government cannot be strong; that this government is not strong enough. But would the honest patriot, in the full tide of successful experiment, abandon a government which has so far kept us free and firm, on the theoretic and visionary fear that this government, the world's best hope, may by possibility want energy to preserve itself? I trust not. I believe this, on the contrary, the strongest government on earth. I believe it is the only one where every man, at the call of the laws, would fly to the standard of the law, and would meet invasions of the public order as his own personal concern. Sometimes it is said that man cannot be trusted with the government of himself. Can he, then, be trusted with the government of others? Or have we found angels in the forms of kings to govern him? Let history answer this question.

Let us, then, with courage and confidence pursue our own federal and republican principles, our attachment to our union and representative government. Kindly separated by nature and a wide ocean from the exterminating havoc of one quarter of the globe; too high-minded to endure the degradations of the others; possessing a chosen country, with room enough for our descendants to the thousandth and thousandth generation; entertaining a due sense of our equal right to the use of our own faculties, to the acquisitions of our industry, to honor and confidence from our fellow citizens, resulting not from birth but from our actions and their sense of them; enlightened by a benign religion, professed, indeed, and practiced in various forms, yet all of them including honesty, truth, temperance, gratitude, and the love of man; acknowledging and adoring an overruling Providence, which by all its dispensations proves that it delights in the happiness of man here and his greater happiness hereafter; with all these blessings, what more is necessary to make us a happy and prosperous people? Still one thing more, fellow citizens—a wise and frugal government, which shall restrain men from injuring one another, which shall leave them otherwise free to regulate their own pursuits of industry and improvement, and shall not take from the mouth of labor the bread it has earned. This is the sum of good government, and this is necessary to close the circle of our felicities.

About to enter, fellow citizens, on the exercise of duties which comprehend everything dear and valuable to you, it is proper that you should understand what I deem the essential principles of our government, and consequently those which ought to shape its administration. I will compress them within the narrowest compass they will bear, stating the general principle, but not all its limitations. Equal and exact justice to all men, of whatever state or persuasion, religious or political; peace, commerce, and honest friendship, with all nations—entangling alliances with none; the support of the state governments in all their rights, as the most competent administrations for our domestic concerns and the surest bulwarks against anti-republican tendencies; the preservation of the general government in its whole constitutional vigor, as the sheet anchor of our peace at home and safety abroad; a jealous care of the right of election by the people—a mild and safe corrective of abuses which are lopped by the sword of the revolution where peaceable remedies are unprovided; absolute acquiescence in the decisions of the majority—the vital principle of republics, from which there is no appeal but to force, the vital principle and immediate parent of despotism; a well-disciplined militia—our best reliance in peace and for the first moments of war, till regulars may relieve them; the supremacy of the civil over the military authority; economy in the public expense, that labor may be lightly burdened; the honest payment of our debts and sacred preservation of the public faith; encouragement of agriculture, and of commerce as its handmaid; the diffusion of information and the arraignment of all abuses at the bar of public reason; freedom of religion; freedom of the press; freedom of person under the protection of the *habeas corpus;* and trial by juries impartially selected—these principles form the bright constellation which has gone before us, and guided our steps through an age of revolution and reformation. The wisdom of our sages and the blood of our heroes have been devoted to their attainment. They should be the creed of our political faith—the text of civil instruction—the touchstone by which to try the services of those we trust; and should we wander from them in moments of error or alarm, let us hasten to retrace our steps and to regain the road which alone leads to peace, liberty, and safety.

I repair, then, fellow citizens, to the post you have assigned me. With experience enough in subordinate offices to have seen the difficulties of this, the greatest of all, I have learned to expect that it will rarely fall to the lot of imperfect man to retire from this station with the reputation and the favor which bring him into it. Without pretensions to that high confidence reposed in our first and great revolutionary character, whose preëminent services had entitled him to the first place in his country's love, and destined for him the fairest page in the volume of faithful history, I ask so much confidence only as may give firmness and effect to the legal administration of your affairs. I shall often go wrong through defect of judgment. When right, I shall often be thought wrong by those whose positions will not command a view of the whole ground. I ask your indulgence for my own errors, which will never be intentional; and your support against the errors of others, who may condemn what they would not if seen in all its parts. The approbation implied by your suffrage is a consolation to me for the past; and my future solicitude will be to retain the good opinion of those who have bestowed it in advance, to conciliate that of others by doing them all the good in my power, and to be instrumental to the happiness and freedom of all.

Relying, then, on the patronage of your good will, I advance with obedience to the work, ready to retire from it whenever you become sensible how much better choice it is in your power to make. And may that Infinite Power which rules the destinies of the universe, lead our councils to what is best, and give them a favorable issue for your peace and prosperity.

To Elias Shipman and Others, a Committee of the Merchants of New Haven[1]

Washington, July 12, 1801.

GENTLEMEN,—I have received the remonstrance you were pleased to address to me, on the appointment of Samuel Bishop to the office of collector of New Haven, lately vacated by the death of David Austin. The right of our fellow citizens to represent to the public functionaries their opinion on proceedings interesting to them, is unquestionably a constitutional right, often useful, sometimes necessary, and will always be respectfully acknoleged by me.

Of the various executive duties, no one excites more anxious concern than that of placing the interests of our fellow citizens in the hands of honest men, with understandings sufficient for their station. No duty, at the same time, is more difficult to fulfil. The knolege of characters possessed by a single individual is, of necessity, limited. To seek out the best through the whole Union, we must resort to other information, which, from the best of men,

1 This official letter, communicated to the press, is better known as "The Reply to the New Haven Remonstrance." New Haven's merchants were aroused by Jefferson's nomination of Samuel Bishop, a Republican, as collector of the port in place of Elizur Goodrich, one of President Adams' "midnight appointments" which Jefferson considered null. He seized the occasion for a public statement of his patronage policy. [Ed.]

acting disinterestedly and with the purest motives, is sometimes incorrect. In the case of Samuel Bishop, however, the subject of your remonstrance, time was taken, information was sought, & such obtained as could leave no room for doubt of his fitness. From private sources it was learnt that his understanding was sound, his integrity pure, his character unstained. And the offices confided to him within his own State, are public evidences of the estimation in which he is held by the State in general, and the city & township particularly in which he lives. He is said to be the town clerk, a justice of the peace, mayor of the city of New Haven, an office held at the will of the legislature, chief judge of the court of common pleas for New Haven county, a court of high criminal and civil jurisdiction wherein most causes are decided without the right of appeal or review, and sole judge of the court of probates, wherein he singly decides all questions of wills, settlement of estates, testate and intestate, appoints guardians, settles their accounts, and in fact has under his jurisdiction and care all the property real and personal of persons dying. The two last offices, in the annual gift of the legislature, were given to him in May last. Is it possible that the man to whom the legislature of Connecticut has so recently committed trusts of such difficulty & magnitude, is 'unfit to be the collector of the district of New Haven,' tho' acknoleged in the same writing, to have obtained all this confidence 'by a long life of usefulness?' It is objected, indeed, in the remonstrance, that he is 77 years of age; but at a much more advanced age, our Franklin was the ornament of human nature. He may not be able to perform in person, all the details of his office; but if he gives us the benefit of his understanding, his integrity, his watchfulness, and takes care that all the details are well performed by himself or his necessary assistants, all public purposes will be answered. The remonstrance, indeed, does not allege that the office *has been* illy conducted, but only apprehends that it *will be* so. Should this happen in event, be assured I will do in it what shall be just and necessary for the public service. In the meantime he should be tried without being prejudged.

The removal, as it is called, of Mr. Goodrich, forms another subject of complaint. Declarations by myself in favor of *political tolerance*, exhortations to *harmony* and affection in social intercourse, and to respect for the *equal rights* of the minority, have, on certain occasions, been quoted & misconstrued into assurances that the tenure of offices was to be undisturbed. But could candor apply such a construction? It is not indeed in the remonstrance that we find it; but it leads to the explanations which that calls for. When it is considered, that during the late administration, those who were not of a particular sect of politics were excluded from all office; when, by a steady pursuit of this measure, nearly the whole offices of the U S were monopolized by that sect; when the public sentiment at length declared itself, and burst open the doors of honor and confidence to those whose opinions they more approved, was it to be imagined that this monopoly of office was still to be continued in the hands of the minority? Does it violate their *equal rights*, to assert some rights in the majority also? Is it *political intolerance* to claim a proportionate share in the direction of the public affairs? Can they not *harmonize* in society unless they have everything in their own hands? If the will of the nation, manifested by their various elections, calls for an administration of government according with the opinions of those elected; if, for the fulfilment of that will, displacements are necessary, with whom can they so justly begin as with persons appointed in the last moments of an administration, not for its own aid, but to begin a career at the same time with their successors, by whom they had never been approved, and who could scarcely expect from them a cordial cooperation? Mr. Goodrich was one of these. Was it proper for him to place himself in office, without knowing whether those whose agent he was to be would have confidence in his agency? Can the preference of another, as the successor to Mr. Austin, be candidly called a removal of Mr. Goodrich? If a due participation of office is a matter of right, how are vacancies to be obtained? Those by death are few; by resignation, none. Can any other mode than that of removal be proposed? This is a painful office; but it is made my duty, and I meet it as such. I proceed in the operation with deliberation & inquiry, that it may injure the best men least, and effect the purposes of justice & public utility with the least private distress; that it may be thrown, as much as possible, on delinquency, on oppression, on intolerance, on incompetence, on ante-revolutionary adherence to our enemies.

The remonstrance laments "that a change in the administration must produce a change in the subordinate officers;" in other words, that it should be deemed necessary for all officers to think with their principal. But on whom does this imputation bear? On those who have excluded from office every shade of opinion which was not theirs? Or on those who have been so excluded? I lament sincerely that unessential differences of political opinion should ever have been deemed sufficient to interdict half the society from the rights and the blessings of self-government, to proscribe them as characters unworthy of every trust. It would have been to me a circumstance of great relief, had I found a moderate participation of office in the hands of the majority. I would gladly have left to time and accident to raise them to their just share. But their total exclusion calls for prompter correctives. I shall correct the procedure; but that done, disdain to follow it, shall return with joy to that state of things, when the only questions concerning a candidate shall be, is he honest? Is he capable? Is he faithful to the Constitution?

I tender you the homage of my high respect.

First Annual Message to Congress[1]

I lay before you the result of the census lately taken of our inhabitants, to a conformity with which we are to reduce the ensuing rates of representation and taxation. You will perceive that the increase of numbers during the last ten years, proceeding in geometrical ratio, promises a duplication in little more than twenty-two years. We contemplate this rapid growth, and the prospect it holds up to us, not with a view to the injuries it may enable us to do to others in some future day, but to the settlement of the extensive country still remaining vacant within our limits, to the multiplications of men susceptible of happiness, educated in the love of order, habituated to self-government, and valuing its blessings above all price.

Other circumstances, combined with the increase of numbers, have produced an augmentation of revenue arising from consumption, in a ratio far beyond that of population alone, and though the changes of foreign relations now taking place so desirably for the world, may for a season affect this branch of revenue, yet, weighing all probabilities of expense, as well as of income, there is

[1] Jefferson had no talent for public speaking and also believed that the practice of his predecessors of addressing Congress in person smacked too much of the monarch's speech from the throne. He communicated his "State of the Union" message in writing, thus setting a precedent that endured for more than a century. Only that part of the address primarily devoted to financial policy is given here. [Ed.]

reasonable ground of confidence that we may now safely dispense with all the internal taxes, comprehending excises, stamps, auctions, licenses, carriages, and refined sugars, to which the postage on newspapers may be added, to facilitate the progress of information, and that the remaining sources of revenue will be sufficient to provide for the support of government, to pay the interest on the public debts, and to discharge the principals in shorter periods than the laws or the general expectations had contemplated. War, indeed, and untoward events, may change this prospect of things, and call for expenses which the imposts could not meet; but sound principles will not justify our taxing the industry of our fellow citizens to accumulate treasure for wars to happen we know not when, and which might not perhaps happen but from the temptations offered by that treasure.

These views, however, of reducing our burdens, are formed on the expectation that a sensible, and at the same time a salutary reduction, may take place in our habitual expenditures. For this purpose those of the civil government, the army, and navy, will need revisal.

When we consider that this government is charged with the external and mutual relations only of these states; that the states themselves have principal care of our persons, our property, and our reputation, constituting the great field of human concerns, we may well doubt whether our organization is not too complicated, too expensive; whether offices and officers have not been multiplied unnecessarily, and sometimes injuriously to the service they were meant to promote. I will cause to be laid before you an essay toward a statement of those who, under public employment of various kinds, draw money from the treasury or from our citizens. . . . Considering the general tendency to multiply offices and dependencies, and to increase expense to the ultimate term of burden which the citizen can bear, it behooves us to avail ourselves of every occasion which presents itself for taking off the surcharge; that it never may be seen here that, after leaving to labor the smallest portion of its earnings on which it can subsist, government shall itself consume the residue of what it was instituted to guard.

In our care, too, of the public contributions intrusted to our direction, it would be prudent to multiply barriers against their dissipation, by appropriating specific sums to every specific purpose susceptible of definition; by disallowing all applications of money varying from the appropriation in object, or transcending it in amount; by reducing the undefined field of contingencies, and thereby circumscribing discretionary powers over money; and by bringing back to a single department all accountabilities for money where the examination may be prompt, efficacious, and uniform. . . .

To Nehemiah Dodge and Others, A Committee of the Danbury Baptist Association, in the State of Connecticut[1]

Washington, January 1, 1802

GENTLEMEN:—The affectionate sentiments of esteem and approbation which you are so good as to express towards me, on behalf of the Danbury Baptist Association, give me the highest satisfaction. My duties dictate a faithful and zealous pursuit of the interests of my constituents, and in proportion as they are persuaded of my fidelity to those duties, the discharge of them becomes more and more pleasing.

Believing with you that religion is a matter which lies solely between man and his God, that he owes account to none other for his faith or his worship, that the legislative powers of government reach actions only, and not opinions, I contemplate with sovereign reverence that act of the whole American people which declared that their legislature should "make no law respecting an establishment of religion, or prohibiting the free exercise thereof," thus building a wall of separation between Church and State. Adhering to this expression of the supreme will of the na-

---

[1] The Baptists were leaders in the struggle for religious liberty, which was far from finished in New England, and they admired Jefferson for his work in this cause. His letter to the Danbury Baptists is the *locus classicus* of the principle of "a wall of separation between Church and State." [Ed.]

tion in behalf of the rights of conscience, I shall see with sincere satisfaction the progress of those sentiments which tend to restore to man all his natural rights, convinced he has no natural right in opposition to his social duties.

I reciprocate your kind prayers for the protection and blessing of the common Father and Creator of man, and tender you for yourselves and your religious association, assurances of my high respect and esteem.

To Brother Handsome Lake[1]

Washington, November 3, 1802

BROTHER HANDSOME LAKE

I have received the message in writing which you sent me
through Captain Irvine, our confidential agent, placed near
you for the purpose of communicating and transacting between us, whatever may be useful for both nations. I am
happy to learn you have been so far favored by the divine
spirit as to be made sensible to those things which are for
your good and that of your people, and of those which are
harmful to you; and particularly that you see the ruinous
effects which the abuse of spirituous liquors have produced
upon them. It has weakened their bodies, enervated their
minds, exposed them to hunger, cold, nakedness, and poverty, kept them in perpetual broils, and reduced their population. I do not wonder, then, brother, at your censures,
not only on your own people, who have voluntarily gone
into these fatal habits, but on all the nations of white people who have supplied their calls for the article. But these
nations have done to you only what they do among themselves. They have sold what individuals wish to buy, leaving to every one to be the guardian of his own health and
happiness. Spirituous liquors are not in themselves bad.
They are often found to be an excellent medicine for the
sick. It is the improper and intemperate use of them, by

[1] Handsome Lake was a Seneca chief and prophet of a new
religion. Jefferson made scores of addresses to Indians, many of
them more ceremonial than this letter (a manuscript in his
papers) but all inculcating the same sentiments. [Ed.]

those in health, which makes them injurious. But as you find that your people cannot refrain from an ill use of them, I greatly applaud your resolution not to use them at all. We have too affectionate a concern for your happiness to place the paltry gain on the sale of these articles in competition with the injury they do you. And as it is the desire of your nation that no spirits should be sent among them, and I am authorized by the great council of the U. S. to prohibit them, I will sincerely cooperate with your wise men in any proper measures for this purpose which shall be agreeable to them.

You remind me, brother, of what I said to you, when you visited us last winter, that the lands you then held would remain yours, and should never go from you but when you should be disposed to sell. This I now repeat, and will ever abide by. We indeed are always ready to buy lands but we will never ask but when you wish to sell. And our laws, in order to protect you against impositions, have forbidden individuals to purchase lands from you, and have rendered it necessary, when you desire to sell, even to state, that an agent from the U.S. should attend the sale, see that your consent is freely given, a satisfactory price paid, and report to us what has been done, for our approbation. This was done in the late case of which you complain. The deputies of your nation came forward, in all the forms which we have been used to consider as evidence of the will of your nation. They proposed to sell to the state of New York certain parcels of land, of small extent, and detached from the body of your lands. The state of New York was desirous to buy. I sent an agent, in whom we could trust, to see that your nation was free, and the sale fair. All was reported to be free and fair. The lands were your property. The right to sell is one of the rights of property. To forbid you the exercise of that right would be wrong to your nation. Nor do I think, brother, that the sale of lands is, under all circumstances, injurious to your people. While they depended on hunting, the more extensive the forests around them, the more game they would yield. But, going into a state of agriculture, it may be advantageous to a society, as it is to an individual, who has more land than he can improve, to sell a part, and lay the money in stocks and implements of agriculture for the better improvement of the residue. A little land, well stocked and improved, will yield more than a great deal without stock or improvement. I hope therefore on further reflection you will see this transaction in a more favorable light, both as it concerns the interest of your nation, and the exercise of that superintending care which I am seriously anxious to employ for their subsistence and happiness. Go on then, brother, in the great reformation you have undertaken. Persuade our red brethren to be sober and to cultivate their lands, and their women to spin and weave for their families. You will soon see your women and children well fed and clothed, your men living happily in peace and plenty, and your numbers increasing from year to year. It will be a great glory to you to have been the instrument of so happy a change and your children's children, from generation to generation, will repeat your name with love and gratitude for ever. In all the enterprises for the good of your people, you may count with confidence on the aid and protection of the United States, and on the sincerity and zeal with which I am myself animated in the furthering of this humane work. You are our brethren of the same land: we wish to see your prosperity as brethren should do. Farewell.

Instructions to Captain Lewis[1]

[*June 20, 1803*]

To Captain Meriwether Lewis esq. Capt. of the 1st regimt. of Infantry of the U.S. of A.

Your situation as Secretary of the President of the U.S. has made you acquainted with the objects of my confidential message of Jan. 18, 1803 to the legislature; you have seen the act they passed, which, tho' expressed in general terms, was meant to sanction those objects, and you are appointed to carry them into execution.

Instruments for ascertaining, by celestial observations, the geography of the country through which you will pass, have been already provided. Light articles for barter and presents among the Indians, arms for your attendants, say for from 10. to 12. men, boats, tents, & other travelling apparatus, with ammunition, medicine, surgical instruments and provisions you will have prepared with such aids as the Secretary at War can yield in his department; & from him also you will receive authority to engage among our troops, by voluntary agreement, the number of attendants above mentioned, over whom you, as their commanding

1 Jefferson had known Lewis, a native of Albemarle, since his youth, had made him his private secretary in 1801, and then seen to his scientific education in Philadelphia in preparation for the Western expedition. These final instructions were written two weeks before Lewis left Washington for the Mississippi. The selection is taken from Donald Jackson, ed., *Letters of the Lewis and Clark Expedition* (Urbana, Ill., 1962). [Ed.]

officer, are invested with all the powers the laws give in such a case.

As your movements while within the limits of the U.S. will be better directed by occasional communications, adapted to circumstances as they arise, they will not be noticed here. What follows will respect your proceedings after your departure from the United states.

Your mission has been communicated to the ministers here from France, Spain & Great Britain, and through them to their governments; & such assurances given them as to it's objects, as we trust will satisfy them. The country [of Louisiana] having been ceded by Spain to France, the passport you have from the minister of France, the representative of the present sovereign of the country, will be a protection with all it's subjects; & that from the minister of England will entitle you to the friendly aid of any traders of that allegiance with whom you may happen to meet.

The object of your mission is to explore the Missouri river, & such principal stream of it, as, by it's course and communication with the waters of the Pacific ocean, whether the Columbia, Oregan, Colorado or any other river may offer the most direct & practicable water communication across this continent for the purposes of commerce.

Beginning at the mouth of the Missouri, you will take observations of latitude & longitude, at all remarkeable points on the river, & especially at the mouths of rivers, at rapids, at islands, & other places & objects distinguished by such natural marks & characters of a durable kind, as that they may with certainty be recognised hereafter. The courses of the river between these points of observation may be supplied by the compass the log-line & by time, corrected by the observations themselves. The variations of the compass too, in different places, should be noticed.

The interesting points of the portage between the heads of the Missouri, & of the water offering the best communication with the Pacific ocean, should also be fixed by observation, & the course of that water to the ocean, in the same manner as that of the Missouri.

Your observations are to be taken with great pains & accuracy, to be entered distinctly & intelligibly for others as well as yourself, to comprehend all the elements necessary, with the aid of the usual tables, to fix the latitude and longitude of the places at which they were taken, and are to be rendered to the war-office, for the purpose of having the calculations made concurrently by proper persons within the U.S. Several copies of these as well as of your other notes should be made at leisure times, & put into the care of the most trust-worthy of your attendants, to guard, by multiplying them, against the accidental losses to which they will be exposed. A further guard would be that one of these copies be on the paper of the birch, as less liable to injury from damp than common paper.

The commerce which may be carried on with the people inhabiting the line you will pursue, renders a knolege of those people important. You will therefore endeavor to make yourself acquainted, as far as a diligent pursuit of your journey shall admit, with the names of the nations & their numbers;

the extent & limits of their possessions;

their relations with other tribes of nations;

their language, traditions, monuments;

their ordinary occupations in agriculture, fishing, hunting, war, arts, & the implements for these;

their food, clothing, & domestic accommodations;

the diseases prevalent among them, & the remedies they use;

moral & physical circumstances which distinguish them from the tribes we know;

peculiarities in their laws, customs & dispositions;

and articles of commerce they may need or furnish, & to what extent.

And, considering the interest which every nation has in extending & strengthening the authority of reason & justice among the people around them, it will be useful to acquire

what knolege you can of the state of morality, religion, &
information among them; as it may better enable those who
may endeavor to civilize & instruct them, to adapt their
measures to the existing notions & practices of those on
whom they are to operate.

Other objects worthy of notice will be

the soil & face of the country, it's growth & vegetable
productions, especially those not of the U.S.

the animals of the country generally, & especially those
not known in the U.S.

the remains or accounts of any which may be deemed
rare or extinct;

the mineral productions of every kind; but more particularly metals, limestone, pit coal, & saltpetre; salines
& mineral waters, noting the temperature of the last,
& such circumstances as may indicate their character;

volcanic appearances;

climate, as characterised by the thermometer, by the
proportion of rainy, cloudy, & clear days, by lightning, hail, snow, ice, by the access & recess of frost,
by the winds prevailing at different seasons, the dates
at which particular plants put forth or lose their
flower, or leaf, times of appearance of particular birds,
reptiles or insects.

Altho' your route will be along the channel of the Missouri, yet you will endeavor to inform yourself, by enquiry, of the character & extent of the country watered
by it's branches, & especially on it's Southern side. The
North river or Rio Bravo which runs into the gulph of
Mexico, and the North river, or Rio colorado which runs
into the gulph of California, are understood to be the
principal streams heading opposite to the waters of the
Missouri, and running Southwardly. Whether the dividing
grounds between the Missouri & them are mountains or
flat lands, what are their distance from the Missouri, the
character of the intermediate country, & the people inhabiting it, are worthy of particular enquiry. The Northern waters of the Missouri are less to be enquired after,

because they have been ascertained to a considerable degree, & are still in a course of ascertainment by English traders, and travellers. But if you can learn any thing certain of the most Northern source of the Missisipi, & of it's position relatively to the lake of the woods, it will be interesting to us. Some account too of the path of the Canadian traders from the Missisipi, at the mouth of the Ouisconsing to where it strikes the Missouri, & of the soil and rivers in it's course, is desireable.

In all your intercourse with the natives, treat them in the most friendly & conciliatory manner which their own conduct will admit; allay all jealousies as to the object of your journey, satisfy them of it's innocence, make them acquainted with the position, extent, character, peaceable & commercial dispositions of the U.S., of our wish to be neighborly, friendly & useful to them, & of our dispositions to a commercial intercourse with them; confer with them on the points most convenient as mutual emporiums, and the articles of most desireable interchange for them & us. If a few of their influential chiefs, within practicable distance, wish to visit us, arrange such a visit with them, and furnish them with authority to call on our officers, on their entering the U.S. to have them conveyed to this place at the public expence. If any of them should wish to have some of their young people brought up with us, & taught such arts as may be useful to them, we will receive, instruct & take care of them. Such a mission, whether of influential chiefs or of young people, would give some security to your own party. Carry with you some matter of the kine-pox; inform those of them with whom you may be, of it's efficacy as a preservative from the smallpox; & instruct & encourage them in the use of it. This may be especially done wherever you winter.

As it is impossible for us to foresee in what manner you will be received by those people, whether with hospitality or hostility, so is it impossible to prescribe the exact degree of perseverance with which you are to pursue your journey. We value too much the lives of citizens to offer them to probable destruction. Your numbers will be sufficient to secure you against the unauthorised opposition of individuals or of small parties: but if a superior force, authorised, or not authorised, by a nation, should be arrayed against your further passage, and inflexibly determined to arrest it, you must decline it's farther pursuit, and return. In the loss of yourselves, we should lose also the information you will have acquired. By returning safely with that, you may enable us to renew the essay with better calculated means. To your own discretion therefore must be left the degree of danger you may risk, and the point at which you should decline, only saying we wish you to err on the side of your safety, and to bring back your party safe even if it be with less information.

As far up the Missouri as the white settlements extend, an intercourse will probably be found to exist between them & the Spanish posts of St. Louis opposite Cahokia, or Ste. Genevieve opposite Kaskaskia. From still further up the river, the traders may furnish a conveyance for letters. Beyond that, you may perhaps be able to engage Indians to bring letters for the government to Cahokia or Kaskaskia, on promising that they shall there receive such special compensation as you shall have stipulated with them. Avail yourself of these means to communicate to us, at seasonable intervals, a copy of your journal, notes & observations, of every kind, putting into cypher whatever might do injury if betrayed.

Should you reach the Pacific ocean inform yourself of the circumstances which may decide whether the furs of those parts may not be collected as advantageously at the head of the Missouri (convenient as is supposed to the waters of the Colorado & Oregan or Columbia) as at Nootka sound, or any other point of that coast; and that trade be consequently conducted through the Missouri & U.S. more beneficially than by the circumnavigation now practised.

On your arrival on that coast endeavor to learn if there be any port within your reach frequented by the sea-vessels of any nation, & to send two of your trusty people back by sea, in such way as shall appear practicable, with a copy of your notes: and should you be of opinion that the return of your party by the way they went will be eminently dangerous, then ship the whole, & return by sea, by the way either of cape Horn, or the cape of good Hope, as you shall be able. As you will be without money, clothes or provisions, you must endeavor to use the credit of the U.S. to obtain them, for which purpose open letters of credit shall be furnished you, authorising you to draw upon the Executive of the U.S. or any of it's officers, in any part of the world, on which draughts can be disposed of, & to apply with our recommendations to the Consuls, agents, merchants, or citizens of any nation with which we have intercourse, assuring them, in our name, that any aids they may furnish you, shall be honorably repaid, and on demand. Our consuls Thomas Hewes at Batavia in Java, Wm. Buchanan in the Isles of France & Bourbon & John Elmslie at the Cape of good Hope will be able to supply your necessities by draughts on us.

Should you find it safe to return by the way you go, after sending two of your party round by sea, or with your whole party, if no conveyance by sea can be found, do so; making such observations on your return, as may serve to supply, correct or confirm those made on your outward journey.

On re-entering the U.S. and reaching a place of safety, discharge any of your attendants who may desire & deserve it, procuring for them immediate paiment of all arrears of pay & cloathing which may have incurred since their departure, and assure them that they shall be recommended to the liberality of the legislature for the grant of a souldier's portion of land each, as proposed in my message to Congress; & repair yourself with your papers to the seat of government.

To provide, on the accident of your death, against anarchy, dispersion, & the consequent danger to your party, and total failure of the enterprize, you are hereby authorised, by any instrument signed & written in your own hand, to name the person among them who shall succeed to the command on your decease, and by like instruments to change the nomination from time to time as further experience of the characters accompanying you shall point out superior fitness: and all the powers and authorities given to yourself are, in the event of your death, transferred to, & vested in the successor so named, with further power to him, and his successors in like manner to name each his successor, who, on the death of his predecessor, shall be invested with all the powers & authorities given to yourself.

Given under my hand at the city of Washington this 20th day of June 1803.

Second Inaugural Address[1]

March 4, 1805

In the transaction of your foreign affairs, we have endeavored to cultivate the friendship of all nations, and especially of those with which we have the most important relations. We have done them justice on all occasions, favored where favor was lawful, and cherished mutual interests and intercourse on fair and equal terms. We are firmly convinced, and we act on that conviction, that with nations, as with individuals, our interests soundly calculated, will ever be found inseparable from our moral duties; and history bears witness to the fact, that a just nation is taken on its word, when recourse is had to armaments and wars to bridle others.

At home, fellow citizens, you best know whether we have done well or ill. The suppression of unnecessary offices, of useless establishments and expenses, enabled us to discontinue our internal taxes. These covering our land with officers, and opening our doors to their intrusions, had already begun that process of domiciliary vexation which, once entered, is scarcely to be restrained from reaching successively every article of produce and property. If among these taxes some minor ones fell which had

[1] The First Inaugural was *promise*, Jefferson said, while this one was a report on *performance*. The original draft was much bolder, but it was cautiously pruned and softened on the advice of his colleagues lest the address give unnecessary offense to the "anti-philosophers" of New England. The opening and the close have been omitted. [Ed.]

not been inconvenient, it was because their amount would not have paid the officers who collected them, and because, if they had any merit, the state authorities might adopt them, instead of others less approved.

The remaining revenue on the consumption of foreign articles, is paid cheerfully by those who can afford to add foreign luxuries to domestic comforts, being collected on our seaboards and frontiers only, and incorporated with the transactions of our mercantile citizens, it may be the pleasure and pride of an American to ask, what farmer, what mechanic, what laborer, ever sees a tax-gatherer of the United States? These contributions enable us to support the current expenses of the government, to fulfil contracts with foreign nations, to extinguish the native right of soil within our limits, to extend those limits, and to apply such a surplus to our public debts, as places at a short day their final redemption, and that redemption once effected, the revenue thereby liberated may, by a just repartition among the states, and a corresponding amendment of the constitution, be applied, *in time of peace*, to rivers, canals, roads, arts, manufactures, education, and other great objects within each state. *In time of war*, if injustice, by ourselves or others, must sometimes produce war, increased as the same revenue will be increased by population and consumption, and aided by other resources reserved for that crisis, it may meet within the year all the expenses of the year, without encroaching on the rights of future generations, by burdening them with the debts of the past. War will then be but a suspension of useful works, and a return to a state of peace, a return to the progress of improvement.

I have said, fellow citizens, that the income reserved had enabled us to extend our limits; but that extension may possibly pay for itself before we are called on, and in the meantime, may keep down the accruing interest; in all events, it will repay the advances we have made. I know that the acquisition of Louisiana has been disapproved by some, from a candid apprehension that the enlargement of our territory would endanger its union. But who can limit the extent to which the federative principle may operate effectively? The larger our association, the less will it be shaken by local passions; and in any view, is it not better that the opposite bank of the Mississippi should be settled by our own brethren and children, than by strangers of another family? With which shall we be most likely to live in harmony and friendly intercourse?

In matters of religion, I have considered that its free exercise is placed by the constitution independent of the powers of the general government. I have therefore undertaken, on no occasion, to prescribe the religious exercises suited to it; but have left them, as the constitution found them, under the direction and discipline of State or Church authorities acknowledged by the several religious societies.

The aboriginal inhabitants of these countries I have regarded with the commiseration their history inspires. Endowed with the faculties and the rights of men, breathing an ardent love of liberty and independence, and occupying a country which left them no desire but to be undisturbed, the stream of overflowing population from other regions directed itself on these shores; without power to divert, or habits to contend against, they have been overwhelmed by the current, or driven before it; now reduced within limits too narrow for the hunter's state, humanity enjoins us to teach them agriculture and the domestic arts; to encourage them to that industry which alone can enable them to maintain their place in existence, and to prepare them in time for that state of society, which to bodily comforts adds the improvement of the mind and morals. We have therefore liberally furnished them with the implements of husbandry and household use; we have placed among them instructors in the arts of first necessity; and they are covered with the ægis of the law against aggressors from among ourselves.

But the endeavors to enlighten them on the fate which awaits their present course of life, to induce them to exercise their reason, follow its dictates, and change their pursuits with the change of circumstances, have powerful obstacles to encounter; they are combated by the habits of their bodies, prejudice of their minds, ignorance, pride, and the influence of interested and crafty individuals among them, who feel themselves something in the present order of things, and fear to become nothing in any other. These persons inculcate a sanctimonious reverence for the customs of their ancestors; that whatsoever they did, must be done through all time; that reason is a false guide, and to advance under its counsel, in their physical, moral, or political condition, is perilous innovation; that their duty is to remain as their Creator made them, ignorance being safety, and knowledge full of danger; in short, my friends, among them is seen the action and counteraction of good sense and bigotry; they, too, have their anti-philosophers, who find an interest in keeping things in their present state, who dread reformation, and exert all their faculties to maintain the ascendency of habit over the duty of improving our reason, and obeying its mandates.

In giving these outlines, I do not mean, fellow citizens, to arrogate to myself the merit of the measures; that is due, in the first place, to the reflecting character of our citizens at large, who, by the weight of public opinion, influence and strengthen the public measures; it is due to the sound discretion with which they select from among themselves those to whom they confide the legislative duties; it is due to the zeal and wisdom of the characters thus selected, who lay the foundations of public happiness in wholesome laws, the execution of which alone remains for others; and it is due to the able and faithful auxiliaries, whose patriotism has associated with me in the executive functions.

During this course of administration, and in order to disturb it, the artillery of the press has been levelled against us, charged with whatsoever its licentiousness could devise or dare. These abuses of an institution so important to freedom and science, are deeply to be regretted, inasmuch as they tend to lessen its usefulness, and to sap its safety; they might, indeed, have been corrected by the wholesome punishments reserved and provided by the laws of the several States against falsehood and defamation; but public duties more urgent press on the time of public servants, and the offenders have therefore been left to find their punishment in the public indignation.

Nor was it uninteresting to the world, that an experiment should be fairly and fully made, whether freedom of discussion, unaided by power, is not sufficient for the propagation and protection of truth—whether a government, conducting itself in the true spirit of its constitution, with zeal and purity, and doing no act which it would be unwilling the whole world should witness, can be written down by falsehood and defamation. The experiment has been tried; you have witnessed the scene; our fellow citizens have looked on, cool and collected; they saw the latent source from which these outrages proceeded; they gathered around their public functionaries, and when the constitution called them to the decision by suffrage, they pronounced their verdict, honorable to those who had served them, and consolatory to the friend of man, who believes he may be intrusted with his own affairs.

No inference is here intended, that the laws, provided by the State against false and defamatory publications, should not be enforced; he who has time, renders a service to public morals and public tranquillity, in reforming these abuses by the salutary coercions of the law; but the experiment is noted, to prove that, since truth and reason have maintained their ground against false opinions in league with false facts, the press, confined to truth, needs no other legal restraint; the public judgment will correct false reasonings and opinions, on a full hearing of all parties; and no other definite line can be drawn between the inestimable liberty of the press and its demoralizing licentiousness. If there be still improprieties which this rule would not restrain, its supplement must be sought in the censorship of public opinion.

Contemplating the union of sentiment now manifested

so generally, as auguring harmony and happiness to our future course, I offer to our country sincere congratulations. With those, too, not yet rallied to the same point, the disposition to do so is gaining strength; facts are piercing through the veil drawn over them; and our doubting brethren will at length see, that the mass of their fellow citizens, with whom they cannot yet resolve to act, as to principles and measures, think as they think, and desire what they desire; that our wish, as well as theirs, is, that the public efforts may be directed honestly to the public good, that peace be cultivated, civil and religious liberty unassailed, law and order preserved, equality of rights maintained, and that state of property, equal or unequal, which results to every man from his own industry, or that of his fathers. When satisfied of these views, it is not in human nature that they should not approve and support them; in the meantime, let us cherish them with patient affection; let us do them justice, and more than justice, in all competitions of interest; and we need not doubt that truth, reason, and their own interests, will at length prevail, will gather them into the fold of their country, and will complete their entire union of opinion, which gives to a nation the blessing of harmony, and the benefit of all its strength. . . .

Fifth Annual Message to Congress[1]

December 3, 1805

Since our last meeting the aspect of our foreign relations has considerably changed. Our coasts have been infested and our harbors watched by private armed vessels, some of them without commissions, some with illegal commissions, others with those of legal form but committing piratical acts beyond the authority of their commissions. They have captured in the very entrance of our harbors, as well as on the high seas, not only the vessels of our friends coming to trade with us, but our own also. They have carried them off under pretence of legal adjudication, but not daring to approach a court of justice, they have plundered and sunk them by the way, or in obscure places where no evidence could arise against them; maltreated the crews, and abandoned them in boats in the open sea or on desert shores without food or covering. These enormities appearing to be unreached by any control of their sovereigns, I found it necessary to equip a force to cruise within our own seas, to arrest all vessels of these descriptions found hovering on our coast within the limits of the Gulf Stream, and to bring the offenders in for trial as pirates.

The same system of hovering on our coasts and harbors under color of seeking enemies, has been also carried on by

[1] The message was primarily concerned with foreign affairs. Interpreted by some as "warlike," it set the administration's direction in both foreign and defense policy. Only the more significant passages are printed here. [Ed.]

public armed ships, to the great annoyance and oppression of our commerce. New principles, too, have been inter-loped into the law of nations, founded neither in justice nor the usage or acknowledgment of nations. According to these, a belligerent takes to himself a commerce with its own enemy which it denies to a neutral, on the ground of its aiding that enemy in the war. But reason revolts at such an inconsistency, and the neutral having equal right with the belligerent to decide the question, the interest of our constituents and the duty of maintaining the authority of reason, the only umpire between just nations, impose on us the obligation of providing an effectual and determined opposition to a doctrine so injurious to the rights of peaceable nations. Indeed, the confidence we ought to have in the justice of others, still countenances the hope that a sounder view of those rights will of itself induce from every belligerent a more correct observance of them. . . .

In reviewing these injuries from some of the belligerent powers, the moderation, the firmness, and the wisdom of the legislature will be all called into action. We ought still to hope that time and a more correct estimate of interest, as well as of character, will produce the justice we are bound to expect. But should any nation deceive itself by false calculations, and disappoint that expectation, we must join in the unprofitable contest of trying which party can do the other the most harm. Some of these injuries may perhaps admit a peaceable remedy. Where that is competent it is always the most desirable. But some of them are of a nature to be met by force only, and all of them may lead to it. I cannot, therefore, but recommend such preparations as circumstances call for. The first object is to place our seaport towns out of the danger of insult. Measures have been already taken for furnishing them with heavy cannon for the service of such land batteries as may make a part of their defence against armed vessels approaching them. In aid of these it is desirable that we should have a competent number of gun-boats; and the number, to be competent, must be considerable. If immediately begun, they may be in readiness for service at the opening of the next season. Whether it will be necessary to augment our land forces will be decided by occurrences probably in the course of your session. In the meantime, you will consider whether it would not be expedient, for a state of peace as well as of war, so to organize or class the militia as would enable us, on a sudden emergency, to call for the services of the younger portions, unencumbered with the old and those having families. Upward of three hundred thousand able-bodied men, between the ages of eighteen and twenty-six years, which the last census shows we may now count within our limits, will furnish a competent number for offence or defence in any point where they may be wanted, and will give time for raising regular forces after the necessity of them shall become certain; and the reducing to the early period of life all its active service cannot but be desirable to our younger citizens, of the present as well as future times, inasmuch as it engages to them in more advanced age a quiet and undisturbed respose in the bosom of their families. I cannot, then, but earnestly recommend to your early consideration the expediency of so modifying our militia system as, by a separation of the more active part from that which is less so, we may draw from it, when necessary, an efficient corps fit for real and active service, and to be called to it in regular rotation. . . .

Sixth Annual Message to Congress[1]

December 2, 1806

The duties composing the Mediterranean fund will cease by law at the end of the present season. Considering, however, that they are levied chiefly on luxuries, and that we have an impost on salt, a necessary of life, the free use of which otherwise is so important, I recommend to your consideration the suppression of the duties on salt, and the continuation of the Mediterranean fund, instead thereof, for a short time, after which that also will become unnecessary for any purpose now within contemplation.

When both of these branches of revenue shall in this way be relinquished, there will still ere long be an accumulation of moneys in the treasury beyond the instalments of public debt which we are permitted by contract to pay. They cannot, then, without a modification assented to by the public creditors, be applied to the extinguishment of this debt, and the complete liberation of our revenues—the most desirable of all objects; nor, if our peace continues, will they be wanting for any other existing purpose. The question, therefore, now comes forward,

[1] The message proposed a new departure in domestic policy. With a bulging treasury surplus and debt retirement proceeding on schedule, despite the outlay for Louisiana, Jefferson called upon Congress to turn its attention to internal improvements, which might have been done but for the deepening crisis with Britain. Only this part of the message is given here. The Mediterranean fund, from a surcharge on imports, had been established to finance the Barbary campaign now completed. [Ed.]

—to what other objects shall these surpluses be appropriated, and the whole surplus of impost, after the entire discharge of the public debt, and during those intervals when the purposes of war shall not call for them? Shall we suppress the impost and give that advantage to foreign over domestic manufactures? On a few articles of more general and necessary use, the suppression in due season will doubtless be right, but the great mass of the articles on which impost is paid is foreign luxuries, purchased by those only who are rich enough to afford themselves the use of them. Their patriotism would certainly prefer its continuance and application to the great purposes of the public education, roads, rivers, canals, and such other objects of public improvement as it may be thought proper to add to the constitutional enumeration of federal powers. By these operations new channels of communication will be opened between the States; the lines of separation will disappear, their interests will be identified, and their union cemented by new and indissoluble ties. Education is here placed among the articles of public care, not that it would be proposed to take its ordinary branches out of the hands of private enterprise, which manages so much better all the concerns to which it is equal; but a public institution can alone supply those sciences which, though rarely called for, are yet necessary to complete the circle, all the parts of which contribute to the improvement of the country, and some of them to its preservation. The subject is now proposed for the consideration of Congress, because, if approved by the time the State legislatures shall have deliberated on this extension of the federal trusts, and the laws shall be passed, and other arrangements made for their execution, the necessary funds will be on hand and without employment. I suppose an amendment to the Constitution, by consent of the States, necessary, because the objects now recommended are not among those enumerated in the Constitution, and to which it permits the public moneys to be applied.

The present consideration of a national establishment

for education, particularly, is rendered proper by this circumstance also, that if Congress, approving the proposition, shall yet think it more eligible to found it on a donation of lands, they have it now in their power to endow it with those which will be among the earliest to produce the necessary income. This foundation would have the advantage of being independent on war, which may suspend other improvements by requiring for its own purposes the resources destined for them. . . .

To the Society of Tammany,
or Columbian Order No. 1,
of the City of New York[1]

Washington, February 16, 1808

I have received your address, fellow citizens, and, thankful for the expressions so personally gratifying to myself, I contemplate with high satisfaction the ardent spirit it breathes of love to our country, and of devotion to its liberty and independence. The crisis in which it is placed, cannot but be unwelcome to those who love peace, yet spurn at a tame submission to wrong. So fortunately remote from the theatre of European contests, and carefully avoiding to implicate ourselves in them, we had a right to hope for an exemption from the calamities which have afflicted the contending nations, and to be permitted unoffendingly to pursue paths of industry and peace.

But the ocean, which, like the air, is the common birthright of mankind, is arbitrarily wrested from us, and maxims consecrated by time, by usage, and by an universal sense of right, are trampled on by superior force. To give time for this demoralizing tempest to pass over, one measure only remained which might cover our beloved country from its overwhelming fury: an appeal to the deliberate understanding of our fellow citizens in a cessa-

[1] Of the many brief addresses Jefferson wrote in explanation or defense of the embargo, this is one of the most eloquent. [Ed.]

tion of all intercourse with the belligerent nations, until it can be resumed under the protection of a returning sense of the moral obligations which constitute a law for nations as well as individuals. There can be no question, in a mind truly American, whether it is best to send our citizens and property into certain captivity, and then wage war for their recovery, or to keep them at home, and to turn seriously to that policy which plants the manufacturer and the husbandman side by side, and establishes at the door of every one that exchange of mutual labors and comforts, which we have hitherto sought in distant regions, and under perpetual risk of broils with them. Between these alternatives your address has soundly decided, and I doubt not your aid, and that of every real and faithful citizen, towards carrying into effect the measures of your country, and enforcing the sacred principle, that in opposing foreign wrong there must be but one mind.

I receive with sensibility your kind prayers for my future happiness, and I supplicate a protecting Providence to watch over your own and our country's freedom and welfare.

To the Inhabitants of Albemarle County, in Virginia[1]

April 3, 1809.

Returning to the scenes of my birth and early life, to the
society of those with whom I was raised, and who have
been ever dear to me, I receive, fellow citizens and neighbors, with inexpressible pleasure, the cordial welcome you
are so good as to give me. Long absent on duties which
the history of a wonderful era made incumbent on those
called to them, the pomp, the turmoil, the bustle and
splendor of office, have drawn but deeper sighs for the
tranquil and irresponsible occupations of private life, for
the enjoyment of an affectionate intercourse with you, my
neighbors and friends, and the endearments of family love,
which nature has given us all, as the sweetener of every
hour. For these I gladly lay down the distressing burthen
of power, and seek, with my fellow citizens, repose and
safety under the watchful cares, the labors, and perplexi-
ties of younger and abler minds. The anxieties you express
to administer to my happiness, do, of themselves, confer
that happiness; and the measure will be complete, if my
endeavors to fulfil my duties in the several public stations
to which I have been called, have obtained for me the
approbation of my country. The part which I have acted

[1] Jefferson was deluged with congratulatory addresses upon
his retirement. Not long after he returned home, his friends
and neighbors sent him a formal welcome, to which he made
this reply. [Ed.]

on the theatre of public life, has been before them; and to their sentence I submit it; but the testimony of my native country, of the individuals who have known me in private life, to my conduct in its various duties and relations, is the more grateful, as proceeding from eye witnesses and observers, from triers of the vicinage. Of you, then, my neighbors, I may ask, in the face of the world, "whose ox have I taken, or whom have I defrauded? Whom have I oppressed, or of whose hand have I received a bribe to blind mine eyes therewith?" On your verdict I rest with conscious security. Your wishes for my happiness are received with just sensibility, and I offer sincere prayers for your own welfare and prosperity.

Report of the Commissioners for the University of Virginia[1]

[*August 4, 1818*]

2. The Board having thus agreed on a proper site for the University, to be reported to the Legislature, proceed to the second of the duties assigned to them—that of proposing a plan for its buildings—and they are of opinion that it should consist of distinct houses or pavilions, arranged at proper distances on each side of a lawn of a proper breadth, and of indefinite extent, in one direction, at least; in each of which should be a lecturing room, with from two to four apartments, for the accommodation of a professor and his family; that these pavilions should be united by a range of dormitories, sufficient each for the accommodation of two students only, this provision being deemed advantageous to morals, to order, and to uninterrupted study; and that a passage of some kind, under cover from the weather, should give a communication along the whole range. It is supposed that such pavilions, on an average of the larger and smaller, will cost each about $5000; each dormitory about $350, and hotels of a

---

[1] The commission appointed by the governor to choose the site and develop a plan for the University of Virginia met in a tavern at Rockfish Gap on the Blue Ridge, August 1–4, 1818. Jefferson chaired the meeting and wrote the Report. It is perhaps the best comprehensive statement of his educational philosophy. The commissioners chose Central College, near Charlottesville, as the site (this first recommendation of the Report is omitted here) and went on to other matters. [Ed.]

single room, for a refectory, and two rooms for the tenant, necessary for dieting the students, will cost about $3500 each. The number of these pavilions will depend on the number of professors, and that of the dormitories and hotels on the number of students to be lodged and dieted. The advantages of this plan are: greater security against fire and infection; tranquillity and comfort to the professors and their families thus insulated; retirement to the students; and the admission of enlargement to any degree to which the institution may extend in future times. It is supposed probable, that a building of somewhat more size in the middle of the grounds may be called for in time, in which may be rooms for religious worship, under such impartial regulations as the Visitors shall prescribe, for public examinations, for a library, for the schools of music, drawing, and other associated purposes.

3, 4. In proceeding to the third and fourth duties prescribed by the Legislature, of reporting "the branches of learning, which should be taught in the University, and the number and description of the professorships they will require," the Commissioners were first to consider at what point it was understood that university education should commence? Certainly not with the alphabet, for reasons of expediency and impracticability, as well from the obvious sense of the Legislature, who, in the same act, make other provision for the primary instruction of the poor children, expecting, doubtless, that in other cases it would be provided by the parent, or become, perhaps, subject of future and further attention of the Legislature. The objects of this primary education determine its character and limits. These objects would be,

To give to every citizen the information he needs for the transaction of his own business;

To enable him to calculate for himself, and to express and preserve his ideas, his contracts and accounts, in writing;

To improve, by reading, his morals and faculties;

To understand his duties to his neighbors and country,

and to discharge with competence the functions confided to him by either;

To know his rights; to exercise with order and justice those he retains; to choose with discretion the fiduciary of those he delegates; and to notice their conduct with diligence, with candor, and judgment;

And, in general, to observe with intelligence and faithfulness all the social relations under which he shall be placed.

To instruct the mass of our citizens in these, their rights, interests and duties, as men and citizens, being then the objects of education in the primary schools, whether private or public, in them should be taught reading, writing and numerical arithmetic, the elements of mensuration, (useful in so many callings,) and the outlines of geography and history. And this brings us to the point at which are to commence the higher branches of education, of which the Legislature require the development; those, for example, which are,

To form the statesmen, legislators and judges, on whom public prosperity and individual happiness are so much to depend;

To expound the principles and structure of government, the laws which regulate the intercourse of nations, those formed municipally for our own government, and a sound spirit of legislation, which, banishing all arbitrary and unnecessary restraint on individual action, shall leave us free to do whatever does not violate the equal rights of another;

To harmonize and promote the interests of agriculture, manufactures and commerce, and by well informed views of political economy to give a free scope to the public industry;

To develop the reasoning faculties of our youth, enlarge their minds, cultivate their morals, and instill into them the precepts of virtue and order;

To enlighten them with mathematical and physical sciences, which advance the arts, and administer to the health, the subsistence, and comforts of human life;

And, generally, to form them to habits of reflection and correct action, rendering them examples of virtue to others, and of happiness within themselves.

These are the objects of that higher grade of education, the benefits and blessings of which the Legislature now propose to provide for the good and ornament of their country, the gratification and happiness of their fellow-citizens, of the parent especially, and his progeny, on which all his affections are concentrated.

In entering on this field, the Commissioners are aware that they have to encounter much difference of opinion as to the extent which it is expedient that this institution should occupy. Some good men, and even of respectable information, consider the learned sciences as useless acquirements; some think that they do not better the condition of man; and others that education, like private and individual concerns, should be left to private individual effort; not reflecting that an establishment embracing all the sciences which may be useful and even necessary in the various vocations of life, with the buildings and apparatus belonging to each, are far beyond the reach of individual means, and must either derive existence from public patronage, or not exist at all. This would leave us, then, without those callings which depend on education, or send us to other countries to seek the instruction they require. But the Commissioners are happy in considering the statute under which they are assembled as proof that the Legislature is far from the abandonment of objects so interesting. They are sensible that the advantages of well-directed education, moral, political and economical, are truly above all estimate. Education generates habits of application, of order, and the love of virtue; and controls, by the force of habit, any innate obliquities in our moral organization. We should be far, too, from the discouraging persuasion that man is fixed, by the law of his nature, at a given point; that his improvement is a chimera, and the hope delusive of rendering ourselves wiser, happier or better than our forefathers were. As well might it be urged that the wild and uncultivated tree, hitherto yielding sour and bitter fruit only, can never be made to yield better; yet we know that the grafting art implants a new tree on the savage stock, producing what is most estimable both in kind and degree. Education, in like manner, engrafts a new man on the native stock, and improves what in his nature was vicious and perverse into qualities of virtue and social worth. And it cannot be but that each generation succeeding to the knowledge acquired by all those who preceded it, adding to it their own acquisitions and discoveries, and handing the mass down for successive and constant accumulation, must advance the knowledge and well-being of mankind, not *infinitely*, as some have said, but *indefinitely*, and to a term which no one can fix and foresee. Indeed, we need look back half a century, to times which many now living remember well, and see the wonderful advances in the sciences and arts which have been made within that period. Some of these have rendered the elements themselves subservient to the purposes of man, have harnessed them to the yoke of his labors, and effected the great blessings of moderating his own, of accomplishing what was beyond his feeble force, and extending the comforts of life to a much enlarged circle, to those who had before known its necessaries only. That these are not the vain dreams of sanguine hope, we have before our eyes real and living examples. What, but education, has advanced us beyond the condition of our indigenous neighbors? And what chains them to their present state of barbarism and wretchedness, but a bigotted veneration for the supposed superlative wisdom of their fathers, and the preposterous idea that they are to look backward for better things, and not forward, longing, as it should seem, to return to the days of eating acorns and roots, rather than indulge in the degeneracies of civilization? And how much more encouraging to the achievements of science and improvement is this, than the desponding view that the condition of man cannot be ameliorated, that what has been must ever be, and that to secure ourselves where we are, we must tread with awful reverence in the footsteps of our fathers. This doctrine is the genuine fruit of the alliance between Church and State; the tenants of which, finding themselves but too well in their present condition, oppose all advances which might unmask their usurpations, and monopolies of honors, wealth, and power, and fear every change, as endangering the comforts they now hold. Nor must we omit to mention, among the benefits of education, the incalculable advantage of training up able counsellors to administer the affairs of our country in all its departments, legislative, executive and judiciary, and to bear their proper share in the councils of our national government; nothing more than education advancing the prosperity, the power, and the happiness of a nation.

Encouraged, therefore, by the sentiments of the Legislature, manifested in this statute, we present the following tabular statement of the branches of learning which we think should be taught in the University, forming them into groups, each of which are within the powers of a single professor:

I. Languages, ancient:
   Latin,
   Greek,
   Hebrew.

II. Languages, modern:
   French,
   Spanish,
   Italian,
   German,
   Anglo-Saxon.

III. Mathematics, pure:
   Algebra,
   Fluxions,

Geometry, Elementary, Transcendental.
Architecture, Military, Naval.

IV. Physico-Mathematics:
Mechanics,
Statics,
Dynamics,
Pneumatics,
Acoustics,
Optics,
Astronomy,
Geography.

V. Physics, or Natural Philosophy:
Chemistry,
Mineralogy.

VI. Botany,
Zoology.

VII. Anatomy,
Medicine.

VIII. Government,
Political Economy,
Law of Nature and Nations,
History, being interwoven with Politics and Law.

IX. Law, municipal.

X. Ideology,
General Grammar,
Ethics,
Rhetoric,
Belles Lettres, and the fine arts.

Some of the terms used in this table being subject to a difference of acceptation, it is proper to define the meaning and comprehension intended to be given them here:

Geometry, Elementary, is that of straight lines and of the circle. Transcendental, is that of all other curves; it includes, of course, *Projectiles*, a leading branch of the military art. Military Architecture includes Fortification, another branch of that art.

Statics respect matter generally, in a state of rest, and include Hydrostatics, or the laws of fluids particularly, at rest or in equilibrio.

Dynamics, used as a general term, include

Dynamics proper, or the laws of *solids* in motion; and
Hydrodynamics, or Hydraulics, those of *fluids* in motion.

Pneumatics teach the theory of air, its weight, motion, condensation, rarefaction, &c.

Acoustics, or Phonics, the theory of sound.

Optics, the laws of light and vision.

Physics, or Physiology, in a general sense, mean the doctrine of the physical objects of our senses.

Chemistry is meant, with its other usual branches, to comprehend the theory of agriculture.

Mineralogy, in addition to its peculiar subjects, is here understood to embrace what is real in geology.

Ideology is the doctrine of thought.

General Grammar explains the construction of language.

Some articles in this distribution of sciences will need observation. A professor is proposed for ancient languages, the Latin, Greek, and Hebrew, particularly; but these languages being the foundation common to all the sciences, it is difficult to foresee what may be the extent of this school. At the same time, no greater obstruction to industrious study could be proposed than the presence, the intrusions and the noisy turbulence of a multitude of small boys; and if they are to be placed here for the rudiments of the languages, they may be so numerous that its character and value as an University will be merged in those of a Grammar school. It is therefore, greatly to be wished, that preliminary schools, either on private or public establishment, could be distributed in districts through the State, as preparatory to the entrance of students into the University. The tender age at which this part of education commences, generally about the tenth year, would weigh heavily with parents in sending their sons to a school so distant as the central establishment would be from most of them. Districts of such extent as that every parent should be within a day's journey of his son at school, would be desirable in cases of sickness, and convenient for supplying their ordinary wants, and might be made to lessen sensibly the expense of this part of their education. And where a sparse population would not, within such a compass, furnish subjects sufficient to maintain a school, a competent enlargement of district must, of necessity, there be submitted to. At these district schools or colleges, boys should be rendered able to read the easier authors, Latin and Greek. This would be useful and sufficient for many not intended for an University education. At these, too, might be taught English grammar, the higher branches of numerical arithmetic, the geometry of straight lines and of the circle, the elements of navigation, and geography to a sufficient degree, and thus afford to greater numbers the means of being qualified for the various vocations of life, needing more instruction than merely menial or prædial labor, and the same advantages to youths whose education may have been neglected until too late to lay a foundation in the learned languages. These institutions, intermediate between the primary schools and University, might then be the passage of entrance for youths into the University, where their classical learning might be critically completed, by a study of the authors of highest degree; and it is at this stage only that they should be received at the University. Giving then a portion of their time to a finished knowledge of the Latin and Greek, the rest might be appropriated to the modern languages, or to the commencement of the course of science for which they should be destined. This would generally be about the fifteenth year of their age, when they might go with more safety and contentment to that distance from their parents. Until this preparatory provision shall be made, either the University will be overwhelmed with the grammar school, or a separate establishment, under one or more ushers, for its lower classes, will be advisable, at a mile or two distant from the general one; where, too, may be exercised the stricter government necessary for young boys, but unsuitable for youths arrived at years of discretion.

The considerations which have governed the specification of languages to be taught by the professor of modern languages were, that the French is the language of general intercourse among nations, and as a depository of human science, is unsurpassed by any other language, living or dead; that the Spanish is highly interesting to us, as the language spoken by so great a portion of the inhabitants of our continents, with whom we shall probably have great intercourse ere long, and is that also in which is written the greater part of the earlier history of America. The Italian abounds with works of very superior order, valuable for their matter, and still more distinguished as models of the finest taste in style and composition. And the German now stands in a line with that of the most learned nations in richness of erudition and advance in the sciences. It is too of common descent with the language of our own country, a branch of the same original Gothic stock, and furnishes valuable illustrations for us. But in this point of view, the Anglo-Saxon is of peculiar value. We have placed it among the modern languages, because it is in fact that which we speak, in the earliest form in which we have knowledge of it. It has been undergoing, with time, those gradual changes which all languages, ancient and modern, have experienced; and even now needs only to be printed in the modern character and orthography to be intelligible, in a considerable degree, to an English reader. It has this value, too, above the Greek and Latin, that while it gives the radix of the mass of our language, they explain its innovations only. Obvious proofs of this have been presented to the modern reader in the disquisitions of Horn Tooke[2]; and Fortescue Aland[3] has well explained the great instruction which may be derived from it to a full understanding of our ancient common law, on which, as a stock, our whole system of law is engrafted. It will form the first link in the chain of an historical review of our language through all its successive changes to the present day, will constitute the foundation of that critical instruction in it which ought to be found in a seminary of general learning, and thus reward amply the few weeks of attention which would alone be requisite for its attainment; a language already fraught with all the eminent science of our parent country, the future vehicle of whatever we may ourselves achieve, and destined to occupy so much space on the globe, claims distinguished attention in American education.

Medicine, where fully taught, is usually subdivided into several professorships, but this cannot well be without the accessory of an hospital, where the student can have the benefit of attending clinical lectures, and of assisting at operations of surgery. With this accessory, the seat of our University is not yet prepared, either by its population or by the numbers of poor who would leave their own houses, and accept of the charities of an hospital. For the present, therefore, we propose but a single professor for both medicine and anatomy. By him the medical science may be taught, with a history and explanations of all its successive theories from Hippocrates to the present day; and anatomy may be fully treated. Vegetable pharmacy will make a part of the botanical course, and mineral and chemical pharmacy of those of mineralogy and chemistry.

[2] John Horne Tooke, English philologist, author of *The Diversions of Purley* (1786–1805). [Ed.]

[3] Sir John Fortescue Aland, whose eighteenth-century edition of his ancestor's *The Difference between Absolute and Limited Monarchy* contained a plea for the study of the Saxon language. [Ed.]

This degree of medical information is such as the mass of scientific students would wish to possess, as enabling them in their course through life, to estimate with satisfaction the extent and limits of the aid to human life and health, which they may understandingly expect from that art; and it constitutes such a foundation for those intended for the profession, that the finishing course of practice at the bed-sides of the sick, and at the operations of surgery in a hospital, can neither be long nor expensive. To seek this finishing elsewhere, must therefore be submitted to for a while.

In conformity with the principles of our Constitution, which places all sects of religion on an equal footing, with the jealousies of the different sects in guarding that equality from encroachment and surprise, and with the sentiments of the Legislature in favor of freedom of religion, manifested on former occasions, we have proposed no professor of divinity; and the rather as the proofs of the being of a God, the creator, preserver, and supreme ruler of the universe, the author of all the relations of morality, and of the laws and obligations these infer, will be within the province of the professor of ethics to which adding the developments of these moral obligations, of those in which all sects agree, with a knowledge of the languages, Hebrew, Greek, and Latin, a basis will be formed common to all sects. Proceeding thus far without offence to the Constitution, we have thought it proper at this point to leave every sect to provide, as they think fittest, the means of further instruction in their own peculiar tenets.

We are further of opinion, that after declaring by law that certain sciences shall be taught in the University, fixing the number of professors they require, which we think should, at present, be ten, limiting (except as to the professors who shall be first engaged in each branch,) a maximum for their salaries, (which should be a certain but moderate subsistence, to be made up by liberal tuition fees, as an excitement to assiduity,) it will be best to leave to the discretion of the visitors, the grouping of these sciences together, according to the accidental qualifications of the professors; and the introduction also of other branches of science, when enabled by private donations, or by public provision, and called for by the increase of population, or other change of circumstances; to establish beginnings, in short, to be developed by time, as those who come after us shall find expedient. They will be more advanced than we are in science and in useful arts, and will know best what will suit the circumstances of their day.

We have proposed no formal provision for the gymnastics of the school, although a proper object of attention for every institution of youth. These exercises with ancient nations, constituted the principal part of the education of their youth. Their arms and mode of warfare rendered them severe in the extreme; ours, on the same correct principle, should be adapted to our arms and warfare; and the manual exercise, military manœuvres, and tactics generally, should be the frequent exercises of the students, in their hours of recreation. It is at that age of aptness, docility, and emulation of the practices of manhood, that such things are soonest learnt and longest remembered. The use of tools too in the manual arts is worthy of encouragement, by facilitating to such as choose it, an admission into the neighboring workshops. To these should be added the arts which embellish life, dancing, music, and drawing; the last more especially, as an important part of military education. These innocent arts furnish amusement and happiness to those who, having time on their hands, might less inoffensively employ it. Needing, at the same time, no regular incorporation with the institution, they may be left to accessory teachers, who will be paid by the individuals employing them, the University only providing proper apartments for their exercise.

The fifth duty prescribed to the Commissioners, is to propose such general provisions as may be properly enacted by the Legislature, for the better organizing and governing the University.

In the education of youth, provision is to be made for, 1, tuition; 2, diet; 3, lodging; 4, government; and 5, honorary excitements. The first of these constitutes the proper functions of the professors; 2, the dieting of the students should be left to private boarding houses of their own choice, and at their own expense; to be regulated by the Visitors from time to time, the house only being provided by the University within its own precincts, and thereby of course subjected to the general regimen, moral or sumptuary, which they shall prescribe. 3. They should be lodged in dormitories, making a part of the general system of buildings. 4. The best mode of government for youth, in large collections, is certainly a desideratum not yet attained with us. It may be well questioned whether *fear* after a certain age, is a motive to which we should have ordinary recourse. The human character is susceptible of other incitements to correct conduct, more worthy of employ, and of better effect. Pride of character, laudable ambition, and moral dispositions are innate correctives of the indiscretions of that lively age; and when strengthened by habitual appeal and exercise, have a happier effect on future character than the degrading motive of fear. Hardening them to disgrace, to corporal punishments, and servile humiliations cannot be the best process for producing erect character. The affectionate deportment between father and son, offers in truth the best example for that of tutor and pupil; and the experience and practice of other[4] countries, in this respect, may be worthy of enquiry and consideration with us. It will then be for the wisdom and discretion of the Visitors to devise and perfect a proper system of government, which, if it be

[4] A police exercised by the students themselves, under proper discretion, has been tried with success in some countries, and the rather as forming them for initiation into the duties and practices of civil life.

founded in reason and comity, will be more likely to nourish in the minds of our youth the combined spirit of order and self-respect, so congenial with our political institutions, and so important to be woven into the American character. 5. What qualifications shall be required to entitle to entrance into the University, the arrangement of the days and hours of lecturing for the different schools, so as to facilitate to the students the circle of attendance on them; the establishment of periodical and public examinations, the premiums to be given for distinguished merit; whether honorary degrees shall be conferred, and by what appellations; whether the title to these shall depend on the time the candidate has been at the University, or, where nature has given a greater share of understanding, attention, and application; whether he shall not be allowed the advantages resulting from these endowments, with other minor items of government, we are of opinion should be entrusted to the Visitors. . . .

IV

Letters

To Robert Skipwith

Monticello. Aug. 3. 1771.

Th: Jefferson to R. Shipwith

I sat down with a design of executing your request to form a catalogue of books amounting to about 30. lib. sterl. but could by no means satisfy myself with any partial choice I could make.[1] Thinking therefore it might be as agreeable to you, I have framed such a general collection as I think you would wish, and might in time find convenient, to procure. Out of this you will chuse for yourself to the amount you mentioned for the present year, and may hereafter as shall be convenient proceed in completing the whole. A view of the second column in this catalogue would I suppose extort a smile from the face of gravity. Peace to it's wisdom! Let me not awaken it. A little attention however to the nature of the human mind evinces that the entertainments of fiction are useful as well as pleasant. That they are pleasant when well written, every person feels who reads. But wherein is it's utility, asks the reverend sage, big with the notion that nothing can be useful but the learned lumber of Greek and Roman reading with which his head is stored? I answer, every thing is useful which contributes to fix us in the principles and practice of virtue. When any signal act of charity or of gratitude, for instance, is presented either to our sight or imagination, we are deeply impressed with it's beauty and feel a strong desire in ourselves of doing charitable and grateful acts also. On the contrary when we see or read of any atrocious deed, we

[1] The catalogue, omitted here, contained approximately 120 titles in the following classifications: Fine Arts (mainly *belles lettres*), Criticism on the Fine Arts, Politics and Trade, Religion, Law, Ancient History, Modern History, Natural Philosophy and Natural History, and Miscellaneous. [Ed.]

are disgusted with it's deformity and conceive an abhorrence of vice. Now every emotion of this kind is an exercise of our virtuous dispositions; and dispositions of the mind, like limbs of the body, acquire strength by exercise. But exercise produces habit; and in the instance of which we speak, the exercise being of the moral feelings, produces a habit of thinking and acting virtuously. We never reflect whether the story we read be truth or fiction. If the painting be lively, and a tolerable picture of nature, we are thrown into a reverie, from which if we awaken it is the fault of the writer. I appeal to every reader of feeling and sentiment whether the fictitious murther of Duncan by Macbeth in Shakespeare does not excite in him as great horror of villainy, as the real one of Henry IV by Ravaillac as related by Davila? And whether the fidelity of Nelson, and generosity of Blandford in Marmontel do not dilate his breast, and elevate his sentiments as much as any similar incident which real history can furnish? Does he not in fact feel himself a better man while reading them, and privately covenant to copy the fair example? We neither know nor care whether Lawrence Sterne really went to France, whether he was there accosted by the poor Franciscan, at first rebuked him unkindly, and then gave him a peace offering; or whether the whole be not a fiction. In either case we are equally sorrowful at the rebuke, and secretly resolve *we* will never do so: we are pleased with the subsequent atonement, and view with emulation a soul candidly acknowleging it's fault, and making a just reparation. Considering history as a moral exercise, her lessons would be too unfrequent if confined to real life. Of those recorded by historians few incidents have been attended with such circumstances as to excite in any high degree this sympathetic emotion of virtue. We are therefore wisely framed to be as warmly interested for a fictitious as for a real personage. The spacious field of imagination is thus laid open to our use, and lessons may be formed to illustrate and carry home to the mind every moral rule of life. Thus a lively and lasting sense of filial duty is more effectually impressed on the mind of a son or daughter by reading King Lear, than by all the dry volumes of ethics and divinity that ever were written. This is my idea of well-written Romance, of Tragedy, Comedy, and Epic Poetry.—If you are fond of speculation, the books under the head of Criticism, will afford you much pleasure. Of Politicks and Trade I have given you a few only of the best books, as you would probably chuse to be not unacquainted with those commercial principles which bring wealth into our country, and the constitutional security we have for the enjoiment of that wealth. In Law I mention a few systematical books, as a knowledge of the minutiae of that science is not necessary for a private gentleman. In Religion, History, Natural philosophy, I have followed the same plan in general. —But whence the necessity of this collection? Come to the new Rowanty, from which you may reach your hand to a library formed on a more extensive plan. Separated from each other but a few paces, the possessions of each would be open to the other. A spring, centrically situated, might be the scene of every evening's joy. There we should talk over the lessons of the day, or lose them in Musick, Chess, or the merriments of our family companions. The heart thus lightened, our pillows would be soft, and health and long life would attend the happy scene. Come then and bring our dear Tibby with you; the first in your affections, and second in mine. Offer prayers for me too at that shrine to which, tho' absent, I pay continual devotion. In every scheme of happiness she is placed in the fore-ground of the picture as the principal figure. Take that away, and it is no picture for me. Bear my affections to Wintipock, cloathed in the warmest expressions of sincerity; and to yourself be every human felicity. Adieu.

To John Randolph[1]

Monticello. Aug. 25. 1775.

Dear Sir

I received your message by Mr. Braxton and immediately gave him an order on the Treasurer for the money, which the Treasurer assured me should be answered on his return. I now send the bearer for the violin and such musick appurtaining to her as may be of no use to the young ladies. I believe you had no case to her. If so, be so good as to direct Watt Lenox to get from Prentis's some bays or other coarse woollen to wrap her in, and then to pack her securely in a wooden box.

I am sorry the situation of our country should render it not eligible to you to remain longer in it. I hope the returning wisdom of Great Britain will e'er long put an end to this unnatural contest. There may be people to whose tempers and dispositions Contention may be pleasing, and who may therefore wish a continuance of confusion. But to me it is of all states, but one, the most horrid. My first wish is a restoration of our just rights; my second a return of the happy period when, consistently with duty, I may withdraw myself totally from the public stage and pass the rest of my days in domestic ease and tranquillity, banishing every desire of afterwards even hearing what passes in the world. Perhaps ardour for the latter may add considerably to the warmth of the former wish. Looking with fondness towards a reconciliation with Great Britain, I cannot help hoping you may be able to contribute towards expediting this good work. I think it must be evident to yourself that the ministry have been deceived by their officers on this side the water, who (for

---

[1] Randolph, the King's Attorney General in Virginia, and a Loyalist, was departing for England, which led to the consummation of a bargain for a violin previously made with Jefferson. [Ed.]

what purposes I cannot tell) have constantly represented the American opposition as that of a small faction, in which the body of the people took little part. This you can inform them of your own knolege to be untrue. They have taken it into their heads too that we are cowards and shall surrender at discretion to an armed force. The past and future operations of the war must confirm or undeceive them on that head. I wish they were thoroughly and minutely acquainted with every circumstance relative to America as it exists in truth. I am persuaded this would go far towards disposing them to reconciliation. Even those in parliament who are called friends to America seem to know nothing of our real determinations. I observe they pronounced in the last parliament that the Congress of 1774 did not mean to insist rigorously on the terms they held out, but kept something in reserve to give up; and in fact that they would give up everything but the article of taxation. Now the truth is far from this, as I can affirm, and put my honor to the assertion; and their continuance in this error may perhaps have very ill consequences. The Congress stated the lowest terms they thought possible to be accepted in order to convince the world they were not unreasonable. They gave up the monopoly and regulation of trade, and all the acts of parliament prior to 1764. leaving to British generosity to render these at some future time as easy to America as the interest of Britain would admit. But this was before blood was spilt. I cannot affirm, but have reason to think, these terms would not now be accepted. I wish no false sense of honor, no ignorance of our real intentions, no vain hope that partial concessions of right will be accepted may induce the ministry to trifle with accomodation till it shall be put even out of our own power ever to accomodate. If indeed Great Britain, disjoined from her colonies, be a match for the most potent nations of Europe with the colonies thrown into their scale, they may go on securely. But if they are not assured of this, it would cer-

tainly be unwise, by trying the event of another campaign, to risque our accepting a foreign aid which perhaps
may not be obtainable but on a condition of everlasting
avulsion from Great Britain. This would be thought a
hard condition to those who still wish for reunion with
their parent country. I am sincerely one of those, and
would rather be in dependance on Great Britain, properly
limited, than on any nation upon earth, or than on no
nation. But I am one of those too who rather than submit
to the right of legislating for us assumed by the British
parliament, and which late experience has shewn they will
so cruelly exercise, would lend my hand to sink the whole
island in the ocean.

If undeceiving the minister as to matters of fact may
change his dispositions, it will perhaps be in your power
by assisting to do this, to render service to the whole empire, at the most critical time certainly that it has ever
seen. Whether Britain shall continue the head of the greatest empire on earth, or shall return to her original station
in the political scale of Europe depends perhaps on the
resolutions of the succeeding winter. God send they may
be wise and salutary for us all!

I shall be glad to hear from you as often as you may be
disposed to think of things here. You may be at liberty I
expect to communicate some things consistently with your
honor and the duties you will owe to a protecting nation.
Such a communication among individuals may be mutually
beneficial to the contending parties. On this or any future
occasion if I affirm to you any facts, your knolege of me
will enable you to decide on their credibility; if I hazard
opinions on the dispositions of men, or other speculative
points, you can only know they are my opinions. My best
wishes for your felicity attend you wherever you go, and
beleive me to be assuredly Your friend & servt.

P.S. My collection of classics and of books of parliamentary learning particularly is not so complete as I could

wish. As you are going to the land of literature and of books you may be willing to dispose of some of yours here and replace them there in better editions. I should be willing to treat on this head with any body you may think proper to empower for that purpose.

To Edmund Pendleton

Philadelphia. Aug. 26. 1776.

DEAR SIR

Yours of the 10th. inst. came to hand about three days ago, the post having brought no mail with him the last week. You seem to have misapprehended my proposition for the choice of a Senate.[1] I had two things in view: to get the wisest men chosen, and to make them perfectly independent when chosen. I have ever observed that a choice by the people themselves is not generally distinguished for it's wisdom. This first secretion from them is usually crude and heterogeneous. But give to those so chosen by the people a second choice themselves, and they generally will chuse wise men. For this reason it was that I proposed the representatives (and not the people) should chuse the Senate, and thought I had notwithstanding that made the Senators (when chosen) perfectly independent of their electors. However I should have no objection to the mode of election proposed in the printed plan of your committee, to wit, that the people of each county should chuse twelve electors, who should meet those of the other counties in the same district and chuse a senator. I should prefer this too for another reason, that the upper as well as lower house should have an opportunity of superintending and judging of the situation of the whole state and be not all of one neighborhood as our upper house used to be. So much for the wisdom of the Senate. To make them independent, I had proposed that they should

[1] In Jefferson's proposed constitution for Virginia. [Ed.]

hold their places for nine years, and then go out (one third every three years) and be incapable for ever of being re-elected to that house. My idea was that if they might be re-elected, they would be casting their eyes forward to the period of election (however distant) and be currying favor with the electors, and consequently dependent on them. My reason for fixing them in office for a term of years rather than for life, was that they might have in idea that they were at a certain period to return into the mass of the people and become the governed instead of the governors which might still keep alive that regard to the public good that otherwise they might perhaps be induced by their independance to forget. Yet I could submit, tho' not so willingly to an appointment for life, or to any thing rather than a mere creation by and dependance on the people. I think the present mode of election objectionable because the larger county will be able to send and will always send a man (less fit perhaps) of their own county to the exclusion of a fitter who may chance to live in a smaller county. I wish experience may contradict my fears. That the Senate as well as lower [or shall I speak truth and call it upper] house should hold no office of profit I am clear; but not that they should of necessity possess distinguished property. You have lived longer than I have and perhaps may have formed a different judgment on better grounds; but my observations do not enable me to say I think integrity the characteristic of wealth. In general I believe the decisions of the people, in a body, will be more honest and more disinterested than those of wealthy men: and I can never doubt an attachment to his country in any man who has his family and peculium in it.—Now as to the representative house which ought to be so constructed as to answer that character truly. I was for extending the right of suffrage (or in other words the rights of a citizen) to all who had a permanent intention of living in the country. Take what circumstances you please as evidence of this, either the having resided a certain time, or having a family, or having property, any or all of them. Whoever intends to live in a country must wish that country well, and has a natural right of assisting in the preservation of it. I think you cannot distinguish between such a person residing in the country and having no fixed property, and one residing in a township whom you say you would admit to a vote. —The other point of equal representation I think capital and fundamental. I am glad you think an alteration may be attempted in that matter.—The fantastical idea of virtue and the public good being a sufficient security to the state against the commission of crimes, which you say you have heard insisted on by some, I assure you was never mine. It is only the sanguinary hue of our penal laws which I meant to object to. Punishments I know are necessary, and I would provide them, strict and inflexible, but proportioned to the crime. Death might be inflicted for murther and perhaps for treason if you would take out of the description of treason all crimes which are not such in their nature. Rape, buggery &c. punish by castration. All other crimes by working on high roads, rivers, gallies &c. a certain time proportioned to the offence. But as this would be no punishment or change of condition to slaves (me miserum!) let them be sent to other countries. By these means we should be freed from the wickedness of the latter, and the former would be living monuments of public vengeance. Laws thus proportionate and mild should never be dispensed with. Let mercy be the character of the law-giver, but let the judge be a mere machine. The mercies of the law will be dispensed equally and impartially to every description of men; those of the judge, or of the executive power, will be the eccentric impulses of whimsical, capricious designing man. . . .

To Giovanni Fabbroni

Williamsburgh in Virginia June. 8. 1778

SIR

Your letter of Sep. 15, 1776 from Paris came safe to hand. We have not however had the pleasure of seeing Mr. De Crenis, the bearer of it in this country, as he joined the army in Pennsylvania as soon as he arrived. I should have taken particular pleasure in serving him on your recommendation. From the kind anxiety expressed in your letters as well as from other sources of information we discover that our enemies have filled Europe with Thrasonic accounts of victories they had never won and conquests they were fated never to make. While these accounts alarmed our friends in Europe they afforded us diversion. We have long been out of all fear for the event of the war. I inclose you a list of the killed, wounded, and captives of the enemy from the Commencement of hostilities at Lexington in April 1775. till November 1777. since which there has been no event of any consequence.[1] This is the best history of the war which can be brought within the compass of a letter. I believe the account to be near the truth, tho' it is difficult to get at the numbers lost by an enemy with absolute precision. Many of the articles have been communicated to us from England as taken from the official returns made by their General. I wish it were in my power to send you as just an account of our [losses] but this cannot be done without an application to the war office which being in another country is at this time out of my reach. I think that upon the whole it has been about one half the number lost by them. In some instances more, but in others less. This difference is ascribed to our superiority in taking aim when we fire;

---

[1] The enclosure, omitted here, showed a total of 18,710 "Men already Lost to England." [Ed.]

every soldier in our army having been intimate with his gun from his infancy. If there could have been a doubt before as to the event of the war, it is now totally removed by the interposition of France; and the generous alliance she has entered into with us.

Tho' much of my time is employed in the councils of America I have yet a little leisure to indulge my fondness for philosophical studies. I could wish to correspond with you on subjects of that kind. It might not be unacceptable to you to be informed for instance of the true power of our climate as discoverable from the Thermometer, from the force and direction of the winds, the quantity of rain, the plants which grow without shelter in the winter &c. On the other hand we should be much pleased with cotemporary observations on the same particulars in your country, which will give us a comparative view of the two climates. Farenheit's thermometer is the only one in use with us. I make my daily observations as early as possible in the morning and again about 4 o'clock in the afternoon, these generally showing the maxima of cold and heat in the course of 24 hours. I wish I could gratify your Botanical taste; but I am acquainted with nothing more than the first principles of that science, yet myself and my friends may furnish you with any Botanical subjects which this country affords, and are not to be had with you: and I shall take pleasure in procuring them when pointed out by you. The greatest difficulty will be the means of conveyance during the continuance of the war.

If there is a gratification which I envy any people in this world it is to your country[2] its music. This is the favorite passion of my soul, and fortune has cast my lot in a country where it is in a state of deplorable barbarism. From the line of life in which we conjecture you to be, I have for some time lost the hope of seeing you here. Should the event prove so, I shall ask your assistance in procur-

[2] Italy. [Ed.]

ing a substitute who may be a proficient in singing and on the harpsichord. I should be contented to receive such an one two or three years hence, when it is hoped he may come more safely, and find here a greater plenty of those useful things which commerce alone can furnish. The bounds of an American fortune will not admit the indulgence of a domestic band of musicians. Yet I have thought that a passion for music might be reconciled with that oeconomy which we are obliged to observe. I retain for instance among my domestic servants a gardener (Ortolano), weaver (Tessitore di lino e lano), a cabinet maker (Stipettaio) and a stonecutter (scalpellino lavorante in piano) to which I would add a Vigneron. In a country where, like yours, music is cultivated and practised by every class of men I suppose there might be found persons of those trades who could perform on the French horn, clarinet or hautboy and bassoon, so that one might have a band of two French horns, two clarinets and hautboys and a bassoon, without enlarging their domestic expences. A certainty of employment for a half dozen years, and at the end of that time to find them if they chose it a conveyance to their own country might induce them to come here on reasonable wages. Without meaning to give you trouble, perhaps it might be practicable for you in your ordinary intercourse with your people to find out such men disposed to come to America. Sobriety and good nature would be desireable parts of their characters. If you think such a plan practicable, and will be so kind as to inform me what will be necessary to be done on my part, I will take care that it shall be done. The necessary expences, when informed of them, I can remit before they are wanting, to any port in France with which country alone we have safe correspondence.

I am Sir with much esteem your humble servt.

To David Rittenhouse

Monticello in Albemarle. Virginia. July 19. 1778.

DEAR SIR

I sincerely congratulate you on the recovery of Philadelphia, and wish it may be found uninjured by the enemy.
How far the interests of literature may have suffered by
the injury or removal of the Orrery (as it is miscalled),
the publick libraries, your papers and implements, are
doubts which still excite anxiety. We were much disappointed in Virginia generally on the day of the great
eclipse, which proved to be cloudy. In Williamsburgh,
where it was total, I understand only the beginning was
seen. At this place which is in Lat. 38° 8' and Longitude
West from Williamsburgh about 1° 45' as is conjectured,
eleven digits only were supposed to be covered. It was
not seen at all till the moon had advanced nearly one third
over the sun's disc. Afterwards it was seen at intervals
through the whole. The egress particularly was visible. It
proved however of little use to me for want of a time
peice that could be depended on; which circumstance, together with the subsequent restoration of Philadelphia to
you, has induced me to trouble you with this letter to
remind you of your kind promise of making me an accurate clock, which being intended for astronomical purposes only, I would have divested of all apparatus for
striking or for any other purpose, which by increasing
it's complication might disturb it's accuracy. A companion to it, for keeping seconds, and which might be moved
easily, would greatly add to it's value. The theodolite, for
which I spoke to you also, I can now dispense with, having since purchased a most excellent one.

Writing to a philosopher, I may hope to be pardoned
for intruding some thoughts of my own, tho' they relate
to him personally. Your time for two years past has, I
beleive, been principally employed in the civil govern-

ment of your country. Tho' I have been aware of the authority our cause would acquire with the world from it's being known that yourself and Doctr. Franklin were zealous friends to it, and am myself duly impressed with a sense of the arduousness of government, and the obligation those are under who are able to conduct it, yet I am also satisfied there is an order of geniusses above that obligation, and therefore exempted from it. No body can conceive that nature ever intended to throw away a Newton upon the occupations of a crown. It would have been a prodigality for which even the conduct of providence might have been arraigned, had he been by birth annexed to what was so far below him. Cooperating with nature in her ordinary œconomy, we should dispose of and employ the geniusses of men according to their several orders and degrees. I doubt not there are in your country many persons equal to the task of conducting government: but you should consider that the world has but one Ryttenhouse, and that it never had one before. The amazing mechanical representation of the solar system which you conceived and executed, has never been surpassed by any but the work of which it is a copy. Are those powers then, which being intended for the erudition of the world, like air and light, the world's common property, to be taken from their proper pursuit to do the commonplace drudgery of governing a single state, a work which may be executed by men of an ordinary stature, such as are always and every where to be found? Without having ascended mount Sina for inspiration, I can pronounce that the precept, in the decalogue of the vulgar, that they shall not make to themselves 'the likeness of any thing that is in the heavens above' is reversed for you, and that you will fulfill the highest purposes of your creation by employing yourself in the perpetual breach of that inhibition. For my own country in particular you must remember something like a promise that it should be adorned with one of them. The taking of your city by the enemy has hitherto prevented the proposition from being made and approved by our legislature. The zeal of a true Whig in science must excuse the hazarding these free thoughts, which flow from a desire of promoting the diffusion of knowledge and of your fame, and from one who can assure you truly that he is with much sincerity & esteem Your most obedt. & most humble servt.

To James Monroe

Monticello May 20. 1782.

DEAR SIR

I have been gratified with the receipt of your two favours of the 6th. and 11th. inst. It gives me pleasure that your county has been wise enough to enlist your talents into their service. I am much obliged by the kind wishes you express of seeing me also in Richmond, and am always mortified when any thing is expected from me which I cannot fulfill, and more especially if it relate to the public service. Before I ventured to declare to my countrymen my determination to retire from public employment I examined well my heart to know whether it were thoroughly cured of every principle of political ambition, whether no lurking particle remained which might leave me uneasy when reduced within the limits of mere private life. I became satisfied that every fibre of that passion was thoroughly eradicated. I examined also in other views my right to withdraw. I considered that I had been thirteen years engaged in public service, that during that time I had so totally abandoned all attention to my private affairs as to permit them to run into great disorder and ruin, that I had now a family advanced to years which require my attention and instruction, that to this was added the hopeful offspring of a deceased friend whose memory must be forever dear to me who have no other reliance for being rendered useful to themselves and their country, that by a constant sacrifice of time, labor, loss, parental and friendly duties, I had been so far from gaining the affection of my countrymen which was the only reward I ever asked or could have felt, that I had even lost the small estimation I before possessed: that however I might have comforted myself under the disapprobation of the well-meaning but uninformed people yet that of their representatives was a shock on which I had not calculated: that this indeed had been followed by an exculpatory declaration, but in the mean time I had been suspected and suspended in the eyes of the world without the least hint then or afterwards made public which might restrain them from supposing I stood arraigned for treasons of the heart and not mere weaknesses of the head. And I felt that these injuries, for such they have been since acknowleged, had inflicted a wound on my spirit which will only be cured by the all-healing grave. If reason and inclination unite in justifying my retirement, the laws of my country are equally in favor of it. Whether the state may command the political services of all its members to an indefinite extent, or if these be among the rights never wholly ceded to the public power, is a question which I do not find expressly decided in England. Obiter dictums on the subject I have indeed met with, but the complection of the times in which these have dropped would generally answer them, and besides that, this species of authority is not acknowleged in our profession. In this country however since the present government has been established the point has been settled by uniform, pointed, and multiplied precedents. Offices of every kind and given by every power, have been daily and hourly declined and resigned from the declaration of independance to this moment. The General assembly has accepted these without discrimination of office, and without ever questioning them in point of right. If a difference between the office of a delegate and any other could ever have been supposed, yet in the case of Mr. Thompson Mason who declined the office of delegate and was permitted by the house so to do that supposition has been proved to be groundless. But indeed no such distinction of offices can be admitted; reason and the opinions of the lawyers putting all on a footing as to this question and giving to the delegate the aid of all the precedents of the refusal of other offices, the law then does not warrant the assumption of such a power by the state over it's members. For if it does where is that law? Nor yet does reason, for tho' I will admit that this does subject every individual if called on to an equal tour of political duty yet it can never go so far as to submit to it his whole existence. If we are made in some degree for others, yet in a greater are we made for ourselves. It were contrary to feeling and indeed ridiculous to suppose a man had less right in himself than one of his neighbors or all of them put together. This would be slavery and not that liberty which the bill of rights has made inviolable and for the preservation of which our government has been changed. Nothing could so completely divest us of that liberty as the establishment of the opinion that the state has a *perpetual* right to the services of all it's members. This to men of certain ways of thinking would be to annihilate the blessing of existence; to contradict the giver of life who gave it for happiness and not for wretchedness, and certainly to such it were better that they had never been born. However with these I may think public service and private misery inseparably linked together, I have not the vanity to count myself among those whom the state would think worth oppressing with perpetual service. I have received a sufficient memento to the contrary. I am persuaded that having hitherto dedicated to them the whole of the active and useful part of my life I shall be permitted to pass the rest in mental quiet. I hope too that I did not mistake the mode any more than the matter of right when I preferred a simple act of renunciation to the taking sanctuary under those many disqualifications (provided by the law for other purposes indeed but) which afford asylum also for rest to the wearied. I dare say you did not expect by the few words you dropped on the right of renunciation to expose yourself to the fatigue of so long a letter, but I wished you to see that if I had done wrong I had been betrayed by a semblance of right at least. . . .

To Martha Jefferson[1]

Annapolis Nov. 28. 1783.

MY DEAR PATSY

After four days journey I arrived here without any accident and in as good health as when I left Philadelphia. The conviction that you would be more improved in the situation I have placed you than if still with me, has solaced me on my parting with you, which my love for you has rendered a difficult thing. The acquirements which I hope you will make under the tutors I have provided for you will render you more worthy of my love, and if they cannot increase it they will prevent it's diminution. Consider the good lady who has taken you under her roof, who has undertaken to see that you perform all your exercises, and to admonish you in all those wanderings from what is right or what is clever to which your inexperience would expose you, consider her I say as your mother, as the only person to whom, since the loss with which heaven has been pleased to afflict you, you can now look up; and that her displeasure or disapprobation on any occasion will be an immense misfortune which should you be so unhappy as to incur by any unguarded act, think no concession too much to regain her good will. With respect to the distribution of your time the following is what I should approve.

from 8. to 10 o'clock practise music.
from 10. to 1. dance one day and draw another
from 1. to 2. draw on the day you dance, and write a letter the next day.

---

[1] His eldest daughter, aged eleven. [Ed.]

from 3. to 4. read French.
from 4. to 5. exercise yourself in music.
from 5. till bedtime read English, write &c.

Communicate this plan to Mrs. Hopkinson and if she approves of it pursue it. As long as Mrs. Trist remains in Philadelphia cultivate her affections. She has been a valuable friend to you and her good sense and good heart make her valued by all who know her and by nobody on earth more than by me. I expect you will write to me by every post. Inform me what books you read, what tunes you learn, and inclose me your best copy of every lesson in drawing. Write also one letter every week either to your aunt Eppes, your aunt Skipwith, your aunt Carr, or the little lady from whom I now inclose a letter, and always put the letter you so write under cover to me. Take care that you never spell a word wrong. Always before you write a word consider how it is spelt, and if you do not remember it, turn to a dictionary. It produces great praise to a lady to spell well. I have placed my happiness on seeing you good and accomplished, and no distress which this world can now bring on me could equal that of your disappointing my hopes. If you love me then, strive to be good under every situation and to all living creatures, and to acquire those accomplishments which I have put in your power, and which will go far towards ensuring you the warmest love of your affectionate father.

P.S. keep my letters and read them at times that you may always have present in your mind those things which will endear you to me.

To George Washington

Annapolis April. 16. 1784.

DEAR SIR

I received your favor of the 8th. inst. by Colo. Harrison. The subject of it is interesting, and, so far as you have stood connected with it, has been matter of anxiety to me: because whatever may be the ultimate fate of the institution of the Cincinnati, as in it's course it draws to it some degree of disapprobation, I have wished to see you stand on ground separated from it; and that the character which will be handed to future ages at the head of our revolution may in no instance be compromitted in subordinate altercations. The subject has been at the point of my pen in every letter I have written to you; but has been still restrained by a reflection that you had among your friends more able counsellors, and in yourself one abler than them all. Your letter has now rendered a duty what was before a desire, and I cannot better merit your confidence than by a full and free communication of facts and sentiments as far as they have come within my observation.

When the army was about to be disbanded, and the officers to take final leave, perhaps never again to meet, it was natural for men who had accompanied each other through so many scenes of hardship, of difficulty and danger, who in a variety of instances must have been rendered mutually dear by those aids and good offices to which their situations had given occasion, it was natural I say for these to seize with fondness any propositions which promised to bring them together again at certain and regular periods. And this I take for granted was the origin and object of this institution: and I have no suspicion that they foresaw, much less intended those mischeifs which exist perhaps in the forebodings of politicians only. I doubt however whether in it's execution it would be found to answer the wishes of those who framed it, and to foster those friendships it was intended to preserve. The numbers would be brought together at their annual assemblies no longer to encounter a common enemy, but to encounter one another in debate and sentiment. Something I suppose is to be done at those meetings, and however unimportant, it will suffice to produce difference of opinion, contradiction and irritation. The way to make friends quarrel is to pit them in disputation under the public eye. An experience of near twenty years has taught me that few friendships stand this test; and that public assemblies where every one is free to speak and to act, are the most powerful looseners of the bands of private friendship. I think therefore that this institution would fail of it's principal object, the perpetuation of the personal friendships contracted thro' the war.

The objections of those opposed to the institution shall be briefly sketched; you will readily fill them up. They urge that it is against the Confederation; against the letter of some of our constitutions; against the spirit of them all, that the foundation, on which all these are built, is the natural equality of man, the denial of every preeminence but that annexed to legal office, and particularly the denial of a preeminence by birth;—that however, in their present dispositions, citizens might decline accepting honorary instalments into the order, a time may come when a change of dispositions would render these flattering; when a well directed distribution of them might draw into the order all the men of talents, of office and wealth; and in this case would probably procure an ingraftment into the government; that in this they will be supported by their foreign members, and the wishes and influence of foreign courts; that experience has shewn that the hereditary branches of modern governments are the patrons of privilege and prerogative, and not of the natural rights of the people, whose oppressors they generally are; that besides these evils which are remote, others may take place more immediately; that a distinction is kept up between the civil and military which it is for the happiness of both to obliterate; that when the members assemble they will be proposing to do something, and what that something may be will depend on actual circumstances; that being an organized body, under habits of subordination, the first obstructions to enterprize will be already surmounted; that the moderation and virtue of a single character has probably prevented this revolution from being closed as most others have been by a subversion of that liberty it was intended to establish; that he is not immortal, and his successor or some one of his successors at the head of this institution may adopt a more mistaken road to glory.

What are the sentiments of Congress on this subject, and what line they will pursue can only be stated conjecturally. Congress as a body, if left to themselves, will in my opinion say nothing on the subject. They may however be forced into a declaration by instructions from some of the states or by other incidents. Their sentiments, if forced from them, will be unfriendly to the institution. If permitted to pursue their own tract, they will check it by side blows whenever it comes in their way, and in competitions for office on equal or nearly equal ground will give silent preferences to those who are not of the fraternity. My reasons for thinking this are: 1. The grounds on which they lately declined the foreign order proposed to be conferred on some of our citizens. 2. The fourth of the fundamental articles of constitution for the new states. I inclose you the report. It has been considered by Congress, recommitted and reformed by a Committee according to the sentiments expressed on other parts of it, but the principle referred to having not been controverted at all, stands in this as in the original report. It is not yet confirmed by Congress. 3. Private conversations on this subject with the members. Since the receipt of your letter I have taken occasion to extend these; not indeed to the military members, because being of the order delicacy forbade it; but to the others pretty generally; and among these I have found but one who is not opposed to the institution, and that with an anguish of mind, tho' covered under a guarded silence, which I have not seen produced by any circumstance before. I arrived at Philadelphia before the separation of the last Congress, and saw there and at Princeton some of it's members not now in delegation. Burke's peice happened to come out at that time which occasioned this institution to be the subject of conversation. I found the same impression made on them which their successors have received. I hear from other quarters that it is disagreeable generally to such citizens as have attended to it, and therefore will probably be so to all when any circumstance shall present it to the notice of all.

This Sir is as faithful an account of sentiments and facts as I am able to give you. You know the extent of the circle within which my observations are at present circumscribed; and can estimate how far, as forming a part of the general opinion, it may merit notice, or ought to influence your particular conduct. It remains now to pay obedience to that part of your letter which requests sentiments on the most eligible measures to be pursued by the society at their next meeting. I must be far from pretending to be a judge of what would *in fact* be the most eligible measures for the society. I can only give you the opinions of those with whom I have conversed, and who, as I have before observed, are unfriendly to it. They lead to these conclusions. 1. If the society proceeds according to it's institution, it will be better to make no applications to Congress on that subject, or on any other in their associated character. 2. If they should propose to modify it so as to render it unobjectionable, I think this would not be effected without such a modification as would amount almost to annihilation; for such would it be to part with it's inheritability, it's organisation and its assemblies. 3. If they should be disposed to discontinue the whole it would remain with them to determine whether they would chuse it to be done by their own act only, or by a reference of the matter to Congress, which would infallibly produce a recommendation of total discontinuance.

You will be sensible, Sir, that these communications are without all reserve. I supposed such to be your wish, and mean them but as materials, with such others as you may collect, for your better judgment to work on. I consider the whole matter as between ourselves alone, having determined to take no active part in this or any thing else which may lead to altercation, or disturb that quiet and tranquillity of mind to which I consign the remaining portion of my life. I have been thrown back by events on a stage where I had never more thought to appear. It is but for a time however, and as a day labourer, free to withdraw or be withdrawn at will. While I remain I shall pursue in silence the path of right; but in every situation public or private shall be gratified by all occasions of rendering you service and of convincing you there is no one to whom your reputation and happiness are dearer than to, Sir, Your most obedient & most humble servt.

To Richard Price

Paris, Feb. 1, 1785

Sir

The copy of your Observations on the American Revolution which you were so kind as to direct to me came duly to hand, and I should sooner have acknowledged the receipt of it but that I awaited a private coveiance for my letter, having experienced much delay and uncertainty in the posts between this place and London. I have read it with very great pleasure, as have done many others to whom I have communicated it. The spirit which it breathes is as affectionate as the observations themselves are wise and just. I have no doubt it will be reprinted in America and produce much good there. The want of power in the federal head was early perceived, and foreseen to be the flaw in our constitution which might endanger its destruction. I have the pleasure to inform you that when I left America in July the people were becoming universally sensible of this, and a spirit to enlarge the powers of Congress was becoming general. Letters and other information recently received shew that this has continued to increase, and that they are likely to remedy this evil effectually. The happiness of governments like ours, wherein the people are truly the mainspring, is that they are never to be despaired of. When an evil becomes so glaring as to strike them generally, they arrouse themselves, and it is redressed. He only is then the popular man and can get into office who shews the best dispositions to reform the evil. This truth was obvious on several occasions during the late war, and this character in our governments saved us. Calamity was our best physician. Since the peace it was observed that some nations of Europe, counting on the weakness of Congress and the little probability of a union in measure among the States, were proposing to grasp at unequal advantages in our commerce. The people are become sensible of this, and you may be assured that this evil will be immediately redressed, and redressed radically. I doubt still whether in this moment they will enlarge those powers in Congress which are necessary to keep the peace among the States. I think it possible that this may be suffered to lie till some two States commit hostilities on each other, but in that moment the hand of the union will be lifted up and interposed, and the people will themselves demand a general concession to Congress of means to prevent similar mischiefs. Our motto is truly "nil desperandum." The apprehensions you express of danger from the want of powers in Congress, led me to note to you this character in our governments, which, since the retreat behind the Delaware, and the capture of Charlestown, has kept my mind in perfect quiet as to the ultimate fate of our union; and I am sure, from the spirit which breathes thro your book, that whatever promises permanence to that will be a comfort to your mind. I have the honour to be, with very sincere esteem and respect, Sir, Your most obedient and most humble servt.

To James Monroe

Paris, June 17. 1785.

. . . I will take the liberty of hazarding to you some thoughts on the policy of entering into treaties with the European nations, and the nature of them. I am not wedded to these ideas, and therefore shall relinquish them chearfully when Congress shall adopt others, and zealously endeavor to carry theirs into effect. First as to the policy of making treaties. Congress, by the Confederation have no original and inherent power over the commerce of the states. But by the 9th. article they are authorised to enter into treaties of commerce. The moment these treaties are concluded the jurisdiction of Congress over the commerce of the states springs into existence, and that of the particular states is superseded so far as the articles of the treaty may have taken up the subject. There are two restrictions only on the exercise of the powers of treaty by Congress. 1st. That they shall not by such treaty restrain the legislatures of the state from imposing such duties on foreigners as their own people are subjected to: 2dly. nor from prohibiting the exportation or importation of any particular species of goods. Leaving these two points free, Congress may by treaty establish any system of commerce they please. But, as I before observed, it is by treaty alone they can do it. Tho' they may exercise their other powers by resolution or ordinance, those over commerce can only be exercised by forming a treaty and this probably by an accidental wording of our confederation. If therefore it is better for the states that Congress should regulate their commerce, it is proper that they should form treaties with all nations with whom we may possibly trade. You see that my primary object in the formation of treaties is to take the commerce of the states out of the hands of the states, and to place it under the superintendance of Congress, so far as the imperfect provisions of our constitution will admit, and until the states shall by new compact make them more perfect. I would say then to every nation on earth, *by treaty*, your people shall trade freely with us, and ours with you, paying no more than the most favoured nation, in order to put an end to the right of individual states acting by fits and starts to interrupt our commerce or to embroil us with any nation. As to the terms of these treaties, the question becomes more difficult. I will mention three different plans. 1. That no duties shall be laid by either party on the productions of the other. 2. That each may be permitted to equalize their duties to those laid by the other. 3. That each shall pay in the ports of the other such duties only as the most favoured nations pay. 1. Were the nations of Europe as free and unembarrassed of established system as we are, I do verily beleive they would concur with us in the first plan. But it is impossible. These establishments are fixed upon them, they are interwoven with the body of their laws and the organisation of their government, and they make a great part of their revenue; they cannot then get rid of them. 2. The plan of equal imposts presents difficulties insurmountable. For how are the equal imposts to be effected? Is it by laying in the ports of A an equal percent on the goods of B. with that which B has laid in his ports on the goods of A? But how are we to find what is that percent? For this is not the usual form of imposts. They generally pay by the ton, by the measure, by the weight, and not by the value. Besides if A. sends a million's worth of goods to B. and takes back but the half of that, and each pays the same percent, it is evident that A. pays the double of what he recovers in the same way with B. This would be our case with Spain. Shall we endeavour to effect equality then by saying A may levy so much on the sum of B's importations into his ports, as B does on the sum of A's importations into the ports of B? But how find out that sum? Will either party lay open their customhouse books candidly to evince this sum? Does either keep their books so exactly as to trouble to do it? This proposition was started in Congress when our instructions were formed, as you may remember, and the impossibility of executing it occasioned it to be disapproved. Besides who should have a right of deciding when the imposts were equal. A. would say to B. my imposts do not raise so much as yours; I raise them therefore. B. would then say you have made them greater than mine, I will raise mine, and thus a kind of auction would be carried on between them, and a mutual irritation, which would end in any thing sooner than equality, and right. 3. I confess then to you that I see no alternative left but that which Congress adopted, of each party placing the other on the footing of the most favoured nation. If the nations of Europe from their actual establishments are not at liberty to say to America that she shall trade in their ports duty free, they may say she may trade there paying no higher duties than the most favoured nation and this is valuable in many of these countries where a very great difference is made between different nations. There is no difficulty in the execution of this contract, because there is not a merchant who does not know, or may not know, the duty paid by every nation on every article. This stipulation leaves each party at liberty to regulate their own commerce by general rules; while it secures the other from partial and oppressive discriminations. The difficulty which arises in our case is, with the nations having American territory. Access to the West Indies is indispensably necessary to us. Yet how to gain it when it is the established system of these nations to exclude all foreigners from their colonies. The only chance seems to be this. Our commerce to the mother countries is valuable to them. We must endeavor then to make this the price of an admission into their West Indies, and to those who refuse the admission we must refuse our commerce or load theirs by odious discriminations in our ports. We have this circumstance in our favor too that what one grants us in their islands the others will not find it worth their while to refuse. The misfortune is that with this country we gave this price for their aid in the war, and we have now nothing more to offer. She being withdrawn from the competition leaves Gr. Britain much more at liberty to hold out against us. This is the difficult part of the business of treaty, and I own it does not hold out the most flattering prospect.—I wish you would consider this subject and write me your thoughts on it. Mr. Gherry wrote me on the same subject. Will you give me leave to impose on you the trouble of communicating this to him? It is long, and will save me much labour in copying. I hope he will be so indulgent as to consider it as an answer to that part of his letter, and will give me his further thoughts on it.

Shall I send you so much of the Encyclopedie as is already published or reserve it here till you come? It is about 40. vols., which probably is about half the work. Give yourself no uneasiness about the money. Perhaps I may find it convenient to ask you to pay trifles occasionally for me in America. I sincerely wish you may find it convenient to come here. The pleasure of the trip will be less than you expect but the utility greater. It will make you adore your own country, it's soil, it's climate, it's equality, liberty, laws, people and manners. My god! How little do my countrymen know what precious blessings they are in possession of, and which no other people on earth enjoy. I confess I had no idea of it myself. While we shall see multiplied instances of Europeans going to live in America, I will venture to say no man now living will ever see an instance of an American removing to settle in Europe and continuing there. Come then and see the proofs of this, and on your return add your testimony to that of every thinking American, in order to satisfy our countrymen how much it is their interest to preserve uninfected by contagion those peculiarities in their government and manners to which they are indebted for these blessings. Adieu my dear friend. Present me affectionately to your collegues. If any of them think me worth writing to, they may be assured that in the epistolary account I will keep the debit side against them. Once more Adieu.

To the Virginia Delegates in Congress

Paris July 12. 1785.

GENTLEMEN

In consequence of the orders of the Legislative and Executive bodies of Virginia, I have engaged Monsr. Houdon to make the Statue of Genl. Washington. For this purpose it is necessary for him to see the General. He therefore goes with Doctr. Franklin, and will have the honor of delivering you this himself. As his journey is at the expence of the state according to our contract, I will pray you to favor him with your patronage and counsels, and to protect him as much as possible from those impositions to which strangers are but too much exposed. I have advised him to proceed in the stages to the General's. I have also agreed, if he can see Generals Greene and Gates, whose busts he has a desire to make, that he may make a moderate deviation for this purpose, after he is done with General Washington.

But the most important object with him is to be employed to make General Washington's equestrian statue for Congress. Nothing but the expectation of this could have engaged him to have undertaken this voiage, as the pedestrian statue for Virginia will not make it worth the business he loses by absenting himself. I was therefore obliged to assure him of my recommendations for this greater work. Having acted in this for the state, you will I hope think yourselves in some measure bound to patronize and urge his being employed by Congress. I would not have done this myself, nor asked you to do it, did I not see that it would be better for Congress to put this business into his hands, than into those of any other person living, for these reasons: 1. He is without rivalship the first statuary of this age; as a proof of which he receives orders from every other country for things intended to be capital. 2. He will have seen General Washington, have taken his measures in every part, and of course whatever he does of him will have the merit of being original, from which other workmen can only furnish copies. 3. He is in possession of the house, the furnaces, and all the apparatus provided for making the statue of Louis XV. If any other workman is employed, this will all be to be provided anew and of course to be added to the price of the statue, for no man can ever expect to make two equestrian statues. The addition which this would be to the price will much exceed the expectation of any person who has not seen that apparatus. In truth it is immense. As to the price of the work it will be much greater than Congress is aware of, probably. I have enquired somewhat into this circumstance, and find the prices of those made for two centuries past have been from 120,000 guineas down to 16,000 guineas, according to the size. And as far as I have seen, the smaller they are, the more agreeable. The smallest yet made is infinitely above the size of the life, and they all appear outré and monstrous. That of Louis XV is probably the best in the world, and it is the smallest here. Yet it is impossible to find a point of view from which it does not appear a monster, unless you go so far as to lose sight of the features and finer lineaments of the face and body. A statue is not made, like a mountain, to be seen at a great distance. To perceive those minuter circumstances which constitute it's beauty you must be near it, and, in that case, it should be so little above the size of the life, as to appear actually of that size from your point of view. I should not therefore fear to propose that the one intended by Congress should be considerably smaller than any of those to be seen here; as I think it will be more beautiful, and also cheaper. I have troubled you with these observations as they have been suggested to me from an actual sight of works in this kind, and supposed they might assist you in making up your minds on this subject. . . .

To Peter Carr[1]

Paris Aug. 19. 1785.

DEAR PETER

I received by Mr. Mazzei your letter of April 20. I am much mortified to hear that you have lost so much time, and that when you arrived in Williamsburgh you were not at all advanced from what you were when you left Monticello. Time now begins to be precious to you. Every day you lose, will retard a day your entrance on that public stage whereon you may begin to be useful to yourself. However the way to repair the loss is to improve the future time. I trust that with your dispositions even the acquisition of science is a pleasing employment. I can assure you that the possession of it is what (next to an honest heart) will above all things render you dear to your friends, and give you fame and promotion in your own country. When your mind shall be well improved with science, nothing will be necessary to place you in the highest points of view but to pursue the interests of your country, the interests of your friends, and your own interests also with the purest integrity, the most chaste honour. The defect of these virtues can never be made up by all the other acquirements of body and mind. Make these then your first object. Give up money, give up fame, give up science, give [up] the earth itself and all it contains rather than do an immoral act. And never suppose that in any possible situation or under any circumstances that it is best for you to do a dishonourable thing however slightly so it may appear to you. Whenever you are to do a thing tho' it can never be known but to yourself, ask yourself

1 Jefferson's nephew and ward, age fifteen. [Ed.]

how you would act were all the world looking at you, and act accordingly. Encourage all your virtuous dispositions, and exercise them whenever an opportunity arises, being assured that they will gain strength by exercise as a limb of the body does, and that exercise will make them habitual. From the practice of the purest virtue you may be assured you will derive the most sublime comforts in every moment of life and in the moment of death. If ever you find yourself environed with difficulties and perplexing circumstances, out of which you are at a loss how to extricate yourself, do what is right, and be assured that that will extricate you the best out of the worst situations. Tho' you cannot see when you fetch one step, what will be the next, yet follow truth, justice, and plain-dealing, and never fear their leading you out of the labyrinth in the easiest manner possible. The knot which you thought a Gordian one will untie itself before you. Nothing is so mistaken as the supposition that a person is to extricate himself from a difficulty, by intrigue, by chicanery, by dissimulation, by trimming, by an untruth, by an injustice. This increases the difficulties tenfold, and those who pursue these methods, get themselves so involved at length that they can turn no way but their infamy becomes more exposed. It is of great importance to set a resolution, not to be shaken, never to tell an untruth. There is no vice so mean, so pitiful, so contemptible and he who permits himself to tell a lie once, finds it much easier to do it a second and third time, till at length it becomes habitual, he tells lies without attending to it, and truths without the world's beleiving him. This falshood of the tongue leads to that of the heart, and in time depraves all it's good dispositions.

An honest heart being the first blessing, a knowing head is the second. It is time for you now to begin to be choice in your reading, to begin to pursue a regular course in it and not to suffer yourself to be turned to the right or left by reading any thing out of that course. I have long ago digested a plan for you, suited to the circumstances in which you will be placed. This I will detail to you from time to time as you advance. For the present I advise you to begin a course of antient history, reading every thing in the original and not in translations. First read Goldsmith's history of Greece. This will give you a digested view of that feild. Then take up antient history in the detail, reading the following books in the following order. Herodotus. Thucydides. Xenophontis hellenica. Xenophontis Anabasis. Quintus Curtius. Justin. This shall form the first stage of your historical reading, and is all I need mention to you now. The next will be of Roman history. From that we will come down to Modern history. In Greek and Latin poetry, you have read or will read at school Virgil, Terence, Horace, Anacreon, Theocritus, Homer. Read also Milton's paradise lost, Ossian, Pope's works, Swift's works in order to form your style in your own language. In morality read Epictetus, Xenophontis memorabilia, Plato's Socratic dialogues, Cicero's philosophies. In order to assure a certain progress in this reading, consider what hours you have free from the school and the exercises of the school. Give about two of them every day to exercise; for health must not be sacrificed to learning. A strong body makes the mind strong. As to the species of exercise, I advise the gun. While this gives a moderate exercise to the body, it gives boldness, enterprize, and independance to the mind. Games played with the ball and others of that nature, are too violent for the body and stamp no character on the mind. Let your gun therefore be the constant companion of your walks. Never think of taking a book with you. The object of walking is to relax the mind. You should therefore not permit yourself even to think while you walk. But divert your attention by the objects surrounding you. Walking is the best possible exercise. Habituate yourself to walk very far. The Europeans value themselves on having subdued the horse to the uses of man. But I doubt whether we have not lost more than we have gained by the use of this animal. No one has occasioned so much the degeneracy of the human body. An Indian goes on foot nearly as far in a day, for a long journey, as an enfeebled white does on his horse, and he will tire the best horses. There is no habit you will value so much as that of walking far without fatigue. I would advise you to take your exercise in the afternoon. Not because it is the best time for exercise for certainly it is not: but because it is the best time to spare from your studies; and habit will soon reconcile it to health, and render it nearly as useful as if you gave to that the more precious hours of the day. A little walk of half an hour in the morning when you first rise is advisable also. It shakes off sleep, and produces other good effects in the animal œconomy. Rise at a fixed and an early hour, and go to bed at a fixed and early hour also. Sitting up late at night is injurious to the health, and not useful to the mind.—Having ascribed proper hours to exercise, divide what remain (I mean of your vacant hours) into three portions. Give the principal to history, the other two, which should be shorter, to Philosophy and Poetry. Write me once every month or two and let me know the progress you make. Tell me in what manner you employ every hour in the day. The plan I have proposed for you is adapted to your present situation only. When that is changed, I shall propose a corresponding change of plan. . . .

To John Jay[1]

Paris Aug. 23, 1785.

DEAR SIR

I shall sometimes ask your permission to write you letters, not official but private. The present is of this kind, and is occasioned by the question proposed in yours of June 14 "Whether it would be useful to us to carry all our own

[1] Secretary of Foreign Affairs. [Ed.]

productions, or none?" Were we perfectly free to decide this question, I should reason as follows. We have now lands enough to employ an infinite number of people in their cultivation. Cultivators of the earth are the most valuable citizens. They are the most vigorous, the most independant, the most virtuous, and they are tied to their country and wedded to it's liberty and interests by the most lasting bands. As long therefore as they can find emploiment in this line, I would not convert them into mariners, artisans, or any thing else. But our citizens will find emploiment in this line till their numbers, and of course their productions, become too great for the demand both internal and foreign. This is not the case as yet, and probably will not be for a considerable time. As soon as it is, the surplus of hands must be turned to something else. I should then perhaps wish to turn them to the sea in preference to manufactures, because comparing the characters of the two classes I find the former the most valuable citizens. I consider the class of artificers as the panders of vice and the instruments by which the liberties of a country are generally overturned. However we are not free to decide this question on principles of theory only. Our people are decided in the opinion that it is necessary for us to take a share in the occupation of the ocean, and their established habits induce them to require that the sea be kept open to them, and that that line of policy be pursued which will render the use of that element as great as possible to them. I think it a duty in those entrusted with the administration of their affairs to conform themselves to the decided choice of their constituents: and that therefore we should in every instance preserve an equality of right to them in the transportation of commodities, in the right of fishing, and in the other uses of the sea. But what will be the consequence? Frequent wars without a doubt. Their property will be violated on the sea, and in foreign ports, their persons will be insulted, emprisoned &c. for pretended debts, contracts, crimes, contraband &c. &c. These insults must be resented, even if we had no feelings, yet to prevent their eternal repetition. Or in other words, our commerce on the ocean and in other countries must be paid for by frequent war. The justest dispositions possible in ourselves will not secure us against it. It would be necessary that all other nations were just also. Justice indeed on our part will save us from those wars which would have been produced by a contrary disposition. But how to prevent those produced by the wrongs of other nations? By putting ourselves in a condition to punish them. Weakness provokes insult and injury, while a condition to punish it often prevents it. This reasoning leads to the necessity of some naval force, that being the only weapon with which we can reach an enemy. I think it to our interest to punish the first insult: because an insult unpunished is the parent of many others. We are not at this moment in a condition to do it, but we should put ourselves into it as soon as possible. If a war with England should take place it seems to me that the first thing necessary would be a resolution to abandon the carrying trade because we cannot protect it. Foreign nations must in that case be invited to bring us what we want and to take our productions in their own bottoms. This alone could prevent the loss of those productions to us and the acquisition of them to our enemy. Our seamen might be emploied in depredations on their trade. But how dreadfully we shall suffer on our coasts, if we have no force on the water, former experience has taught us. Indeed I look forward with horror to the very possible case of war with an European power, and think there is no protection against them but from the possession of some force on the sea. Our vicinity to their West India possessions and to the fisheries is a bridle which a small naval force on our part would hold in the mouths of the most powerful of these countries. I hope our land office will rid us of our debts, and that our first attention then will be to the beginning a naval force of some sort. This alone can countenance our people as carriers on the water, and I suppose them to be determined to continue such. . . .

To Chastellux

Paris Sep. 2. 1785.

DEAR SIR

You were so kind as to allow me a fortnight to read your journey through Virginia. But you should have thought of this indulgence while you were writing it, and have rendered it less interesting if you meant that your readers should have been longer engaged with it. In fact I devoured it at a single meal, and a second reading scarce allowed me sang froid enough to mark a few errors in the names of persons and places which I note on a paper herein inclosed, with an inconsiderable error or two in facts which I have also noted because I supposed you wished to state them correctly. From this general approbation however you must allow me to except about a dozen pages in the earlier part of the book which I read with a continued blush from beginning to end, as it presented me a lively picture of what I wish to be, but am not.[1] No, my dear Sir, the thousand millionth part of what you there say, is more than I deserve. It might perhaps have passed in Europe at the time you wrote it, and the exaggeration might not have been detected. But consider that the animal is now brought there, and that every one will take his dimensions for himself. The friendly complexion of your mind has betrayed you into a partiality of which the European spectator will be divested. Respect to yourself therefore will require indispensably that you expunge the whole of those pages except your own judicious observations interspersed among them on Animal and physi-

[1] Chastellux's flattering description of Jefferson appeared in *Voyages . . . dans l'Amérique Septentrionale dans les années 1780, 1781 et 1782* (Paris, 1786). Enclosure omitted. [Ed.]

cal subjects. With respect to my countrymen[2] there is surely nothing which can render them uneasy, in the observations made on them. They know that they are not perfect, and will be sensible that you have viewed them with a philanthropic eye. You say much good of them, and less ill than they are conscious may be said with truth. I have studied their character with attention. I have thought them, as you have found them, aristocratical, pompous, clannish, indolent, hospitable, and I should have added, disinterested, but you say attached to their interest. This is the only trait in their character wherein our observations differ. I have always thought them so careless of their interests, so thoughtless in their expences and in all their transactions of business that I had placed it among the vices of their character, as indeed most virtues when carried beyond certain bounds degenerate into vices. I had even ascribed this to it's cause, to that warmth of their climate which unnerves and unmans both body and mind. While on this subject I will give you my idea of the characters of the several states.

In the North they are
cool
sober
laborious
persevering
independant
jealous of their own liberties, and just to those of others
interested
chicaning
superstitious and hypocritical in their religion

In the South they are
fiery
Voluptuary
indolent
unsteady
independant
zealous for their own liberties, but trampling on those of others
generous
candid
without attachment or pretentions to any religion but that of the heart.

[2] In this case, Virginians. [Ed.]

These characteristics grow weaker and weaker by gradation from North to South and South to North, insomuch that an observing traveller, without the aid of the quadrant may always know his latitude by the character of the people among whom he finds himself. It is in Pennsylvania that the two characters seem to meet and blend and to form a people free from the extremes both of vice and virtue. Peculiar circumstances have given to New York the character which climate would have given had she been placed on the South instead of the North side of Pennsylvania. Perhaps too other circumstances may have occasioned in Virginia a transplantation of a particular vice foreign to it's climate. You could judge of this with more impartiality than I could, and the probability is that your estimate of them is the most just. I think it for their good that the vices of their character should be pointed out to them that they may amend them; for a malady of either body or mind once known is half cured.

I wish you would add to this peice your letter to Mr. Madison on the expediency of introducing the arts into America. I found in that a great deal of matter, very many observations, which would be useful to the legislators of America, and to the general mass of citizens. I read it with great pleasure and analysed it's contents that I might fix them in my own mind. I have the honor to be with very sincere esteem Dear Sir Your most obedient & most humble servt.

To James Madison

Paris Sep. 20. 1785.

. . . I received this summer a letter from Messrs. Buchanan and Hay as directors of the public buildings desiring I would have drawn for them plans of sundry buildings, and in the first place of a Capitol. They fixed for their receiving this plan a day which was within one month of that on which their letter came to my hand. I engaged an Architect of capital abilities in this business. Much time was requisite, after the external form was agreed on, to make the internal distribution convenient for the three branches of government. This time was much lengthened by my avocations to other objects which I had no right to neglect. The plan however was settled. The gentlemen had sent me one which they had thought of. The one agreed on here is more convenient, more beautiful, gives more room and will not cost more than two thirds of what that would. We took for our model what is called the Maisonquarrèe of Nismes, one of the most beautiful, if not the most beautiful and precious morsel of architecture left us by antiquity. It was built by Caius and Lucius Caesar and repaired by Louis XIV. and has the suffrage of all the judges of architecture who have seen it, as yielding to no one of the beautiful monuments of Greece, Rome, Palmyra and Balbec which late travellers have communicated to us. It is very simple, but it is noble beyond expression, and would have done honour to our country as presenting to travellers a morsel of taste in our infancy promising much for our maturer age. I have been much mortified with information which I received two days ago from Virginia that the first brick of the Capitol would be laid within a few days. But surely the delay of this peice of a summer would have been repaid by the savings in the plan preparing here, were we to value it's other superiorities as nothing. But how is a taste in this beautiful art to be formed in our countrymen, unless we avail ourselves of every occasion when public buildings are to be erected, of presenting to them models for their study and imitation? Pray try if you can effect the stopping of this work. I have written also to E. R. on the subject. The loss will be only of the laying the bricks already laid, or a part of them. The bricks themselves will do again for the interior walls, and one side wall and one end wall may remain as they will answer equally well for our plan. This loss is not to be weighed against the saving of money which will arise, against the comfort of laying out the public money for something honourable, the satisfaction of seeing an object and proof of national good taste, and the regret and mortification of erecting a monument of our barbarism which will be loaded with execrations as long as it shall endure. The plans are in good forwardness and I hope will be ready within three or four weeks. They could not be stopped now but on paying their whole price which will be considerable. If the Undertakers are afraid to undo what they have done, encourage them to it by a recommendation from the assembly. You see I am an enthusiast on the subject of the arts. But it is an enthusiasm of which I am not ashamed, as it's object is to improve the taste of my countrymen, to increase their reputation, to reconcile to them the respect of the world and procure them it's praise. . . .

To Charles Bellini

Paris Sep. 30. 1785.

. . . Behold me at length on the vaunted scene of Europe! It is not necessary for your information that I should enter into details concerning it. But you are perhaps curious to know how this new scene has struck a savage of the mountains of America. Not advantageously I assure you. I find the general fate of humanity here most deplorable. The truth of Voltaire's observation offers itself perpetually, that every man here must be either the hammer or the anvil. It is a true picture of that country to which they say we shall pass hereafter, and where we are to see god and his angels in splendor, and crouds of the damned trampled under their feet. While the great mass of the people are thus suffering under physical and moral oppression, I have endeavored to examine more nearly the condition of the great, to appreciate the true value of the circumstances in their situation which dazzle the bulk of the spectators, and especially to compare it with that degree of happiness which is enjoyed in America by every class of people. Intrigues of love occupy the younger, and those of ambition the more elderly part of the great. Conjugal love having no existence among them, domestic happiness, of which that is the basis, is utterly unknown. In lieu of this are substituted pursuits which nourish and invigorate all our bad passions, and which offer only moments of extasy amidst days and months of restlessness and torment. Much, very much inferior this to the tranquil permanent felicity with which domestic society in America blesses most of it's inhabitants, leaving them to follow steadily those pursuits which health and reason approve, and rendering truly delicious the intervals of these pursuits. In science, the mass of people is two centuries behind ours, their literati half a dozen years before us. Books, really good, acquire just reputation in that time, and so become known to us and communicate to us all their advances in knowledge. Is not this delay compensated by our being placed out of the reach of that swarm of nonsense which issues daily from a thousand presses and perishes almost in issuing? With respect to what are termed polite manners, without sacrificing too much the sincerity of language, I would wish [my] countrymen to adopt just so much of European politeness as to be ready [to] make all those little sacrifices of self which really render European manners amiable, and relieve society from the disagreeable scenes to which rudeness often exposes it. Here it seems that a man might pass a life without encountering a single rudeness. In the pleasures of the table they are far before us, because with good taste they unite temperance. They do not terminate the most sociable meals by transforming themselves into brutes. I have never yet seen a man drunk in France, even among the lowest of the people. Were I to proceed to tell you how much I enjoy their architecture, sculpture, painting, music, I should want words. It is in these arts they shine.

The last of them particularly is an enjoiment, the depriva-
tion of which with us cannot be calculated. I am almost
ready to say it is the only thing which from my heart I
envy them, and which in spight of all the authority of the
decalogue I do covet. . . .

To John Banister, Jr.

Paris Oct. 15. 1785.

DEAR SIR

I should sooner have answered the paragraph in your
favor of Sep. 19. respecting the best seminary for the education of youth in Europe, but that it was necessary for
me to make enquiries on the subject. The result of these
has been to consider the competition as resting between
Geneva and Rome. They are equally cheap, and probably
are equal in the course of education pursued. The advantage of Geneva is that students acquire there the habits of
speaking French. The advantages of Rome are the acquiring a local knowledge of a spot so classical and so celebrated; the acquiring the true pronuntiation of the Latin
language; the acquiring a just taste in the fine arts, more
particularly those of painting, sculpture, Architecture, and
Music; a familiarity with those objects and processes of
agriculture which experience has shewn best adapted to a
climate like ours; and lastly the advantage of a fine climate
for health. It is probable too that by being boarded in a
French family the habit of speaking that language may be
obtained. I do not count on any advantage to be derived
in Geneva from a familiar acquaintance with the principles
of it's government. The late revolution has rendered it a
tyrannical aristocracy more likely to give ill than good
ideas to an American. I think the balance in favor of Rome.
Pisa is sometimes spoken of as a place of education. But it
does not offer the 1st. and 3d. of the advantages of Rome.

But why send an American youth to Europe for education? What are the objects of an useful American education? Classical knowlege, modern languages and chiefly
French, Spanish, and Italian; Mathematics; Natural philosophy; Natural History; Civil History; Ethics. In Natural philosophy I mean to include Chemistry and Agriculture, and in Natural history to include Botany as well as
the other branches of those departments. It is true that the
habit of speaking the modern languages cannot be so well
acquired in America, but every other article can be as well
acquired at William and Mary College as at any place in
Europe. When College education is done with and a young
man is to prepare himself for public life, he must cast his
eyes (for America) either on Law or Physic. For the
former where can he apply so advantageously as to Mr.
Wythe? For the latter he must come to Europe; the medical class of students therefore is the only one which need
come to Europe. Let us view the disadvantages of sending
a youth to Europe. To enumerate them all would require
a volume. I will select a few. If he goes to England he
learns drinking, horse-racing and boxing. These are the
peculiarities of English education. The following circumstances are common to education in that and the other
countries of Europe. He acquires a fondness for European
luxury and dissipation and a contempt for the simplicity
of his own country; he is fascinated with the privileges of
the European aristocrats, and sees with abhorrence the
lovely equality which the poor enjoys with the rich in his
own country: he contracts a partiality for aristocracy or
monarchy; he forms foreign friendships which will never
be useful to him, and loses the season of life for forming in
his own country those friendships which of all others are
the most faithful and permanent: he is led by the strongest
of all the human passions into a spirit for female intrigue
destructive of his own and others happiness, or a passion
for whores destructive of his health, and in both cases
learns to consider fidelity to the marriage bed as an un-

gentlemanly practice and inconsistent with happiness: he recollects the voluptuary dress and arts of the European women and pities and despises the chaste affections and simplicity of those of his own country; he retains thro' life a fond recollection and a hankering after those places which were the scenes of his first pleasures and of his first connections; he returns to his own country, a foreigner, unacquainted with the practices of domestic œconomy necessary to preserve him from ruin; speaking and writing his native tongue as a foreigner, and therefore unqualified to obtain those distinctions which eloquence of the pen and tongue ensures in a free country; for I would observe to you that what is called style in writing or speaking is formed very early in life while the imagination is warm, and impressions are permanent. I am of opinion that there never was an instance of a man's writing or speaking his native tongue with elegance who passed from 15. to 20. years of age out of the country where it was spoken. Thus no instance exists of a person writing two languages perfectly. That will always appear to be his native language which was most familiar to him in his youth. It appears to me then that an American coming to Europe for education loses in his knowledge, in his morals, in his health, in his habits, and in his happiness. I had entertained only doubts on this head before I came to Europe: what I see and hear since I come here proves more than I had even suspected. Cast your eye over America: who are the men of most learning, of most eloquence, most beloved by their country and most trusted and promoted by them? They are those who have been educated among them, and whose manners, morals and habits are perfectly homogeneous with those of the country.—Did you expect by so short a question to draw such a sermon on yourself? I dare say you did not. But the consequences of foreign education are alarming to me as an American. I sin therefore through zeal whenever I enter on the subject. You are sufficiently American to pardon me for it. Let me hear of your health and be assured of the esteem with which I am Dear Sir Your friend & servant.

To James Madison

Fontainebleau Oct. 28. 1785.

DEAR SIR

Seven o'clock, and retired to my fireside, I have determined to enter into conversation with you; this is a village of about 5,000 inhabitants when the court is not here and 20,000 when they are, occupying a valley thro' which runs a brook, and on each side of it a ridge of small mountains most of which are naked rock. The king comes here in the fall always, to hunt. His court attend him, as do also the foreign diplomatic corps. But as this is not indispensably required, and my finances do not admit the expence of a continued residence here, I propose to come occasionally to attend the king's levees, returning again to Paris, distant 40 miles. This being the first trip, I set out yesterday morning to take a view of the place. For this purpose I shaped my course towards the highest of the mountains in sight, to the top of which was about a league. As soon as I had got clear of the town I fell in with a poor woman walking at the same rate with myself and going the same course. Wishing to know the condition of the labouring poor I entered into conversation with her, which I began by enquiries for the path which would lead me into the mountain: and thence proceeded to enquiries into her vocation, condition and circumstance. She told me she was a day labourer, at 8. sous or 4 d. sterling the day; that she had two children to maintain, and to pay a rent of 30 livres for her house (which would consume the hire of 75 days), that often she could get no emploiment, and of course was without bread. As we had walked together near a mile and she had so far served me as a guide, I gave her, on parting 24 sous. She burst into tears of a gratitude which I could perceive was unfeigned, because she was unable to utter a word. She had probably never before received so great an aid. This little *attendrissement*, with the solitude of my walk led me into a train of reflections on that unequal division of property which occasions the numberless instances of wretchedness which I had observed in this country and is to be observed all over Europe. The property of this country is absolutely concentered in a very few hands, having revenues of from half a million of guineas a year downwards. These employ the flower of the country as servants, some of them having as many as 200 domestics, not labouring. They employ also a great number of manufacturers, and tradesmen, and lastly the class of labouring husbandmen. But after all these comes the most numerous of all the classes, that is, the poor who cannot find work. I asked myself what could be the reason that so many should be permitted to beg who are willing to work, in a country where there is a very considerable proportion of uncultivated lands? These lands are kept idle mostly for the sake of game. It should seem then that it must be because of the enormous wealth of the proprietors which places them above attention to the increase of their revenues by permitting these lands to be laboured. I am conscious that an equal division of property is impracticable. But the consequences of this enormous inequality producing so much misery to the bulk of mankind, legislators cannot invent too many devices for subdividing property, only taking care to let their subdivisions go hand in hand with the natural affections of the human mind. The descent of property of every kind therefore to all the children, or to all the brothers and sisters, or other relations in equal degree is a politic measure, and a practicable one. Another means of silently lessening the inequality of property is to exempt all from taxation below a certain point, and to tax the higher portions of property in geometrical progression as they rise. Whenever there is in any country, uncultivated lands and unemployed poor, it is clear that the laws of property have been so far extended as to violate natural right. The earth is given as a common stock for man to labour and live on. If, for the encouragement of industry we allow it to be appropriated, we must take care that other employment be furnished to those excluded from the appropriation. If we do not the fundamental right to labour the earth returns to the unemployed. It is too soon yet in our country to say that every man who cannot find employment but who can find uncultivated land, shall be at liberty to cultivate it, paying a moderate rent. But it is not too soon to provide by every possible means that as few as possible shall be without a little portion of land. The small landholders are the most precious part of a state.—The next object which struck my attention in my walk was the deer with which the wood abounded. They were of the kind called 'Cerfs' and are certainly of the same species with ours. They are blackish indeed under the belly, and not white as ours, and they are more of the chestnut red: but these are such small differences as would be sure to happen in two races from the same stock, breeding separately a number of ages.—Their hares are totally different from the animal we call by that name: but their rabbet is almost exactly like him. The only difference is in their manners; the land on which I walked for some time being absolutely reduced to a honeycomb by their burrowing. I think there is no instance of ours burrowing.—After descending the hill again I saw a man cutting fern. I went to him under the pretence of asking the shortest road to the town, and afterwards asked for what use he was cutting fern. He told me that this part of the country furnished a great deal of fruit to Paris. That when packed in straw it acquired an ill taste, but that dry fern preserved it perfectly without communicating any taste at all. I treasured this observation for the preservation of my apples on my return to my own country. They have no apple here to compare with our Newtown pipping. They have nothing which deserves the name of a peach; there being not sun enough to ripen the plumbpeach and the best of their soft peaches being like our autumn peaches. Their cherries and strawberries are fair, but I think less flavoured. Their plumbs I think are better; so also the gooseberries, and the pears infinitely beyond any thing we possess. They have no grape better than our sweet-water. But they have a succession of as good from very early in the summer till frost. I am tomorrow to go to Mr. Malsherbes (an uncle of the Chevalr. Luzerne's) about 7. leagues from hence, who is the most curious man in France as to his trees. He is making for me a collection of the vines from which the Burgundy, Champagne, Bourdeaux, Frontignac, and other the most valuable wines of this country are made. Another gentleman is collecting for me the best eating grapes, including what we call the raisin. I propose also to endeavor to colonize their hare, rabbet, red and grey partridge, pheasants of different kinds, and some other birds. But I find that I am wandering beyond the limits of my walk and will therefore bid you Adieu. Yours affectionately.

To George Wythe

Paris Aug. 13. 1786.

. . . The European papers have announced that the assembly of Virginia were occupied on the revisal of their Code of laws. This, with some other similar intelligence, has contributed much to convince the people of Europe, that what the English papers are constantly publishing of our anarchy, is false; as they are sensible that such a work is that of a people only who are in perfect tranquillity. Our act for freedom of religion is extremely applauded. The Ambassadors and ministers of the several nations of Europe resident at this court have asked of me copies of it to send to their sovereigns, and it is inserted at full length in several books now in the press; among others, in the new Encyclopedie. I think it will produce considerable good even in these countries where ignorance, superstition, poverty and oppression of body and mind in every form, are so firmly settled on the mass of the people, that their redemption from them can never be hoped. If the almighty had begotten a thousand sons, instead of one, they would not have sufficed for this task. If all the sovereigns of Europe were to set themselves to work to emancipate the minds of their subjects from their present ignorance and prejudices, and that as zealously as they now endeavor the contrary, a thousand years would not place them on that high ground on which our common people are now setting out. Ours could not have been so fairly put into the hands of their own common sense, had they not been separated from their parent stock and been kept from contamination, either from them, or the other people of the old world, by the intervention of so wide an ocean. To know the worth of this, one must see the want of it here. I think by far the most important bill in our whole code is that for the diffusion of knowlege among the people. No other sure foundation can be devised for the preservation of freedom, and happiness. If any body thinks that kings, nobles, or priests are good conservators of the public happiness, send them here. It is the best school in the universe to cure them of that folly. They will see here with their own eyes that these descriptions of men are an abandoned confederacy against the happiness of the mass of people. The omnipotence of their effect cannot be better proved than in this country particularly, where notwithstanding the finest soil upon earth, the finest climate under heaven, and a people of the most benevolent, the most gay, and amiable character of which the human form is susceptible, where such a people I say, surrounded by so many blessings from nature, are yet loaded with misery by kings, nobles and priests, and by them alone. Preach, my dear Sir, a crusade against ignorance; establish and improve the law for educating the common people. Let our countrymen know that the people alone can protect us against these evils, and that the tax which will be paid for this purpose is not more than the thousandth part of what will be paid to kings, priests and nobles who will rise up among us if we leave the people in ignorance. . . .

To Maria Cosway

Paris Octob. 12 1786

MY DEAR MADAM

Having performed the last sad office of handing you into your carriage at the Pavillon de St. Denis, and seen the wheels get actually into motion, I turned on my heel and walked, more dead than alive, to the opposite door, where my own was awaiting me. Mr. Danquerville was missing. He was sought for, found, and dragged down stairs. We were crammed into the carriage, like recruits for the Bastille, and not having soul enough to give orders to the coachman, he presumed Paris our destination, and drove off. After a considerable interval silence was broke with a '*je suis vraiment affligé du depart de ces bons gens.*' This was the signal for a mutual confession of distress. We began immediately to talk of Mr. and Mrs. Cosway, of their goodness, their talents, their amability, and tho we spoke of nothing else, we seemed hardly to have entered into matter when the coachman announced the rue St. Denis, and that we were opposite Mr. Danquerville's. He insisted on descending there and traversing a short passage to his lodgings. I was carried home. Seated by my fire side, solitary and sad, the following dialogue took place between my Head and my Heart.

Head. Well, friend, you seem to be in a pretty trim.

Heart. I am indeed the most wretched of all earthly beings. Overwhelmed with grief, every fibre of my frame distended beyond it's natural powers to bear, I would willingly meet whatever catastrophe should leave me no more to feel or to fear.

Head. These are the eternal consequences of your warmth and precipitation. This is one of the scrapes into which you are ever leading us. You confess your follies indeed: but still you hug and cherish them, and no reformation can be hoped, where there is no repentance.

Heart. Oh my friend! This is no moment to upbraid my foibles. I am rent into fragments by the force of my grief! If you have any balm, pour it into my wounds: if none, do not harrow them by new torments. Spare me in this awful moment! At any other I will attend with patience to your admonitions.

Head. On the contrary I never found that the moment of triumph with you was the moment of attention to my admonitions. While suffering under your follies you may perhaps be made sensible of them, but, the paroxysm over, you fancy it can never return. Harsh therefore as the medecine may be, it is my office to administer it. You will be pleased to remember that when our friend Trumbull used to be telling us of the merits and talents of these good people, I never ceased whispering to you that we had no occasion for new acquaintance; that the greater their merit and talents, the more dangerous their friendship to our tranquillity, because the regret at parting would be greater.

Heart. Accordingly, Sir, this acquaintance was not the consequence of my doings. It was one of your projects which threw us in the way of it. It was you, remember, and not I, who desired the meeting, at Legrand & Molinos. I never trouble myself with domes nor arches. The Halle aux bleds might have rotted down before I should have gone to see it. But you, forsooth, who are eternally getting us to sleep with your diagrams and crotchets, must go and examine this wonderful piece of architecture. And when you had seen it, oh! it was the most superb thing on earth! What you had seen there was worth all you had yet seen in Paris! I thought so too. But I meant it of the lady and gentleman to whom we had been presented, and not of a parcel of sticks and chips put together in pens. You then,

Sir, and not I, have been the cause of the present distress.

Head. It would have been happy for you if my diagrams and crotchets had gotten you to sleep on that day, as you are pleased to say they eternally do. My visit to Legrand & Molinos had publick utility for it's object. A market is to be built in Richmond. What a commodious plan is that of Legrand & Molinos: especially if we put on it the noble dome of the Halle aux bleds. If such a bridge as they shewed us can be thrown across the Schuylkill at Philadelphia, the floating bridges taken up, and the navigation of that river opened, what a copious resource will be added, of wood and provisions, to warm and feed the poor of that city. While I was occupied with these objects, you were dilating with your new acquaintances, and contriving how to prevent a separation from them. Every soul of you had an engagement for the day. Yet all these were to be sacrificed, that you might dine together. Lying messengers were to be dispatched into every quarter of the city with apologies for your breach of engagement. You particularly had the effrontery to send word to the Dutchess Danville that, in the moment we were setting out to dine with her, dispatches came to hand which required immediate attention. You wanted me to invent a more ingenious excuse; but I knew you were getting into a scrape, and I would have nothing to do with it. Well, after dinner to St. Cloud, from St. Cloud to Ruggieri's, from Ruggieri to Krumfoltz, and if the day had been as long as a Lapland summer day, you would still have contrived means, among you, to have filled it.

Heart. Oh! my dear friend, how you have revived me by recalling to my mind the transactions of that day! How well I remember them all, and that when I came home at night and looked back to the morning, it seemed to have been a month agone. Go on then, like a kind comforter, and paint to me the day we went to St. Germains. How beautiful was every object! the Port de Neuilly, the hills along the Seine, the rainbows of the machine of Marly, the terras of St. Germains, the chateaux, the gardens, the statues of Marly, the pavillon of Lucienne. Recollect too Madrid, Bagatelle, the King's garden, the Dessert. How grand the idea excited by the remains of such a column! The spiral staircase too was beautiful. Every moment was filled with something agreeable. The wheels of time moved on with a rapidity of which those of our carriage gave but a faint idea, and yet in the evening, when one took a retrospect of the day, what a mass of happiness had we travelled over! Retrace all those scenes to me, my good companion, and I will forgive the unkindness with which you were chiding me. The day we went to St. Germains was a little too warm, I think, was not it?

Head. Thou art the most incorrigible of all the beings that ever sinned! I reminded you of the follies of the first day, intending to deduce from thence some useful lessons for you, but instead of listening to these, you kindle at the recollection, you retrace the whole series with a fondness which shews you want nothing but the opportunity to act it over again. I often told you during it's course that you were imprudently engaging your affections under circumstances that must cost you a great deal of pain: that the persons indeed were of the greatest merit, possessing good sense, good humour, honest hearts, honest manners, and eminence in a lovely art: that the lady had moreover qualities and accomplishments, belonging to her sex, which might form a chapter apart for her: such as music, modesty, beauty, and that softness of disposition which is the ornament of her sex and charm of ours. But that all these considerations would increase the pang of separation: that their stay here was to be short: that you rack our whole system when you are parted from those you love, complaining that such a separation is worse than death, inasmuch as this ends our sufferings, whereas that only begins them: and that the separation would in this instance be the more severe as you would probably never see them again.

Heart. But they told me they would come back again the next year.

Head. But in the mean time see what you suffer: and their return too depends on so many circumstances that if you had a grain of prudence you would not count upon it. Upon the whole it is improbable and therefore you should abandon the idea of ever seeing them again.

Heart. May heaven abandon me if I do!

Head. Very well. Suppose then they come back. They are to stay here two months, and when these are expired, what is to follow? Perhaps you flatter yourself they may come to America?

Heart. God only knows what is to happen. I see nothing impossible in that supposition, and I see things wonderfully contrived sometimes to make us happy. Where could they find such objects as in America for the exercise of their enchanting art? especially the lady, who paints landscape so inimitably. She wants only subjects worthy of immortality to render her pencil immortal. The Falling spring, the Cascade of Niagara, the Passage of the Potowmac thro the Blue mountains, the Natural bridge. It is worth a voiage across the Atlantic to see these objects; much more to paint, and make them, and thereby ourselves, known to all ages. And our own dear Monticello, where has nature spread so rich a mantle under the eye? mountains, forests, rocks, rivers. With what majesty do we there ride above the storms! How sublime to look down into the workhouse of nature, to see her clouds, hail, snow, rain, thunder, all fabricated at our feet! And the glorious Sun, when rising as if out of a distant water, just gilding the tops of the mountains, and giving life to all nature!——I hope in god no circumstance may ever make either seek an asylum from grief! With what sincere sympathy I would open every cell of my composition to receive the effusion of their woes! I would pour my tears into their wounds: and if a drop of balm could be found at the top of the Cordilleras, or at the remotest sources of the Missouri, I would go thither myself to seek and to bring it. Deeply practised in the school of affliction, the human heart knows no joy which I have not lost, no sorrow of which I have not drank! Fortune can present no grief of unknown form to me! Who then can so softly bind up the wound of another as he who has felt the same wound himself? But Heaven forbid they should ever know a sorrow!—Let us turn over another leaf, for this has distracted me.

Head. Well. Let us put this possibility to trial then on another point. When you consider the character which is given of our country by the lying newspapers of London, and their credulous copyers in other countries; when you reflect that all Europe is made to believe we are a lawless banditti, in a state of absolute anarchy, cutting one another's throats, and plundering without distinction, how can you expect that any reasonable creature would venture among us?

Heart. But you and I know that all this is false: that there is not a country on earth where there is greater tranquillity, where the laws are milder, or better obeyed: where every one is more attentive to his own business, or meddles less with that of others: where strangers are better received, more hospitably treated, and worth a more sacred respect.

Head. True, you and I know this, but your friends do not know it.

Heart. But they are sensible people who think for themselves. They will ask of impartial foreigners who have been among us, whether they saw or heard on the spot any instances of anarchy. They will judge too that a people occupied as we are in opening rivers, digging navigable canals, making roads, building public schools, establishing academies, erecting busts and statues to our great men, protecting religious freedom, abolishing sanguinary punishments, reforming and improving our laws in general, they will judge I say for themselves whether these are not the occupations of a people at their ease, whether this is

not better evidence of our true state than a London newspaper, hired to lie, and from which no truth can ever be
extracted but by reversing everything it says.

Head. I did not begin this lecture my friend with a view
to learn from you what America is doing. Let us return
then to our point. I wished to make you sensible how im-
prudent it is to place your affections, without reserve, on
objects you must so soon lose, and whose loss when it
comes must cost you such severe pangs. Remember the
last night. You knew your friends were to leave Paris
to-day. This was enough to throw you into agonies. All
night you tossed us from one side of the bed to the other.
No sleep, no rest. The poor crippled wrist too, never left
one moment in the same position, now up, now down, now
here, now there; was it to be wondered at if all it's pains
returned? The Surgeon then was to be called, and to be
rated as an ignoramus because he could not devine the
cause of this extraordinary change.—In fine, my friend,
you must mend your manners. This is not a world to live
at random in as you do. To avoid these eternal distresses,
to which you are for ever exposing us, you must learn to
look forward before you take a step which may interest
our peace. Everything in this world is matter of calculation. Advance then with caution, the balance in your hand.
Put into one scale the pleasures which any object may
offer; but put fairly into the other the pains which are to
follow, and see which preponderates. The making an acquaintance is not a matter of indifference. When a new
one is proposed to you, view it all round. Consider what
advantages it presents, and to what inconveniencies it may
expose you. Do not bite at the bait of pleasure till you
know there is no hook beneath it. The art of life is the art
of avoiding pain: and he is the best pilot who steers clear-
est of the rocks and shoals with which it is beset. Pleasure
is always before us; but misfortune is at our side: while
running after that, this arrests us. The most effectual means
of being secure against pain is to retire within ourselves,

and to suffice for our own happiness. Those, which depend on ourselves, are the only pleasures a wise man will count on: for nothing is ours which another may deprive us of. Hence the inestimable value of intellectual pleasures. Ever in our power, always leading us to something new, never cloying, we ride, serene and sublime, above the concerns of this mortal world, contemplating truth and nature, matter and motion, the laws which bind up their existence, and that eternal being who made and bound them up by these laws. Let this be our employ. Leave the bustle and tumult of society to those who have not talents to occupy themselves without them. Friendship is but another name for an alliance with the follies and the misfortunes of others. Our own share of miseries is sufficient: why enter then as volunteers into those of another? Is there so little gall poured into our own cup that we must needs help to drink that of our neighbor? A friend dies or leaves us: we feel as if a limb was cut off. He is sick: we must watch over him, and participate of his pains. His fortune is shipwrecked: ours must be laid under contribution. He loses a child, a parent or a partner: we must mourn the loss as if it was our own.

Heart. And what more sublime delight than to mingle tears with one whom the hand of heaven hath smitten! To watch over the bed of sickness, and to beguile it's tedious and it's painful moments! To share our bread with one to whom misfortune has left none! This world abounds indeed with misery: to lighten it's burthen we must divide it with one another. But let us now try the virtues of your mathematical balance, and as you have put into one scale the burthens of friendship, let me put it's comforts into the other. When languishing then under disease, how grateful is the solace of our friends! How are we penetrated with their assiduities and attentions! How much are we supported by their encouragements and kind offices! When Heaven has taken from us some object of our love, how sweet is it to have a bosom whereon to recline our heads,

and into which we may pour the torrent of our tears!
Grief, with such a comfort, is almost a luxury! In a life
where we are perpetually exposed to want and accident,
yours is a wonderful proposition, to insulate ourselves, to
retire from all aid, and to wrap ourselves in the mantle of
self-sufficiency! For assuredly nobody will care for him
who cares for nobody. But friendship is precious not only
in the shade but in the sunshine of life: and thanks to a
benevolent arrangement of things, the greater part of life
is sunshine. I will recur for proof to the days we have
lately passed. On these indeed the sun shone brightly! How
gay did the face of nature appear! Hills, vallies, chateaux,
gardens, rivers, every object wore it's liveliest hue!
Whence did they borrow it? From the presence of our
charming companion. They were pleasing, because she
seemed pleased. Alone, the scene would have been dull
and insipid: the participation of it with her gave it relish.
Let the gloomy Monk, sequestered from the world, seek
unsocial pleasures in the bottom of his cell! Let the sub-
limated philosopher grasp visionary happiness while pursuing phantoms dressed in the garb of truth! Their supreme wisdom is supreme folly: and they mistake for
happiness the mere absence of pain. Had they ever felt the
solid pleasure of one generous spasm of the heart, they
would exchange for it all the frigid speculations of their
lives, which you have been vaunting in such elevated terms.
Believe me then, my friend, that that is a miserable arithmetic which would estimate friendship at nothing, or at
less than nothing. Respect for you has induced me to enter
into this discussion, and to hear principles uttered which I
detest and abjure. Respect for myself now obliges me to
recall you into the proper limits of your office. When nature assigned us the same habitation, she gave us over it a
divided empire. To you she allotted the field of science, to
me that of morals. When the circle is to be squared, or
the orbit of a comet to be traced; when the arch of greatest strength, or the solid of least resistance is to be investi-

gated, take you the problem: it is yours: nature has given me no cognisance of it. In like manner in denying to you the feelings of sympathy, of benevolence, of gratitude, of justice, of love, of friendship, she has excluded you from their controul. To these she has adapted the mechanism of the heart. Morals were too essential to the happiness of man to be risked on the incertain combinations of the head. She laid their foundation therefore in sentiment, not in science. That she gave to all, as necessary to all: this to a few only, as sufficing with a few. I know indeed that you pretend authority to the sovereign controul of our conduct in all it's parts: and a respect for your grave saws and maxims, a desire to do what is right, has sometimes induced me to conform to your counsels. A few facts however which I can readily recall to your memory, will suffice to prove to you that nature has not organised you for our moral direction. When the poor wearied souldier, whom we overtook at Chickahominy with his pack on his back, begged us to let him get up behind our chariot, you began to calculate that the road was full of souldiers, and that if all should be taken up our horses would fail in their journey. We drove on therefore. But soon becoming sensible you had made me do wrong, that tho we cannot relieve all the distressed we should relieve as many as we can, I turned about to take up the souldier; but he had entered a bye path, and was no more to be found: and from that moment to this I could never find him out to ask his forgiveness. Again, when the poor woman came to ask a charity in Philadelphia, you whispered that she looked like a drunkard, and that half a dollar was enough to give her for the ale-house. Those who want the dispositions to give, easily find reasons why they ought not to give. When I sought her out afterwards, and did what I should have done at first, you know that she employed the money immediately towards placing her child at school. If our country, when pressed with wrongs at the point of the bayonet, had been governed by it's heads instead of it's hearts, where should we have been now? hanging on a gallows as high as Haman's. You began to calculate and to compare wealth and numbers: we threw up a few pulsations of our warmest blood: we supplied enthusiasm against wealth and numbers: we put our existence to the hazard, when the hazard seemed against us, and we saved our country: justifying at the same time the ways of Providence, whose precept is to do always what is right, and leave the issue to him. In short, my friend, as far as my recollection serves me, I do not know that I ever did a good thing on your suggestion, or a dirty one without it. I do for ever then disclaim your interference in my province. Fill paper as you please with triangles and squares: try how many ways you can hang and combine them together. I shall never envy nor controul your sublime delights. But leave me to decide when and where friendships are to be contracted. You say I contract them at random, so you said the woman at Philadelphia was a drunkard. I receive no one into my esteem till I know they are worthy of it. Wealth, title, office, are no recommendations to my friendship. On the contrary great good qualities are requisite to make amends for their having wealth, title and office. You confess that in the present case I could not have made a worthier choice. You only object that I was so soon to lose them. We are not immortal ourselves, my friend; how can we expect our enjoiments to be so? We have no rose without it's thorn; no pleasure without alloy. It is the law of our existence; and we must acquiesce. It is the condition annexed to all our pleasures, not by us who receive, but by him who gives them. True, this condition is pressing cruelly on me at this moment. I feel more fit for death than life. But when I look back on the pleasures of which it is the consequence, I am conscious they were worth the price I am paying. Notwithstanding your endeavors too to damp my hopes, I comfort myself with expectations of their promised return. Hope is sweeter than despair, and they were too good to mean to deceive me. In the summer, said the gentleman; but in the spring, said the lady: and I should love her forever, were it only for that! Know then, my friend, that I have taken these good people into my bosom: that I have lodged them in the warmest cell I could find: that I love them, and will continue to love them thro life: that if fortune should dispose them on one side the globe, and me on the other, my affections shall pervade it's whole mass to reach them. Knowing then my determination, attempt not to disturb it. If you can at any time furnish matter for their amusement, it will be the office of a good neighbor to do it. I will in like manner seize any occasion which may offer to do the like good turn for you with Condorcet, Rittenhouse, Madison, La Cretelle, or any other of those worthy sons of science whom you so justly prize.

I thought this a favorable proposition whereon to rest the issue of the dialogue. So I put an end to it by calling for my nightcap. Methinks I hear you wish to heaven I had called a little sooner, and so spared you the ennui of such a tedious sermon. I did not interrupt them sooner because I was in a mood for hearing sermons. You too were the subject; and on such a thesis I never think the theme long; not even if I am to write it, and that slowly and awkwardly, as now, with the left hand. But that you may not be discoraged from a correspondence which begins so formidably, I will promise you on my honour that my future letters shall be of a reasonable length. I will even agree to express but half my esteem for you, for fear of cloying you with too full a dose. But, on your part, no curtailing. If your letters are as long as the bible, they will appear short to me. Only let them be brim full of affection. I shall read them with the dispositions with which Arlequin in les deux billets spelt the words 'je t'aime' and wished that the whole alphabet had entered into their composition.

We have had incessant rains since your departure. These

make me fear for your health, as well as that you have had an uncomfortable journey. The same cause has prevented me from being able to give you any account of your friends here. This voiage to Fontainbleau will probably send the Count de Moustier and the Marquise de Brehan to America. Danquerville promised to visit me, but has not done it as yet. De latude comes sometimes to take family soupe with me, and entertains me with anecdotes of his five and thirty years imprisonment. How fertile is the mind of man which can make the Bastille and Dungeon of Vincennes yeild interesting anecdotes. You know this was for making four verses on Mme. de Pompadour. But I think you told me you did not know the verses. They were these. "*Sans esprit, sans sentiment, Sans etre belle, ni neuve, En France on peut avoir le premier amant: Pompadour en est l'epreuve.*" I have read the memoir of his three escapes. As to myself my health is good, except my wrist which mends slowly, and my mind which mends not at all, but broods constantly over your departure. The lateness of the season obliges me to decline my journey into the South of France. Present me in the most friendly terms to Mr. Cosway, and receive me into your own recollection with a partiality and a warmth, proportioned, not to my own poor merit, but to the sentiments of sincere affection and esteem with which I have the honour to be, my dear Madam, your most obedient humble servant.

To St. John de Crèvecoeur

Paris Jan. 15. 1787.

DEAR SIR

I see by the Journal of this morning that they are robbing us of another of our inventions to give it to the English. The writer indeed only admits them to have revived what he thinks was known to the Greeks, that is the making the circumference of a wheel of one single peice. The farmers in New Jersey were the first who practised it, and they practised it commonly. Dr. Franklin, in one of his trips to London, mentioned this practice to the man, now in London, who has the patent for making those wheels (I forget his name.) The idea struck him. The Doctor promised to go to his shop and assist him in trying to make the wheel of one peice. The Jersey farmers did it by cutting a young sapling, and bending it, while green and juicy, into a circle; and leaving it so till it became perfectly seasoned. But in London there are no saplings. The difficulty was then to give to old wood the pliancy of young. The Doctor and the workman laboured together some weeks, and succeeded, and the man obtained a patent for it which has made his fortune. I was in his shop in London, he told me the whole story himself, and acknowledged, not only the origin of the idea, but how much the assistance of Dr. Franklin had contributed to perform the operation on dry wood. He spoke of him with love and gratitude. I think I have had a similar account from Dr. Franklin, but cannot be certain quite. I know that being in Philadelphia when the first set of patent wheels arrived from London, and were spoken of by the gentleman (an Englishman) who brought them as a wonderful discovery. The idea of it's being a new discovery was laughed at by the Philadelphians, who in their Sunday parties across the Delaware had seen every farmer's cart mounted on such wheels. The writer in the paper supposes the English workman got his idea from Homer. But it is more likely that the Jersey farmer got the idea from thence, because ours are the only farmers who can read Homer: because too the Jersey practice is precisely that stated by Homer; the English practice very different. Homer's words are (comparing a young hero killed by Ajax to a poplar felled by a workman)————

ὃ δ' ἐν κονιῃσι, χαμαι, πεϲεν, αιγειρος ὡς,
Ἡ ῥα τ'ἐν ειαμενῃ ελεος μεγαλοιο πεφυκε
Λειη αταρ τε ὁι οζοι επ' ακροτατῃ πεφυαϲι
Την μεν θἁρματοπηγος ανηρ αιθωνι ϲιδηρῳ

Ἐξεταμ' οφρα ιτυν καμψη περικαλλεῖ διφρῳ,
Ἡ μεν τ'αξομενη κειται ποταμοιο παρ οχθας
4. Il. 482.

literally thus 'he fell on the ground, like a poplar, which
has grown, smooth, in the wet part of a great meadow;
with it's branches shooting from it's summit. But the Char-
iot-maker with his sharp axe, has felled it, that he may bend
a wheel for a beautiful chariot. It lies drying on the banks
of the river.' Observe the circumstances which coincide
with the Jersey practice. 1. It is a tree growing in a moist
place, full of juices, and easily bent. 2. It is cut while green.
3. It is bent into the circumference of a wheel. 4. It is left
to dry in that form. You, who write French well and
readily, should write a line for the Journal to reclaim the
honour of our farmers. Adieu. Your's affectionately.

To Edward Carrington

Paris Jan. 16. 1787

. . . The tumults in America,[1] I expected would have
produced in Europe an unfavorable opinion of our political state. But it has not. On the contrary, the small effect
of those tumults seems to have given more confidence in
the firmness of our governments. The interposition of the
people themselves on the side of government has had a
great effect on the opinion here. I am persuaded myself
that the good sense of the people will always be found to
be the best army. They may be led astray for a moment,
but will soon correct themselves. The people are the only
censors of their governors: and even their errors will tend
to keep these to the true principles of their institution. To
punish these errors too severely would be to suppress the
only safeguard of the public liberty. The way to prevent
these irregular interpositions of the people is to give them

[1] Shays's Rebellion, primarily. [Ed.]

full information of their affairs thro' the channel of the public papers, and to contrive that those papers should penetrate the whole mass of the people. The basis of our governments being the opinion of the people, the very first object should be to keep that right; and were it left to me to decide whether we should have a government without newspapers, or newspapers without a government, I should not hesitate a moment to prefer the latter. But I should mean that every man should receive those papers and be capable of reading them. I am convinced that those societies (as the Indians) which live without government enjoy in their general mass an infinitely greater degree of happiness than those who live under European governments. Among the former, public opinion is in the place of law, and restrains morals as powerfully as laws ever did any where. Among the latter, under pretence of governing they have divided their nations into two classes, wolves and sheep. I do not exaggerate. This is a true picture of Europe. Cherish therefore the spirit of our people, and keep alive their attention. Do not be too severe upon their errors, but reclaim them by enlightening them. If once they become inattentive to the public affairs, you and I, and Congress, and Assemblies, judges and governors shall all become wolves. It seems to be the law of our general nature, in spite of individual exceptions; and experience declares that man is the only animal which devours his own kind, for I can apply no milder term to the governments of Europe, and to the general prey of the rich on the poor.

To James Madison

Paris Jan. 30. 1787.

DEAR SIR

My last to you was of the 16th of Dec. since which I have received yours of Nov. 25. and Dec. 4. which

afforded me, as your letters always do, a treat on matters
public, individual and oeconomical. I am impatient to
learn your sentiments on the late troubles in the Eastern
states.[1] So far as I have yet seen, they do not appear to
threaten serious consequences. Those states have suffered
by the stoppage of the channels of their commerce, which
have not yet found other issues. This must render money
scarce, and make the people uneasy. This uneasiness has
produced acts absolutely unjustifiable: but I hope they
will provoke no severities from their governments. A
consciousness of those in power that their administration
of the public affairs has been honest, may perhaps produce
too great a degree of indignation: and those characters
wherein fear predominates over hope may apprehend too
much from these instances of irregularity. They may conclude too hastily that nature has formed man insusceptible
of any other government but that of force, a conclusion
not founded in truth, nor experience. Societies exist under
three forms sufficiently distinguishable. 1. Without government, as among our Indians. 2. Under governments wherein
the will of every one has a just influence, as is the case in
England in a slight degree, and in our states in a great one.
3. Under governments of force: as is the case in all other
monarchies and in most of the other republics. To have an
idea of the curse of existence under these last, they must
be seen. It is a government of wolves over sheep. It is a
problem, not clear in my mind, that the 1st. condition is
not the best. But I believe it to be inconsistent with any
great degree of population. The second state has a great
deal of good in it. The mass of mankind under that enjoys
a precious degree of liberty and happiness. It has it's evils
too: the principal of which is the turbulence to which it
is subject. But weigh this against the oppressions of
monarchy, and it becomes nothing. *Malo periculosam,
libertatem quam quietam servitutem.* Even this evil is
productive of good. It prevents the degeneracy of govern-

[1] Shays's Rebellion. [Ed.]

ment, and nourishes a general attention to the public affairs. I hold it that a little rebellion now and then is a good thing, and as necessary in the political world as storms in the physical. Unsuccessful rebellions indeed generally establish the incroachments on the rights of the people which have produced them. An observation of this truth should render honest republican governors so mild in their punishment of rebellions, as not to discourage them too much. It is a medecine necessary for the sound health of government. If these transactions give me no uneasiness, I feel very differently at another peice of intelligence, to wit, the possibility that the navigation of the Missisipi may be abandoned to Spain. I never had any interest Westward of the Alleghaney; and I never will have any. But I have had great opportunities of knowing the character of the people who inhabit that country. And I will venture to say that the act which abandons the navigation of the Missisipi is an act of separation between the Eastern and Western country. It is a relinquishment of five parts out of eight of the territory of the United States, an abandonment of the fairest subject for the paiment of our public debts, and the chaining those debts on our own necks in perpetuum. I have the utmost confidence in the honest intentions of those who concur in this measure; but I lament their want of acquaintance with the character and physical advantages of the people who, right or wrong, will suppose their interests sacrificed on this occasion to the contrary interests of that part of the confederacy in possession of present power. If they declare themselves a separate people, we are incapable of a single effort to retain them. Our citizens can never be induced, either as militia or as souldiers, to go there to cut the throats of their own brothers and sons, or rather to be themselves the subjects instead of the perpetrators of the parricide. Nor would that country quit the cost of being retained against the will of it's inhabitants, could it be done. But it cannot be done. They are able already to rescue the navigation of the Missisipi out of the hands of Spain, and to add New Orleans to their own territory. They will be joined by the inhabitants of Louisiana. This will bring on a war between them and Spain; and that will produce the question with us whether it will not be worth our while to become parties with them in the war, in order to reunite them with us, and thus correct our error? And were I to permit my forebodings to go one step further, I should predict that the inhabitants of the U.S. would force their rulers to take the affirmative of that question. I wish I may be mistaken in all these opinions. . . .

To Madame de Tessé

Nismes. Mar. 20. 1787.

Here I am, Madam, gazing whole hours at the Maison quarrée, like a lover at his mistress. The stocking-weavers and silk spinners around it consider me as an hypochondriac Englishman, about to write with a pistol the last chapter of his history. This is the second time I have been in love since I left Paris. The first was with a Diana at the Chateau de Laye Epinaye in the Beaujolois, a delicious morsel of sculpture, by Michael Angelo Slodtz. This, you will say, was in rule, to fall in love with a fine woman: but, with a house! It is out of all precedent! No, madam, it is not without a precedent in my own history. While at Paris, I was violently smitten with the hotel de Salm, and used to go to the Thuileries almost daily to look at it. The loueuse des chaises, inattentive to my passion, never had the complaisance to place a chair there; so that, sitting on the parapet, and twisting my neck round to see the object of my admiration, I generally left it with a torticollis. From Lyons to Nismes I have been nourished with the remains of Roman grandeur. They have always brought you to my mind, because I know your affection for whatever is Roman and noble. At Vienne I thought of you. But I am glad you were not there; for you would have seen me more angry than I hope you will ever see me. The Pretorian palace, as it is called, comparable for it's fine proportions to the Maison quarrée, totally defaced by the Barbarians who have coverted it to it's present purpose; it's beautiful, fluted, Corinthian columns cut out in part to make space for Gothic widows, and hewed down in the residue to the plane of the building. At Orange too I thought of you. I was sure you had seen with rapture the sublime triumphal arch at the entrance into the city. I went then to the Arenas. Would you believe Madam, that in this 18th. century, in France, under the reign of Louis XVI, they are at this moment pulling down the circular wall of this superb remain to pave a road? And that too from a hill which is itself an entire mass of stone just as fit, and more accessible. A former Intendant, a Monsr. de Baville has rendered his memory dear to travellers and amateurs by the pains he took to preserve and to restore these monuments of antiquity. The present one (I do not know who he is) is demolishing the object to make a good road to it. I thought of you again, and I was then in great good humour, at the Pont du Gard, a sublime antiquity, and well preserved. But most of all here, where Roman taste, genius, and magnificence excite ideas analogous to yours at every step, I could no longer oppose the inclination to avail myself of your permission to write to you, a permission given with too much complaisance by you, taken advantage of with too much indiscretion by me. Madame de Tott too did me the same honour. But she being only the descendant of some of those puny heroes who boiled their own kettles before the walls of Troy, I shall write to her from a Graecian, rather than a Roman canton; when I shall find myself for example among her Phocean relations at Marseilles. Loving, as you do Madam, the precious remains of antiquity, loving architecture, gardening, a warm sun, and a clear sky, I wonder you have never thought of moving Chaville to Nismes. This is not so

impracticable as you may think. The next time a Surin-
tendant des batiments du roi, after the example of M. Col-
bert, sends persons to Nismes to move the Maison quarrée
to Paris, that they may not come empty-handed, desire
them to bring Chaville with them to replace it. A propos
of Paris. I have now been three weeks from there without
knowing any thing of what has past. I suppose I shall meet
it all at Aix, where I have directed my letters to be lodged
poste restante. My journey has given me leisure to reflect
on this Assemblée des Notables. Under a good and young
king as the present, I think good may be made of it. I
would have the deputies then by all means so conduct
themselves as to encourage him to repeat the calls of this
assembly. Their first step should be to get themselves divided into two chambers, instead of seven, the Noblesse
and the commons separately. The 2d. to persuade the king,
instead of chusing the deputies of the commons himself, to
summon those chosen by the people for the Provincial administrations. The 3d. as the Noblesse is too numerous to
be all admitted into the assemblée, to obtain permission for
that body to chuse it's own deputies. The rest would
follow. Two houses so elected would contain a mass of
wisdom which would make the people happy, and the
king great; would place him in history where no other act
can possibly place him. This is my plan Madam; but I
wish to know yours, which I am sure is better.

From a correspondent at Nismes you will not expect
news. Were I to attempt to give you news, I should tell
you stories a thousand years old. I should detail to you
the intrigues of the courts of the Caesars, how they affect
us here, the oppressions of their Praetors, Praefects &c.
I am immersed in antiquities from morning to night. For
me the city of Rome is actually existing in all the splendor
of its empire. I am filled with alarms for the event of the
irruptions dayly making on us by the Goths, Ostrogoths,
Visigoths and Vandals, lest they should reconquer us to
our original barbarism. If I am sometimes induced to look

forward to the eighteenth century, it is only when recalled to it by the recollection of your goodness and friendship, and by those sentiments of sincere esteem and respect with which I have the honor to be, Madam, your most obedient & most humble servant.

To Lafayette

Nice, April 11, 1787.

Your head, my dear friend, is full of Notable things; and being better employed, therefore I do not expect letters from you. I am constantly roving about, to see what I have never seen before and shall never see again. In the great cities, I go to see what travellers think alone worthy of being seen; but I make a job of it, and generally gulp it all down in a day. On the other hand, I am never satiated with rambling through the fields and farms, examining the culture and cultivators, with a degree of curiosity which makes some take me to be a fool, and others to be much wiser than I am. I have been pleased to find among the people a less degree of physical misery than I had expected. They are generally well clothed, and have a plenty of food, not animal indeed, but vegetable, which is as wholesome. Perhaps they are over worked, the excess of the rent required by the landlord, obliging them to too many hours of labor, in order to produce that, and wherewith to feed and clothe themselves. The soil of Champagne and Burgundy I have found more universally good than I had expected, and as I could not help making a comparison with England, I found that comparison more unfavorable to the latter than is generally admitted. The soil, the climate, and the productions are superior to those of England, and the husbandry as good, except in one point; that of manure. In England, long leases for twenty-one years, or three lives, to wit, that of the farmer, his wife, and son, renewed by the son as soon as he comes to the possession, for his own life, his wife's and eldest child's, and so on, render the farms there almost hereditary, make it worth the farmer's while to manure the lands highly, and give the landlord an opportunity of occasionally making his rent keep pace with the improved state of the lands. Here the leases are either during pleasure, or for three, six, or nine years, which does not give the farmer time to repay himself for the expensive operation of well manuring, and therefore, he manures ill, or not at all. I suppose, that could the practice of leasing for three lives be introduced in the whole kingdom, it would, within the term of your life, increase agricultural productions fifty per cent; or were any one proprietor to do it with his own lands, it would increase his rents fifty per cent, in the course of twenty-five years. But I am told the laws do not permit it. The laws then, in this particular, are unwise and unjust, and ought to give that permission. In the southern provinces, where the soil is poor, the climate hot and dry, and there are few animals, they would learn the art, found so precious in England, of making vegetable manure, and thus improving these provinces in the article in which nature has been least kind to them. Indeed, these provinces afford a singular spectacle. Calculating on the poverty of their soil, and their climate by its latitude only, they should have been the poorest in France. On the contrary, they are the richest, from one fortuitous circumstance. Spurs or ramifications of high mountains, making down from the Alps, and as it were, reticulating these provinces, give to the vallies the protection of a particular inclosure to each, and the benefit of a general stagnation of the northern winds produced by the whole of them, and thus countervail the advantage of several degrees of latitude. From the first olive fields of Pierrelate, to the orangeries of Hieres, has been continued rapture to me. I have often wished for you. I think you have not made this journey. It is a pleasure you have to come, and an improvement to be added to the many you have already made. It will be a great comfort to you to know, from your own inspection, the condition of all the provinces of your own country, and it will be interesting to them at some future day to be known to you. This is perhaps the only moment of your life in which you can acquire that knolege. And to do it most effectually you must be absolutely incognito, you must ferret the people out of their hovels as I have done, look into their kettles, eat their bread, loll on their beds under pretence of resting yourself, but in fact to find if they are soft. You will feel a sublime pleasure in the course of this investigation, and a sublimer one hereafter when you shall be able to apply your knolege to the softening of their beds, or the throwing a morsel of meat into the kettle of vegetables. You will not wonder at the subjects of my letter: they are the only ones which have been present to my mind for some time past, and the waters must always be what are the fountain from which they flow. According to this indeed I should have intermixed from beginning to end warm expressions of friendship to you: but according to the ideas of our country we do not permit ourselves to speak even truths when they may have the air of flattery. I content myself therefore with saying once for all that I love you, your wife and children. Tell them so and Adieu. Your's affectionately.

To Peter Carr

Paris Aug. 10. 1787.

DEAR PETER

I have received your two letters of Decemb. 30. and April 18. and am very happy to find by them, as well as by letters from Mr. Wythe, that you have been so fortunate as to attract his notice and good will: I am sure you will find this to have been one of the most fortunate events of your life, as I have ever been sensible it was of mine. I inclose[1] you a sketch of the sciences to which I would wish you to apply in such order as Mr. Wythe shall advise: I mention also the books in them worth your reading, which submit to his correction. Many of these are among your father's books, which you should have brought to you. As I do not recollect those of them not in his library, you must write to me for them, making out a catalogue of such as you think you shall have occasion for in 18 months from the date of your letter, and consulting Mr. Wythe on the subject. To this sketch I will add a few particular observations.

1. Italian. I fear the learning this language will confound your French and Spanish. Being all of them degenerated dialects of the Latin, they are apt to mix in conversation. I have never seen a person speaking the three languages who did not mix them. It is a delightful language, but late events having rendered the Spanish more useful, lay it aside to prosecute that.

2. Spanish. Bestow great attention on this, and endeavor to acquire an accurate knowledge of it. Our future connections with Spain and Spanish America will render that language a valuable acquisition. The antient history of a great part of America too is written in that language. I send you a dictionary.

3. Moral philosophy. I think it lost time to attend lectures in this branch. He who made us would have been a pitiful bungler if he had made the rules of our moral conduct a matter of science. For one man of science, there are thousands who are not. What would have become of them? Man was destined for society. His morality therefore was to be formed to this object. He was endowed with a sense of right and wrong merely relative to this. This sense is as much a part of his nature as the sense of hearing, seeing, feeling; it is the true foundation of morality, and not the το χαλον truth, &c., as fanciful writers have imagined. The moral sense, or conscience, is as much a part of man

[1] Enclosure omitted. [Ed.]

as his leg or arm. It is given to all human beings in a stronger or weaker degree, as force of members is given them in a greater or less degree. It may be strengthened by exercise, as may any particular limb of the body. This sense is submitted indeed in some degree to the guidance of reason; but it is a small stock which is required for this: even a less one than what we call Common sense. State a moral case to a ploughman and a professor. The former will decide it as well, and often better than the latter, because he has not been led astray by artificial rules. In this branch therefore read good books because they will encourage as well as direct your feelings. The writings of Sterne particularly form the best course of morality that ever was written. Besides these read the books mentioned in the inclosed paper; and above all things lose no occasion of exercising your dispositions to be grateful, to be generous, to be charitable, to be humane, to be true, just, firm, orderly, couragious &c. Consider every act of this kind as an exercise which will strengthen your moral faculties, and increase your worth.

4. Religion. Your reason is now mature enough to receive this object. In the first place divest yourself of all bias in favour of novelty and singularity of opinion. Indulge them in any other subject rather than that of religion. It is too important, and the consequences of error may be too serious. On the other hand shake off all the fears and servile prejudices under which weak minds are servilely crouched. Fix reason firmly in her seat, and call to her tribunal every fact, every opinion. Question with boldness even the existence of a god; because, if there be one, he must more approve the homage of reason, than that of blindfolded fear. You will naturally examine first the religion of your own country. Read the bible then, as you would read Livy or Tacitus. The facts which are within the ordinary course of nature you will believe on the authority of the writer, as you do those of the same kind in Livy and Tacitus. The testimony of the writer weighs in

their favor in one scale, and their not being against the laws of nature does not weigh against them. But those facts in the bible which contradict the laws of nature, must be examined with more care, and under a variety of faces. Here you must recur to the pretensions of the writer to inspiration from god. Examine upon what evidence his pretensions are founded, and whether that evidence is so strong as that it's falshood would be more improbable than a change of the laws of nature in the case he relates. For example in the book of Joshua we are told the sun stood still several hours. Were we to read that fact in Livy or Tacitus we should class it with their showers of blood, speaking of statues, beasts &c., but it is said that the writer of that book was inspired. Examine therefore candidly what evidence there is of his having been inspired. The pretension is entitled to your enquiry, because millions believe it. On the other hand you are Astronomer enough to know how contrary it is to the law of nature that a body revolving on it's axis, as the earth does, should have stopped, should not by that sudden stoppage have prostrated animals, trees, buildings, and should after a certain time have resumed it's revolution, and that without a second general prostration. Is this arrest of the earth's motion, or the evidence which affirms it, most within the law of probabilities? You will next read the new testament. It is the history of a personage called Jesus. Keep in your eye the opposite pretensions. 1. Of those who say he was begotten by god, born of a virgin, suspended and reversed the laws of nature at will, and ascended bodily into heaven: and 2. of those who say he was a man, of illegitimate birth, of a benevolent heart, enthusiastic mind, who set out without pretensions to divinity, ended in believing them, and was punished capitally for sedition by being gibbeted according to the Roman law which punished the first commission of that offence by whipping, and the second by exile or death *in furcâ*. See this law in the Digest Lib. 48. tit. 19 § 28.3. and Lipsius Lib. 2. de cruce.

cap. 2. These questions are examined in the books I have mentioned under the head of religion, and several others. They will assist you in your enquiries, but keep your reason firmly on the watch in reading them all. Do not be frightened from this enquiry by any fear of it's consequences. If it ends in a belief that there is no god, you will find incitements to virtue in the comfort and pleasantness you feel in it's exercise, and the love of others which it will procure you. If you find reason to believe there is a god, a consciousness that you are acting under his eye, and that he approves you, will be a vast additional incitement. If that there be a future state, the hope of a happy existence in that increases the appetite to deserve it; if that Jesus was also a god, you will be comforted by a belief of his aid and love. In fine, I repeat that you must lay aside all prejudice on both sides, and neither believe nor reject any thing because any other person, or description of persons have rejected or believed it. Your own reason is the only oracle given you by heaven, and you are answerable not for the rightness but uprightness of the decision.—I forgot to observe when speaking of the New testament that you should read all the histories of Christ, as well of those whom a council of ecclesiastics have decided for us to be Pseudo-evangelists, as those they named Evangelists, because these Pseudo-evangelists pretended to inspiration as much as the others, and you are to judge their pretensions by your own reason, and not by the reason of those ecclesiastics. Most of these are lost. There are some however still extant, collected by Fabricius which I will endeavor to get and send you.

5. Travelling. This makes men wiser, but less happy. When men of sober age travel, they gather knowledge which they may apply usefully for their country, but they are subject ever after to recollections mixed with regret, their affections are weakened by being extended over more objects, and they learn new habits which cannot be gratified when they return home. Young men who travel

are exposed to all these inconveniences in a higher degree, to others still more serious, and do not acquire that wisdom for which a previous foundation is requisite by repeated and just observations at home. The glare of pomp and pleasure is analogous to the motion of their blood, it absorbs all their affection and attention, they are torn from it as from the only good in this world, and return to their home as to a place of exile and condemnation. Their eyes are for ever turned back to the object they have lost, and it's recollection poisons the residue of their lives. Their first and most delicate passions are hackneyed on unworthy objects here, and they carry home only the dregs, insufficient to make themselves or any body else happy. Add to this that a habit of idleness, an inability to apply themselves to business is acquired and renders them useless to themselves and their country. These observations are founded in experience. There is no place where your pursuit of knowledge will be so little obstructed by foreign objects as in your own country, nor any wherein the virtues of the heart will be less exposed to be weakened. Be good, be learned, and be industrious, and you will not want the aid of travelling to render you precious to your country, dear to your friends, happy within yourself. I repeat my advice to take a great deal of exercise, and on foot. Health is the first requisite after morality. Write to me often and be assured of the interest I take in your success, as well as of the warmth of those sentiments of attachment with which I am, dear Peter, your affectionate friend.

To James Madison

Paris Dec. 20. 1787.

. . . The season admitting only of operations in the Cabinet, and these being in a great measure secret, I have little to fill a letter. I will therefore make up the deficiency by adding a few words on the Constitution proposed by our Convention. I like much the general idea of framing a government which should go on of itself peaceably, without needing continual recurrence to the state legislatures. I like the organization of the government into Legislative, Judiciary and Executive. I like the power given the Legislature to levy taxes; and for that reason solely approve of the greater house being chosen by the people directly. For tho' I think a house chosen by them will be very illy qualified to legislate for the Union, for foreign nations &c. yet this evil does not weigh against the good of preserving inviolate the fundamental principle that the people are not to be taxed but by representatives chosen immediately by themselves. I am captivated by the compromise of the opposite claims of the great and little states, of the latter to equal, and the former to proportional influence. I am much pleased too with the substitution of the method of voting by persons, instead of that of voting by states: and I like the negative given to the Executive with a third of either house, though I should have liked it better had the Judiciary been associated for that purpose, or invested with a similar and separate power. There are other good things of less moment. I will now add what I do not like. First the omission of a bill of rights providing clearly and without the aid of sophisms for freedom of religion, freedom of the press, protection against standing armies, restriction against monopolies, the eternal and unremitting force of the habeas corpus laws, and trials by jury in all matters of fact triable by the laws of the land and not by the law of Nations. To say, as Mr. Wilson does that a bill of rights was not necessary because all is reserved in the case of the general government which is not given, while in the particular ones all is given which is not reserved might do for the Audience to whom it was addressed, but is surely gratis dictum, opposed by strong inferences from the body of the instrument, as well as from the omission of the clause of our present confederation which had declared that in express terms. It was a hard conclusion to say because there has been no uniformity among the states as to the cases triable by jury, because some have been so incautious as to abandon this mode of trial, therefore the most prudent states shall be reduced to the same level of calamity. It would have been much more just and wise to have concluded the other way that as most of the states had judiciously preserved this palladium, those who had wandered should be brought back to it, and to have established general right instead of general wrong. Let me add that a bill of rights is what the people are entitled to against every government on earth, general or particular, and what no just government should refuse, or rest on inference. The second feature I dislike, and greatly dislike, is the abandonment in every instance of the necessity of rotation in office, and most particularly in the case of the President. Experience concurs with reason in concluding that the first magistrate will always be re-elected if the constitution permits it. He is then an officer for life. This once observed it becomes of so much consequence to certain nations to have a friend or a foe at the head of our affairs that they will interfere with money and with arms. A Galloman or an Angloman will be supported by the nation he befriends. If once elected, and at a second or third election outvoted by one or two votes, he will pretend false votes, foul play, hold possession of the reins of government, be supported by the states voting for him, especially if they are the central ones lying in a compact body themselves and separating their opponents: and they will be aided by one nation of Europe, while the majority are aided by another. The election of a President of America some years hence will be much more interesting to certain nations of Europe than ever the election of a king of Poland was. Reflect on all the instances in history antient and modern, of elective monarchies, and say if they do not give foundation for my fears, the Roman emperors, the popes, while they were of any importance, the German emperors till they became hereditary in practice, the kings of Poland, the Deys of the Ottoman dependancies. It may be said that if elections are to be attended with these disorders, the seldomer they are renewed the better. But experience shews that the only way to prevent disorder is to render them uninteresting by frequent changes. An incapacity to be elected a second time would have been the only effectual preventative. The power of removing him every fourth year by the vote of the people is a power which will not be exercised. The king of Poland is removeable every day by the Diet, yet he is never removed.—Smaller objections are the Appeal in fact as well as law, and the binding all persons Legislative, Executive and Judiciary by oath to maintain that constitution. I do not pretend to decide what would be the best method of procuring the establishment of the manifold good things in this constitution, and of getting rid of the bad. Whether by adopting it in hopes of future amendment, or, after it has been duly weighed and canvassed by the people, after seeing the parts they generally dislike, and those they generally approve, to say to them 'We see now what you wish. Send together your deputies again, let them frame a constitution for you omitting what you have condemned, and establishing the powers you approve. Even these will be a great addition to the energy of your government.'—At all events I hope you will not be discouraged from other trials, if the present one should fail of it's full effect.—I have thus told you freely what I like and dislike: merely as a matter of curiosity for I know your own judgment has been formed on all these points after having heard every thing which could be urged on them. I own I am not a friend to a very energetic government. It is always oppressive. The late rebellion in Massachusetts has given more alarm than I think it should have done. Calculate that one rebellion in 13 states in the course of 11 years, is but one for each state in a century and a half. No country should be so long without one. Nor will any degree of power in the hands of government prevent insurrections. France with all it's despotism, and two or three hundred thousand men always in arms has had three insurrections in the three years I have been here in every one of which greater numbers were engaged than in Massachusetts and a great deal more blood was spilt. In Turkey, which Montesquieu supposes more despotic, insurrections are the events of every day. In England, where the hand of power is lighter than here, but heavier than with us they happen every half dozen years. Compare again the ferocious depredations of their insurgents with the order, the moderation and the almost self extinguishment of ours.—After all, it is my principle that the will of the Majority should always prevail. If they approve the proposed Convention in all it's parts, I shall concur in it chearfully, in hopes that they will amend it whenever they shall find it work wrong. I think our governments will remain virtuous for many centuries; as long as they are chiefly agricultural; and this will be as long as there shall be vacant lands in any part of America. When they get piled upon one another in large cities, as in Europe, they will become corrupt as in Europe. Above all things I hope the education of the common people will be attended to; convinced that on their good sense we may rely with the most security for the preservation of a due degree of liberty. I have tired you by this time with my disquisitions and will therefore only add assurances of the sincerity of those sentiments of esteem and attachment with which I am Dear Sir your affectionate friend & servant.

P.S. The instability of our laws is really an immense evil. I think it would be well to provide in our constitutions that there shall always be a twelvemonth between the ingrossing a bill and passing it: that it should then be offered to it's passage without changing a word: and that if circumstances should be thought to require a speedier passage, it should take two thirds of both houses instead of a bare majority.

Travel Notes for Messrs. Rutledge and Shippen

[Paris June 19. 1788]

OBJECTS OF ATTENTION FOR AN AMERICAN [1]

1. Agriculture. Every thing belonging to this art, and whatever has a near relation to it. Useful or agreeable animals which might be transported to America. New species of plants for the farm or garden, according to the climate of the different states.

2. Mechanical arts, so far as they respect things necessary in America, and inconvenient to be transported thither ready made. Such are forges, stonequarries, boats, bridges (very specially) &c. &c.

3. Lighter mechanical arts and manufactures. Some of these will be worth a superficial view. But circumstances rendering it impossible that America should become a manufacturing country during the time of any man now living, it would be a waste of attention to examine these minutely.

4. Gardens. Peculiarly worth the attention of an American, because it is the country of all others where the noblest gardens may be made without expence. We have only to cut out the superabundant plants.

5. Architecture worth great attention. As we double our numbers every 20 years we must double our houses. Besides we build of such perishable materials that one half of our houses must be rebuilt in every space of 20 years. So that in that term, houses are to be built for three fourths of our inhabitants. It is then among the most important

[1] One section of the notes "hastily scribbled" for two young Americans, John Rutledge, Jr., and Thomas Lee Shippen. [Ed.]

arts: and it is desireable to introduce taste into an art which shews so much.

6. Painting, statuary. Too expensive for the state of wealth among us. It would be useless therefore and preposterous for us to endeavor to make ourselves connoisseurs in those arts. They are worth seeing, but not studying.

7. Politics of each country. Well worth studying so far as respects internal affairs. Examine their influence on the happiness of the people: take every possible occasion of entering into the hovels of the labourers, and especially at the moments of their repast, see what they eat, how they are cloathed, whether they are obliged to labour too hard; whether the government or their landlord takes from them an unjust proportion of their labour; on what footing stands the property they call their own, their personal liberty &c.

8. Courts. To be seen as you would see the tower of London or Menagerie of Versailles with their Lions, tygers, hyaenas and other beasts of prey, standing in the same relation to their fellows. A slight acquaintance with them will suffice to shew you that, under the most imposing exterior, they are the weakest and worst part of mankind. Their manners, could you ape them, would not make you beloved in your own country, nor would they improve it could you introduce them there to the exclusion of that honest simplicity now prevailing in America, and worthy of being cherished.

To John Trumbull

Paris Feb. 15. 1789.

Dear Sir

I have duly received your favor of the 5th. inst. with respect to the busts and pictures. I will put off till my return from America all of them except Bacon, Locke and Newton, whose pictures I will trouble you to have copied for me: and as I consider them as the three greatest men that have ever lived, without any exception, and as having laid the foundation of those superstructures which have been raised in the Physical and Moral sciences, I would wish to form them into a knot on the same canvas, that they may not be confounded at all with the herd of other great men. To do this I suppose we need only desire the copyist to draw the three busts in three ovals all contained in a larger oval in some such forms as this each bust to be the size of the life. The large oval would I suppose be about between four and five feet. Perhaps you can suggest a better way of accomplishing my idea. In your hands be it, as well as the

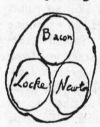

subaltern expences you mention. I trouble you with a letter to Mrs. Church. We have no important news here but of the revolution of Geneva which is not yet sufficiently explained. But they have certainly reformed their government. I am with great esteem Dr. Sir Your affectionate friend & humble servt.

To Francis Hopkinson

Paris Mar, 13. 1789

. . . You say that I have been dished up to you as an anti-federalist, and ask me if it be just. My opinion was never worthy enough of notice to merit citing: but since you ask it I will tell it you. I am not a Federalist, because I never submitted the whole system of my opinions to the creed of any party of men whatever in religion, in philosophy, in politics, or in any thing else where I was capable of thinking for myself. Such an addiction is the last degradation of a free and moral agent. If I could not go to heaven but with a party, I would not go there at all. Therefore I protest to you I am not of the party of federalists.

But I am much farther from that of the Antifederalists. I approved from the first moment, of the great mass of what is in the new constitution, the consolidation of the government, the organisation into Executive, legislative and judiciary, the subdivision of the legislative, the happy compromise of interests between the great and little states by the different manner of voting in the different houses, the voting by persons instead of states, the qualified negative on laws given to the Executive which however I should have liked better if associated with the judiciary also as in New York, and the power of taxation. I thought at first that the latter might have been limited. A little reflection soon convinced me it ought not to be. What I disapproved from the first moment also was the want of a bill of rights to guard liberty against the legislative as well as executive branches of the government, that is to say to secure freedom in religion, freedom of the press, freedom from monopolies, freedom from unlawful imprisonment, freedom from a permanent military, and a trial by jury in all cases determinable by the laws of the land. I disapproved also the perpetual reeligibility of the President. To these points of disapprobation I adhere. My first wish was that the 9. first conventions might accept the constitution, as the means of securing to us the great mass of good it contained, and that the 4. last might reject it, as the means of obtaining amendments. But I was corrected in this wish the moment I saw the much better plan of Massachusets[1] and which had never occurred to me. With respect to the declaration of rights I suppose the majority of the United states are of my opinion: for I apprehend all the antifederalists, and a very respectable proportion of the federalists think that such a declaration should now be annexed. The enlightened part of Europe have given us the greatest credit for inventing this instrument of security for the rights of the people, and have been not a little surprised to

[1] The Massachusetts convention called for unconditional ratification with recommended amendments. [Ed.]

see us so soon give it up. With respect to the re-eligibility of the president, I find myself differing from the majority of my countrymen, for I think there are but three states of the 11. which have desired an alteration of this. And indeed, since the thing is established, I would wish it not to be altered during the life of our great leader, whose executive talents are superior to those I beleive of any man in the world, and who alone by the authority of his name and the confidence reposed in his perfect integrity, is fully qualified to put the new government so under way as to secure it against the efforts of opposition. But having derived from our error all the good there was in it I hope we shall correct it the moment we can no longer have the same person at the helm. These, my dear friend, are my sentiments, by which you will see I was right in saying I am neither federalist nor antifederalist; that I am of neither party, nor yet a trimmer between parties. These my opinions I wrote within a few hours after I had read the constitution, to one or two friends in America. I had not then read one single word printed on the subject. I never had an opinion in politics or religion which I was afraid to own. A costive reserve on these subjects might have procured me more esteem from some people, but less from myself. My great wish is to go on in a strict but silent performance of my duty: to avoid attracting notice and to keep my name out of newspapers, because I find the pain of a little censure, even when it is unfounded, is more acute than the pleasure of much praise. The attaching circumstance of my present office is that I can do it's duties unseen by those for whom they are done.—You did not think, by so short a phrase in your letter, to have drawn on yourself such an egoistical dissertation. I beg your pardon for it, and will endeavor to merit that pardon by the constant sentiments of esteem & attachment with which I am Dear Sir, Your sincere friend & servant.

To James Madison

Paris Mar. 15. 1789.

. . . Your thoughts on the subject of the Declaration of
rights in the letter of Oct. 17. I have weighed with great
satisfaction. Some of them had not occurred to me before,
but were acknoleged just in the moment they were presented to my mind. In the arguments in favor of a declaration of rights, you omit one which has great weight with
me, the legal check which it puts into the hands of the
judiciary. This is a body, which if rendered independent,
and kept strictly to their own department merits great
confidence for their learning and integrity. In fact what
degree of confidence would be too much for a body composed of such men as Wythe, Blair, and Pendleton? On
characters like these the *'civium ardor prava jubentium'*
would make no impression. I am happy to find that on the
whole you are a friend to this amendment. The Declaration of rights is like all other human blessings alloyed with
some inconveniences, and not accomplishing fully it's object. But the good in this instance vastly overweighs the
evil. I cannot refrain from making short answers to the
objections which your letter states to have been raised. 1.
That the rights in question are reserved by the manner in
which the federal powers are granted. Answer. A constitutive act may certainly be so formed as to need no declaration of rights. The act itself has the force of a declaration as far as it goes: and if it goes to all material points
nothing more is wanting. In the draught of a constitution
which I had once a thought of proposing in Virginia, and
printed afterwards, I endeavored to reach all the great
objects of public liberty, and did not mean to add a declaration of rights. Probably the object was imperfectly
executed: but the deficiencies would have been supplied
by others in the course of discussion. But in a constitutive
act which leaves some precious articles unnoticed, and

raises implications against others, a declaration of rights becomes necessary by way of supplement. This is the case of our new federal constitution. This instrument forms us into one state as to certain objects, and gives us a legislative and executive body for these objects. It should therefore guard us against their abuses of power within the feild submitted to them. 2. A positive declaration of some essential rights could not be obtained in the requisite latitude. Answer. Half a loaf is better than no bread. If we cannot secure all our rights, let us secure what we can. 3. The limited powers of the federal government and jealousy of the subordinate governments afford a security which exists in no other instance. Answer. The first member of this seems resolvable into the 1st. objection before stated. The jealousy of the subordinate governments is a precious reliance. But observe that those governments are only agents. They must have principles furnished them whereon to found their opposition. The declaration of rights will be the text whereby they will try all the acts of the federal government. In this view it is necessary to the federal government also: as by the same text they may try the opposition of the subordinate governments. 4. Experience proves the inefficacy of a bill of rights. True. But tho it is not absolutely efficacious under all circumstances, it is of great potency always, and rarely inefficacious. A brace the more will often keep up the building which would have fallen with that brace the less. There is a remarkeable difference between the characters of the Inconveniencies which attend a Declaration of rights, and those which attend the want of it. The inconveniences of the Declaration are that it may cramp government in it's useful exertions. But the evil of this is shortlived, moderate, and reparable. The inconveniencies of the want of a Declaration are permanent, afflicting and irreparable: they are in constant progression from bad to worse. The executive in our governments is not the sole, it is scarcely the principal object of my jealousy. The tyranny of the legislatures is the most formidable dread at present, and will be for long years. That of the executive will come in it's turn, but it will be at a remote period. I know there are some among us who would now establish a monarchy. But they are inconsiderable in number and weight of character. The rising race are all republicans. We were educated in royalism: no wonder if some of us retain that idolatry still. Our young people are educated in republicanism. An apostacy from that to royalism is unprecedented and impossible. I am much pleased with the prospect that a declaration of rights will be added: and hope it will be done in that way which will not endanger the whole frame of the government, or any essential part of it. . . .

To Rabaut de St. Etienne

Paris June 3, 1789.

Sir

After you quitted us yesterday evening, we continued our conversation (Monsr. de la Fayette, Mr. Short and myself) on the subject of the difficulties which environ you. The desireable object being to secure the good which the King has offered and to avoid the ill which seems to threaten, an idea was suggested, which appearing to make an impression on Monsr. de la Fayette, I was encouraged to pursue it on my return to Paris, to put it into form, and now to send it to you and him. It is this, that the king in a *seance royale,* should come forward with a Charter of Rights in his hand, to be signed by himself and by every member of the three orders. This charter to contain the five great points which the Resultat of December offered on the part of the king, the abolition of pecuniary privileges offered by the privileged orders, and the adoption of the National debt and a grant of the sum of money asked from the nation. This last will be a cheap price for the preceding articles, and let the same act declare your immediate separation till the next anniversary meeting. You will carry back to your constituents more good than ever was effected before without violence, and you will stop exactly at the point where violence would otherwise begin. Time will be gained, the public mind will continue to ripen and to be informed, a basis of support may be prepared with the people themselves, and expedients occur for gaining still something further at your next meeting, and for stopping again at the point of force. I have ventured to send to yourself and Monsieur de la Fayette a sketch of my ideas of what this act might contain without endangering any dispute. But it is offered merely as a canvas for you to work on, if it be fit to work on at all. I know too little of the subject, and you know too much of it to justify me in offering any thing but a hint. I have done it too in a hurry: insomuch that since committing it to writing it occurs to me that the 5th. article may give alarm, that it is in a good degree included in the 4th. and is therefore useless. But after all what excuse can I make, Sir, for this presumption. I have none but an unmeasurable love for your nation and a painful anxiety lest Despotism, after an unaccepted offer to bind it's own hands, should seize you again with tenfold fury. Permit me to add to these very sincere assurances of the sentiments of esteem & respect with which I have the honor to be Sir Your most obedt. & most humble servt.

ENCLOSURE

A Charter of Rights solemnly established by the King and Nation.

1. The States general shall assemble, uncalled, on the 1st. day of November annually, and shall remain together so long as they shall see cause. They shall regulate their own elections and proceedings, and until they shall ordain otherwise, their elections shall be in the forms observed in the present year, and shall be triennial.

2. The States-general alone shall levy money on the nation, and shall appropriate it.

3. Laws shall be made by the States-general only, with the consent of the king.

4. No person shall be restrained of his liberty but by regular process from a court of justice, authorized by a general law: [except that a Noble may be imprisoned by order of a court of justice on the prayer of 12. of his nearest relations.] On complaint of an unlawful imprisonment, to any judge whatever, he shall have the prisoner immediately brought before him, and shall discharge him if his imprisonment be unlawful. The office in whose custody the prisoner is shall obey the orders of the judge, and both judge and officer shall be responsible civilly and criminally for a failure of duty herein.

5. The Military shall be subordinate to the Civil authority.[1]

6. Printers shall be liable to legal prosecution for printing and publishing false facts injurious to the party prosecuting: but they shall be under no other restraint.

7. All pecuniary privileges and exemptions enjoyed by any description of persons are abolished.

8. All debts already contracted by the king are hereby made the debts of the nation: and the faith thereof is pledged for their paiment in due time.

9. 80. millions of livres are now granted to the king, to be raised by loan and reimbursed by the nation: and the taxes heretofore paid shall continue to be paid to the end of the present year, and no longer.

10. The States general shall now separate and meet again on the 1st. day of November next.

Done, on behalf of the whole nation, by the King and their representatives in the States general, at Versailles, this —— day of June 1789.

Signed by the king, and by every member individually, and in his presence.

[1] Interlined by Jefferson. [Ed.]

To Diodati

Paris August 3. 1789.

. . . I presume that your correspondents here have given
you a history of all the events which have happened. The
Leyden gazette, tho' it contains several inconsiderable
errors gives on the whole a just enough idea. It is impossible to conceive a greater fermentation than has worked
in Paris, nor do I believe that so great a fermentation ever
produced so little injury in any other place. I have been
thro' it daily, have observed the mobs with my own eyes
in order to be satisfied of their objects, and declare to you
that I saw so plainly the legitimacy of them, that I have
slept in my house as quietly thro' the whole as ever I did
in the most peaceable moments. So strongly fortified was
the despotism of this government by long possession, by
the respect and the fears of the people, by possessing the
public force, by the imposing authority of forms and of
taste, that had it held itself on the defensive only, the
national assembly with all their good sense, could probably
have only obtained a considerable improvement of the
government, not a total revision of it. But, ill informed of
the spirit of their nation, the despots around the throne had
recourse to violent measures, the forerunners of force. In
this they have been completely overthrown, and the nation has made a total resumption of rights, which they had
certainly never before ventured even to think of. The National assembly have now as clean a canvas to work on
here as we had in America. Such has been the firmness and
wisdom of their proceedings in moments of adversity as
well as prosperity, that I have the highest confidence that
they will use their power justly. As far as I can collect from
conversation with their members, the constitution they
will propose will resemble that of England in it's outlines,
but not in it's defects. They will certainly leave the king
possessed completely of the Executive powers, and par-

ticularly of the public force. Their legislature will consist of one order only, and not of two as in England: the representation will be equal and not abominably partial as that of England: it will be guarded against corruption, instead of having a majority sold to the king, and rendering his will absolute: whether it will be in one chamber, or broke into two cannot be foreseen. They will meet at certain epochs and sit as long as they please, instead of meeting only when, and sitting only as long as, the king pleases as in England. There is a difference of opinion whether the king shall have an absolute, or only a qualified Negative on their acts. The parliaments will probably be suppressed; and juries provided in criminal cases perhaps even in civil ones. This is what appears probable at present. The Assembly is this day discussing the question whether they will have a declaration of rights. Paris has been led by events to assume the government of itself. It has hitherto worn too much the appearance of conformity to continue thus independently of the will of the nation. Reflection will probably make them sensible that the security of all depends on the dependance of all on the national legislature. I have so much confidence in the good sense of man, and his qualifications for self-government, that I am never afraid of the issue where reason is left free to exert her force; and I will agree to be stoned as a false prophet if all does not end well in this country. Nor will it end with this country. Here is but the first chapter of the history of European liberty. . . .

To James Madison

Paris September 6. 1789.

DEAR SIR

I sit down to write to you without knowing by what occasion I shall send my letter. I do it because a subject comes into my head which I would wish to develope a little more than is practicable in the hurry of the moment of making up general dispatches.

The question Whether one generation of men has a right to bind another, seems never to have been started either on this or our side of the water. Yet it is a question of such consequences as not only to merit decision, but place also, among the fundamental principles of every government. The course of reflection in which we are immersed here on the elementary principles of society has presented this question to my mind; and that no such obligation can be so transmitted I think very capable of proof.—I set out on this ground, which I suppose to be self evident, '*that the earth belongs in usufruct to the living*': that the dead have neither powers nor rights over it. The portion occupied by any individual ceases to be his when himself ceases to be, and reverts to the society. If the society has formed no rules for the appropriation of it's lands in severality, it will be taken by the first occupants. These will generally be the wife and children of the decedent. If they have formed rules of appropriation, those rules may give it to the wife and children, or to some one of them, or to the legatee of the deceased. So they may give it to his creditor. But the child, the legatee, or creditor takes it, not by any natural right, but by a law of the society of which they are members, and to which they are subject. Then no man can, by *natural right*, oblige the lands he occupied, or the persons who succeed him in that occupation, to the paiment of debts contracted by him. For if he could, he might, during his own life, eat up the usufruct of the lands for several generations to come, and then the lands would belong to the dead, and not to the living, which would be the reverse of our principle.

What is true of every member of the society individually, is true of them all collectively, since the rights of the whole can be no more than the sum of the rights of the individuals.—To keep our ideas clear when applying them to a multitude, let us suppose a whole generation of men to be born on the same day, to attain mature age on the same day, and to die on the same day, leaving a succeeding generation in the moment of attaining their mature age all together. Let the ripe age be supposed of 21. years, and their period of life 34. years more, that being the average term given by the bills of mortality to persons who have already attained 21. years of age. Each successive generation would, in this way, come on, and go off the stage at a fixed moment, as individuals do now. Then I say the earth belongs to each of these generations, during it's course, fully, and in their own right. The 2d. generation receives it clear of the debts and incumberances of the 1st. the 3d of the 2d. and so on. For if the 1st. could charge it with a debt, then the earth would belong to the dead and not the living generation. Then no generation can contract debts greater than may be paid during the course of it's own existence. At 21. years of age they may bind themselves and their lands for 34. years to come: at 22. for 33: at 23. for 32. and at 54. for one year only; because these are the terms of life which remain to them at those respective epochs.—But a material difference must be noted between the succession of an individual, and that of a whole generation. Individuals are parts only of a society, subject to the laws of the whole. These laws may appropriate the portion of land occupied by a decedent to his creditor rather than to any other, or to his child on condition he satisfies the creditor. But when a whole generation, that is, the whole society dies, as in the case we have supposed, and another generation or society succeeds, this forms a whole, and there is no superior who can give their territory to a third society, who may have lent money to their predecessors beyond their faculties of paying.

What is true of a generation all arriving to self-government on the same day, and dying all on the same day, is true of those in a constant course of decay and renewal, with this only difference. A generation coming in and going out entire, as in the first case, would have a right in the 1st. year of their self-dominion to contract a debt for 33. years, in the 10th. for 24. in the 20th. for 14. in the 30th. for 4. whereas generations, changing daily by daily deaths and births, have one constant term, beginning at the date of their contract, and ending when a majority of those of full age at that date shall be dead. The length of that term may be estimated from the tables of mortality, corrected by the circumstances of climate, occupation &c. peculiar to the country of the contractors. Take, for instance, the table of M. de Buffon wherein he states 23,994 deaths, and the ages at which they happened. Suppose a society in which 23,994 persons are born every year, and live to the ages stated in this table. The conditions of that society will be as follows. 1st. It will consist constantly of 617,703. persons of all ages. 2ly. Of those living at any one instant of time, one half will be dead in 24. years 8. months. 3dly. 10,675 will arrive every year at the age of 21. years complete. 4ly. It will constantly have 348,417 persons of all ages above 21. years. 5ly. And the half of those of 21. years and upwards living at any one instant of time will be dead in 18. years 8. months, or say 19. years as the nearest integral number. Then 19. years is the term beyond which neither the representatives of a nation, nor even the whole nation itself assembled, can validly extend a debt.

To render this conclusion palpable by example, suppose that Louis XIV. and XV. had contracted debts in the name of the French nation to the amount of 10,000 milliards of livres, and that the whole had been contracted in Genoa. The interest of this sum would be 500. milliards, which is said to be the whole rent roll or nett proceeds of the territory of France. Must the present generation of men have retired from the territory in which nature produced them, and ceded it to the Genoese creditors? No. They have the same rights over the soil on which they were produced, as the preceding generations had. They derive these rights not from their predecessors, but from nature. They then and their soil are by nature clear of the debts of their predecessors.

Again suppose Louis XV. and his cotemporary generation had said to the money-lenders of Genoa, give us money that we may eat, drink, and be merry in our day; and on condition you will demand no interest till the end of 19. years you shall then for ever after receive an annual interest of 12⅝ per cent.[1] The money is lent on these conditions, is divided among the living, eaten, drank, and squandered. Would the present generation be obliged to apply the produce of the earth and of their labour to replace their dissipations? Not at all.

I suppose that the recieved opinion, that the public debts of one generation devolve on the next, has been suggested by our seeing habitually in private life that he who succeeds to lands is required to pay the debts of his ancestor or testator: without considering that this requisition is municipal only, not moral; flowing from the will of the society, which has found it convenient to appropriate lands, become vacant by the death of their occupant, on the condition of a paiment of his debts: but that between society and society, or generation and generation, there is no municipal obligation, no umpire but the law of nature. We seem not to have perceived that, by the law of nature, one generation is to another as one independant nation to another.

The interest of the national debt of France being in fact but a two thousandth part of it's rent roll, the paiment of it is practicable enough: and so becomes a question merely of honor, or of expediency. But with respect to future debts, would it not be wise and just for that nation to declare, in the constitution they are forming, that neither

---

[1] 100 £, at a compound interest of 5. per cent, makes at the end of 19. years, an aggregate of principal and interest of £252–14, the interest of which is 12 £–12s–7d which is nearly 12⅝ per cent on the first capital of 100. £.

the legislature, nor the nation itself, can validly contract more debt than they may pay within their own age, or within the term of 19. years? And that all future contracts will be deemed void as to what shall remain unpaid at the end of 19. years from their date? This would put the lenders, and the borrowers also, on their guard. By reducing too the faculty of borrowing within it's natural limits, it would bridle the spirit of war, to which too free a course has been procured by the inattention of money-lenders to this law of nature, that succeeding generations are not responsible for the preceding.

On similar ground it may be proved that no society can make a perpetual constitution, or even a perpetual law. The earth belongs always to the living generation. They may manage it then, and what proceeds from it, as they please, during their usufruct. They are masters too of their own persons, and consequently may govern them as they please. But persons and property make the sum of the objects of government. The constitution and the laws of their predecessors [are] extinguished then in their natural course with those who gave them being. This could preserve that being till it ceased to be itself, and no longer. Every constitution then, and every law, naturally expires at the end of 19 years. If it be enforced longer, it is an act of force, and not of right.—It may be said that the succeeding generation exercising in fact the power of repeal, this leaves them as free as if the constitution or law had been expressly limited to 19 years only. In the first place, this objection admits the right, in proposing an equivalent. But the power of repeal is not an equivalent. It might be indeed if every form of government were so perfectly contrived that the will of the majority could always be obtained fairly and without impediment. But this is true of no form. The people cannot assemble themselves. Their representation is unequal and vicious. Various checks are opposed to every legislative proposition. Factions get possession of the public councils. Bribery corrupts them.

Personal interests lead them astray from the general interests of their constituents: and other impediments arise so as to prove to every practical man that a law of limited duration is much more manageable than one which needs a repeal.

This principle that the earth belongs to the living, and not to the dead, is of very extensive application and consequences, in every country, and most especially in France. It enters into the resolution of the questions Whether the nation may change the descent of lands holden in tail? Whether they may change the appropriation of lands given antiently to the church, to hospitals, colleges, orders of chivalry, and otherwise in perpetuity? Whether they may abolish the charges and privileges attached on lands, including the whole catalogue ecclesiastical and feudal? It goes to hereditary offices, authorities and jurisdictions; to hereditary orders, distinctions and appellations; to perpetual monopolies in commerce, the arts and sciences; with a long train of et ceteras: and it renders the question of reimbursement a question of generosity and not of right. In all these cases, the legislature of the day could authorize such appropriations and establishments for their own time, but no longer; and the present holders, even where they, or their ancestors, have purchased, are in the case of bonâ fide purchasers of what the seller had no right to convey.

Turn this subject in your mind, my dear Sir, and particularly as to the power of contracting debts; and develope it with that perspicuity and cogent logic so peculiarly yours. Your station in the councils of our country gives you an opportunity of producing it to public consideration, of forcing it into discussion. At first blush it may be rallied, as a theoretical speculation: but examination will prove it to be solid and salutary. It would furnish matter for a fine preamble to our first law for appropriating the public revenue; and it will exclude at the threshold of our new government the contagious and ruinous errors of this quarter of the globe, which have armed despots with means, not sanctioned by nature, for binding in chains their fellow men. We have already given in example one effectual check to the Dog of war by transferring the power of letting him loose from the Executive to the Legislative body, from those who are to spend to those who are to pay. I should be pleased to see this second obstacle held out by us also in the first instance. No nation can make a declaration against the validity of long-contracted debts so disinterestedly as we, since we do not owe a shilling which may not be paid with ease, principal and interest, within the time of our own lives.—Establish the principle also in the new law to be passed for protecting copyrights and new inventions, by securing the exclusive right for 19. instead of 14. years. Besides familiarising us to this term, it will be an instance the more of our taking reason for our guide, instead of English precedent, the habit of which fetters us with all the political heresies of a nation equally remarkeable for it's early excitement from some errors, and long slumbering under others.

I write you no news, because, when an occasion occurs, I shall write a separate letter for that. I am always with great & sincere esteem, dear Sir Your affectionate friend & servt.

To Madame d'Enville

New York April. 2. 1790.

I had hoped, Madame la Duchesse, to have again had the honor of paying my respects to you in Paris, but the wish of our government that I should take a share in it's administration, has become a law to me. Could I have persuaded myself that public offices were made for private convenience, I should undoubtedly have preferred a continuance in that which placed me nearer to you: but believing on the contrary that a good citizen should take his stand where the public authority marshals him, I have acquiesced. Among the circumstances which reconcile me to my new position, the most powerful is the opportunities it will give me of cementing the friendship between our two nations. Be assured that to do this is the first wish of my heart. I have but one system of ethics for men and for nations. To be grateful, to be faithful to all engagements and under all circumstances, to be open and generous, promotes in the long run even the interests of both: and I am sure it promotes their happiness. The change in your government will approximate us more to one another. You have had some checks, some horrors since I left you. But the way to heaven, you know, has always been said to be strewed with thorns. Why your nation have had fewer than any other on earth, I do not know, unless it be that it is the best on earth. If I assure you, Madam, moreover that I consider yourself personally as with the foremost of your nation in every virtue, it is not flattery, my heart knows not that, it is a homage to sacred truth, it is a tribute I pay with cordiality to a character in which I saw but one error; it was that of treating me with a degree of favor I did not merit. Be assured that I shall ever retain a lively sense of all your goodness to me, which was a circumstance of principal happiness to me during my stay in Paris. I hope that by this time you have seen that my prognostications of a successful issue to your revolution have been verified. I feared for you during a short interval. But after the declaration of the army, tho there might be episodes of distress, the denouement was out of doubt. Heaven send that the glorious example of your country may be but the beginning of the history of European liberty, and that you may live many years in health and happiness to see at length that heaven did not make man in it's wrath. Accept the homage of those sentiments of sincere and respectful esteem with which I have the honor to be, Madame la Duchesse, your most affectionate & obedient humble servant.

To Major Pierre Charles L'Enfant

Philadelphia, April 10, 1791.

SIR

I am favored with your letter of the 4th instant, and in compliance with your request, I have examined my papers, and found the plans of Frankfort-on-the-Mayne, Carlsruhe, Amsterdam, Strasburg, Paris, Orleans, Bordeaux, Lyons, Montpelier, Marseilles, Turin, and Milan, which I send in a roll by the post. They are on large and accurate scales, having been procured by me while in those respective cities myself. As they are connected with the notes I made in my travels, and often necessary to explain them to myself, I will beg your care of them, and to return them when no longer useful to you, leaving you absolutely free to keep them as long as useful. I am happy that the President has left the planning of the town[1] in such good hands, and have no doubt it will be done to general satisfaction. Considering that the grounds to be reserved for the public are to be paid for by the acre, I think very liberal reservations should be made for them; and if this be about the Tyber and on the back of the town, it will be of no injury to the commerce of the place, which will undoubtedly establish itself on the deep waters towards the eastern branch and mouth of Rock Creek; the water about the mouth of the Tyber not being of any depth. Those connected with the government will prefer fixing themselves near the public grounds in the centre, which will also be convenient to be resorted to as walks from the lower and upper town. Having communicated to the President, before he went away, such general ideas on the subject of the town as occurred to me, I make no doubt that, in explaining himself to you on the subject, he has interwoven with his own ideas, such of mine as he approved. For fear of repeating therefore what he did not

[1] Washington, D.C. [Ed.]

approve, and having more confidence in the unbiassed state of his mind, than in my own, I avoided interfering with what he may have expressed to you. Whenever it is proposed to prepare plans for the Capitol, I should prefer the adoption of some one of the models of antiquity, which have had the approbation of thousands of years; and for the President's house, I should prefer the celebrated fronts of modern buildings, which have already received the approbation of all good judges. Such are the Galerie du Louire, the Gardes meubles, and two fronts of the Hotel de Salm. But of this it is yet time enough to consider. In the meantime I am, with great esteem, Sir, your most obedient humble servant.

To Benjamin Banneker[1]

Philadelphia Aug. 30. 1791.

SIR

I thank you sincerely for your letter of the 19th instant and for the Almanac it contained. No body wishes more than I do to see such proofs as you exhibit, that nature has given to our black brethren, talents equal to those of the other colors of men, and that the appearance of a want of them is owing merely to the degraded condition of their existence, both in Africa & America. I can add with truth, that no body wishes more ardently to see a good system commenced for raising the condition both of their body & mind to what it ought to be, as fast as the imbecility of their present existence, and other circumstances which cannot be neglected, will admit. I have taken the liberty of sending your Almanac to Monsieur de Condorcet, Secretary of the Academy of Sciences at Paris, and member of the Philanthropic society, because I con-

---

[1] Banneker, of Maryland, was a free-born black, a mathematician, astronomer, and almanac maker. Jefferson was responsible for his appointment to survey the District of Columbia. [Ed.]

sidered it as a document to which your whole colour had
a right for their justification against the doubts which have
been entertained of them. I am with great esteem, Sir Your
most obed^t humble serv^t.

To the President of the United States
(George Washington)

Monticello Sep. 9. 1792.

. . . I now take the liberty of proceeding to that part of
your letter wherein you notice the internal dissentions
which have taken place within our government, & their
disagreeable effect on it's movements. That such dissentions have taken place is certain, & even among those who
are nearest to you in the administration. To no one have
they given deeper concern than myself: to no one equal
mortification at being myself a part of them. Tho' I take
to myself no more than my share of the general observations of your letter, yet I am so desirous ever that you
should know the whole truth, & believe no more than the
truth, that I am glad to seize every occasion of developing to you whatever I do or think relative to the government; & shall therefore ask permission to be more lengthy
now than the occasion particularly calls for, or could otherwise perhaps justify.

When I embarked in the government, it was with a
determination to intermeddle not at all with the legislature,
& as little as possible with my co-departments. The first
and only instance of variance from the former part of
my resolution, I was duped into by the Secretary of the
Treasury and made a tool for forwarding his schemes, not
then sufficiently understood by me; and of all the errors
of my political life, this has occasioned me the deepest
regret.[1] It has ever been my purpose to explain this to

[1] The "bargain" on the assumption of State debts in 1790.
[Ed.]

you, when, from being actors on the scene, we shall have become uninterested spectators only. The second part of my resolution has been religiously observed with the war department; & as to that of the Treasury, has never been farther swerved from than by the mere enunciation of my sentiments in conversation, and chiefly among those who, expressing the same sentiments, drew mine from me. If it has been supposed that I have ever intrigued among the members of the legislatures to defeat the plans of the Secretary of the Treasury, it is contrary to all truth. As I never had the desire to influence the members, so neither had I any other means than my friendships, which I valued too highly to risk by usurpations on their freedom of judgment, & the conscientious pursuit of their own sense of duty. That I have utterly, in my private conversations, disapproved of the system of the Secretary of the treasury, I ackolege & avow: and this was not merely a speculative difference. His system flowed from principles adverse to liberty, & was calculated to undermine and demolish the republic, by creating an influence of his department over the members of the legislature. I saw this influence actually produced, & it's first fruits to be the establishment of the great outlines of his project by the votes of the very persons who, having swallowed his bait were laying themselves out to profit by his plans: & that had these persons withdrawn, as those interested in a question ever should, the vote of the disinterested majority was clearly the reverse of what they made it. These were no longer the votes then of the representatives of the people, but of deserters from the rights & interests of the people: & it was impossible to consider their decisions, which had nothing in view but to enrich themselves, as the measures of the fair majority, which ought always to be respected.—If what was actually doing begat uneasiness in those who wished for virtuous government, what was further proposed was not less threatening to the friends of the Constitution. For, in a Report on the subject of manufactures (still to be acted on) it was expressly assumed that the general government has a right to exercise all powers which may be for the *general welfare*, that is to say, all the legitimate powers of government: since no government has a legitimate right to do what is not for the welfare of the governed. There was indeed a sham-limitation of the universality of this power *to cases where money is to be employed*. But about what is it that money cannot be employed? Thus the object of these plans taken together is to draw all the powers of government into the hands of the general legislature, to establish means for corrupting a sufficient corps in that legislature to divide the honest votes & preponderate, by their own, the scale which suited, & to have that corps under the command of the Secretary of the Treasury for the purpose of subverting step by step the principles of the constitution, which he has so often declared to be a thing of nothing which must be changed. Such views might have justified something more than mere expressions of dissent, beyond which, nevertheless, I never went.—Has abstinence from the department committed to me been equally observed by him? To say nothing of other interferences equally known, in the case of the two nations with which we have the most intimate connections, France & England, my system was to give some satisfactory distinctions to the former, of little cost to us, in return for the solid advantages yielded us by them; & to have met the English with some restrictions which might induce them to abate their severities against our commerce. I have always supposed this coincided with your sentiments. Yet the Secretary of the treasury, by his cabals with members of the legislature, & by high-toned declamation on other occasions, has forced down his own system, which was exactly the reverse. He undertook, of his own authority, the conferences with the ministers of those two nations, & was, on every consultation, provided with some report of a conversation with the one or the other of them, adapted to his views. These views, thus made to prevail, their execution fell of course to me; & I can safely appeal to you, who have seen all my letters & proceedings, whether I have not carried them into execution as sincerely as if they had been my own, tho' I ever considered them as inconsistent with the honor & interest of our country. That they have been inconsistent with our interest is but too fatally proved by the stab to our navigation given by the French.—So that if the question be By whose fault is it that Colo Hamilton & myself have not drawn together? the answer will depend on that to two other questions; whose principles of administration best justify, by their purity, conscientious adherence? and which of us has, notwithstanding, stepped farthest into the controul of the department of the other?

To this justification of opinions, expressed in the way of conversation, against the views of Colo Hamilton, I beg leave to add some notice of his late charges against me in Fenno's gazette; for neither the stile, matter, nor venom of the pieces alluded to can leave a doubt of their author. Spelling my name & character at full length to the public, while he conceals his own under the signature of "an American" he charges me 1. With having written letters from Europe to my friends to oppose the present constitution while depending. 2. With a desire of not paying the public debt. 3. With setting up a paper to decry & slander the government. 1. The first charge is most false. No man in the U. S. I suppose, approved of every title in the constitution: no one, I believe approved more of it than I did: and more of it was certainly disproved by my accuser than by me, and of it's parts most vitally republican. Of this the few letters I wrote on the subject (not half a dozen I believe) will be a proof: & for my own satisfaction & justification, I must tax you with the reading of them when I return to where they are. You will there see that my objection to the constitution was that it wanted a bill of rights securing freedom of religion, freedom of the press, freedom from standing armies, trial

by jury, & a constant Habeas corpus act. Colo Hamilton's
was that it wanted a king and house of lords. The sense
of America has approved my objection & added the bill
of rights, not the king and lords. I also thought a longer
term of service, insusceptible of renewal, would have made
a President more independant. My country has thought
otherwise, & I have acquiesced implicitly. He wishes the
general government should have power to make laws binding the states in all cases whatsoever. Our country has
thought otherwise: has he acquiesced? Notwithstanding my
wish for a bill of rights, my letters strongly urged the adoption of the constitution, by nine states at least, to secure the
good it contained. I at first thought that the best method of
securing the bill of rights would be for four states to hold
off till such a bill should be agreed to. But the moment I
saw Mr. Hancock's proposition to pass the constitution as
it stood, and give perpetual instructions to the representatives of every state to insist on a bill of rights, I
acknoleged the superiority of his plan, & advocated universal adoption. 2. The second charge is equally untrue. My
whole correspondence while in France, & every word,
letter, & act on the subject since my return, prove that no
man is more ardently intent to see the public debt soon &
sacredly paid off than I am. This exactly marks the difference between Colo Hamilton's views & mine, that I
would wish the debt paid tomorrow; he wishes it never to
be paid, but always to be a thing where with to corrupt &
manage the legislature. 3. I have never enquired what
number of sons, relations & friends of Senators, representatives, printers or other useful partisans Colo Hamilton has provided for among the hundred clerks of his department, the thousand excisemen, custom-house officers,
loan officers &c. &c. appointed by him, or at his nod,
and spread over the Union; nor could ever have imagined
that the man who has the shuffling of millions backwards
& forwards from paper into money & money into paper,
from Europe to America, & America to Europe, the deal-

ing out of Treasury-secrets among his friends in what time & measure he pleases, and who never slips an occasion of making friends with his means, that such an one I say would have brought forward a charge against me for having appointed the poet Freneau translating clerk to my office, with a salary of 250. dollars a year. That fact stands thus. While the government was at New York I was applied to on behalf of Freneau to know if there was any place within my department to which he could be appointed. I answered there were but four clerkships, all of which I found full, and continued without any change. When we removed to Philadelphia, Mr. Pintard the translating clerk, did not chuse to remove with us. His office then became vacant. I was again applied to there for Freneau, & had no hesitation to promise the clerkship for him. I cannot recollect whether it was at the same time, or afterwards, that I was told he had a thought of setting up a newspaper there. But whether then, or afterwards, I considered it as a circumstance of some value, as it might enable me to do, what I had long wished to have done, that is, to have the material parts of the Leyden gazette brought under your eye & that of the public, in order to possess yourself & them of a juster view of the affairs of Europe than could be obtained from any other public source. This I had ineffectually attempted through the press of Mr. Fenno while in New York, selecting & translating passages myself at first then having it done by Mr. Pintard the translating clerk, but they found their way too slowly into Mr. Fenno's papers. Mr. Bache essayed it for me in Philadelphia, but his being a daily paper, did not circulate sufficiently in the other states. He even tried, at my request, the plan of a weekly paper of recapitulation from his daily paper, in hopes that that might go into the other states, but in this too we failed. Freneau, as translating clerk, & the printer of a periodical paper likely to circulate thro' the states (uniting in one person the parts of Pintard & Fenno) revived my hopes that the thing could at length be effected. On the establishment of his paper therefore, I furnished him with the Leyden gazettes, with an expression of my wish that he could always translate & publish the material intelligence they contained; & have continued to furnish them from time to time, as regularly as I received them. But as to any other direction or indication of my wish how his press should be conducted, what sort of intelligence he should give, what essays encourage, I can protest in the presence of heaven, that I never did by myself or any other, directly or indirectly, say a syllable, nor attempt any kind of influence. I can further protest, in the same awful presence, that I never did by myself or any other, directly or indirectly, write, dictate or procure any one sentence or sentiment to be inserted *in his, or any other gazette*, to which my name was not affixed or that of my office.—I surely need not except here a thing so foreign to the present subject as a little paragraph about our Algerine captives, which I put once into Fenno's paper.—Freneau's proposition to publish a paper, having been about the time that the writings of Publicola, & the discourses on Davila had a good deal excited the public attention, I took for granted from Freneau's character, which had been marked as that of a good whig, that he would give free place to pieces written against the aristocratical & monarchical principles these papers had inculcated. This having been in my mind, it is likely enough I may have expressed it in conversation with others; tho' I do not recollect that I did. To Freneau I think I could not, because I had still seen him but once, & that was at a public table, at breakfast, at Mrs. Elsworth's, as I passed thro' New York the last year. And I can safely declare that my expectations looked only to the chastisement of the aristocratical & monarchical writers, & not to any criticisms on the proceedings of government: Colo Hamilton can see no motive for any appointment but that of making a convenient partizan. But you Sir, who have received from me recommendations of a Rittenhouse, Barlow, Paine, will believe that talents & science are sufficient motives with me in appointments to which they are fitted: & that Freneau, as a man of genius, might find a preference in my eye to be a translating clerk, & make good title to the little aids I could give him as the editor of a gazette, by procuring subscriptions to his paper, as I did some, before it appeared, & as I have with pleasure done for the labours of other men of genius. I hold it to be one of the distinguishing excellencies of elective over hereditary successions, that the talents, which nature has provided in sufficient proportion, should be selected by the society for the government of their affairs, rather than that this should be transmitted through the loins of knaves & fools passing from the debauches of the table to those of the bed. Colo Hamilton, alias "Plain facts," says that Freneau's salary began before he resided in Philadelphia. I do not know what quibble he may have in reserve on the word "residence." He may mean to include under that idea the removal of his family; for I believe he removed, himself, before his family did, to Philadelphia. But no act of mine gave commencement to his salary before he so far took up his abode in Philadelphia as to be sufficiently in readiness for the duties of the office. As to the merits or demerits of his paper, they certainly concern me not. He & Fenno are rivals for the public favor. The one courts them by flattery, the other by censure, & I believe it will be admitted that the one has been as servile, as the other severe. But is not the dignity, & even decency of government committed, when one of it's principal ministers enlists himself as an anonymous writer or paragraphist for either the one or the other of them? —No government ought to be without censors: & where the press is free, no one ever will. If virtuous, it need not fear the fair operation of attack & defence. Nature has given to man no other means of sifting out the truth either in religion, law, or politics. I think it as honorable to the government neither to know, nor notice, it's sycophants or censors, as it would be undignified & criminal to pamper the former & persecute the latter.—So much for the past. A word now of the future.

When I came into this office, it was with a resolution to retire from it as soon as I could with decency. It pretty early appeared to me that the proper moment would be the first of those epochs at which the constitution seems to have contemplated a periodical change or renewal of the public servants. In this I was confirmed by your resolution respecting the same period; from which however I am happy in hoping you have departed. I look to that period with the longing of a wave-worn mariner, who has at length the land in view, & shall count the days & hours which still lie between me & it. In the meanwhile my main object will be to wind up the business of my office avoiding as much as possible all new enterprize. With the affairs of the legislature, as I never did intermeddle, so I certainly shall not now begin. I am more desirous to predispose everything for the repose to which I am withdrawing, than expose it to be disturbed by newspaper contests. If these however cannot be avoided altogether, yet a regard for your quiet will be a sufficient motive for my deferring it till I become merely a private citizen, when the propriety or impropriety of what I may say or do may fall on myself alone. I may then too avoid the charge of misapplying that time which now belonging to those who employ me, should be wholly devoted to their service. If my own justification, or the interests of the republic shall require it, I reserve to myself the right of then appealing to my country, subscribing my name to whatever I write, & using with freedom & truth the facts & names necessary to place the cause in it's just form before that tribunal. To a thorough disregard of the honors & emoluments of office I join as great a value for the esteem of my countrymen, & conscious of having merited it by an integrity which cannot be reproached, & by an enthusiastic devotion to their rights & liberty, I will not suffer my retirement to be clouded by the slanders of a man whose history, from the moment at which history can stoop to notice him, is a tissue of machinations against the liberty of the country which has not only received and given him bread, but heaped it's honors on his head.—Still however I repeat the hope that it will not be necessary to make such an appeal. Though little known to the people of America, I believe that, as far as I am known, it is not as an enemy to the republic, nor an intriguer against it, nor a waster of it's revenue, nor prostitutor of it to the purposes of corruption, as the American represents me; and I confide that yourself are satisfied that, as to dissensions in the newspapers, not a syllable of them has ever proceeded from me; & that no cabals or intrigues of mine have produced those in the legislature, & I hope I may promise, both to you & myself, that none will receive aliment from me during the short space I have to remain in office, which will find ample employment in closing the present business of the department. . . .

To William Short[1]

Philadelphia Jan. 3. 1793.

. . . The tone of your letters had for some time given me pain, on account of the extreme warmth with which they censured the proceedings of the Jacobins of France. I considered that sect as the same with the Republican patriots, & the Feuillants as the Monarchical patriots, well known in the early part of the revolution, & but little distant in their views, both having in object the establishment of a free constitution, & differing only on the question whether their chief Executive should be hereditary or not. The Jacobins (as since called) yielded to the Feuillants & tried the experiment of retaining their hereditary Executive. The experiment failed completely, and would have brought on the reestablishment of despotism had it

---

[1] United States Minister at The Hague. [Ed.]

been pursued. The Jacobins saw this, and that the expunging that officer was of absolute necessity. And the Nation was with them in opinion, for however they might have been formerly for the constitution framed by the first assembly, they were come over from their hope in it, and were now generally Jacobins. In the struggle which was necessary, many guilty persons fell without the forms of trial, and with them some innocent. These I deplore as much as any body, & shall deplore some of them to the day of my death. But I deplore them as I should have done had they fallen in battle. It was necessary to use the arm of the people, a machine not quite so blind as balls and bombs, but blind to a certain degree. A few of their cordial friends met at their hands the fate of enemies. But time and truth will rescue & embalm their memories, while their posterity will be enjoying that very liberty for which they would never have hesitated to offer up their lives. The liberty of the whole earth was depending on the issue of the contest, and was ever such a prize won with so little innocent blood? My own affections have been deeply wounded by some of the martyrs to this cause, but rather than it should have failed, I would have seen half the earth desolated. Were there but an Adam & an Eve left in every country, & left free, it would be better than as it now is. I have expressed to you my sentiments, because they are really those of 99. in an hundred of our citizens. The universal feasts, and rejoicings which have lately been had on account of the successes of the French shewed the genuine effusions of their hearts. You have been wounded by the sufferings of your friends, and have by this circumstance been hurried into a temper of mind which would be extremely disrelished if known to your countrymen. The reserve of the President of the United States had never permitted me to discover the light in which he viewed it, and as I was more anxious that you should satisfy him than me, I had still avoided explanations with you on the subject. But your 113. induced him to break silence and to notice the extreme acrimony of your expressions. He added that he had been informed the sentiments you expressed in your conversations were equally offensive to our allies, & that you should consider yourself as the representative of your country and that what you say might be imputed to your constituents. He desired me therefore to write to you on this subject. He added that he considered France as the sheet anchor of this country and its friendship as a first object. There are in the U. S. some characters of opposite principles; some of them are high in office, others possessing great wealth, and all of them hostile to France and fondly looking to England as the staff of their hope. These I named to you on a former occasion. Their prospects have certainly not brightened. Excepting them, this country is entirely republican, friends to the constitution, anxious to preserve it and to have it administered according to it's own republican principles. The little party above mentioned have espoused it only as a stepping stone to monarchy, and have endeavored to approximate it to that in it's administration in order to render it's final transition more easy. The successes of republicanism in France have given the coup de grace to their prospects, and I hope to their projects. . . .

To James Madison

[*Philadelphia. March 24, 1793*]

The idea seems to gain credit that the naval powers combining against France will prohibit supplies even of provisions to that country. Should this be formally notified I should suppose Congress would be called, because it is a justifiable cause of war, and as the Executive cannot decide the question of war on the affirmative side, neither ought it to do so on the negative side, by preventing the competent body from deliberating on the question. But I should hope that war would not be their choice. I think it

will furnish us a happy opportunity of setting another
precious example to the world, by shewing that nations
may be brought to justice by appeals to their interests as
well as by appeals to arms. I should hope that Congress
instead of a denunciation[1] of war, would instantly exclude
from our ports all the manufactures, produce, vessels and
subjects of the nations committing this aggression, during the continuance of the aggression and till full satisfaction made for it. This would work well in many ways,
safely in all, and introduce between nations another umpire than arms. It would relieve us too from the risks and
the horrors of cutting throats. The death of the King of
France has not produced as open condemnations from the
Monocrats as I expected. I dined the other day in a company where the subject was discussed. I will name the
company in the order in which they manifested their partialities beginning with the warmest Jacobinism and proceeding by shade to the most heartfelt aristocracy. Smith
(N.Y.) Coxe. Stewart. T. Shippen. Bingham. Peters. Breck.
Meredith. Wolcott. It is certain that the ladies of this
city, of the first circle, are all open-mouthed against the
murderers of a sovereign, and they generally speak those
sentiments which the more cautious husband smothers. . . .

To James Madison

Monticello, Dec. 28, 1794.

. . . The denunciation of the democratic societies[2] is one
of the extraordinary acts of boldness of which we have
seen so many from the fraction of monocrats. It is wonderful indeed, that the President should have permitted him-

---

[1] Public announcement. [Ed.]

[2] In his annual message to Congress, November 19, 1794,
Washington condemned the "self-created" democratic societies
which had sprung up during the preceding year and a half and
linked their agitation to the Whisky Rebellion in western
Pennsylvania. [Ed.]

self to be the organ of such an attack on the freedom of discussion, the freedom of writing, printing & publishing. It must be a matter of rare curiosity to get at the modifications of these rights proposed by them, and to see what line their ingenuity would draw between democratical societies, whose avowed object is the nourishment of the republican principles of our constitution, and the society of the Cincinnati, *a self-created* one, carving out for itself hereditary distinctions, lowering over our Constitution eternally, meeting together in all parts of the Union, periodically, with closed doors, accumulating a capital in their separate treasury, corresponding secretly & regularly, & of which society the very persons denouncing the democrats are themselves the fathers, founders, & high officers. Their sight must be perfectly dazzled by the glittering of crowns & coronets, not to see the extravagance of the proposition to suppress the friends of general freedom, while those who wish to confine that freedom to the few, are permitted to go on in their principles & practices. I here put out of sight the persons whose misbehavior has been taken advantage of to slander the friends of popular rights; and I am happy to observe, that as far as the circle of my observation & information extends, everybody has lost sight of them, and views the abstract attempt on their natural & constitutional rights in all it's nakedness. I have never heard, or heard of, a single expression or opinion which did not condemn it as an inexcusable aggression. And with respect to the transactions against the excise law, it appears to me that you are all swept away in the torrent of governmental opinions, or that we do not know what these transactions have been. We know of none which, according to the definitions of the law, have been anything more than riotous. There was indeed a meeting to consult about a separation. But to consult on a question does not amount to a determination of that question in the affirmative, still less to the acting on such a determination; but we shall see, I suppose, what the court lawyers, & courtly judges,

& would-be ambassadors will make of it. The excise law is an infernal one. The first error was to admit it by the Constitution; the 2d., to act on that admission; the 3d & last will be, to make it the instrument of dismembering the Union, & setting us all afloat to chuse which part of it we will adhere to. The information of our militia, returned from the Westward, is uniform, that tho the people there let them pass quietly, they were objects of their laughter, not of their fear; that 1000 men could have cut off their whole force in a thousand places of the Alleganey; that their detestation of the excise law is universal, and has now associated to it a detestation of the government; & that separation which perhaps was a very distant & problematical event, is now near, & certain, & determined in the mind of every man. I expected to have seen some justification of arming one part of the society against another; of declaring a civil war the moment before the meeting of that body which has the sole right of declaring war; of being so patient of the kicks & scoffs of our enemies, & rising at a feather against our friends; of adding a million to the public debt & deriding us with recommendations to pay it if we can &c., &c. But the part of the speech which was to be taken as a justification of the armament, reminded me of parson Saunders' demonstration why minus into minus make plus. After a parcel of shreds of stuff from Æsop's fables, and Tom Thumb, he jumps all at once into his Ergo, minus multiplied into minus make plus. Just so the 15,000 men enter after the fables, in the speech.—However, the time is coming when we shall fetch up the leeway of our vessel. The changes in your house, I see, are going on for the better, and even the Augean herd over your heads are slowly purging off their impurities. Hold on then, my dear friend, that we may not shipwreck in the meanwhile. I do not see, in the minds of those with whom I converse, a greater affliction than the fear of your retirement; but this must not be, unless to a more splendid & a more efficacious post. There I should rejoice to see you; I hope I may say,

I shall rejoice to see you. I have long had much in my mind to say to you on that subject. But double delicacies have kept me silent. I ought perhaps to say, while I would not give up my own retirement for the empire of the universe, how I can justify wishing one whose happiness I have so much at heart as yours, to take the front of the battle which is fighting for my security. This would be easy enough to be done, but not at the heel of a lengthy epistle. . . .

To Phillip Mazzei

Monticello, April 24, 1796.

. . . The aspect of our politics has wonderfully changed since you left us. In place of that noble love of liberty and republican government which carried us triumphantly through the war, an Anglican monarchical aristocratical party has sprung up, whose avowed object is to draw over us the substance, as they have already done the forms, of the British government. The main body of our citizens, however, remain true to their republican principles; the whole landed interest is republican, and so is a great mass of talents. Against us are the Executive, the Judiciary, two out of three branches of the Legislature, all the officers of the government, all who want to be officers, all timid men who prefer the calm of despostism to the boisterous sea of liberty, British merchants and Americans trading on British capital, speculators and holders in the banks and public funds, a contrivance invented for the purposes of corruption, and for assimilating us in all things to the rotten as well as the sound parts of the English model. It would give you a fever were I to name to you the apostates who have gone over to these heresies, men who were Samsons in the field and Solomons in the council, but who have had their heads shorn by the harlot England. In short, we are likely to preserve the liberty we have obtained only by unremitting labors and perils. But we shall preserve it; and our mass of weight and wealth on the good side is so great, as to leave no danger that force will ever be attempted against us. We have only to awake and snap the Lilliputian cords with which they have been entangling us during the first sleep which succeeded our labors. . . .

To Elbridge Gerry

Philadelphia, May 13, 97.

. . . I entirely commend your dispositions towards Mr. Adams; knowing his worth as intimately and esteeming it as much as any one, and acknoleging the preference of his claims, if any I could have had, to the high office conferred on him. But in truth, I had neither claims nor wishes on the subject, tho I know it will be difficult to obtain belief of this. When I retired from this place & the office of Secy of state, it was in the firmest contemplation of never more returning here. There had indeed been suggestions in the public papers, that I was looking towards a succession to the President's chair, but feeling a consciousness of their falsehood, and observing that the suggestions came from hostile quarters, I considered them as intended merely to excite public odium against me. I never in my life exchanged a word with any person, on the subject, till I found my name brought forward generally, in competition with that of Mr. Adams. Those with whom I then communicated, could say, if it were necessary, whether I met the call with desire, or even with a ready acquiescence, and whether from the moment of my first acquiescence, I did not devoutly pray that the very thing might happen which has happened. The second office of this government is honorable & easy, the first is but a splendid misery.

You express apprehensions that stratagems will be used, to produce a misunderstanding between the President and myself. Tho not a word having this tendency has ever been hazarded to me by any one, yet I consider as a certainty that nothing will be left untried to alienate him from me. These machinations will proceed from the Hamiltons by whom he is surrounded, and who are only a little less hostile to him than to me. It cannot but damp the pleasure of cordiality, when we suspect that it is suspected. I cannot help fearing, that it is impossible for Mr. Adams to believe that the state of my mind is what it really is; that he may think I view him as an obstacle in my way. I have no supernatural power to impress truth on the mind of another, nor he any to discover that the estimate which he may form, on a just view of the human mind as generally constituted, may not be just in its application to a special constitution. This may be a source of private uneasiness to us; I honestly confess that it is so to me at this time. But neither of us are capable of letting it have effect on our public duties. Those who may endeavor to separate us, are probably excited by the fear that I might have influence on the executive councils; but when they shall know that I consider my office as constitutionally confined to legislative functions, and that I could not take any part whatever in executive consultations, even were it proposed, their fears may perhaps subside, & their object be found not worth a machination.

I do sincerely wish with you, that we could take our stand on a ground perfectly neutral & independent towards all nations. It has been my constant object thro public life; and with respect to the English & French, particularly, I have too often expressed to the former my wishes, & made to them propositions verbally & in writing, officially & privately, to official & private characters, for them to doubt of my views, if they would be content with equality. Of this they are in possession of several written & formal proofs, in my own hand writing. But they have wished a monopoly of commerce & influence with us; and they have in fact obtained it. When we take notice that theirs is the workshop to which we go for all we want;

that with them centre either immediately or ultimately all the labors of our hands and lands; that to them belongs either openly or secretly the great mass of our navigation; that even the factorage of their affairs here, is kept to themselves by factitious citizenships; that these foreign & false citizens now constitute the great body of what are called our merchants, fill our sea ports, are planted in every little town & district of the interior country, sway everything in the former places by their own votes, & those of their dependants, in the latter, by their insinuations & the influence of their ledgers; that they are advancing fast to a monopoly of our banks & public funds, and thereby placing our public finances under their control; that they have in their alliance the most influential characters in & out of office; when they have shewn that by all these bearings on the different branches of the government, they can force it to proceed in whatever direction they dictate, and bend the interests of this country entirely to the will of another; when all this, I say, is attended to, it is impossible for us to say we stand on independent ground, impossible for a free mind not to see & to groan under the bondage in which it is bound. If anything after this could excite surprise, it would be that they have been able so far to throw dust in the eyes of our own citizens, as to fix on those who wish merely to recover self-government the charge of subserving one foreign influence, because they resist submission to another. But they possess our printing presses, a powerful engine in their government of us. At this very moment, they would have drawn us into a war on the side of England, had it not been for the failure of her bank. Such was their open & loud cry, & that of their gazettes till this event. After plunging us in all the broils of the European nations, there would remain but one act to close our tragedy, that is, to break up our Union; and even this they have ventured seriously & solemnly to propose & maintain by arguments in a Connecticut paper. I have been happy, however, in believing, from the stifling of this effort, that that dose was found too strong, & excited as much repugnance there as it did horror in other parts of our country, & that whatever follies we may be led into as to foreign nations, we shall never give up our Union, the last anchor of our hope, & that alone which is to prevent this heavenly country from becoming an arena of gladiators. Much as I abhor war, and view it as the greatest scourge of mankind, and anxiously as I wish to keep out of the broils of Europe, I would yet go with my brethren into these, rather than separate from them. But I hope we may still keep clear of them, notwithstanding our present thraldom, & that time may be given us to reflect on the awful crisis we have passed through, and to find some means of shielding ourselves in future from foreign influence, political, commercial, or in whatever other form it may be attempted. I can scarcely withhold myself from joining in the wish of Silas Deane, that there were an ocean of fire between us & the old world. . . .

To John Taylor

Philadelphia, June 1, 1798.

. . . Mr. New showed me your letter on the subject of the patent, which gave me an opportunity of observing what you said as to the effect, with you, of public proceedings, and that it was not unusual now to estimate the separate mass of Virginia and North Carolina, with a view to their separate existence. It is true that we are completely under the saddle of Massachusetts and Connecticut, and that they ride us very hard, cruelly insulting our feelings, as well as exhausting our strength and subsistence. Their natural friends, the three other eastern States, join them from a sort of family pride, and they have the art to divide certain other parts of the Union, so as to make use of them to govern the whole. This is not new, it is the old practice of despots; to use a part of the people to keep the rest in order. And those who have once got an ascendancy, and possessed themselves of all the resources of the nation, their revenues and offices, have immense means for retaining their advantage. But our present situation is not a natural one. The republicans, through every part of the Union, say, that it was the irresistible influence and popularity of General Washington played off by the cunning of Hamilton, which turned the government over to anti-republican hands, or turned the republicans chosen by the people into anti-republicans. He delivered it over to his successor in this state, and very untoward events since, improved with great artifice, have produced on the public mind the impressions we see. But still I repeat it, this is not the natural state. Time alone would bring round an order of things more correspondent to the sentiments of our constituents. But are there no events impending, which will do it within a few months? The crisis with England, the public and authentic avowal of sentiments hostile to the leading principles of our Constitution, the prospect of a war, in which we shall stand alone, land tax, stamp tax, increase of public debt, &c. Be this as it may, in every free and deliberating society, there must, from the nature of man, be opposite parties, and violent dissensions and discords; and one of these, for the most part, must prevail over the other for a longer or shorter time. Perhaps this party division is necessary to induce each to watch and delate to the people the proceedings of the other. But if on a temporary superiority of the one party, the other is to resort to a scission of the Union, no federal government can ever exist. If to rid ourselves of the present rule of Massachusetts and Connecticut, we break the Union, will the evil stop there? Suppose the New England States alone cut off, will our nature be changed? Are we not men still to the south of that, and with all the passions of men? Immediately, we shall see a Pennsylvania and a Virginia party arise in the residuary confederacy, and the public mind will be distracted with the same party spirit. What a game too will the one party have in their hands, by eternally threatening the other that unless they do so and so, they will join their northern neighbors. If we reduce our Union to Virginia and North Carolina, immediately the conflict will be established between the representatives of these two States, and they will end by breaking into their simple units. Seeing, therefore, that an association of men who will not quarrel with one another is a thing which never yet existed, from the greatest confederacy of nations down to a town meeting or a vestry; seeing that we must have somebody to quarrel with, I had rather keep our New England associates for that purpose, than to see our bickerings transferred to others. They are circumscribed within such narrow limits, and their population so full, that their numbers will ever be the minority, and they are marked, like the Jews, with such a perversity of character, as to constitute, from that circumstance, the natural division of our parties. A little patience, and we shall see the reign of witches pass over, their spells dissolved, and the people recovering their true sight, restoring their government to its true principles. It is true, that in the meantime, we are suffering deeply in spirit, and incurring the horrors of a war, and long oppressions of enormous public debt. But who can say what would be the evils of a scission, and when and where they would end? Better keep together as we are, haul off from Europe as soon as we can, and from all attachments to any portions of it; and if they show their power just sufficiently to hoop us together, it will be the happiest situation in which we can exist. If the game runs sometimes against us at home, we must have patience till luck turns, and then we shall have an opportunity of winning back the *principles* we have lost. For this is a game where principles are the stake. Better luck, therefore, to us all, and health, happiness and friendly salutations to yourself. Adieu.

P. S. It is hardly necessary to caution you to let nothing of mine get before the public; a single sentence got hold of by the Porcupines, will suffice to abuse and persecute me in their papers for months.

To Elbridge Gerry

Philadelphia, Jan 26, 1799.

MY DEAR SIR

Your favor of Nov. 12 was safely delivered to me by Mr. Binney, but not till Dec. 28, as I arrived here only three days before that date. It was received with great satisfaction. Our very long intimacy as fellow-laborers in the same cause, the recent expressions of mutual confidence which had preceded your mission,[1] the interesting course which that had taken, & particularly & personally as it regarded yourself, made me anxious to hear from you on your return. I was the more so too, as I had myself during the whole of your absence, as well as since your return, been a constant butt for every shaft of calumny which malice & falsehood could form, & the presses, public speakers, or private letters disseminate. . . . In confutation of these and all future calumnies, by way of anticipation, I shall make to you a profession of my political faith; in confidence that you will consider every future imputation on me of a contrary complexion, as bearing on its front the mark of falsehood & calumny.

I do then, with sincere zeal, wish an inviolable preservation of our present federal constitution, according to the true sense in which it was adopted by the States, that in which it was advocated by it's friends, & not that which it's enemies apprehended, who therefore became it's enemies; and I am opposed to the monarchising it's features by the forms of it's administration, with a view to conciliate a first transition to a President & Senate for life, & from that to a hereditary tenure of these offices, & thus to

[1] A member of Adams' three-man commission to France, Gerry had lingered in Paris and tried to cushion the shock of the XYZ Affair. [Ed.]

worm out the elective principle. I am for preserving to the States the powers not yielded by them to the Union, & to the legislature of the Union it's constitutional share in the division of powers; and I am not for transferring all the powers of the States to the general government, & all those of that government to the Executive branch. I am for a government rigorously frugal & simple, applying all the possible savings of the public revenue to the discharge of the national debt; and not for a multiplication of officers & salaries merely to make partisans, & for increasing, by every device, the public debt, on the principle of it's being a public blessing. I am for relying, for internal defence, on our militia solely, till actual invasion, and for such a naval force only as may protect our coasts and harbors from such depredations as we have experienced; and not for a standing army in time of peace, which may overawe the public sentiment; nor for a navy, which, by it's own expenses and the eternal wars in which it will implicate us, will grind us with public burthens, & sink us under them. I am for free commerce with all nations; political connection with none; & little or no diplomatic establishment. And I am not for linking ourselves by new treaties with the quarrels of Europe; entering that field of slaughter to preserve their balance, or joining in the confederacy of kings to war against the principles of liberty. I am for freedom of religion, & against all maneuvres to bring about a legal ascendancy of one sect over another: for freedom of the press, & against all violations of the constitution to silence by force & not by reason the complaints or criticisms, just or unjust, of our citizens against the conduct of their agents. And I am for encouraging the progress of science in all it's branches; and not for raising a hue and cry against the sacred name of philosophy; for awing the human mind by stories of raw-head & bloody bones to a distrust of its own vision, & to repose implicitly on that of others; to go backwards instead of forwards to look for improvement; to believe that government, religion, morality, & every other science were in the highest perfection in ages of the darkest ignorance, and that nothing can ever be devised more perfect than what was established by our forefathers. To these I will add, that I was a sincere well-wisher to the success of the French revolution, and still wish it may end in the establishment of a free & well-ordered republic; but I have not been insensible under the atrocious depredations they have committed on our commerce. The first object of my heart is my own country. In that is embarked my family, my fortune, & my own existence. I have not one farthing of interest, nor one fibre of attachment out of it, nor a single motive of preference of any one nation to another, but in proportion as they are more or less friendly to us. But though deeply feeling the injuries of France, I did not think war the surest means of redressing them. I did believe, that a mission sincerely disposed to preserve peace, would obtain for us a peaceable & honorable settlement & retribution; and I appeal to you to say, whether this might not have been obtained, if either of your colleagues had been of the same sentiment with yourself.

These, my friend, are my principles; they are unquestionably the principles of the great body of our fellow citizens, and I know there is not one of them which is not yours also. In truth, we never differed but on one ground, the funding system; and as, from the moment of it's being adopted by the constituted authorities, I became religiously principled in the sacred discharge of it to the uttermost farthing, we are united now even on that single ground of difference. . . .

To Edmund Randolph

Monticello, Aug. 18, 99.

DEAR SIR

I received only two days ago your favor of the 12th, and as it was on the eve of the return of our post, it was not possible to make so prompt a despatch of the answer. Of all the doctrines which have ever been broached by the federal government, the novel one, of the common law being in force & cognizable as an existing law in their courts, is to me the most formidable. All their other assumptions of un-given powers have been in the detail. The bank law, the treaty doctrine, the sedition act, alien act, the undertaking to change the state laws of evidence in the state courts by certain parts of the stamp act, &c., &c., have been solitary, unconsequential, timid things, in comparison with the audacious, barefaced and sweeping pretension to a system of law for the U S, without the adoption of their legislature, and so infinitively beyond their power to adopt. If this assumption be yielded to, the state courts may be shut up, as there will then be nothing to hinder citizens of the same state suing each other in the federal courts in every case, as on a bond for instance, because the common law obliges payment of it, & the common law they say is their law. I am happy you have taken up the subject; & I have carefully perused & considered the notes you enclosed, and find but a single paragraph which I do not approve. It is that wherein (page 2.) you say, that laws being emanations from the legislative department, &, when once enacted, continuing in force from a presumption that their will so continues, that that presumption fails & the laws of course fall, on the destruction of that legislative department. I do not think this is the true bottom on which laws & the administering them rest. The whole body of the nation is the sovereign legislative, judiciary and executive power for itself. The inconvenience of meeting to exercise these powers in person, and their inaptitude to exercise them, induce them to appoint special organs to declare their legislative will, to judge & to execute it. It is the will of the nation which makes the law obligatory; it is their will which creates or annihilates the organ which is to declare & announce it. They may do it by a single person, as an Emperor of Russia, (constituting his declarations evidence of their will,) or by a few persons, as the Aristocracy of Venice, or by a complication of councils, as in our former regal government, or our present republican one. The law being law because it is the will of the nation, is not changed by their changing the organ through which they chuse to announce their future will; no more than the acts I have done by one attorney lose their obligation by my changing or discontinuing that attorney. This doctrine has been, in a certain degree sanctioned by the federal executive. For it is precisely that on which the continuance of obligation from our treaty with France was established, and the doctrine was particularly developed in a letter to Gouverneur Morris,[1] written with the approbation of President Washington and his cabinet. Mercer once prevailed on the Virginia Assembly to declare a different doctrine in some resolutions. These met universal disapprobation in this, as well as the other States, and if I mistake not, a subsequent Assembly did something to do away the authority of their former unguarded resolutions. In this case, as in all others, the true principle will be quite as effectual to establish the just deductions, for before the revolution, the nation of Virginia had, by the organs they then thought proper to constitute, established a system of laws, which they divided into three denominations of 1, common law; 2, statute law; 3, Chancery: or if you please, into two only, of 1, common law; 2, Chancery. When, by the declaration of Independence, they chose to abolish their former organs of declaring their will, the acts of will already formally & constitutionally declared, remained untouched. For the nation was not dissolved, was not annihilated; it's will, therefore, remained in full vigor; and on the establishing the new organs, first of a convention, & afterwards a more complicated legislature, the old acts of national will continued in force, until the nation should, by its new organs, declare it's will changed. The common law, therefore,

[1] As United States Minister to France in 1792. [Ed.]

which was not in force when we landed here, nor till we had formed ourselves into a nation, and had manifested by the organs we constituted that the common law was to be our law, continued to be our law, because the nation continued in being, & because though it changed the organs for the future declarations of its will, yet it did not change its former declarations that the common law was it's law. Apply these principles to the present case. Before the revolution there existed no such nation as the U S; they then first associated as a nation, but for special purposes only. They had all their laws to make, as Virginia had on her first establishment as a nation. But they did not, as Virginia had done, proceed to adopt a whole system of laws ready made to their hand. As their association as a nation was only for special purposes, to wit, for the management of their concerns with one another & with foreign nations, and the states composing the association chose to give it powers for those purposes & no others, they could not adopt any general system, because it would have embraced objects on which this association had no right to form or declare a will. It was not the organ for declaring a national will in these cases. In the cases confided to them, they were free to declare the will of the nation, the law; but till it was declared there could be no law. So that the common law did not become, ipso facto, law on the new association; it could only become so by a positive adoption, & so far only as they were authorized to adopt.

I think it will be of great importance, when you come to the proper part, to portray at full length the consequences of this new doctrine, that the common law is the law of the U S, & that their courts have, of course, jurisdiction co-extensive with that law, that is to say, general over all cases & persons. But, great heavens! Who could have conceived in 1789 that within ten years we should have to combat such windmills. Adieu. Yours affectionately.

To Doctor Joseph Priestley

Washington, Mar 21, 1801.

DEAR SIR

I learnt some time ago that you were in Philadelphia, but that it was only for a fortnight; & supposed you were gone. It was not till yesterday I received information that you were still there, had been very ill, but were on the recovery. I sincerely rejoice that you are so. Yours is one of the few lives precious to mankind, & for the continuance of which every thinking man is solicitous. Bigots may be an exception. What an effort, my dear Sir, of bigotry in Politics & Religion have we gone through! The barbarians really flattered themselves they should be able to bring back the time of Vandalism, when ignorance put everything into the hands of power & priestcraft. All advances in science were proscribed as innovations. They pretended to praise and encourage education, but it was to be the education of our ancestors. We were to look backwards, not forwards, for improvement; the President himself declaring, in one of his answers to addresses, that we were never to expect to go beyond them in real science. This was the real ground of all the attacks on you. Those who live by mystery & *charlatanerie*, fearing you would render them useless by simplifying the Christian philosophy,—the most sublime & benevolent, but most perverted system that ever shone on man,—endeavored to crush your well-earnt & well-deserved fame. But it was the Lilliputians upon Gulliver. Our countrymen have recovered from the alarm into which art & industry had thrown them; sicence & honesty are replaced on their high ground; and you, my dear Sir, as their great apostle, are on it's pinnacle. It is with heartfelt satisfaction that, in the first moments of my public action, I can hail you with welcome to our land, tender to you the homage of it's respect & esteem, cover you under the protection of those laws which were made for the wise and good like you, and disdain the legitimacy of that libel on legislation, which, under the form of a law, was for some time placed among them.[1]

As the storm is now subsiding, and the horizon becoming serene, it is pleasant to consider the phenomenon with attention. We can no longer say there is nothing new under the sun. For this whole chapter in the history of man is new. The great extent of our Republic is new. Its sparse habitation is new. The mighty wave of public opinion which has rolled over it is new. But the most pleasing novelty is, it's so quickly subsiding over such an extent of surface to it's true level again. The order & good sense displayed in this recovery from delusion, and in the momentous crisis which lately arose, really bespeak a strength of character in our nation which augurs well for the duration of our Republic; & I am much better satisfied now of it's stability than I was before it was tried. I have been, above all things, solaced by the prospect which opened on us, in the event of a non-election of a President; in which case, the federal government would have been in the situation of a clock or watch run down. There was no idea of force, nor of any occasion for it. A convention, invited by the Republican members of Congress, with the virtual President & Vice President, would have been on the ground in 8. weeks, would have repaired the Constitution where it was defective, & wound it up again. This peaceable & legitimate resource, to which we are in the habit of implicit obedience, superseding all appeal to force, and being always within our reach, shows a precious principle of self-preservation in our composition, till a change of circumstances shall take place, which is not within prospect at any definite period.

But I have got into a long disquisition on politics, when I only meant to express my sympathy in the state of your

[1] The Alien Law. [Ed.]

health, and to tender you all the affections of public &
private hospitality. . . .

To Robert R. Livingston[1]

Washington, Apr. 18, 1802.

. . . The cession of Louisiana and the Floridas by Spain
to France works most sorely on the U. S. On this subject
the Secretary of State has written to you fully. Yet I cannot forbear recurring to it personally, so deep is the impression it makes in my mind. It compleatly reverses all
the political relations of the U. S. and will form a new
epoch in our political course. Of all nations of any consideration France is the one which hitherto has offered the
fewest points on which we could have any conflict of right,
and the most points of a communion of interests. From
these causes we have ever looked to her as our *natural
friend*, as one with which we never could have an occasion of difference. Her growth therefore we viewed as our
own, her misfortunes ours. There is on the globe one single spot, the possessor of which is our natural and habitual
enemy. It is New Orleans, through which the produce of
three-eighths of our territory must pass to market, and
from its fertility it will ere long yield more than half of
our whole produce and contain more than half our inhabitants. France placing herself in that door assumes to us the
attitude of defiance. Spain might have retained it quietly
for years. Her pacific dispositions, her feeble state, would
induce her to increase our facilities there, so that her possession of the place would be hardly felt by us, and it
would not perhaps be very long before some circumstance
might arise which might make the cession of it to us the
price of something of more worth to her. Not so can it
ever be in the hands of France. The impetuosity of her
temper, the energy and restlessness of her character, placed

[1] United States Minister to France. [Ed.]

in a point of eternal friction with us, and our character, which though quiet, and loving peace and the pursuit of wealth, is high-minded, despising wealth in competition with insult or injury, enterprising and energetic as any nation on earth, these circumstances render it impossible that France and the U. S. can continue long friends when they meet in so irritable a position. They as well as we must be blind if they do not see this; and we must be very improvident if we do not begin to make arrangements on that hypothesis. The day that France takes possession of N. Orleans fixes the sentence which is to restrain her forever within her low water mark. It seals the union of two nations who in conjunction can maintain exclusive possession of the ocean. From that moment we must marry ourselves to the British fleet and nation. We must turn all our attentions to a maritime force, for which our resources place us on very high grounds: and having formed and cemented together a power which may render reinforcement of her settlements here impossible to France, make the first cannon, which shall be fired in Europe the signal for tearing up any settlement she may have made, and for holding the two continents of America in sequestration for the common purposes of the united British and American nations. This is not a state of things we seek or desire. It is one which this measure, if adopted by France, forces on us, as necessarily as any other cause, by the laws of nature, brings on its necessary effect. It is not from a fear of France that we deprecate this measure proposed by her. For however greater her force is than ours compared in the abstract, it is nothing in comparison of ours when to be exerted on our soil. But it is from a sincere love of peace, and a firm persuasion that bound to France by the interests and the strong sympathies still existing in the minds of our citizens, and holding relative positions which ensure their continuance we are secure of a long course of peace. Whereas the change of friends, which will be rendered necessary if France changes that position, embarks us necessarily as a belligerent power in the first war of Europe. In that case France will have held possession of New Orleans during the interval of a peace, long or short, at the end of which it will be wrested from her. Will this short-lived possession have been an equivalent to her for the transfer of such a weight into the scale of her enemy? Will not the amalgamation of a young, thriving nation continue to that enemy the health and force which are at present so evidently on the decline? And will a few years possession of N. Orleans add equally to the strength of France? She may say she needs Louisiana for the supply of her West Indies. She does not need it in time of peace. And in war she could not depend on them because they would be so easily intercepted. I should suppose that all these considerations might in some proper form be brought into view of the government of France. Tho' stated by us, it ought not to give offence; because we do not bring them forward as a menace, but as consequences not controulable by us, but inevitable from the course of things. We mention them not as things which we desire by any means, but as things we deprecate; and we beseech a friend to look forward and to prevent them for our common interests.

If France considers Louisiana however as indispensable for her views she might perhaps be willing to look about for arrangements which might reconcile it to our interests. If anything could do this it would be the ceding to us the island of New Orleans and the Floridas. This would certainly in a great degree remove the causes of jarring and irritation between us, and perhaps for such a length of time as might produce other means of making the measure permanently conciliatory to our interests and friendships. It would at any rate relieve us from the necessity of taking immediate measures for countervailing such an operation by arrangements in another quarter. Still we should consider N. Orleans and the Floridas as equivalent for the risk of a quarrel with France produced by her vicinage. I have no doubt you have urged these considerations on every proper occasion with the government where you are. They are such as must have effect if you can find the means of producing thorough reflection on them by that government. The idea here is that the troops sent to St. Domingo, were to proceed to Louisiana after finishing their work in that island. If this were the arrangement, it will give you time to return again and again to the charge, for the conquest of St. Domingo will not be a short work. It will take considerable time to wear down a great number of souldiers. Every eye in the U. S. is now fixed on this affair of Louisiana. Perhaps nothing since the revolutionary war has produced more uneasy sensations through the body of the nation. . . .

To Benjamin H. Latrobe

Washington Nov. 2. 1802.

DEAR SIR

The placing of a navy in a state of perfect preservation, so that at the beginning of a subsequent war it shall be as sound as at the end of the preceding one when laid up, and the lessening the expence of repairs, perpetually necessary while they lie in the water, are objects of the first importance to a nation which to a certain degree must be maritime. The dry docks of Europe, being below the level of tide water, are very expensive in their construction and in the manner of keeping them clear of water, and are only practicable at all where they have high tides: insomuch that no nation has ever proposed to lay up their whole navy in dry docks. But if the dry dock were above the level of tide water, and there be any means of raising the vessels up into them, and of covering the dock with a roof, thus withdrawn from the rot and the sun, they would last as long as the interior timbers, doors and floors of a house. The vast command of running water at this place, at different heights from 30 to 200 feet above tide water, enables us to effect this desirable object by forming a lower bason into which the tide water shall float the vessel and then have its gates closed, and adjoining to this, but 24 feet higher, an upper bason 275 feet wide, and 800 f. long (sufficient to contain 12 frigates) into which running water can be introduced from above, so that filling both basons (as in a lock) the vessel shall be raised up and floated into the upper one, and the water being discharged leave her dry. Over a bason not wider than 175 feet, a roof can be thrown, in the manner of that of the Halle au blé at Paris, which needing no underworks to support it, will permit the bason to be entirely open and free for the movement of the vessels. I mean to propose the construction of one of these to the National legislature, convinced it will be a work of no great cost, that it will save us great annual expence, and be an encouragement to prepare in peace the vessels we shall need in war, when we find they can be kept in a state of perfect preservation and without expence.

The first thing to be done is to chuse from which of the streams we will derive our water for the lock. These are the Eastern branch, Tyber, Rock creek, and the Potomak itself. Then to trace the canal, draw plans of that and of the two basons, and calculate the expence of the whole, that we may lead the legislature to no expence in the execution of which they shall not be apprised in the beginning. For this I ask your aid, which will require your coming here. Some surveys and elevations have been already made by Mr. N. King, a very accurate man in that line, and who will assist in any thing you desire, and execute on the ground any tracings you may direct, unless you prefer doing them yourself. It is very material too that this should be done immediately, as we have little more than 4 weeks to the meeting of the legislature, and there will then be but 2 weeks for them to consider and decide before the day arrives (Jan. 1) at which alone any number of labourers can be hired here. Should that pass either the work must lie over for a year, or be executed by day labourers at double expence. I propose that such a force shall be provided as to compleat the work in one year. If this results, as it will receive all our present ships, the next work will be a second one, to build and lay up additional ships. On the subject of your superintending the execution of the work it would be premature to say any thing till the legislature shall have declared their will. Be so good as to let me hear from you immediately, if you cannot come so soon as you can write. Accept my best wishes and respects.

To Doctor Benjamin Rush

Washington, April 21, 1803.

DEAR SIR

In some of the delightful conversations with you, in the evenings of 1798-99, and which served as an anodyne to the afflictions of the crisis through which our country was then laboring, the Christian religion was sometimes our topic; and I then promised you, that one day or other, I would give you my views of it. They are the result of a life of inquiry and reflection, and very different from that anti-Christian system imputed to me by those who know nothing of my opinions. To the corruptions of Christianity I am, indeed, opposed; but not to the genuine precepts of Jesus himself. I am a Christian, in the only sense in which he wished any one to be; sincerely attached to his doctrines, in preference to all others; ascribing to himself every *human* excellence; and believing he never claimed any other. At the short interval since these conversations, when I could justifiably abstract my mind from public affairs, the subject has been under my contemplation. But the more I considered it, the more it expanded beyond the measure of either my time or information. In the moment of my late departure from Monticello,

I received from Dr. Priestley, his little treatise of "Socrates and Jesus Compared." This being a section of the general view I had taken of the field, it became a subject of reflection while on the road, and unoccupied otherwise. The result was, to arrange in my mind a syllabus, or outline of such an estimate of the comparative merits of Christianity, as I wished to see executed by some one of more leisure and information for the task, than myself. This I now send you, as the only discharge of my promise I can probably ever execute. And in confiding it to you, I know it will not be exposed to the malignant perversions of those who make every word from me a text for new misrepresentations and calumnies. I am moreover averse to the communication of my religious tenets to the public; because it would countenance the presumption of those who have endeavored to draw them before that tribunal, and to seduce public opinion to erect itself into that inquisition over the rights of conscience, which the laws have so justly proscribed. It behooves every man who values liberty of conscience for himself, to resist invasions of it in the case of others; or their case may, by change of circumstances, become his own. It behooves him, too, in his own case, to give no example of concession, betraying the common right of independent opinion, by answering questions of faith, which the laws have left between God and himself. Accept my affectionate salutations.

Syllabus of an Estimate of the Merit of the Doctrines of Jesus, compared with those of others.

In a comparative view of the Ethics of the enlightened nations of antiquity, of the Jews and of Jesus, no notice should be taken of the corruptions of reason among the ancients, to wit, the idolatry and superstition of the vulgar, nor of the corruptions of Christianity by the learned among its professors.

Let a just view be taken of the moral principles inculcated by the most esteemed of the sects of ancient philosophy, or of their individuals; particularly Pythagoras, Socrates, Epicurus, Cicero, Epictetus, Seneca, Antoninus.

I. Philosophers. 1. Their precepts related chiefly to ourselves, and the government of those passions which, unrestrained, would disturb our tranquillity of mind.[1] In this branch of philosophy they were really great.

2. In developing our duties to others, they were short and defective. They embraced, indeed, the circles of kindred and friends, and inculcated patriotism, or the love of our country in the aggregate, as a primary obligation: towards our neighbors and countrymen they taught justice, but scarcely viewed them as within the circle of benevolence. Still less have they inculcated peace, charity and love to our fellow men, or embraced with benevolence the whole family of mankind.

II. Jews. 1. Their system was Deism; that is, the belief in one only God. But their ideas of him and of his attributes were degrading and injurious.

2. Their Ethics were not only imperfect, but often irreconcilable with the sound dictates of reason and morality, as they respect intercourse with those around us; and repulsive and anti-social, as respecting other nations. They needed reformation, therefore, in an eminent degree.

III. Jesus. In this state of things among the Jews, Jesus appeared. His parentage was obscure; his condition poor; his education null; his natural endowments great; his life

---

[1] To explain, I will exhibit the heads of Seneca's and Cicero's philosophical works, the most extensive of any we have received from the ancients. Of ten heads in Seneca, seven relate to ourselves, viz. *de ira, consolatio, de tranquilitate, de constantia sapientis, de otio sapientis, de vita beata, de brevitate vitae;* two relate to others, *de clementia, de beneficiis;* and one relates to the government of the world, *de providentia.* Of eleven tracts of Cicero, five respect ourselves, viz. *de finibus, Tusculana, academica, paradoxa, de Senectute;* one, *de officiis,* relates partly to ourselves, partly to others; one, *de amicitia,* relates to others; and four are on different subjects, to wit, *de natura deorum, de divinatione, de fato,* and *somnium Scipionis.*

correct and innocent: he was meek, benevolent, patient, firm, disinterested, and of the sublimest eloquence.

The disadvantages under which his doctrines appear are remarkable.

1. Like Socrates and Epictetus, he wrote nothing himself.

2. But he had not, like them, a Xenophon or an Arrian to write for him. I name not Plato, who only used the name of Socrates to cover the whimsies of his own brain. On the contrary, all the learned of his country, entrenched in its power and riches, were opposed to him, lest his labors should undermine their advantages; and the committing to writing his life and doctrines fell on unlettered and ignorant men; who wrote, too, from memory, and not till long after the transactions had passed.

3. According to the ordinary fate of those who attempt to enlighten and reform mankind, he fell an early victim to the jealousy and combination of the altar and the throne, at about thirty-three years of age, his reason having not yet attained the *maximum* of its energy, nor the course of his preaching, which was but of three years at most, presented occasions for developing a complete system of morals.

4. Hence the doctrines which he really delivered were defective as a whole, and fragments only of what he did deliver have come to us mutilated, misstated, and often unintelligible.

5. They have been still more disfigured by the corruptions of schismatizing followers, who have found an interest in sophisticating and perverting the simple doctrines he taught, by engrafting on them the mysticisms of a Grecian sophist, frittering them into subtleties, and obscuring them with jargon, until they have caused good men to reject the whole in disgust, and to view Jesus himself as an impostor.

Notwithstanding these disadvantages, a system of morals is presented to us, which, if filled up in the style and spirit of the rich fragments he left us, would be the most perfect and sublime that has ever been taught by man.

The question of his being a member of the Godhead, or in direct communication with it, claimed for him by some of his followers, and denied by others, is foreign to the present view, which is merely an estimate of the intrinsic merits of his doctrines.

1. He corrected the Deism of the Jews, confirming them in their belief of one only God, and giving them juster notions of his attributes and government.

2. His moral doctrines, relating to kindred and friends, were more pure and perfect than those of the most correct of the philosophers, and greatly more so than those of the Jews; and they went far beyond both in inculcating universal philanthropy, not only to kindred and friends, to neighbors and countrymen, but to all mankind, gathering all into one family, under the bonds of love, charity, peace, common wants and common aids. A development of this head will evince the peculiar superiority of the system of Jesus over all others.

3. The precepts of philosophy, and of the Hebrew code, laid hold of actions only. He pushed his scrutinies into the heart of man; erected his tribunal in the region of his thoughts, and purified the waters at the fountain head.

4. He taught, emphatically, the doctrines of a future state, which was either doubted, or disbelieved by the Jews; and wielded it with efficacy, as an important incentive, supplementary to the other motives to moral conduct.

To John Breckinridge[1]

Monticello, August 12, 1803.

DEAR SIR

The enclosed letter, though directed to you, was intended to me also, and was left open with a request, that when forwarded, I would forward it to you. It gives

[1] United States Senator from Kentucky. [Ed.]

me occasion to write a word to you on the subject of Louisiana, which being a new one, an interchange of sentiments may produce correct ideas before we are to act on them.

Our information as to the country is very incomplete; we have taken measures to obtain it full as to the settled part, which I hope to receive in time for Congress. The boundaries, which I deem not admitting question, are the high lands on the western side of the Mississippi enclosing all its waters, the Missouri of course, and terminating in the line drawn from the northwestern point of the Lake of the Woods to the nearest source of the Mississippi, as lately settled between Great Britain and the United States. We have some claims, to extend on the seacoast westwardly to the Rio Norte or Bravo, and better, to go eastwardly to the Rio Perdido, between Mobile and Pensacola, the ancient boundary of Louisiana. These claims will be a subject of negotiation with Spain, and if, as soon as she is at war, we push them strongly with one hand, holding out a price in the other, we shall certainly obtain the Floridas, and all in good time. In the meanwhile, without waiting for permission, we shall enter into the exercise of the natural right we have always insisted on with Spain, to wit, that of a nation holding the upper part of streams, having a right of innocent passage through them to the ocean. We shall prepare her to see us practise on this, and she will not oppose it by force.

Objections are raising to the eastward against the vast extent of our boundaries, and propositions are made to exchange Louisiana, or a part of it, for the Floridas. But, as I have said, we shall get the Floridas without, and I would not give one inch of the waters of the Mississippi to any nation, because I see in a light very important to our peace the exclusive right to its navigation, and the admission of no nation into it, but as into the Potomac or Delaware, with our consent and under our police. These federalists see in this acquisition the formation of a new confederacy,

embracing all the waters of the Mississippi, on both sides
of it, and a separation of its eastern waters from us. These
combinations depend on so many circumstances which we
cannot foresee, that I place little reliance on them. We
have seldom seen neighborhood produce affection among
nations. The reverse is almost the universal truth. Besides,
if it should become the great interest of those nations to
separate from this, if their happiness should depend on it
so strongly as to induce them to go through that convulsion, why should the Atlantic States dread it? But especially why should we, their present inhabitants, take side
in such a question? When I view the Atlantic States, procuring for those on the eastern waters of the Mississippi
friendly instead of hostile neighbors on its western waters,
I do not view it as an Englishman would be procuring future blessings for the French nation, with whom he has no
relations of blood or affection. The future inhabitants of
the Atlantic and Mississippi States will be our sons. We
leave them in distinct but bordering establishments. We
think we see their happiness in their union, and we wish
it. Events may prove it otherwise; and if they see their
interest in separation, why should we take side with our
Atlantic rather than our Mississippi descendants? It is the
elder and the younger son differing. God bless them both,
and keep them in union, if it be for their good, but separate them, if it be better. The inhabited part of Louisiana,
from Point Coupée to the sea, will of course be immediately a territorial government, and soon a State. But above
that, the best use we can make of the country for some
time, will be to give establishments in it to the Indians on
the east side of the Mississippi, in exchange for their present country, and open land offices in the last, and thus
make this acquisition the means of filling up the eastern
side, instead of drawing off its population. When we shall
be full on this side, we may lay off a range of States on
the western bank from the head to the mouth, and so,
range after range, advancing compactly as we multiply.

This treaty must of course be laid before both Houses, because both have important functions to exercise respecting it. They, I presume, will see their duty to their country in ratifying and paying for it, so as to secure a good which would otherwise probably be never again in their power. But I suppose they must then appeal to *the nation* for an additional article to the Constitution, approving and confirming an act which the nation had not previously authorized. The Constitution has made no provision for our holding foreign territory, still less for incorporating foreign nations into our Union. The executive in seizing the fugitive occurrence which so much advances the good of their country, have done an act beyond the Constitution. The Legislature in casting behind them metaphysical subtleties, and risking themselves like faithful servants, must ratify and pay for it, and throw themselves on their country for doing for them unauthorized, what we know they would have done for themselves had they been in a situation to do it. It is the case of a guardian, investing the money of his ward in purchasing an important adjacent territory; and saying to him when of age, I did this for your good; I pretend to no right to bind you: you may disavow me, and I must get out of the scrape as I can: I thought it my duty to risk myself for you. But we shall not be disavowed by the nation, and their act of indemnity will confirm and not weaken the Constitution, by more strongly marking out its lines. . . .

To Jean Baptiste Say

Washington, February 1, 1804.

DEAR SIR

I have to acknowledge the receipt of your obliging letter, and with it, of two very interesting volumes on Political Economy. These found me engaged in giving the leisure moments I rarely find, to the perusal of Malthus' work on population, a work of sound logic, in which some of the opinions of Adam Smith, as well as of the economists, are ably examined. I was pleased, on turning to some chapters where you treat the same questions, to find his opinions corroborated by yours. I shall proceed to the reading of your work with great pleasure. In the meantime, the present conveyance, by a gentleman of my family going to Paris, is too safe to hazard a delay in making my acknowledgments for this mark of attention, and for having afforded to me a satisfaction, which the ordinary course of literary communications could not have given me for a considerable time.

The differences of circumstance between this and the old countries of Europe, furnish differences of fact whereon to reason, in questions of political economy, and will consequently produce sometimes a difference of result. There, for instance, the quantity of food is fixed, or increasing in a slow and only arithmetical ratio, and the proportion is limited by the same ratio. Supernumerary births consequently add only to your mortality. Here the immense extent of uncultivated and fertile lands enables every one who will labor, to marry young, and to raise a family of any size. Our food, then, may increase geometrically with our laborers, and our births, however multiplied, become effective. Again, there the best distribution of labor is supposed to be that which places the manufacturing hands alongside the agricultural; so that the one part shall feed both, and the other part furnish both with clothes and other comforts. Would that be best here? Egoism and first appearances say yes. Or would it be better that all our laborers should be employed in agriculture? In this case a double or treble portion of fertile lands would be brought into culture; a double or treble creation of food be produced, and its surplus go to nourish the now perishing births of Europe, who in return would manufacture and send us in exchange our clothes and other comforts. Morality listens to this, and so invariably do the laws of nature create our duties and interests, that when they seem to be at variance, we ought to suspect some fallacy in our reasonings. In solving this question, too, we should allow its just weight to the moral and physical preference of the agricultural, over the manufacturing, man. My occupations permit me only to ask questions. They deny me the time, if I had the information, to answer them. Perhaps, as worthy the attention of the author of the *Traité d'Economie Politique*, I shall find them answered in that work. If they are not, the reason will have been that you wrote for Europe; while I shall have asked them because I think for America. Accept, Sir, my respectful salutations, and assurances of great consideration.

To Governor William C. C. Claiborne[1]

Washington, July 7. 1804.

. . . The position of New Orleans certainly entitles it to be the greatest city the world has ever seen. There is no spot on the globe to which the produce of so great an extent of fertile country must necessarily come. It is three times the greater than that on the Eastern side of the Allegany which is to be divided among all the seaports of the Atlantic states. There is also no spot where yellow fever is so much to be apprehended. In the middle and Northern parts of Europe where the sun rarely shines, they can safely build cities in solid blocks without generating disease. But under the cloudless skies of America where there is so constant an accumulation of heat, men cannot be piled on one another with impunity. Accordingly we find this disease confined to the solid-built parts of our towns and the parts on the waterside where there is most matter for putrefaction, rarely extending into the thin-

[1] Acting Governor of Orleans Territory. [Ed.]

built parts of the town, and never known into the country. In these latter places it cannot be communicated. In order to catch it you must go into the local atmosphere where it prevails. Is not this a strong indication that we ought not to contend with the laws of nature, but should decide at once that all our cities shall be thin-built? You will perhaps remember that in 1793 yourself, the present governor Harrison with another young gentleman, dining with me in Philadelphia, the then late yellow fever being the subject of conversation, and its in-communicability in the country, I observed that in building cities in the U.S. we should take the chequer board for our plan, leaving the white squares open and unbuilt for ever, and planted with trees. Harrison treasured this idea in his mind, and having to lay off a city 2 or 3 years ago on the banks of Ohio, opposite to Louisville,[2] he laid it off on this plan. As it is probable that N. Orleans must be very soon enlarged, I inclose you the same plan for consideration. I have great confidence that howsoever the yellow fever may prevail in the old part of the town, it would not be communicable in that part which should be built on this plan; because this would be all like the thin-built parts of our towns, where experience has taught us that a person may carry it, after catching it in its local region, but can never communicate it out of that. Having very sincerely at heart, that the prosperity of N. Orleans should be unchecked, and great faith founded as I think in experience of the effect of this mode of building against a disease which is such a scourge to our close built cities, I could not deny myself the communication of the plan, leaving to you to bring it into real existence if those more interested should think as favorably of it as I do. For beauty, pleasure and convenience it will certainly be eminent. . . .

[2] Jeffersonville, Indiana. [Ed.]

To Doctor Edward Jenner

Monticello, May 14, 1806.

Sir,

I have received a copy of the evidence at large respecting the discovery of the vaccine inoculation which you have been pleased to send me, and for which I return you my thanks. Having been among the early converts, in this part of the globe, to its efficiency, I took an early part in recommending it to my countrymen. I avail myself of this occasion of rendering you a portion of the tribute of gratitude due to you from the whole human family. Medicine has never before produced any single improvement of such utility. Harvey's discovery of the circulation of the blood was a beautiful addition to our knowledge of the animal economy, but on a review of the practice of medicine before and since that epoch, I do not see any great amelioration which has been derived from that discovery. You have erased from the calendar of human afflictions one of its greatest. Yours is the comfortable reflection that mankind can never forget that you have lived. Future nations will know by history only that the loathsome smallpox has existed and by you has been extirpated.

Accept my fervent wishes for your health and happiness and assurances of the greatest respect and consideration.

To William Hamilton

Washington, July, 1806

. . . Having decisively made up my mind for retirement at the end of my present term, my views and attentions are all turned homewards. I have hitherto been engaged in my buildings which will be finished in the course of the present year. The improvement of my grounds has been reserved for my occupation on my return home. For this reason it is that I have put off to the fall of the year after next the collection of such curious trees as will bear our winters in the open air.

The grounds which I destine to improve in the style of the English gardens are in a form very difficult to be managed. They compose the northern quadrant of a mountain for about ⅔ of its height & then spread for the upper third over its whole crown. They contain about three hundred acres, washed at the foot for about a mile, by a river of the size of the Schuylkill. The hill is generally too steep for direct ascent, but we make level walks successively along it's side, which in it's upper part encircle the hill & intersect these again by others of easy ascent in various parts. They are chiefly still in their native woods, which are majestic, and very generally a close undergrowth, which I have not suffered to be touched, knowing how much easier it is to cut away than to fill up. The upper third is chiefly open, but to the South is covered with a dense thicket of Scotch broom (Spartium scoparium Lin.) which being favorably spread before the sun will admit of advantageous arrangement for winter enjoyment. You are sensible that this disposition of the ground takes from me the first beauty in gardening, the variety of hill & dale, & leaves me as an awkward substitute a few hanging hollows & ridges. This subject is so unique and at the same time refractory, that to make a disposition analogous to its character would require much more of the genius of the landscape painter & gardener than I pretend to. I had once hoped to get Parkins to go and give me some outlines, but I was disappointed. Certainly I could never wish your health to be such as to render travelling necessary; but should a journey at any time promise improvement to it, there is no one on which you would be received with more pleasure than at Monticello. Should I be there you will have an opportunity of indulging on a new field some of the taste which has made the Woodlands the only rival which I have known in America to what may be seen in England.

Thither without doubt we are to go for models in this art. Their sunless climate has permitted them to adopt what is certainly a beauty of the very first order in landscape. Their canvas is of open ground, variegated with clumps of trees distributed with taste. They need no more of wood than will serve to embrace a lawn or a glade. But under the beaming, constant and almost vertical sun of Virginia, shade is our Elysium. In the absence of this no beauty of the eye can be enjoyed. This organ must yield it's gratification to that of the other senses; without the hope of any equivalent to the beauty relinquished. The only substitute I have been able to imagine is this. Let your ground be covered with trees of the loftiest stature. Trim up their bodies as high as the constitution & form of the tree will bear, but so as that their tops shall still unite & yield dense shade. A wood, so open below, will have nearly the appearance of open grounds. Then, when in the open ground you would plant a clump of trees, place a thicket of shrubs presenting a hemisphere the crown of which shall distinctly show itself under the branches of the trees. This may be effected by a due selection & arrangement of the shrubs, & will I think offer a group not much inferior to that of trees. The thickets may be varied too by making some of them of evergreens altogether, our red cedar made to grow in a bush, evergreen privet, pyrocanthus, Kalmia, Scotch broom. Holly would be elegant but it does not grow in my part of the country.

Of prospect I have a rich profusion and offering itself at every point of the compass. Mountains distant & near, smooth & shaggy, single & in ridges, a little river hiding itself among the hills so as to shew in lagoons only, cultivated grounds under the eye and two small villages. To prevent a satiety of this is the principal difficulty. It may be successively offered, & in different portions through vistas, or which will be better, between thickets so disposed as to serve as vistas, with the advantage of shifting the scenes as you advance on your way.

You will be sensible by this time of the truth of my information that my views are turned so steadfastly homeward that the subject runs away with me whenever I get on it. I sat down to thank you for kindnesses received, & to bespeak permission to ask further contributions from your collection & I have written you a treatise on gardening generally, in which art lessons would come with more justice from you to me.

To John Norvell

Washington, June 14, 1807.

SIR

Your letter of May 9 has been duly received. The subject it proposes would require time & space for even moderate development. My occupations limit me to a very short notice of them. I think there does not exist a good elementary work on the organization of society into civil government: I mean a work which presents in one full & comprehensive view the system of principles on which such an organization should be founded, according to the rights of nature. For want of a single work of that character, I should recommend Locke on Government, Sidney, Priestley's Essay on the first Principles of Government, Chipman's Principles of Government, & the Federalist. Adding, perhaps, Beccaria on crimes & punishments, because of the demonstrative manner in which he has treated that branch of the subject. If your views of political inquiry go further, to the subjects of money & commerce, Smith's Wealth of Nations is the best book to be read, unless Say's Political Economy can be had, which treats the same subject on the same principles, but in a shorter compass & more lucid manner. But I believe this work has not been translated into our language.

History, in general, only informs us what bad government is. But as we have employed some of the best materials of the British constitution in the construction of our own government, a knolege of British history becomes useful to the American politician. There is, however, no general history of that country which can be recommended. The elegant one of Hume seems intended to disguise & discredit the good principles of the government, and is so plausible & pleasing in it's style & manner, as to instil it's errors & heresies insensibly into the minds of unwary readers. Baxter has performed a good operation on it. He has taken the text of Hume as his ground work, abridging it by the omission of some details of little interest, and wherever he has found him endeavoring to mislead, by either the suppression of a truth or by giving it a false coloring, he has changed the text to what it should be, so that we may properly call it Hume's history republicanised. He has moreover continued the history (but indifferently) from where Hume left it, to the year 1800. The work is not popular in England, because it is republican; and but a few copies have ever reached America. It is a single quarto volume. Adding to this Ludlow's Memoirs, Mrs. M'Cauley's & Belknap's histories, a sufficient view will be presented of the free principles of the English constitution.

To your request of my opinion of the manner in which a newspaper should be conducted, so as to be most useful, I should answer, 'by restraining it to true facts & sound principles only.' Yet I fear such a paper would find few subscribers. It is a melancholy truth, that a suppression of the press could not more compleatly deprive the nation of its benefits, than is done by it's abandoned prostitution to falsehood. Nothing can now be believed which is seen in a newspaper. Truth itself becomes suspicious by being put into that polluted vehicle. The real extent of this state of misinformation is known only to those who are in situations to confront facts within their knolege with the lies of the day. I really look with commiseration over the great body of my fellow citizens, who, reading newspapers, live & die in the belief, that they have known something of what has been passing in the world in their time; whereas the accounts they have read in newspapers are just as true a history of any other period of the world as of the present, except that the real names of the day are affixed to their fables. General facts may indeed be collected from them, such as that Europe is now at war, that Bonaparte has been a successful warrior, that he has subjected a great portion of Europe to his will, &c., &c.; but no details can be relied on. I will add, that the man who never looks into a newspaper is better informed than he who reads them; inasmuch as he who knows nothing is nearer to truth than he whose mind is filled with falsehoods & errors. He who reads nothing will still learn the great facts, and the details are all false.

Perhaps an editor might begin a reformation in some such way as this. Divide his paper into 4 chapters, heading the 1st, Truths. 2d, Probabilities. 3d, Possibilities. 4th, Lies. The first chapter would be very short, as it would contain little more than authentic papers, and information from such sources, as the editor would be willing to risk his own reputation for their truth. The 2d would contain what, from a mature consideration of all circumstances, his judgment should conclude to be probably true. This, however, should rather contain too little than too much. The 3d & 4th should be professedly for those readers who would rather have lies for their money than the blank paper they would occupy.

Such an editor too, would have to set his face against the demoralising practice of feeding the public mind habitually on slander, & the depravity of taste which this nauseous ailment induces. Defamation is becoming a necessary of life; insomuch, that a dish of tea in the morning or evening cannot be digested without this stimulant. Even those who do not believe these abominations, still read them with complaisance to their auditors, and instead of the abhorrence & indignation which should fill a virtuous mind, betray a secret pleasure in the possibility that some may believe them, tho they do not themselves. It seems to escape them, that it is not he who prints, but he who pays for printing a slander, who is it's real author.

These thoughts on the subjects of your letter are hazarded at your request. Repeated instances of the publication of what has not been intended for the public eye, and the malignity with which political enemies torture every sentence from me into meanings imagined by their own wickedness only, justify my expressing a solicitude, that this hasty communication may in nowise be permitted to find it's way into the public papers. Not fearing these political bull-dogs, I yet avoid putting myself in the way of being baited by them, and do not wish to volunteer away that portion of tranquillity, which a firm execution of my duties will permit me to enjoy.

I tender you my salutations, and best wishes for your success.

To George Hay[1]

Washington, June 20, 1807

. . . I did not see till last night the opinion of the Judge on the *subpœna duces tecum* against the President. Considering the question there as *coram non judice*, I did not read his argument with much attention. Yet I saw readily enough, that, as is usual where an opinion is to be supported, right or wrong, he dwells much on smaller objections, and passes over those which are solid. Laying down the position generally, that all persons owe obedience to subpœnas, he admits no exception unless it can be produced in his law books. But if the Constitution enjoins on a particular officer to be always engaged in a particular

[1] United States attorney and chief prosecutor in the trial of Aaron Burr for treason. The presiding judge was John Marshall. [Ed.]

set of duties imposed on him, does not this supersede the general law, subjecting him to minor duties inconsistent with these? The Constitution enjoins his constant agency in the concerns of six millions of people. Is the law paramount to this, which calls on him on behalf of a single one? Let us apply the Judge's own doctrine to the case of himself and his brethren. The sheriff of Henrico summons him from the bench, to quell a riot somewhere in his county. The federal judge is, by the general law, a part of the *posse* of the State sheriff. Would the Judge abandon major duties to perform lesser ones? Again; the court of Orleans or Maine commands, by subpœnas, the attendance of all the judges of the Supreme Court. Would they abandon their posts as judges, and the interests of millions committed to them, to serve the purposes of a single individual? The leading principle of our Constitution is the independence of the legislature, executive and judiciary of each other, and none are more jealous of this than the judiciary. But would the executive be independent of the judiciary, if he were subject to the *commands* of the latter, and to imprisonment for disobedience; if the several courts could bandy him from pillar to post, keep him constantly trudging from north to south and east to west, and withdraw him entirely from his constitutional duties? The intention of the Constitution, that each branch should be independent of the others, is further manifested by the means it has furnished to each, to protect itself from enterprises of force attempted on them by the others, and to none has it given more effectual or diversified means than to the executive. Again; because ministers can go into a court in London as witnesses, without interruption to their executive duties, it is inferred that they would go to a court one thousand or one thousand five hundred miles off, and that ours are to be dragged from Maine to Orleans by every criminal who will swear that their testimony "may be of use to him." The Judge says, "*it is apparent* that the President's duties as chief magistrate do not demand his whole time, and are not unremitting." If he alludes to our annual retirement from the seat of government, during the sickly season, he should be told that such arrangements are made for carrying on the public business, at and between the several stations we take, that it goes on as unremittingly there, as if we were at the seat of government. I pass more hours in public business at Monticello than I do here, every day; and it is much more laborious, because all must be done in writing. Our stations being known, all communications come to them regularly, as to fixed points. It would be very different were we always on the road, or placed in the noisy and crowded taverns where courts are held. . . .

To Lacépède

Washington, July 14, 1808.

SIR

If my recollection does not deceive me, the collection of the remains of the animal incognitum of the Ohio (sometimes called mammoth), possessed by the Cabinet of Natural History at Paris, is not very copious. Under this impression, and presuming that this Cabinet is allied to the National Institute, to which I am desirous of rendering some service, I have lately availed myself of an opportunity of collecting some of those remains. General Clarke (the companion of Governor Lewis in his expedition to the Pacific Ocean) being, on a late journey, to pass by the Big-bone Lick of the Ohio, was kind enough to undertake to employ for me a number of laborers, and to direct their operations in digging for these bones at this important deposit of them. The result of these researches will appear in the enclosed catalogue of specimens which I am now able to place at the disposal of the National Institute.[1] An aviso being to leave this place for some port of France on public service, I deliver the packages to

---

[1] The catalogue is omitted. [Ed.]

Captain Haley, to be deposited with the Consul of the United States, at whatever port he may land. They are addressed to Mr. Warden of our legation at Paris, for the National Institute, and he will have the honor of delivering them. To these I have added the horns of an animal called by the natives the Mountain Ram, resembling the sheep by his head, but more nearly the deer in his other parts; as also the skin of another animal, resembling the sheep by his fleece but the goat in his other parts. This is called by the natives the Fleecy Goat, or in the style of the natural historian, the Pokotragos. I suspect it to be nearly related to the Pacos, and were we to group the fleecy animals together, it would stand perhaps with the Vigogne, Pacos, and Sheep. The Mountain Ram was found in abundance by Messrs. Lewis and Clarke on their western tour, and was frequently an article of food for their party, and esteemed more delicate than the deer. The Fleecy Goat they did not see, but procured two skins from the Indians, of which this is one. Their description will be given in the work of Governor Lewis, the journal and geographical part of which may be soon expected from the press; but the parts relating to the plants and animals observed in his tour, will be delayed by the engravings. In the meantime, the plants of which he brought seeds, have been very successfully raised in the botanical garden of Mr. Hamilton of the Woodlands, and by Mr. McMahon, a gardener of Philadelphia; and on the whole, it is with pleasure I can assure you that the addition to our knowledge in every department, resulting from this tour of Messrs. Lewis and Clarke, has entirely fulfilled my expectations in setting it on foot, and that the world will find that those travellers have well earned its favor. I will take care that the Institute as well as yourself shall receive Governor Lewis's work as it appears.

It is with pleasure I embrace this occasion of returning you my thanks for the favor of your very valuable works, *sur les poissons et les cetacées.* . . .

To Thomas Jefferson Randolph[1]

Washington November 24, 1808.

MY DEAR JEFFERSON

I have just received the enclosed letter under cover from Mr. Bankhead which I presume is from Anne, and will inform you she is well. Mr. Bankhead has consented to go & pursue his studies at Monticello, and live with us till his pursuits or circumstances may require a separate establishment. Your situation, thrown at such a distance from us, & alone, cannot but give us all great anxieties for you. As much has been secured for you, by your particular position and the acquaintance to which you have been recommended, as could be done towards shielding you from the dangers which surround you. But thrown on a wide world, among entire strangers, without a friend or guardian to advise, so young too and with so little experience of mankind, your dangers are great, & still your safety must rest on yourself. A determination never to do what is wrong, prudence and good humor, will go far towards securing to you the estimation of the world. When I recollect that at 14 years of age, the whole care & direction of myself was thrown on myself entirely, without a relation or friend qualified to advise or guide me, and recollect the various sorts of bad company with which I associated from time to time, I am astonished I did not turn off with some of them, & become as worthless to society as they were. I had the good fortune to become acquainted very early with some characters of very high standing, and to feel the incessant wish that I could ever become what they were. Under temptations & difficulties, I would ask myself what would Dr. Small, Mr. Wythe, Peyton Randolph do in this situation? What course in it will insure me their approbation? I am certain that this

---

[1] His grandson. [Ed.]

mode of deciding on my conduct, tended more to its correctness than any reasoning powers I possessed. Knowing the even & dignified line they pursued, I could never doubt for a moment which of two courses would be in character for them. Whereas, seeking the same object through a process of moral reasoning, & with the jaundiced eye of youth, I should often have erred. From the circumstances of my position, I was often thrown into the society of horse racers, card players, fox hunters, scientific & professional men, and of dignified men; and many a time have I asked myself, in the enthusiastic moment of the death of a fox, the victory of a favorite horse, the issue of a question eloquently argued at the bar, or in the great council of the nation, well, which of these kinds of reputation should I prefer? That of a horse jockey? a fox hunter? an orator? or the honest advocate of my country's rights? Be assured, my dear Jefferson, that these little returns into ourselves, this self-catechising habit, is not trifling nor useless, but leads to the prudent selection & steady pursuit of what is right.

I have mentioned good humor as one of the preservatives of our peace & tranquillity. It is among the most effectual, and its effect is so well imitated and aided, artificially, by politeness, that this also becomes an acquisition of first rate value. In truth, politeness is artificial good humor, it covers the natural want of it, & ends by rendering habitual a substitute nearly equivalent to the real virtue. It is the practice of sacrificing to those whom we meet in society, all the little conveniences & preferences which will gratify them, & deprive us of nothing worth a moment's consideration; it is the giving a pleasing & flattering turn to our expressions, which will conciliate others, and make them pleased with us as well as themselves. How cheap a price for the good will of another! When this is in return for a rude thing said by another, it brings him to his senses, it mortifies & corrects him in the most salutary way, and places him at the feet of your good nature, in the eyes of the company. But in stating prudential rules for our government in society, I must not omit the important one of never entering into dispute or argument with another. I never saw an instance of one of two disputants convincing the other by argument. I have seen many, on their getting warm, becoming rude, & shooting one another. Conviction is the effect of our own dispassionate reasoning, either in solitude, or weighing within ourselves, dispassionately, what we hear from others, standing uncommitted in argument ourselves. It was one of the rules which, above all others, made Doctor Franklin the most amiable of men in society, "never to contradict anybody." If he was urged to announce an opinion, he did it rather by asking questions, as if for information, or by suggesting doubts. When I hear another express an opinion which is not mine, I say to myself, he has a right to his opinion, as I to mine; why should I question it? His error does me no injury, and shall I become a Don Quixote, to bring all men by force of argument to one opinion? If a fact be misstated, it is probable he is gratified by a belief of it, & I have no right to deprive him of the gratification. If he wants information, he will ask it, & then I will give it in measured terms; but if he still believes his own story, & shows a desire to dispute the fact with me, I hear him & say nothing. It is his affair, not mine, if he prefers error. There are two classes of disputants most frequently to be met with among us. The first is of young students, just entered the threshold of science, with a first view of its outlines, not yet filled up with the details & modifications which a further progress would bring to their knoledge. The other consists of the ill-tempered & rude men in society, who have taken up a passion for politics. (Good humor & politeness never introduce into mixed society, a question on which they foresee there will be a difference of opinion.) From both of those classes of disputants, my dear Jefferson, keep aloof, as you would from the infected subjects of yellow fever or pestilence. Consider yourself, when with them, as among the patients of Bedlam, needing medical more than moral counsel. Be a listener only, keep within yourself, and endeavor to establish with yourself the habit of silence, especially on politics. In the fevered state of our country, no good can ever result from any attempt to set one of these fiery zealots to rights, either in fact or principle. They are determined as to the facts they will believe, and the opinions on which they will act. Get by them, therefore, as you would by an angry bull; it is not for a man of sense to dispute the road with such an animal. You will be more exposed than others to have these animals shaking their horns at you, because of the relation in which you stand with me. Full of political venom, and willing to see me & to hate me as a chief in the antagonist party, your presence will be to them what the vomit grass is to the sick dog, a nostrum for producing ejaculation. Look upon them exactly with that eye, and pity them as objects to whom you can administer only occasional ease. My character is not within their power. It is in the hands of my fellow citizens at large, and will be consigned to honor or infamy by the verdict of the republican mass of our country, according to what themselves will have seen, not what their enemies and mine shall have said. Never, therefore, consider these puppies in politics as requiring any notice from you, & always show that you are not afraid to leave my character to the umpirage of public opinion. Look steadily to the pursuits which have carried you to Philadelphia, be very select in the society you attach yourself to, avoid taverns, drinkers, smokers, idlers, & dissipated persons generally; for it is with such that broils & contentions arise; and you will find your path more easy and tranquil. The limits of my paper warn me that it is time for me to close with my affectionate adieu.

To John Hollins

Washington, February 19, 1809.

DEAR SIR

A little transaction of mine, as innocent a one as I ever entered into, and where an improper construction was never less expected, is making some noise, I observe, in your city. I beg leave to explain it to you, because I mean to ask your agency in it. The last year, the Agricultural Society of Paris, of which I am a member, having had a plough presented to them, which, on trial with a graduated instrument, did equal work with half the force of their best ploughs, they thought it would be a benefit to mankind to communicate it. They accordingly sent one to me, with a view to its being made known here, and they sent one to the Duke of Bedford also, who is one of their members, to be made use of for England, although the two nations were then at war. By the Mentor, now going to France, I have given permission to two individuals in Delaware and New York, to import two parcels of Merino sheep from France, which they have procured there, and to some gentlemen in Boston, to import a very valuable machine which spins cotton, wool, and flax equally. The last spring, the Society informed me they were cultivating the cotton of the Levant and other parts of the Mediterranean, and wished to try also that of our southern States. I immediately got a friend to have two tierces of seed forwarded to me. They were consigned to Messrs. Falls and Brown of Baltimore, and notice of it being given me, I immediately wrote to them to re-ship them to New York, to be sent by the Mentor. Their first object was to make a show of my letter, as something very criminal, and to carry the subject into the newspapers. I had, on a like request, some time ago, (but before the embargo) from the President of the Board of Agriculture of London, of which I am also a member, to send them some of the genuine May wheat of Virginia, forwarded to them two or three barrels of it.

General Washington, in his time, received from the same Society the seed of the perennial succory, which Arthur Young had carried over from France to England, and I have since received from a member of it the seed of the famous turnip of Sweden, now so well known here. I mention these things, to show the nature of the correspondence which is carried on between societies instituted for the benevolent purpose of communicating to all parts of the world whatever useful is discovered in any one of them. These societies are always in peace, however their nations may be at war. Like the republic of letters, they form a great fraternity spreading over the whole earth, and their correspondence is never interrupted by any civilized nation. Vaccination has been a late and remarkable instance of the liberal diffusion of a blessing newly discovered. It is really painful, it is mortifying, to be obliged to note these things, which are known to every one who knows anything, and felt with approbation by every one who has any feeling. But we have a faction, to whose hostile passions the torture even of right into wrong is a delicious gratification. Their malice I have long learned to disregard, their censure to deem praise. But I observe that some republicans are not satisfied (even while we are receiving liberally from others) that this small return should be made. They will think more justly at another day; but, in the meantime, I wish to avoid offence. My prayer to you, therefore, is, that you will be so good, under the enclosed order, as to receive these two tierces of seed from Falls and Brown, and pay them their disbursements for freight, etc., which I will immediately remit you on knowing the amount. Of the seed, when received, be so good as to make manure for your garden. When rotted with a due mixture of stable manure or earth, it is the best in the world. I rely on your friendship to excuse this trouble, it being necessary I should not commit myself again to persons of whose honor, or the want of it, I know nothing.

Accept the assurances of my constant esteem and respect.

To Henri Grégoire

Washington, February 25, 1809.

SIR

I have received the favor of your letter of August 17th, and with it the volume you were so kind as to send me on the "Literature of Negroes." Be assured that no person living wishes more sincerely than I do, to see a complete refutation of the doubts I have myself entertained and expressed on the grade of understanding allotted to them by nature, and to find that in this respect they are on a par with ourselves. My doubts were the result of personal observation on the limited sphere of my own State, where the opportunities for the development of their genius were not favorable, and those of exercising it still less so. I expressed them therefore with great hesitation; but whatever be their degree of talent it is no measure of their rights. Because Sir Isaac Newton was superior to others in understanding, he was not therefore lord of the person or property of others. On this subject they are gaining daily in the opinions of nations, and hopeful advances are making towards their re-establishment on an equal footing with the other colors of the human family. I pray you therefore to accept my thanks for the many instances you have enabled me to observe of respectable intelligence in that race of men, which cannot fail to have effect in hastening the day of their relief; and to be assured of the sentiments of high and just esteem and consideration which I tender to yourself with all sincerity.

To Doctor Benjamin S. Barton

Monticello, September 21, 1809.

DEAR SIR

I received last night your favor of the 14th, and would with all possible pleasure have communicated to you any part or the whole of the Indian vocabularies which I had collected, but an irreparable misfortune has deprived me of them. I have now been thirty years availing myself of every possible opportunity of procuring Indian vocabularies to the same set of words; my opportunities were probably better than will ever occur again to any person having the same desire. I had collected about fifty, and had digested most of them in collateral columns, and meant to have printed them the last of my stay in Washington. But not having yet digested Captain Lewis' collection, nor having leisure then to do it, I put it off till I should return home. The whole, as well digest as originals, were packed in a trunk of stationery, and sent round by water with about thirty other packages of my effects from Washington, and while ascending James river, this package on account of its weight and presumed precious contents, was singled out and stolen. The thief being disappointed on opening it, threw into the river all its contents, of which he thought he could make no use. Among them were the whole of the vocabularies. Some leaves floated ashore and were found in the mud; but these were very few, and so defaced by the mud and water that no general use can be made of them. On the receipt of your letter I turned to them, and was very happy to find, that the only morsel of an original vocabulary among them, was Captain Lewis' of the Pani language, of which you say you have not one word. I therefore enclose it to you as it is, and a little fragment of some other, which I see is in his handwriting, but no indication remains on it of what language it is. It is a specimen of the condition of the little which was recovered. I am the more concerned at this accident, as of the two hundred and fifty words of my vocabularies, and the one hundred and thirty words of the great Russian vocabularies of the languages of the other quarters of the globe, seventy-three were common to both, and would have furnished materials for a comparison from which something might have resulted. Although I believe no general

use can ever be made of the wrecks of my loss, yet I
will ask the return of the Pani vocabulary when you are
done with it. Perhaps I may make another attempt to collect, although I am too old to expect to make much progress
in it.

I learn with pleasure your acquisition of the pamphlet
on the astronomy of the ancient Mexicans. . . .

To Cæsar A. Rodney[1]

Monticello, February 10, 1810.

MY DEAR SIR

I have to thank you for your favor of the 31st ultimo,
which is just now received. It has been peculiarly unfortunate for us, personally, that the portion in the history of
mankind, at which we were called to take a share in the
direction of their affairs, was such an one as history has
never before presented. At any other period, the evenhanded justice we have observed towards all nations, the
efforts we have made to merit their esteem by every act
which candor or liberality could exercise, would have
preserved our peace, and secured the unqualified confidence of all other nations in our faith and probity. But
the hurricane which is now blasting the world, physical
and moral, has prostrated all the mounds of reason as well
as right. All those calculations which, at any other period,
would have been deemed honorable, of the existence of a
moral sense in man, individually or associated, of the connection which the laws of nature have established between
his duties and his interests, of a regard for honest fame
and the esteem of our fellow men, have been a matter of
reproach on us, as evidences of imbecility. As if it could
be a folly for an honest man to suppose that others could
be honest also, when it is their interest to be so. And when
is this state of things to end? The death of Bonaparte

[1] Attorney General of the United States. [Ed.]

would, to be sure, remove the first and chiefest apostle of the desolation of men and morals, and might withdraw the scourge of the land. But what is to restore order and safety on the ocean? The death of George III? Not at all. He is only stupid; and his ministers, however weak and profligate in morals, are ephemeral. But his nation is permanent, and it is that which is the tyrant of the ocean. The principle that force is right, is become the principle of the nation itself. They would not permit an honest minister, were accident to bring such an one into power, to relax their system of lawless piracy. These were the difficulties when I was with you. I know they are not lessened, and I pity you.

It is a blessing, however, that our people are reasonable; that they are kept so well informed of the state of things as to judge for themselves, to see the true sources of their difficulties, and to maintain their confidence undiminished in the wisdom and integrity of their functionaries. *Macte virtute* therefore. Continue to go straight forward, pursuing always that which is right, as the only clue which can lead us out of the labyrinth. Let nothing be spared of either reason or passion, to preserve the public confidence entire, as the only rock of our safety. In times of peace the people look most to their representatives; but in war, to the executive solely. It is visible that their confidence is even now veering in that direction; that they are looking to the executive to give the proper direction to their affairs, with a confidence as auspicious as it is well founded. . . .

To Destutt de Tracy[1]

Monticello, January 26, 1811

. . . One of its doctrines, indeed, the preference of a plural over a singular executive, will probably not be as-

[1] The letter concerns Tracy's *A Commentary and Review of Montesquieu's Spirit of Laws*, which Jefferson helped to translate and publish and to which he contributed an anonymous preface. [Ed.]

sented to here. When our present government was first established, we had many doubts on this question, and many leanings towards a supreme executive council. It happened that at that time the experiment of such an one was commenced in France, while the single executive was under trial here. We watched the motions and effects of these two rival plans, with an interest and anxiety proportioned to the importance of a choice between them. The experiment in France failed after a short course, and not from any circumstance peculiar to the times or nation, but from those internal jealousies and dissensions in the Directory, which will ever arise among men equal in power, without a principal to decide and control their differences. We had tried a similar experiment in 1784, by establishing a committee of the States, composed of a member from every State, then thirteen, to exercise the executive functions during the recess of Congress. They fell immediately into schisms and dissensions, which became at length so inveterate as to render all co-operation among them impracticable: they dissolved themselves, abandoning the helm of government and it continued without a head, until Congress met the ensuing winter. This was then imputed to the temper of two or three individuals; but the wise ascribed it to the nature of man. The failure of the French Directory, and from the same cause, seems to have authorized a belief that the form of a plurality, however promising in theory, is impracticable with men constituted with the ordinary passions. While the tranquil and steady tenor of our single executive, during a course of twenty-two years of the most tempestuous times the history of the world has ever presented, gives a rational hope that this important problem is at length solved. Aided by the counsels of a cabinet of heads of departments, originally four, but now five, with whom the President consults, either singly or altogether, he has the benefit of their wisdom and information, brings their views to one centre, and produces an unity of action and direction in all the branches of the government. The excellence of this construction of the executive power has already manifested itself here under very opposite circumstances. During the administration of our first President, his cabinet of four members was equally divided by as marked an opposition of principle as monarchism and republicanism could bring into conflict. Had that cabinet been a directory, like positive and negative quantities in algebra, the opposing wills would have balanced each other and produced a state of absolute inaction. But the President heard with calmness the opinions and reasons of each, decided the course to be pursued, and kept the government steadily in it, unaffected by the agitation. The public knew well the dissensions of the cabinet, but never had an uneasy thought on their account, because they knew also they had provided a regulating power which would keep the machine in steady movement. I speak with an intimate knowledge of these scenes, *quorum pars fui;* as I may of others of a character entirely opposite. The third administration, which was of eight years, presented an example of harmony in a cabinet of six persons, to which perhaps history has furnished no parallel. There never arose, during the whole time, an instance of an unpleasant thought or word between the members. We sometimes met under differences of opinion, but scarcely ever failed, by conversing and reasoning, so to modify each other's ideas, as to produce an unanimous result. Yet, able and amicable as these members were, I am not certain this would have been the case, had each possessed equal and independent powers. Ill-defined limits of their respective departments, jealousies, trifling at first, but nourished and strengthened by repetition of occasions, intrigues without doors of designing persons to build an importance to themselves on the divisions of others, might, from small beginnings, have produced persevering oppositions. But the power of decision in the President left no object for internal dissension, and external intrigue was stifled in embryo by the knowledge which incendiaries possessed, that no division they could foment would change the course of the executive power. I am not conscious that my participations in executive authority have produced any bias in favor of the single executive; because the parts I have acted have been in the subordinate, as well as superior stations, and because, if I know myself, what I have felt, and what I have wished, I know that I have never been so well pleased, as when I could shift power from my own, on the shoulders of others; nor have I ever been able to conceive how any rational being could propose happiness to himself from the exercise of power over others.

I am still, however, sensible of the solidity of your principle, that, to insure the safety of the public liberty, its depository should be subject to be changed with the greatest ease possible, and without suspending or disturbing for a moment the movements of the machine of government. You apprehend that a single executive, with eminence of talent, and destitution of principle, equal to the object, might, by usurpation, render his powers hereditary. Yet I think history furnishes as many examples of a single usurper arising out of a government by a plurality, as of temporary trusts of power in a single hand rendered permanent by usurpation. I do not believe, therefore, that this danger is lessened in the hands of a plural executive. Perhaps it is greatly increased, by the state of inefficiency to which they are liable from feuds and divisions among themselves. The conservative body you propose might be so constituted, as, while it would be an admirable sedative in a variety of smaller cases, might also be a valuable sentinel and check on the liberticide views of an ambitious individual. I am friendly to this idea. But the true barriers of our liberty in this country are our State governments; and the wisest conservative power ever contrived by man, is that of which our Revolution and present government found us possessed. Seventeen distinct States, amalgamated into one as to their foreign concerns, but single and independent as to their internal administration, regularly organized with legislature and governor resting on the choice of the people, and enlightened by a free press, can never be so fascinated by the arts of one man, as to submit voluntarily to his usurpation. Nor can they be constrained to it by any force he can possess. While that may paralyze the single State in which it happens to be encamped, sixteen others, spread over a country of two thousand miles diameter, rise up on every side, ready organized for deliberation by a constitutional legislature, and for action by their governor, constitutionally the commander of the militia of the State, that is to say, of every man in it able to bear arms; and that militia, too, regularly formed into regiments and battalions, into infantry, cavalry and artillery, trained under officers general and subordinate, legally appointed, always in readiness, and to whom they are already in habits of obedience. The republican government of France was lost without a struggle, because the party of "un et indivisible" had prevailed; no provincial organizations existed to which the people might rally under authority of the laws, the seats of the directory were virtually vacant, and a small force sufficed to turn the legislature out of their chamber, and to salute its leader chief of the nation. But with us, sixteen out of seventeen States rising in mass, under regular organization, and legal commanders, united in object and action by their Congress, or, if that be in duresse, by a special convention, present such obstacles to an usurper as forever to stifle ambition in the first conception of that object.

Dangers of another kind might more reasonably be apprehended from this perfect and distinct organization, civil and military, of the States; to wit, that certain States from local and occasional discontents, might attempt to secede from the Union. This is certainly possible; and would be befriended by this regular organization. But it is not probable that local discontents can spread to such an extent, as to be able to face the sound parts of so extensive an Union; and if ever they should reach the majority, they would then become the regular government, acquire the ascendency in Congress, and be able to redress their own grievances by laws peaceably and constitutionally passed. And even the States in which local discontents might engender a commencement of fermentation, would be paralyzed and self-checked by that very division into parties into which we have fallen, into which all States must fall wherein men are at liberty to think, speak, and act freely, according to the diversities of their individual conformations, and which are, perhaps, essential to preserve the purity of the government, by the censorship which these parties habitually exercise over each other. . . .

To Isaac McPherson

Monticello, August 13, 1813.

SIR

Your letter of August 3d asking information on the subject of Mr. Oliver Evans' exclusive right to the use of what he calls his Elevators, Conveyers, and Hopperboys, has been duly received. My wish to see new inventions encouraged, and old ones brought again into useful notice, has made me regret the circumstances which have followed the expiration of his first patent. . . .

Your letter, however, points to a much broader question, whether what have received from Mr. Evans the new and proper name of Elevators, are of his invention. Because, if they are not, his patent gives him no right to obstruct others in the use of what they possessed before. I assume it is a Lemma, that it is the invention of the machine itself, which is to give a patent right, and not the application of it to any particular purpose, of which it is susceptible. If one person invents a knife convenient for pointing our pens, another cannot have a patent right for the same knife to point our pencils. A compass was invented for navigating the sea; another could not have a patent right for using it to survey land. A machine for threshing *wheat* has been invented in Scotland; a second person cannot get a patent right for the same machine to thresh *oats*, a third *rye*, a fourth *peas*, a fifth *clover*, etc. A string of buckets is invented and used for raising water, ore, etc.; can a second have a patent right to the same machine for raising wheat, a third oats, a fourth rye, a fifth peas, etc.? The question then whether such a string of buckets was invented first by Oliver Evans, is a mere question of fact in mathematical history. Now, turning to such books only as I happen to possess, I find abundant proof that this simple machinery has been in use from time immemorial. Doctor Shaw, who visited Egypt and the Barbary coast in the years 1727-8-9, in the margin of his map of Egypt, gives us the figure of what he calls a Persian wheel, which is a string of round cups or buckets hanging on a pulley, over which they revolved, bringing up water from a well and delivering it into a trough above. He found this used at Cairo, in a well 264 feet deep, which the inhabitants believe to have been the work of the patriarch Joseph. Shaw's travels, 341, Oxford edition of 1738 in folio, and the Universal History, I. 416, speaking of the manner of watering the higher lands in Egypt, says, "formerly they made use of Archimedes' screw, thence named the Egyptian pump, but they now generally use wheels (wallowers) which carry a rope or chain of earthen pots holding about seven or eight quarts apiece, and draw the water from the canals. There are besides a vast number of wells in Egypt, from which the water is drawn in the same manner to water the gardens and fruit trees; so that it is no exaggeration to say, that there are in Egypt above 200,000 oxen daily employed in this labor." Shaw's name of Persian wheel has been since given more particularly to a wheel with buckets, either fixed or suspended on pins, at its periphery. Mortimer's husbandry, I. 18, Duhamel III. II., Ferguson's Mechanic's plate, XIII;

but his figure, and the verbal description of the Universal History, prove that the string of buckets is meant under that name. His figure differs from Evans' construction in the circumstances of the buckets being round, and strung through their bottom on a chain. But it is the principle, to wit, a string of buckets, which constitutes the invention, not the form of the buckets, round, square, or hexagon; nor the manner of attaching them, nor the material of the connecting band, whether chain, rope, or leather. Vitruvius, L. x. c. 9, describes this machinery as a windlass, on which is a chain descending to the water, with vessels of copper attached to it; the windlass being turned, the chain moving on it will raise the vessel, which in passing over the windlass will empty the water they have brought up into a reservoir. And Perrault, in his edition of Vitruvius, Paris, 1684, folio plates 61, 62, gives us three forms of these water elevators, in one of which the buckets are square, as Mr. Evans' are. Bossuet, Histoire des Mathematiques, i. 86, says, "the drum wheel, the wheel with buckets and the *Chapelets*, are hydraulic machines which come to us from the ancients. But we are ignorant of the time when they began to be put into use." The *Chapelets* are the revolving bands of the buckets which Shaw calls the Persian wheel, the moderns a chain-pump, and Mr. Evans elevators. The next of my books in which I find these elevators is Wolf's Cours de Mathematiques, i. 370, and plate 1, Paris, 1747, 8vo; here are two forms. In one of them the buckets are square, attached to two chains, passing over a cylinder or wallower at top, and under another at bottom, by which they are made to revolve. It is a nearly exact representation of Evans' Elevators. But a more exact one is to be seen in Desaguliers's Experimental Philosophy, ii. plate 34; in the Encyclopedie de Diderot et D'Alembert, 8vo edition of Lausanne, first volume of plates in the four subscribed Hydraulique. Norie, is one where round eastern pots are tied by their collars between two endless ropes suspended on a revolving lantern or wallower. This is said to have been used for raising ore out of a mine. In a book which I do not possess, L'Architecture Hidraulique de Belidor, the second volume of which is said [De la Lande's continuation of Montuclas' Histoire de Mathematiques, iii. 711] to contain a detail of all the pumps, ancient and modern, hydraulic machines, fountains, wells, etc., I have no doubt this Persian wheel, chain pump, chapelets, elevators, by whichever name you choose to call it, will be found in various forms. The last book I have to quote for it is Prony's Architecture Hydraulique i., Avertissement vii., and § 648, 649, 650. In the latter of which passages he observes that the first idea which occurs for raising water is to lift it in a bucket by hand. When the water lies too deep to be reached by hand, the bucket is suspended by a chain and let down over a pulley or windlass. If it be desired to raise a continued stream of water, the simplest means which offers itself to the mind is to attach to an endless chain or cord a number of pots or buckets, so disposed that, the chain being suspended on a lanthorn or wallower above, and plunged in water below, the buckets may descend and ascend alternately, filling themselves at bottom and emptying at a certain height above, so as to give a constant stream. Some years before the date of Mr. Evans' patent, a Mr. Martin of Caroline county in this State, constructed a drill-plough, in which he used the band of buckets for elevating the grain from the box into the funnel, which let them down into the furrow. He had bands with different sets of buckets adapted to the size of peas, of turnip seed, etc. I have used this machine for sowing Benni seed also, and propose to have a band of buckets for drilling Indian corn, and another for wheat. Is it possible that in doing this I shall infringe Mr. Evans' patent? That I can be debarred of any use to which I might have applied my drill, when I bought it, by a patent issued after I bought it?

These verbal descriptions, applying so exactly to Mr. Evans' elevators, and the drawings exhibited to the eye, flash conviction both on reason and the senses that there is nothing new in these elevators but their being strung together on a strap of leather. If this strap of leather be an invention, entitling the inventor to a patent right, it can only extend to the strap, and the use of the string of buckets must remain free to be connected by chains, ropes, a strap of hempen girthing, or any other substance except leather. But, indeed, Mr. Martin had before used the strap of leather.

The screw of Archimedes is as ancient, at least, as the age of that mathematician, who died more than 2,000 years ago. Diodorus Siculus speaks of it, L. i., p. 21, and L. v., p. 217, of Stevens' edition of 1559, folio; and Vitruvius, xii. The cutting of its spiral worm into sections for conveying flour or grain, seems to have been an invention of Mr. Evans, and to be a fair subject of a patent right. But it cannot take away from others the use of Archimedes' screw with its perpetual spiral, for any purposes of which it is susceptible.

The hopper-boy is an useful machine, and so far as I know, original.

It has been pretended by some, (and in England especially,) that inventors have a natural and exclusive right to their inventions, and not merely for their own lives, but inheritable to their heirs. But while it is a moot question whether the origin of any kind of property is derived from nature at all, it would be singular to admit a natural and even an hereditary right to inventors. It is agreed by those who have seriously considered the subject, that no individual has, of natural right, a separate property in an acre of land, for instance. By an universal law, indeed, whatever, whether fixed or movable, belongs to all men equally and in common, is the property for the moment of him who occupies it, but when he relinquishes the occupation, the property goes with it. Stable ownership is the gift of social law, and is given late in the progress of society. It would be curious then, if an idea, the fugitive fermentation of an individual brain, could, of natural right, be claimed in exclusive and stable property. If nature has made any one thing less susceptible than all others of exclusive property, it is the action of the thinking power called an idea, which an individual may exclusively possess as long as he keeps it to himself; but the moment it is divulged, it forces itself into the possession of every one, and the receiver cannot dispossess himself of it. Its peculiar character, too, is that no one possesses the less, because every other possesses the whole of it. He who receives an idea from me, receives instruction himself without lessening mine; as he who lights his taper at mine, receives light without darkening me. That ideas should freely spread from one to another over the globe, for the moral and mutual instruction of man, and improvement of his condition, seems to have been peculiarly and benevolently designed by nature, when she made them, like fire, expansible over all space, without lessening their density in any point, and like the air in which we breathe, move, and have our physical being, incapable of confinement or exclusive appropriation. Inventions then cannot, in nature, be a subject of property. Society may give an exclusive right to the profits arising from them, as an encouragement to men to pursue ideas which may produce utility, but this may or may not be done, according to the will and convenience of the society, without claim or complaint from anybody. Accordingly, it is a fact, as far as I am informed, that England was, until we copied her, the only country on earth which ever, by a general law, gave a legal right to the exclusive use of an idea. In some other countries it is sometimes done, in a great case, and by a special and personal act, but, generally speaking, other nations have thought that these monopolies produce more embarrassment than advantage to society; and it may be observed that the nations which refuse monopolies of invention, are as fruitful as England in new and useful devices.

Considering the exclusive right to invention as given not of natural right, but for the benefit of society, I know well the difficulty of drawing a line between the things which are worth to the public the embarrassment of an exclusive patent, and those which are not. As a member of the patent board for several years, while the law authorized a board to grant or refuse patents, I saw with what slow progress a system of general rules could be matured. Some, however, were established by that board. One of these was, that a machine of which we were possessed, might be applied by every man to any use of which it is susceptible, and that this right ought not to be taken from him and given to a monopolist, because the first perhaps had occasion so to apply it. Thus a screw for crushing plaster might be employed for crushing corn-cobs. And a chain-pump for raising water might be used for raising wheat: this being merely a change of application. Another rule was that a change of material should not give title to a patent. As the making a ploughshare of cast rather than of wrought iron; a comb of iron instead of horn or of ivory, or the connecting buckets by a band of leather rather than of hemp or iron. A third was that a mere change of form should give no right to a patent, as a high-quartered shoe instead of a low one; a round hat instead of a three-square; or a square bucket instead of a round one. But for this rule, all the changes of fashion in dress would have been under the tax of patentees. These were among the rules which the uniform decisions of the board had already established, and under each of them Mr. Evans' patent would have been refused. First, because it was a mere change of application of the chain-pump, from raising water to raise wheat. Secondly, because the using a leathern instead of a hempen band, was a mere change of material; and thirdly, square buckets instead of round, are only a change of form, and the ancient forms, too, appear to have been indifferently square or round. But there were still abundance of cases which could not be brought under rule, until they should have presented themselves under all their aspects; and these investigations occupying more time of the members of the board than they could spare from higher duties, the whole was turned over to the judiciary, to be matured into a system, under which every one might know when his actions were safe and lawful. Instead of refusing a patent in the first instance, as the board was authorized to do, the patent now issues of course, subject to be declared void on such principles as should be established by the courts of law. This business, however, is but little analogous to their course of reading, since we might in vain turn over all the lubberly volumes of the law to find a single ray which would lighten the path of the mechanic or the mathematician. It is more within the information of a board of academical professors, and a previous refusal of patent would better guard our citizens against harassment by lawsuits. But England had given it to her judges, and the usual predominancy of her examples carried it to ours.

It happened that I had myself a mill built in the interval between Mr. Evans' first and second patents. I was living in Washington, and left the construction to the millwright. I did not even know he had erected elevators, conveyers and hopper-boys, until I learnt it by an application from Mr. Evans' agent for the patent price. Although I had no idea he had a right to it by law, (for no judicial decision had then been given,) yet I did not hesitate to remit to Mr. Evans the old and moderate patent price, which was what he then asked, from a wish to encourage even the useful revival of ancient inventions. But I then expressed my opinion of the law in a letter, either to Mr. Evans or to his agent.

I have thus, Sir, at your request, given you the facts and ideas which occur to me on this subject. . . .

To John Adams

Monticello, October 28, 1813.

DEAR SIR

According to the reservation between us, of taking up one of the subjects of our correspondence at a time, I turn to your letters of August the 16th and September the 2d.

The passage you quote from Theognis, I think has an ethical rather than a political object. The whole piece is a moral *exhortation*, παραινεσις, and this passage particularly seems to be a reproof to man, who, while with his domestic animals he is curious to improve the race, by employing always the finest male, pays no attention to the improvement of his own race, but intermarries with the vicious, the ugly, or the old, for considerations of wealth or ambition. It is in conformity with the principle adopted afterwards by the Pythagoreans, and expressed by Ocellus in another form; περι δε τῆς 'εκ τῶν αλληλων ανθρωπων γενεσεως etc.,— ουχ ηδονης ενεκα η μιξις which, as literally as intelligibility will admit, may be thus translated: "concerning the interprocreation of men, how, and of whom it shall be, in a perfect manner, and according to the laws of modesty and sanctity, conjointly, this is what I think right. First to lay it down that we do not commix for the sake of pleasure, but of the procreation of children. For the powers, the organs and desires for coition have not been given by God to man for the sake of pleasure, but for the procreation of the race. For as it were incongruous, for a mortal born to partake of divine life, the immortality of the race being taken away, God fulfilled the purpose by making the generations uninterrupted and continuous. This, therefore, we are especially to lay down as a principle, that coition is not for the sake of pleasure." But nature, not trusting to this moral and abstract motive, seems to have provided more securely for the perpetuation of the species, by making it the effect of the *oestrum* implanted in the constitution of both sexes. And not only has the commerce of love been indulged on this unhallowed impulse, but made subservient also to wealth and ambition by marriage, without regard to the beauty, the healthiness, the understanding, or virtue of the subject from which we are to breed. The selecting the best male for a harem of well-chosen females also, which Theognis seems to recommend from the example of our sheep and asses, would doubtless improve the human, as it does the brute animal, and produce a race of veritable ραιστοι. For experience proves, that the moral and physical qualities of man, whether good or evil, are transmissible in a certain degree from father to son. But I suspect that the equal rights of men will rise up against this privileged Solomon and his harem, and oblige us to continue acquiescence under the "Αμαυρωσις γενεος αστων" which Theognis complains of, and to content ourselves with the accidental aristoi produced by the fortuitous concourse of breeders. For I agree with you that there is a natural aristocracy among men. The grounds of this are virtue and talents. Formerly, bodily powers gave place among the aristoi. But since the invention of gunpowder has armed the weak as well as the strong with missile death, bodily strength, like beauty, good humor, politeness and other accomplishments, has become but an auxiliary ground of distinction. There is also an artificial aristocracy, founded on wealth and birth, without either virtue or talents; for with these it would belong to the first class. The natural aristocracy I consider as the most precious gift of nature, for the instruction, the trusts, and government of society. And indeed, it would have been inconsistent in creation to have formed man for the social state, and not to have provided virtue and wisdom enough to manage the concerns of the society. May we not even say, that that form of government is the best, which provides the most effectually for a pure selection of these natural aristoi into the offices of government? The artificial aristocracy is a mischievous ingredient in government, and provision should be made to prevent its ascendency. On the question, what is the best provision, you and I differ; but we differ as rational friends, using the free exercise of our own reason, and mutually indulging its errors. You think it best to put the pseudo-aristoi into a separate chamber of legislation, where they may be hindered from doing mischief by their co-ordinate branches, and where, also, they may be a protection to wealth against the agrarian and plundering enterprises of the majority of the people. I think that to give them power in order to prevent them from doing mischief, is arming them for it, and increasing instead of remedying the evil. For if the co-ordinate branches can arrest their action, so may they that of the co-ordinates. Mischief may be done negatively as well as positively. Of this, a cabal in the Senate of the United States has furnished many proofs. Nor do I believe them necessary to protect the wealthy; because enough of these will find their way into every branch of the legislation, to protect themselves. From fifteen to twenty legislatures of our own, in action for thirty years past, have proved that no fears of an equalization of property are to be apprehended from them. I think the best remedy is exactly that provided by all our constitutions, to leave to the citizens the free election and separation of the aristoi from the pseudo-aristoi, of the wheat from the chaff. In general they will elect the really good and wise. In some instances, wealth may corrupt, and birth blind them; but not in sufficient degree to endanger the society.

It is probable that our difference of opinion may, in some measure, be produced by a difference of character in those among whom we live. From what I have seen of Massachusetts and Connecticut myself, and still more from what I have heard, and the character given of the former by yourself, (volume 1, page 111,)[1] who know them so much better, there seems to be in those two States a traditionary reverence for certain families, which has rendered the offices of the government nearly hereditary in those families. I presume that from an early period of your history, members of those families happening to possess virtue and talents, have honestly exercised them for the good of the people, and by their services have endeared their names to them. In coupling Connecticut with you, I mean it politically only, not morally. For having made the Bible the common law of their land, they seem to have modeled their morality on the story of Jacob and Laban. But although this hereditary succession to office with you, may, in some degree, be founded in real family merit, yet in a much higher degree, it has proceeded from your strict alliance of Church and State. These families are canonized in the eyes of the people on common principles, "you tickle me, and I will tickle you." In Virginia we have nothing of this. Our clergy, before the revolution, having been secured against rivalship by fixed salaries, did not give themselves the trouble of acquiring influence over the people. Of wealth, there were great accumulations in particular families, handed down from generation to generation, under the English law of entails. But the only object of ambition for the wealthy was a seat in the King's Council. All their court then was paid to the crown and its creatures; and they Philipized in all collisions between the King and the people. Hence they were unpopular; and that unpopularity continues attached to their names. A Randolph, a Carter, or a Burwell must have great personal superiority over a common competitor to be elected by the people even at this day. At the first session of our legislature after the Declaration of Independence, we passed a law abolishing entails. And this was followed by one abolishing the privilege of

[1] A reference to Adams's *Defence of the Constitutions*. . . . [Ed.]

primogeniture, and dividing the lands of intestates equally among all their children, or other representatives. These laws, drawn by myself, laid the axe to the foot of pseudo-aristocracy. And had another which I prepared been adopted by the legislature, our work would have been complete. It was a bill for the more general diffusion of learning. This proposed to divide every county into wards of five or six miles square, like your townships; to establish in each ward a free school for reading, writing and common arithmetic; to provide for the annual selection of the best subjects from these schools, who might receive, at the public expense, a higher degree of education at a district school; and from these district schools to select a certain number of the most promising subjects, to be completed at an university, where all the useful sciences should be taught. Worth and genius would thus have been sought out from every condition of life, and completely prepared by education for defeating the competition of wealth and birth for public trusts. My proposition had, for a further object, to impart to these wards those portions of self-government for which they are best qualified, by confiding to them the care of their poor, their roads, police, elections, the nomination of jurors, administration of justice in small cases, elementary exercises of militia; in short, to have made them little republics, with a warden at the head of each, for all those concerns which, being under their eye, they would better manage than the larger republics of the county or State. A general call of ward meetings by their wardens on the same day through the State, would at any time produce the genuine sense of the people on any required point, and would enable the State to act in mass, as your people have so often done, and with so much effect by their town meetings. The law for religious freedom, which made a part of this system, having put down the aristocracy of the clergy, and restored to the citizen the freedom of the mind, and those of entails and descents nurturing an equality of condition among them, this on education would have raised the mass of the people to the high ground of moral respectability necessary to their own safety, and to orderly government; and would have completed the great object of qualifying them to select the veritable aristoi, for the trusts of government, to the exclusion of the pseudalists; and the same Theognis who has furnished the epigraphs of your two letters, assures us that "Ουδεμιαν πω, Κυρν', αγαθοι πολιν ωλεσαν ανδρες." Although this law has not yet been acted on but in a small and inefficient degree, it is still considered as before the legislature, with other bills of the revised code, not yet taken up, and I have great hope that some patriotic spirit will, at a favorable moment, call it up, and make it the keystone of the arch of our government.

With respect to aristocracy, we should further consider, that before the establishment of the American States, nothing was known to history but the man of the old world, crowded within limits either small or overcharged, and steeped in the vices which that situation generates. A government adapted to such men would be one thing; but a very different one, that for the man of these States. Here every one may have land to labor for himself, if he chooses; or, preferring the exercise of any other industry, may exact for it such compensation as not only to afford a comfortable subsistence, but wherewith to provide for a cessation from labor in old age. Every one, by his property, or by his satisfactory situation, is interested in the support of law and order. And such men may safely and advantageously reserve to themselves a wholesome control over their public affairs, and a degree of freedom, which, in the hands of the *canaille* of the cities of Europe, would be instantly perverted to the demolition and destruction of everything public and private. The history of the last twenty-five years of France, and of the last forty years in America, nay of its last two hundred years, proves the truth of both parts of this observation.

But even in Europe a change has sensibly taken place

in the mind of man. Science had liberated the ideas of those who read and reflect, and the American example had kindled feelings of right in the people. An insurrection has consequently begun, of science, talents, and courage, against rank and birth, which have fallen into contempt. It has failed in its first effort, because the mobs of the cities, the instrument used for its accomplishment, debased by ignorance, poverty, and vice, could not be restrained to rational action. But the world will recover from the panic of this first catastrophe. Science is progressive, and talents and enterprise on the alert. Resort may be had to the people of the country, a more governable power from their principles and subordination; and rank, and birth, and tinsel-aristocracy will finally shrink into insignificance, even there. This, however, we have no right to meddle with. It suffices for us, if the moral and physical condition of our own citizens qualifies them to select the able and good for the direction of their government, with a recurrence of elections at such short periods as will enable them to displace an unfaithful servant, before the mischief he meditates may be irremediable.

I have thus stated my opinion on a point on which we differ, not with a view to controversy, for we are both too old to change opinions which are the result of a long life of inquiry and reflection; but on the suggestions of a former letter of yours, that we ought not to die before we have explained ourselves to each other. We acted in perfect harmony, through a long and perilous contest for our liberty and independence. A constitution has been acquired, which, though neither of us thinks perfect, yet both consider as competent to render our fellow citizens the happiest and the securest on whom the sun has ever shone. If we do not think exactly alike as to its imperfections, it matters little to our country, which, after devoting to it long lives of disinterested labor, we have delivered over to our successors in life, who will be able to take care of it and of themselves. . . .

To Thomas Law

Poplar Forest, June 13, 1814.

DEAR SIR

The copy of your Second Thoughts on Instinctive Impulses, with the letter accompanying it, was received just as I was setting out on a journey to this place, two or three days distant from Monticello. I brought it with me and read it with great satisfaction, and with the more as it contained exactly my own creed on the foundation of morality in man. It is really curious that on a question so fundamental, such a variety of opinions should have prevailed among men, and those, too, of the most exemplary virtue and first order of understanding. It shows how necessary was the care of the Creator in making the moral principle so much a part of our constitution as that no errors of reasoning or of speculation might lead us astray from its observance in practice. Of all the theories on this question, the most whimsical seems to have been that of Wollaston, who considers *truth* as the foundation of morality. The thief who steals your guinea does wrong only inasmuch as he acts a lie in using your guinea as if it were his own. Truth is certainly a branch of morality, and a very important one to society. But presented as its foundation, it is as if a tree taken up by the roots, had its stem reversed in the air, and one of its branches planted in the ground. Some have made the *love of God* the foundation of morality. This, too, is but a branch of our moral duties, which are generally divided into duties to God and duties to man. If we did a good act merely from the love of God and a belief that it is pleasing to Him, whence arises the morality of the Atheist? It is idle to say, as some do, that no such being exists. We have the same evidence of the fact as of most of those we act on, to wit: their own affirmations, and their reasonings in support of them. I have observed, indeed, generally, that while in

Protestant countries the defections from the Platonic Christianity of the priests is to Deism, in Catholic countries they are to Atheism. Diderot, D'Alembert, D'Holbach, Condorcet, are known to have been among the most virtuous of men. Their virtue, then, must have had some other foundation than the love of God.

The Το κυλον of others is founded in a different faculty, that of taste, which is not even a branch of morality. We have indeed an innate sense of what we call beautiful, but that is exercised chiefly on subjects addressed to the fancy, whether through the eye in visible forms, as landscape, animal figure, dress, drapery, architecture, the composition of colors, etc., or to the imagination directly, as imagery, style, or measure in prose or poetry, or whatever else constitutes the domain of criticism or taste, a faculty entirely distinct from the moral one. Self-interest, or rather self-love, or *egoism*, has been more plausibly substituted as the basis of morality. But I consider our relations with others as constituting the boundaries of morality. With ourselves we stand on the ground of identity, not of relation, which last, requiring two subjects, excludes self-love confined to a single one. To ourselves, in strict language, we can owe no duties, obligation requiring also two parties. Self-love, therefore, is no part of morality. Indeed it is exactly its counterpart. It is the sole antagonist of virtue, leading us constantly by our propensities to self-gratification in violation of our moral duties to others. Accordingly, it is against this enemy that are erected the batteries of moralists and religionists, as the only obstacle to the practice of morality. Take from man his selfish propensities, and he can have nothing to seduce him from the practice of virtue. Or subdue those propensities by education, instruction or restraint, and virtue remains without a competitor. Egoism, in a broader sense, has been thus presented as the source of moral action. It has been said that we feed the hungry, clothe the naked, bind up the wounds of the man beaten by thieves, pour oil and wine into them, set him on our own beast and bring him to the inn, because we receive ourselves pleasure from these acts. So Helvetius, one of the best men on earth, and the most ingenious advocate of this principle, after defining "interest" to mean not merely that which is pecuniary, but whatever may procure us pleasure or withdraw us from pain, [*de l'esprit* 2, 1,] says, [ib. 2, 2,] "the humane man is he to whom the sight of misfortune is insupportable, and who to rescue himself from this spectacle, is forced to succor the unfortunate object." This indeed is true. But it is one step short of the ultimate question. These good acts give us pleasure, but how happens it that they give us pleasure? Because nature hath implanted in our breasts a love of others, a sense of duty to them, a moral instinct, in short, which prompts us irresistibly to feel and to succor their distresses, and protests against the language of Helvetius, [ib. 2, 5,] "what other motive than self-interest could determine a man to generous actions? It is as impossible for him to love what is good for the sake of good, as to love evil for the sake of evil." The Creator would indeed have been a bungling artist, had he intended man for a social animal, without planting in him social dispositions. It is true they are not planted in every man, because there is no rule without exceptions; but it is false reasoning which converts exceptions into the general rule. Some men are born without the organs of sight, or of hearing, or without hands. Yet it would be wrong to say that man is born without these faculties, and sight, hearing, and hands may with truth enter into the general definition of man.

The want or imperfection of the moral sense in some men, like the want or imperfection of the senses of sight and hearing in others, is no proof that it is a general characteristic of the species. When it is wanting, we endeavor to supply the defect by education, by appeals to reason and calculation, by presenting to the being so unhappily conformed, other motives to do good and to eschew evil, such as the love, or the hatred, or rejection of those among whom he lives, and whose society is necessary to his happiness and even existence; demonstrations by sound calculation that honesty promotes interest in the long run; the rewards and penalties established by the laws; and ultimately the prospects of a future state of retribution for the evil as well as the good done while here. These are the correctives which are supplied by education, and which exercise the functions of the moralist, the preacher, and legislator; and they lead into a course of correct action all those whose disparity is not too profound to be eradicated. Some have argued against the existence of a moral sense, by saying that if nature had given us such a sense, impelling us to virtuous actions, and warning us against those which are vicious, then nature would also have designated, by some particular ear-marks, the two sets of actions which are, in themselves, the one virtuous and the other vicious. Whereas, we find, in fact, that the same actions are deemed virtuous in one country and vicious in another. The answer is, that nature has constituted *utility* to man, the standard and test of virtue. Men living in different countries, under different circumstances, different habits and regimens, may have different utilities; the same act, therefore, may be useful, and consequently virtuous in one country which is injurious and vicious in another differently circumstanced. I sincerely, then, believe with you in the general existence of a moral instinct. I think it the brightest gem with which the human character is studded, and the want of it as more degrading than the most hideous of the bodily deformities. I am happy in reviewing the roll of associates in this principle which you present in your second letter, some of which I had not before met with. To these might be added Lord Kaims, one of the ablest of our advocates, who goes so far as to say, in his Principles of Natural Religion, that a man owes no duty to which he is not urged by some impulsive feeling. This is correct, if referred to the standard of general feeling in the given case, and not to the feeling of a single individual.

Perhaps I may misquote him, it being fifty years since I read his book.

The leisure and solitude of my situation here has led me to the indiscretion of taxing you with a long letter on a subject whereon nothing new can be offered you. I will indulge myself no farther than to repeat the assurances of my continued esteem and respect.

To Edward Coles

Monticello, August 25th, '14

DEAR SIR

Your favour of July 31, was duly received, and was read with peculiar pleasure. The sentiments breathed through the whole do honor to both the head and heart of the writer. Mine on the subject of slavery of negroes have long since been in possession of the public, and time has only served to give them stronger root. The love of justice and the love of country plead equally the cause of these people, and it is a moral reproach to us that they should have pleaded it so long in vain, and should have produced not a single effort, nay I fear not much serious willingness to relieve them & ourselves from our present condition of moral & political reprobation. From those of the former generation who were in the fulness of age when I came into public life, which was while our controversy with England was on paper only, I soon saw that nothing was to be hoped. Nursed and educated in the daily habit of seeing the degraded condition, both bodily and mental, of those unfortunate beings, not reflecting that that degradation was very much the work of themselves & their fathers, few minds have yet doubted but that they were as legitimate subjects of property as their horses and cattle. The quiet and monotonous course of colonial life has been disturbed by no alarm, and little reflection on the value of liberty. And when alarm was taken at an enterprize on

their own, it was not easy to carry them to the whole
length of the principles which they invoked for themselves.
In the first or second session of the Legislature after I became a member, I drew to this subject the attention of·Col.
Bland, one of the oldest, ablest, & most respected members,
and he undertook to move for certain moderate extensions
of the protection of the laws to these people. I seconded
his motion, and, as a younger member, was more spared in
the debate; but he was denounced as an enemy of his country, & was treated with the grossest indecorum. From an
early stage of our revolution other & more distant duties
were assigned to me, so that from that time till my return
from Europe in 1789, and I may say till I returned to reside at home in 1809, I had little opportunity of knowing
the progress of public sentiment here on this subject. I had
always hoped that the younger generation receiving their
early impressions after the flame of liberty had been kindled in every breast, & had become as it were the vital
spirit of every American, that the generous temperament
of youth, analogous to the motion of their blood, and
above the suggestions of avarice, would have sympathized
with oppression wherever found, and proved their love of
liberty beyond their own share of it. But my intercourse
with them, since my return has not been sufficient to ascer-
tain that they had made towards this point the progress I
had hoped. Your solitary but welcome voice is the first
which has brought this sound to my ear; and I have considered the general silence which prevails on this subject
as indicating an apathy unfavorable to every hope. Yet the
hour of emancipation is advancing, in the march of time.
It will come; and whether brought on by the generous
energy of our own minds; or by the bloody process of St
Domingo, excited and conducted by the power of our
present enemy, if once stationed permanently within our
Country, and offering asylum & arms to the oppressed, is
a leaf of our history not yet turned over. As to the method
by which this difficult work is to be effected, if permitted

to be done by ourselves, I have seen no proposition so expedient on the whole, as that as emancipation of those born after a given day, and of their education and expatriation after a given age. This would give time for a gradual extinction of that species of labour & substitution of another, and lessen the severity of the shock which an operation so fundamental cannot fail to produce. For men probably of any color, but of this color we know, brought from their infancy without necessity for thought or forecast, are by their habits rendered as incapable as children of taking care of themselves, and are extinguished promptly wherever industry is necessary for raising young. In the mean time they are pests in society by their idleness, and the depredations to which this leads them. Their amalgamation with the other color produces a degradation to which no lover of his country, no lover of excellence in the human character can innocently consent. I am sensible of the partialities with which you have looked towards me as the person who should undertake this salutary but arduous work. But this, my dear sir, is like bidding old Priam to buckle the armour of Hector *"trementibus æquo humeris et inutile ferruncingi."* No, I have overlived the generation with which mutual labors & perils begat mutual confidence and influence. This enterprise is for the young; for those who can follow it up, and bear it through to its consummation. It shall have all my prayers, & these are the only weapons of an old man. But in the mean time are you right in abandoning this property, and your country with it? I think not. My opinion has ever been that, until more can be done for them, we should endeavor, with those whom fortune has thrown on our hands, to feed and clothe them well, protect them from all ill usage, require such reasonable labor only as is performed voluntarily by freemen, & be led by no repugnancies to abdicate them, and our duties to them. The laws do not permit us to turn them loose, if that were for their good: and to commute them for other property is to commit them to those whose usage of them we cannot control. I hope then, my dear sir, you will reconcile yourself to your country and its unfortunate condition; that you will not lessen its stock of sound disposition by withdrawing your portion from the mass. That, on the contrary you will come forward in the public councils, become the missionary of this doctrine truly christian; insinuate & inculcate it softly but steadily, through the medium of writing and conversation; associate others in your labors, and when the phalanx is formed, bring on and press the proposition perseveringly until its accomplishment. It is an encouraging observation that no good measure was ever proposed, which, if duly pursued, failed to prevail in the end. We have proof of this in the history of the endeavors in the English parliament to suppress that very trade which brought this evil on us. And you will be supported by the religious precept, "be not weary in well-doing." That your success may be as speedy & complete, as it will be of honorable & immortal consolation to yourself, I shall as fervently and sincerely pray as I assure you of my great friendship and respect.

To Benjamin Austin

Monticello, January 9, 1816

. . . You tell me I am quoted by those who wish to continue our dependence on England for manufactures. There was a time when I might have been so quoted with more candor, but within the thirty years which have since elapsed, how are circumstances changed! We were then in peace. Our independent place among nations was acknowledged. A commerce which offered the raw material in exchange for the same material after receiving the last touch of industry, was worthy of welcome to all nations. It was expected that those especially to whom manufacturing industry was important, would cherish the friendship of such customers by every favor, by every inducement, and particularly cultivate their peace by every act of justice and friendship. Under this prospect the question seemed legitimate, whether, with such an immensity of un-improved land, courting the hand of husbandry, the in-dustry of agriculture, or that of manufactures, would add most to the national wealth? And the doubt was enter-tained on this consideration chiefly, that to the labor of the husbandman a vast addition is made by the spontane-ous energies of the earth on which it is employed: for one grain of wheat committed to the earth, she renders twenty, thirty, and even fifty fold, whereas to the labor of the manufacturer nothing is added. Pounds of flax, in his hands, yield, on the contrary, but pennyweights of lace. This exchange, too, laborious as it might seem, what a field did it promise for the occupations of the ocean; what a nursery for that class of citizens who were to exercise and maintain our equal rights on that element? This was the state of things in 1785, when the "Notes on Virginia" were first printed; when, the ocean being open to all nations, and their common right in it acknowledged and exercised under regulations sanctioned by the assent and usage of all, it was thought that the doubt might claim some con-sideration. But who in 1785 could foresee the rapid de-pravity which was to render the close of that century the disgrace of the history of man? Who could have imagined that the two most distinguished in the rank of nations, for science and civilization, would have suddenly descended from that honorable eminence, and setting at defiance all those moral laws established by the Author of nature be-tween nation and nation, as between man and man, would cover earth and sea with robberies and piracies, merely because strong enough to do it with temporal impunity; and that under this disbandment of nations from social or-der, we should have been despoiled of a thousand ships, and have thousands of our citizens reduced to Algerine slavery. Yet all this has taken place. One of these nations interdicted to our vessels all harbors of the globe without having first proceeded to some one of hers, there paid a tribute proportioned to the cargo, and obtained her license to proceed to the port of destination. The other declared them to be lawful prize if they had touched at the port, or been visited by a ship of the enemy nation. Thus were we completely excluded from the ocean. Compare this state of things with that of '85, and say whether an opinion founded in the circumstances of that day can be fairly applied to those of the present. We have experienced what we did not then believe, that there exist both profligacy and power enough to exclude us from the field of interchange with other nations: that to be independent for the comforts of life we must fabricate them ourselves. We must now place the manufacturer by the side of the agriculturist. The former question is suppressed, or rather assumes a new form. Shall we make our own comforts, or go without them, at the will of a foreign nation? He, therefore, who is now against domestic manufacture, must be for reducing us either to dependence on that foreign nation, or to be clothed in skins, and to live like wild beasts in dens and caverns. I am not one of these; experience has taught me that manufactures are now as necessary to our independence as to our comfort; and if those who quote me as of a different opinion, will keep pace with me in purchasing nothing foreign where an equivalent of domestic fabric can be obtained, without regard to difference of price, it will not be our fault if we do not soon have a supply at home equal to our demand, and wrest that weapon of distress from the hand which has wielded it. If it shall be proposed to go beyond our own supply, the question of '85 will then recur, will our *surplus* labor be then most beneficially employed in the culture of the earth, or in the fabrications of art? We have time yet for consideration, before that question will press upon us; and the maxim to be applied will depend on the circumstances which shall then exist; for in so complicated a science as political economy, no one axiom can be laid down as wise and expedient for all times and circumstances, and for their contraries. Inattention to this is what has called for this explanation, which reflection would have rendered unnecessary with the candid, while nothing will do it with those who use the former opinion only as a stalking horse, to cover their disloyal propensities to keep us in eternal vassalage to a foreign and unfriendly people.

I salute you with assurances of great respect and esteem.

To John Adams

Monticello, January 11, 1816.

. . . I agree with you in all its[1] eulogies on the eighteenth century. It certainly witnessed the sciences and arts, manners and morals, advanced to a higher degree than the world had ever before seen. And might we not go back to the æra of the Borgias, by which time the barbarous ages had reduced national morality to its lowest point of depravity, and observe that the arts and sciences, rising from that point, advanced gradually through all the sixteenth, seventeenth and eighteenth centuries, softening and correcting the manners and morals of man? I think, too, we may add to the great honor of science and the arts, that their natural effect is, by illuminating public opinion, to erect it into a censor, before which the most exalted tremble for their future, as well as present fame. With some exceptions only, through the seventeenth and eighteenth centuries, morality occupied an honorable chapter in the political code of nations. You must have observed while in Europe, as I thought I did, that those who administered the governments of the greater powers at least, had a respect to faith, and considered the dignity of their government as involved in its integrity. A wound indeed was inflicted on this character of honor in the eighteenth century by the partition of Poland. But this was

[1] Adams' letter of November 13, 1815. [Ed.]

the atrocity of a barbarous government chiefly, in conjunction with a smaller one still scrambling to become great, while one only of those already great, and having character to lose, descended to the baseness of an accomplice in the crime. France, England, Spain, shared in it only inasmuch as they stood aloof and permitted its perpetration.

How then has it happened that these nations, France especially and England, so great, so dignified, so distinguished by science and the arts, plunged all at once into all the depths of human enormity, threw off suddenly and openly all the restraints of morality, all sensation to character, and unblushingly avowed and acted on the principle that power was right? Can this sudden apostasy from national rectitude be accounted for? The treaty of Pilnitz seems to have begun it, suggested perhaps by the baneful precedent of Poland. Was it from the terror of monarchs, alarmed at the light returning on them from the west, and kindling a volcano under their thrones? Was it a combination to extinguish that light, and to bring back, as their best auxiliaries, those enumerated by you, the Sorbonne, the Inquisition, the Index Expurgatorius, and the knights of Loyola? Whatever it was, the close of the century saw the moral world thrown back again to the age of the Borgias, to the point from which it had departed three hundred years before. France, after crushing and punishing the conspiracy of Pilnitz, went herself deeper and deeper into the crimes she had been chastising. I say France and not Bonaparte; for, although he was the head and mouth, the nation furnished the hands which executed his enormities. England, although in opposition, kept full pace with France, not indeed by the manly force of her own arms, but by oppressing the weak and bribing the strong. At length the whole choir joined and divided the weaker nations among them. Your prophecies to Dr. Price proved truer than mine; and yet fell short of the fact, for instead of a million, the destruction of eight or ten millions of human beings has probably been the effect of these convulsions. I did not, in '89, believe they would have lasted so long, nor have cost so much blood. But although your prophecy has proved true so far, I hope it does not preclude a better final result. That same light from our west seems to have spread and illuminated the very engines employed to extinguish it. It has given them a glimmering of their rights and their power. The idea of representative government has taken root and growth among them. Their masters feel it, and are saving themselves by timely offers of this modification of their powers. Belgium, Prussia, Poland, Lombardy, etc., are now offered a representative organization; illusive probably at first, but it will grow into power in the end. Opinion is power, and that opinion will come. Even France will yet attain representative government. You observe it makes the basis of every Constitution which has been demanded or offered,—of that demanded by their Senate; of that offered by Bonaparte; and of that granted by Louis XVIII. The idea then is rooted, and will be established, although rivers of blood may yet flow between them and their object. The allied armies now couching upon them are first to be destroyed, and destroyed they will surely be. A nation united can never be conquered. . . .

To Samuel Kercheval

Monticello, July 12, 1816.

SIR

I duly received your favor of June the 13th, with the copy of the letters on the calling a convention, on which you are pleased to ask my opinion. I have not been in the habit of mysterious reserve on any subject, nor of buttoning up my opinions within my own doublet. On the contrary, while in public service especially, I thought the public entitled to frankness, and intimately to know whom they employed. But I am now retired: I resign myself, as a passenger, with confidence to those at present at the helm, and ask but for rest, peace and good will. The question you propose, on equal representation, has become a party one, in which I wish to take no public share. Yet, if it be asked for your own satisfaction only, and not to be quoted before the public, I have no motive to withhold it, and the less from you, as it coincides with your own. At the birth of our republic, I committed that opinion to the world, in the draught of a constitution annexed to the "Notes on Virginia," in which a provision was inserted for a representation permanently equal. The infancy of the subject at that moment, and our inexperience of self-government, occasioned gross departures in that draught from genuine republican canons. In truth, the abuses of monarchy had so much filled all the space of political contemplation, that we imagined everything republican which was not monarchy. We had not yet penetrated to the mother principle, that "governments are republican only in proportion as they embody the will of their people, and execute it." Hence, our first constitutions had really no leading principles in them. But experience and reflection have but more and more confirmed me in the particular importance of the equal representation then proposed. On that point, then, I am entirely in sentiment with your letters; and only lament that a copyright of your pamphlet prevents their appearance in the newspapers, where alone they would be generally read, and produce general effect. The present vacancy too, of other matter, would give them place in every paper, and bring the question home to every man's conscience.

But inequality of representation in both Houses of our legislature, is not the only republican heresy in this first essay of our Revolutionary patriots at forming a Constitution. For let it be agreed that a government is republican in proportion as every member composing it has his equal voice in the direction of its concerns, (not indeed in person, which would be impracticable beyond the limits of a city, or small township,) but by representatives chosen by himself, and responsible to him at short periods, and let us bring to the test of this canon every branch of our Constitution.

In the legislature, the House of Representatives is chosen by less than half the people, and not at all in proportion to those who do choose. The Senate are still more disproportionate, and for long terms of irresponsibility. In the Executive, the Governor is entirely independent of the choice of the people, and of their control; his Council equally so, and at best but a fifth wheel to a wagon. In the Judiciary, the judges of the highest courts are dependent on none but themselves. In England, where judges were named and removable at the will of an hereditary executive, from which branch most misrule was feared, and has flowed, it was a great point gained, by fixing them for life, to make them independent of that executive. But in a government founded on the public will, this principle operates in an opposite direction, and against that will. There, too, they were still removable on a concurrence of the executive and legislative branches. But we have made them independent of the nation itself. They are irremovable, but by their own body, for any depravities of conduct, and even by their own body for the imbecilities of dotage. The justices of the inferior courts are self-chosen, are for life, and perpetuate their own body in succession forever, so that a faction once possessing themselves of the bench of a county, can never be broken up, but hold their county in chains, forever indissoluble. Yet these justices are the real executive as well as judiciary, in all our minor and most ordinary concerns. They tax us at will; fill the office of sheriff, the most important of all the executive officers of the county; name nearly all our military leaders, which leaders, once named, are removable but by themselves. The juries, our judges of all fact, and of law when they choose it, are not selected by the people, nor amenable to them. They are chosen by an officer named by the court and executive. Chosen, did I say? Picked up by the sheriff from the loungings of the court yard, after everything respectable has retired from it. Where then is our republicanism to be found? Not in our Constitution certainly, but merely in the spirit of our people. That would oblige even a despot to govern us republicanly. Owing to this spirit, and to nothing in the form of our Constitution, all things have gone well. But this fact, so triumphantly misquoted by the enemies of reformation, is not the fruit of our Constitution, but has prevailed in spite of it. Our functionaries have done well, because generally honest men. If any were not so, they feared to show it.

But it will be said, it is easier to find faults than to amend them. I do not think their amendment so difficult as is pretended. Only lay down true principles, and adhere to them inflexibly. Do not be frightened into their surrender by the alarms of the timid, or the croakings of wealth against the ascendency of the people. If experience be called for, appeal to that of our fifteen or twenty governments for forty years, and show me where the people have done half the mischief in these forty years, that a single despot would have done in a single year; or show half the riots and rebellions, the crimes and the punishments, which have taken place in any single nation, under kingly government, during the same period. The true foundation of republican government is the equal right of every citizen, in his person and property, and in their management. Try by this, as a tally, every provision of our Constitution, and see if it hangs directly on the will of the people. Reduce your legislature to a convenient number for full, but orderly discussion. Let every man who fights or pays, exercise his just and equal right in their election. Submit them to approbation or rejection at short intervals. Let the executive be chosen in the same way, and for the same term, by those whose agent he is to be; and leave no screen of a council behind which to skulk from responsibility. It has been thought that the people are not competent electors of judges *learned in the law*. But I do not know that this is true, and, if doubtful, we should follow principle. In this, as in many other elections, they would be guided by reputation, which would not err oftener, perhaps, than the present mode of appointment. In one State of the Union, at least, it has long been tried, and with the most satisfactory success. The judges of Connecticut have been chosen by the people every six months, for nearly two centuries, and I believe there has hardly ever been an instance of change; so powerful is the curb of incessant responsibility. If prejudice, however, derived from a monarchical institution, is still to prevail against the vital elective principle of our own, and if the existing example among ourselves of periodical election of judges by the people be still mistrusted, let us at least not adopt the evil, and reject the good, of the English precedent; let us retain amovability on the concurrence of the executive and legislative branches, and nomination by the executive alone. Nomination to office is an executive function. To give it to the legislature, as we do, is a violation of the principle of the separation of powers. It swerves the members from correctness, by temptations to intrigue for office themselves, and to a corrupt barter of votes; and destroys responsibility by dividing it among a multitude. By leaving nomination in its proper place, among executive functions, the principle of the distribution of power is preserved, and responsibility weighs with its heaviest force on a single head.

The organization of our county administrations may be thought more difficult. But follow principle, and the knot unties itself. Divide the counties into wards of such size as that every citizen can attend, when called on, and act in person. Ascribe to them the government of their wards in all things relating to themselves exclusively. A justice, chosen by themselves, in each, a constable, a military company, a patrol, a school, the care of their own poor, their own portion of the public roads, the choice of one or more jurors to serve in some court, and the delivery, within their own wards, of their own votes for all elective officers of higher sphere, will relieve the county administration of nearly all its business, will have it better done, and by making every citizen an acting member of the government, and in the offices nearest and most interesting to him, will attach him by his strongest feelings to the independence of his country, and its republican Constitution. The justices thus chosen by every ward, would constitute the county court, would do its judiciary business, direct roads and bridges, levy county and poor rates, and administer all the matters of common interest to the whole country. These wards, called townships in New England, are the vital principle of their governments, and have proved themselves the wisest invention ever devised by the wit of man for the perfect exercise of self-government, and for its preservation. We should thus marshal our government into, 1, the general federal republic, for all concerns foreign and federal; 2, that of the State, for what relates to our own citizens exclusively; 3, the county republics, for the duties and concerns of the county; and 4, the ward republics, for the small, and yet numerous and interesting concerns of the neighborhood; and in government, as well as in every other business of life, it is by division and subdivision of duties alone, that all matters, great and small, can be managed to perfection. And the whole is cemented by giving to every citizen, personally, a part in the administration of the public affairs.

The sum of these amendments is, 1. General suffrage. 2. Equal representation in the legislature. 3. An executive chosen by the people. 4. Judges elective or amovable. 5. Justices, jurors, and sheriffs elective. 6. Ward divisions. And 7. Periodical amendments of the Constitution.

I have thrown out these as loose heads of amendment, for consideration and correction; and their object is to secure self-government by the republicanism of our Constitution, as well as by the spirit of the people; and to nourish and perpetuate that spirit. I am not among those who fear the people. They, and not the rich, are our dependence for continued freedom. And to preserve their independence, we must not let our rulers load us with perpetual debt. We must make our election between *economy and liberty*, or *profusion and servitude*. If we run into such debts, as that we must be taxed in our meat and in our drink, in our necessaries and our comforts, in our labors and our amusements, for our callings and our creeds, as the people of England are, our people, like them, must come to labor sixteen hours in the twenty-four, give the earnings of fifteen of these to the government for their debts and daily expenses; and the sixteenth being insufficient to afford us bread, we must live, as they now do, on oatmeal and potatoes; have no time to think, no means of calling the mismanagers to account; but be glad to obtain subsistence by hiring ourselves to rivet their chains on the necks of our fellow sufferers. Our land-holders, too, like theirs, retaining indeed the title and stewardship of estates called theirs, but held really in trust for the treasury, must wander, like theirs, in foreign countries, and be contented with penury, obscurity, exile, and the glory of the nation. This example reads to us the salutary lesson, that private fortunes are destroyed by public as well as by private extravagance. And this is the tendency of all human governments. A departure from principle in one instance becomes a precedent for a second; that second for a third; and so on, till the bulk of the society is reduced to be mere automatons of misery, to have no sensibilities left but for sinning and suffering. Then begins, indeed, the *bellum omnium in omnia*, which some philosophers observing to be so general in this world, have mistaken it for the natural, instead of the abusive state of man. And the fore horse of this frightful team is public debt. Taxation follows that, and in its train wretchedness and oppression.

Some men look at constitutions with sanctimonious reverence, and deem them like the ark of the covenant, too sacred to be touched. They ascribe to the men of the preceding age a wisdom more than human, and suppose what they did to be beyond amendment. I knew that age well; I belonged to it, and labored with it. It deserved well of its country. It was very like the present, but without the experience of the present; and forty years of experience in government is worth a century of book-reading; and this they would say themselves, were they to rise from the dead. I am certainly not an advocate for frequent and untried changes in laws and constitutions. I think moderate imperfections had better be borne with; because, when once known, we accommodate ourselves to them, and find practical means of correcting their ill effects. But I know also, that laws and institutions must go hand in hand with the progress of the human mind. As that becomes more developed, more enlightened, as new discoveries are made, new truths disclosed, and manners and opinions change with the change of circumstances, institutions must advance also, and keep pace with the times. We might as well require a man to wear still the coat which fitted him when a boy, as civilized society to remain ever under the regimen of their barbarous ancestors. It is this preposterous idea which has lately deluged Europe in blood. Their monarchs, instead of wisely yielding to the gradual change of circumstances, of favoring progressive accommodation to progressive improvement, have clung to old abuses, entrenched themselves behind steady habits, and obliged their subjects to seek through blood and violence rash and ruinous innovations, which, had they been referred to the peaceful deliberations and collected wisdom of the nation, would have been put into acceptable and salutary forms. Let us follow no such examples, nor weakly believe that one generation is not as capable as another of taking care of itself, and of ordering its own affairs. Let us, as our sister States have done, avail ourselves of our reason and experience, to correct the crude essays of our first and unexperienced, although wise, virtuous, and well-meaning councils. And lastly, let us provide in our Constitution for its revision at stated periods. What these periods should be, nature herself indicates. By the European tables of mortality, of the adults living at any one moment of time, a majority will be dead in about nineteen years. At the end of that period then, a new majority is come into place; or, in other words, a new generation. Each generation is as independent of the one preceding, as that was of all which had gone before. It has then, like them, a right to choose for itself the form of government it believes most promotive of its own happiness; consequently, to accommodate to the circumstances in which it finds itself, that received from its predecessors; and it is for the peace and good of mankind, that a solemn opportunity of doing this every nineteen or twenty years, should be provided by the Constitution; so that it may be handed on, with periodical repairs, from generation to generation, to the end of time, if anything human can so long endure. It is now forty years since the constitution of Virginia was formed. The same tables inform us, that, within that period, two-thirds of the adults then living are now dead. Have then the remaining third, even if they had the wish, the right to hold in obedience to their will, and to laws heretofore made by them, the other two-thirds, who, with themselves, compose the present mass of adults? If they have not, who has? The dead? But the dead have no rights. They are nothing; and nothing cannot own something. Where there is no substance, there can be no accident. This corporeal globe, and everything upon it, belong to its present corporeal inhabitants, during their generation. They alone have a right to direct what is the concern of themselves alone, and to declare the law of that direction; and this declaration can only be made by their majority. That majority, then, has a right to depute representatives to a convention, and to make the Constitution what they think will be the best for themselves. But how collect their voice? This is the real difficulty. If invited by private authority, or county or district meetings, these divisions are so large that few will attend; and their voice will be imperfectly, or falsely, pronounced. Here, then, would be one of the advantages of the ward divisions I have proposed. The mayor of every ward, on a question like the present, would call his ward together, take the simple yea or nay of its members, convey these to the county court, who would hand on those of all its wards to the proper general authority; and the voice of the whole people would be thus fairly, fully, and peaceably expressed, discussed, and decided by the common reason of the society. If this avenue be shut to the call of sufferance, it will make itself heard through that of force, and we shall go on, as other nations are doing, in the endless circle of oppression, rebellion, reformation; and oppression, rebellion, reformation, again; and so on forever.

These, Sir, are my opinions of the governments we see among men, and of the principles by which alone we may prevent our own from falling into the same dreadful track. I have given them at greater length than your letter called for. But I cannot say things by halves; and I confide them to your honor, so to use them as to preserve me from the gridiron of the public papers. If you shall approve and enforce them, as you have done that of equal representation, they may do some good. If not, keep them to yourself as the effusions of withered age and useless time. I shall, with not the less truth, assure you of my great respect and consideration.

To Judge Spencer Roane[1]

Poplar Forest, September 6, 1819.

DEAR SIR

I had read in the Enquirer, and with great approbation, the pieces signed Hampden, and have read them

[1] Judge of the Virginia Supreme Court of Appeals, whose articles in the Richmond *Enquirer* vigorously opposed the United States Supreme Court's claim to ultimate jurisdiction in federal questions. [Ed.]

again with redoubled approbation, in the copies you have been so kind as to send me. I subscribe to every tittle of them. They contain the true principles of the revolution of 1800, for that was as real a revolution in the principles of our government as that of 1776 was in its form; not effected indeed by the sword, as that, but by the rational and peaceable instrument of reform, the suffrage of the people. The nation declared its will by dismissing functionaries of one principle, and electing those of another, in the two branches, executive and legislature, submitted to their election. Over the judiciary department, the Constitution had deprived them of their control. That, therefore, has continued the reprobated system, and although new matter has been occasionally incorporated into the old, yet the leaven of the old mass seems to assimilate to itself the new, and after twenty years' confirmation of the federated system by the voice of the nation, declared through the medium of elections, we find the judiciary on every occasion, still driving us into consolidation.

In denying the right they usurp of exclusively explaining the Constitution, I go further than you do, if I understand rightly your quotation from the Federalist, of an opinion that "the judiciary is the last resort in relation *to the other departments* of the government, but not in relation to the rights of the parties to the compact under which the judiciary is derived." If this opinion be sound, then indeed is our Constitution a complete *felo de se*. For intending to establish three departments, co-ordinate and independent, that they might check and balance one another, it has given, according to this opinion, to one of them alone, the right to prescribe rules for the government of the others, and to that one too, which is unelected by, and independent of the nation. For experience has already shown that the impeachment it has provided is not even a scare-crow; that such opinions as the one you combat, sent cautiously out, as you observe also, by detachment, not belonging to the case often, but sought for out of it, as if to rally the public opinion beforehand to their views, and to indicate the line they are to walk in, have been so quietly passed over as never to have excited animadversion, even in a speech of any one of the body entrusted with impeachment. The Constitution, on this hypothesis, is a mere thing of wax in the hands of the judiciary, which they may twist and shape into any form they please. It should be remembered, as an axiom of eternal truth in politics, that whatever power in any government is independent, is absolute also; in theory only, at first, while the spirit of the people is up, but in practice, as fast as that relaxes. Independence can be trusted nowhere but with the people in mass. They are inherently independent of all but moral law. My construction of the Constitution is very different from that you quote. It is that each department is truly independent of the others, and has an equal right to decide for itself what is the meaning of the Constitution in the cases submitted to its action; and especially, where it is to act ultimately and without appeal. I will explain myself by examples, which, having occurred while I was in office, are better known to me, and the principles which governed them.

A legislature had passed the sedition law. The federal courts had subjected certain individuals to its penalties of fine and imprisonment. On coming into office, I released these individuals by the power of pardon committed to executive discretion, which could never be more properly exercised than where citizens were suffering without the authority of law, or, which was equivalent, under a law unauthorized by the Constitution, and therefore null. In the case of Marbury and Madison, the federal judges declared that commissions, signed and sealed by the President, were valid, although not delivered. I deemed delivery essential to complete a deed, which, as long as it remains in the hands of the party, is as yet no deed; it is *in posse* only, but not *in esse*, and I withheld delivery of the commissions. They cannot issue a mandamus to the President or legislature, or to any of their officers.[2] When the British treaty of [1806] arrived, without any provision against the impressment of our seamen, I determined not to ratify it. The Senate thought I should ask their advice. I thought that would be a mockery of them, when I was predetermined against following it, should they advise its ratification. The Constitution had made their advice necessary to confirm a treaty, but not to reject it. This has been blamed by some; but I have never doubted its soundness. . . .

To William Short

Monticello, October 31, 1819.

. . . As you say of yourself, I too am an Epicurian. I consider the genuine (not the imputed) doctrines of Epicurus as containing everything rational in moral philosophy which Greece and Rome have left us. Epictetus indeed, has given us what was good of the Stoics; all beyond, of their dogmas, being hypocrisy and grimace. Their great crime was in their calumnies of Epicurus and misrepresentations of his doctrines; in which we lament to see the candid character of Cicero engaging as an accomplice. Diffuse, vapid, rhetorical, but enchanting. His prototype Plato, eloquent as himself, dealing out mysticisms incomprehensible to the human mind, has been deified by certain sects usurping the name of Christians; because, in his foggy conceptions, they found a basis of impenetrable darkness whereon to rear fabrications as delirious, of their own invention. These they fathered blasphemously on Him whom they claimed as their Founder, but who would disclaim them with the indignation which their caricatures of His religion so justly excite. Of Socrates we have nothing genuine but in the Memorabilia of Xenophon; for Plato

[2] The Constitution controlling the common law in this particular.

makes him one of his Collocutors merely to cover his own whimsies under the mantle of his name; a liberty of which we are told Socrates himself complained. Seneca is indeed a fine moralist, disfiguring his work at times with some Stoicisms, and affecting too much of antithesis and point, yet giving us on the whole a great deal of sound and practical morality. But the greatest of all the reformers of the depraved religion of His own country, was Jesus of Nazareth. Abstracting what is really His from the rubbish in which it is buried, easily distinguished by its lustre from the dross of His biographers, and as separable from that as the diamond from the dunghill, we have the outlines of a system of the most sublime morality which has ever fallen from the lips of man; outlines which it is lamentable He did not live to fill up. Epictetus and Epicurus give laws for governing ourselves, Jesus a supplement of the duties and charities we owe to others. The establishment of the innocent and genuine character of this benevolent Moralist, and the rescuing it from the imputation of imposture, which has resulted from artificial systems;[1] invented by ultra-Christian sects, unauthorized by a single word ever uttered by Him, is a most desirable object, and one to which Priestley has successfully devoted his labors and learning. It would in time, it is to be hoped, effect a quiet euthanasia of the heresies of bigotry and fanaticism which have so long triumphed over human reason, and so generally and deeply afflicted mankind; but this work is to be begun by winnowing the grain from the chaff of the historians of His life. I have sometimes thought of translating Epictetus (for he has never been tolerably translated into English) by adding the genuine doctrines of Epicurus from the Syntagma of Gassendi, and an abstract from the Evangelists of whatever has the stamp of the eloquence and

[1] *E.*g. The immaculate conception of Jesus, His deification, the creation of the world by Him, His miraculous powers, His resurrection and visible ascension, His corporeal presence in the Eucharist, the Trinity, original sin, atonement, regeneration, election, orders of Hierarchy, etc.

fine imagination of Jesus. The last I attempted too hastily some twelve or fifteen years ago. It was the work of two or three nights only, at Washington, after getting through the evening task of reading the letters and papers of the day. But with one foot in the grave, these are now idle projects for me. My business is to beguile the wearisomeness of declining life, as I endeavor to do, by the delights of classical reading and of mathematical truths, and by the consolations of a sound philosophy, equally indifferent to hope and fear.

I take the liberty of observing that you are not a true disciple of our master Epicurus, in indulging the indolence to which you say you are yielding. One of his canons, you know, was that "that indulgence which presents a greater pleasure, or produces a greater pain, is to be avoided." Your love of repose will lead, in its progress, to a suspension of healthy exercise, a relaxation of mind, an indifference to everything around you, and finally to a debility of body, and hebetude of mind, the farthest of all things from the happiness which the well-regulated indulgences of Epicurus ensure; fortitude, you know, is one of his four cardinal virtues. That teaches us to meet and surmount difficulties; not to fly from them, like cowards; and to fly, too, in vain, for they will meet and arrest us at every turn of our road. . . .

I will place under this a syllabus of the doctrines of Epicurus, somewhat in the lapidary style, which I wrote some twenty years ago; a like one of the philosophy of Jesus, of nearly the same age, is too long to be copied. *Vale, et tibi persuade carissimum te esse mihi.*

Syllabus of the doctrines of Epicurus.

Physical.—The Universe eternal.
Its parts, great and small, interchangeable.
Matter and Void alone.
Motion inherent in matter which is weighty and declining.

Eternal circulation of the elements of bodies.

Gods, an order of beings next superior to man, enjoying in their sphere, their own felicities; but not meddling with the concerns of the scale of beings below them.

Moral.—Happiness the aim of life.

Virtue the foundation of happiness.

Utility the test of virtue.

Pleasure active and In-do-lent.

In-do-lence is the absence of pain, the true felicity.

Active, consists in agreeable motion; it is not happiness, but the means to produce it.

Thus the absence of hunger is an article of felicity; eating the means to obtain it.

The *summum bonum* is to be not pained in body, nor troubled in mind.

i. e. In-do-lence of body, tranquillity of mind.

To procure tranquillity of mind we must avoid desire and fear, the two principal diseases of the mind.

Man is a free agent.

Virtue consists in 1. Prudence. 2. Temperance. 3. Fortitude. 4. Justice.

To which are opposed, 1. Folly. 2. Desire. 3. Fear. 4. Deceit.

To John Holmes[1]

Monticello, April 22, 1820.

I thank you, dear Sir, for the copy you have been so kind as to send me of the letter to your constituents on the Missouri question. It is a perfect justification to them. I had for a long time ceased to read newspapers, or pay any attention to public affairs, confident they were in good hands, and content to be a passenger in our bark to the shore from which I am not distant. But this momentous

[1] Congressman from the District of Maine, Massachusetts. [Ed.]

question, like a fire-bell in the night, awakened and filled
me with terror. I considered it at once as the knell of the
Union. It is hushed, indeed, for the moment. But this is
a reprieve only, not a final sentence. A geographical line,
coinciding with a marked principle, moral and political,
once conceived and held up to the angry passions of men,
will never be obliterated; and every new irritation will
mark it deeper and deeper. I can say, with conscious
truth, that there is not a man on earth who would sacrifice
more than I would to relieve us from this heavy reproach,
in any *practicable* way. The cession of that kind of property, for so it is misnamed, is a bagatelle which would not
cost me a second thought, if, in that way, a general emancipation and *expatriation* could be effected; and, gradually,
and with due sacrifices, I think it might be. But as it is,
we have the wolf by the ears, and we can neither hold
him, nor safely let him go. Justice is in one scale, and
self-preservation in the other. Of one thing I am certain,
that as the passage of slaves from one State to another,
would not make a slave of a single human being who would
not be so without it, so their diffusion over a greater surface would make them individually happier, and pro-
portionally facilitate the accomplishment of their emancipation, by dividing the burden on a greater number of
coadjutors. An abstinence too, from this act of power,
would remove the jealousy excited by the undertaking of
Congress to regulate the condition of the different descriptions of men composing a State. This certainly is the exclusive right of every State, which nothing in the Constitution has taken from them and given to the General
Government. Could Congress, for example, say, that the
non-freemen of Connecticut shall be freemen, or that they
shall not emigrate into any other State?

I regret that I am now to die in the belief, that the
useless sacrifice of themselves by the generation of 1776,
to acquire self-government and happiness to their country,
is to be thrown away by the unwise and unworthy passions

of their sons, and that my only consolation is to be, that I live not to weep over it. If they would but dispassionately weigh the blessings they will throw away, against an abstract principle more likely to be effected by union than by scission, they would pause before they would perpetrate this act of suicide on themselves, and of treason against the hopes of the world. To yourself, as the faithful advocate of the Union, I tender the offering of my high esteem and respect.

To John Adams

Monticello, August 15, 1820.

I am a great defaulter, my dear Sir, in our correspondence, but prostrate health rarely permits me to write; and when it does, matters of business imperiously press their claims. I am getting better however, slowly, swelled legs being now the only serious symptom, and these, I believe, proceed from extreme debility. I can walk but little; but I ride six or eight miles a day without fatigue; and within a few days, I shall endeavor to visit my other home, after a twelvemonth's absence from it.[1] Our University, four miles distant, gives me frequent exercise, and the oftener, as I direct its architecture. Its plan is unique, and it is becoming an object of curiosity for the traveler. I have lately had an opportunity of reading a critique on this institution in your North American Review of January last, having been not without anxiety to see what that able work would say of us; and I was relieved on finding in it much coincidence of opinion, and even where criticisms were indulged, I found they would have been obviated had the developments of our plan been fuller. But these

[1] Poplar Forest, some eighty miles south of Monticello. Jefferson was still recovering from an illness suffered in the fall of 1818. [Ed.]

were restrained by the character of the paper reviewed,[2] being merely a report of outlines, not a detailed treatise, and addressed to a legislative body, not to a learned academy. For example, as an inducement to introduce the Anglo-Saxon into our plan, it was said that it would reward amply the *few weeks* of attention which alone would be requisite for its attainment; leaving both term and degree under an indefinite expression, because I know that not much time is necessary to attain it to an useful degree sufficient to give such instruction in the etymologies of our language as may satisfy ordinary students, while more time would be requisite for those who should propose to attain a critical knowledge of it. In a letter which I had occasion to write to Mr. Crofts, who sent you, I believe, as well as myself, a copy of his treatise on the English and German languages, as preliminary to an etymological dictionary he meditated, I went into explanations with him of an easy process for simplifying the study of the Anglo-Saxon, and lessening the terrors and difficulties presented by its rude alphabet, and unformed orthography. But this is a subject beyond the bounds of a letter, as it was beyond the bounds of a report to the legislature. Mr. Crofts died, I believe, before any progress was made in the work he had projected.

The reviewer expresses doubt, rather than decision, on our placing military and naval architecture in the department of pure mathematics. Military architecture embraces fortification and fieldworks, which, with their bastions, curtains, hornworks, redoubts, etc., are based on a technical combination of lines and angles. These are adapted to offence and defence, with and against the effects of bombs, balls, escalades, etc. But lines and angles make the sum of elementary geometry, a branch of pure mathematics; and the direction of the bombs, balls, and other projectiles, the necessary appendages of military

---

[2] *The Report of the Commissioners for the University of Virginia.* See p. 332. [Ed.]

works, although no part of their architecture, belong to the conic sections, a branch of transcendental geometry. Diderot and D'Alembert, therefore, in their *Arbor Scientiæ*, have placed military architecture in the department of elementary geometry. Naval architecture teaches the best form and construction of vessels; for which best form it has recourse to the question of the solid of least resistance; a problem of transcendental geometry. And its appurtenant projectiles belong to the same branch, as in the preceding case. It is true, that so far as respects the action of the water on the rudder and oars, and of the wind on the sails, it may be placed in the department of mechanics, as Diderot and D'Alembert have done; but belonging quite as much to geometry, and allied in its military character to military architecture, it simplified our plan to place both under the same head. These views are so obvious, that I am sure they would have required but a second thought, to reconcile the reviewer to their *location* under the head of pure mathematics. For this word *location*, see Bailey, Johnson, Sheridan, Walker, etc. But if dictionaries are to be the arbiters of language, in which of them shall we find *neologism?* No matter. It is a good word, well sounding, obvious, and expresses an idea, which would otherwise require circumlocution. The reviewer was justifiable, therefore, in using it; although he noted at the same time, as unauthoritative, *centrality, grade, sparse;* all which have been long used in common speech and writing. I am a friend to *neology*. It is the only way to give to a language copiousness and euphony. Without it we should still be held to the vocabulary of Alfred or of Ulphilas; and held to their state of science also: for I am sure they had no words which could have conveyed the ideas of oxygen, cotyledons, zoophytes, magnetism, electricity, hyaline, and thousands of others expressing ideas not then existing, nor of possible communication in the state of their language. What a language has the French become since the date of their revolution, by the free introduction of new words!

The most copious and eloquent in the living world; and equal to the Greek, had not that been regularly modifiable almost *ad infinitum*. Their rule was, that whenever their language furnished or adopted a root, all its branches, in every part of speech, were legitimated by giving them their appropriate terminations. Αδελφος, αδελφη, αδελφιδιον, αδελφοτης, αδελφιξις, αδελφιδους, αδελφικος, αδελφιζω, αδελφικως.[3] And this should be the law of every language. Thus, having adopted the adjective *fraternal*, it is a root which should legitimate *fraternity, fraternation, fraternisation, fraternism, to fraternate, fraternise, fraternally*. And give the word *neologism* to our language, as a root, and it should give us its fellow substantives, *neology, neologist, neologisation*; its adjectives, *neologous, neological, neologistical*; its verb, *neologise*; and adverb, *neologically*. Dictionaries are but the depositories of words already legitimated by usage. Society is the workshop in which new ones are elaborated. When an individual uses a new word, if ill formed, it is rejected in society; if well formed, adopted, and after due time, laid up in the depository of dictionaries. And if, in this process of sound neologisation, our trans-Atlantic brethren shall not choose to accompany us, we may furnish, after the Ionians, a second example of a colonial dialect improving on its primitive.

But enough of criticism: let me turn to your puzzling letter of May the 12th, on matter, spirit, motion, etc. Its crowd of scepticisms kept me from sleep. I read it, and laid it down; read it, and laid it down, again and again; and to give rest to my mind, I was obliged to recur ultimately to my habitual anodyne, "I feel, therefore I exist." I feel bodies which are not myself: there are other existences then. I call them *matter*. I feel them changing place. This gives me *motion*. Where there is an absence of matter, I call it *void*, or *nothing*, or *immaterial space*.

[3] Brother, sister, little brother, brotherly love, brotherhood, nephew, brotherly (adj.), adopt as a brother, brotherly (adv.). [Ed.]

On the basis of sensation, of matter and motion, we may erect the fabric of all the certainties we can have or need. I can conceive *thought* to be an action of a particular organization of matter, formed for that purpose by its Creator, as well as that *attraction* is an action of matter, or *magnetism* of loadstone. When he who denies to the Creator the power of endowing matter with the mode of action called *thinking*, shall show how He could endow the sun with the mode of action called *attraction*, which reins the planets in the track of their orbits, or how an absence of matter can have a will, and by that will put matter into motion, then the Materialist may be lawfully required to explain the process by which matter exercises the faculty of thinking. When once we quit the basis of sensation, all is in the wind. To talk of *immaterial* existences, is to talk of *nothings*. To say that the human soul, angels, God, are immaterial, is to say, they are *nothings*, or that there is no God, no angels, no soul. I cannot reason otherwise: but I believe I am supported in my creed of materialism by the Lockes, the Tracys and the Stewarts. At what age of the Christian Church this heresy of *immaterialism*, or masked atheism, crept in, I do not exactly know. But a heresy it certainly is. Jesus taught nothing of it. He told us, indeed, that "God is a Spirit," but He has not defined what a spirit is, nor said that it is not *matter*. And the ancient fathers generally, of the three first centuries, held it to be matter, light and thin indeed, an etherial gas; but still matter. . . .

Rejecting all organs of information, therefore, but my senses, I rid myself of the pyrrhonisms with which an indulgence in speculations hyperphysical and antiphysical, so uselessly occupy and disquiet the mind. A single sense may indeed be sometimes deceived, but rarely; and never all our senses together, with their faculty of reasoning. They evidence realities, and there are enough of these for all the purposes of life, without plunging into the fathomless abyss of dreams and phantasms. I am satisfied, and sufficiently occupied with the things which are, without tormenting or troubling myself about those which may indeed be, but of which I have no evidence. I am sure that I really know many, many things, and none more surely than that I love you with all my heart, and pray for the continuance of your life until you shall be tired of it yourself.

To the President of the United States (James Monroe)

Monticello, October 24, 1823.

DEAR SIR

The question presented by the letters you have sent me, is the most momentous which has ever been offered to my contemplation since that of Independence.[1] That made us a nation, this sets our compass and points the course which we are to steer through the ocean of time opening on us. And never could we embark on it under circumstances more auspicious. Our first and fundamental maxim should be, never to entangle ourselves in the broils of Europe. Our second, never to suffer Europe to intermeddle with cis-Atlantic affairs. America, North and South, has a set of interests distinct from those of Europe, and peculiarly her own. She should therefore have a system of her own, separate and apart from that of Europe. While the last is laboring to become the domicile of despotism, our endeavor should surely be, to make our hemisphere that of freedom. One nation, most of all, could disturb us in this pursuit; she now offers to lead, aid, and accompany us in it. By acceding to her proposition, we detach her from the bands, bring her mighty weight into the scale of free

[1] That is, the question of whether the United States should join with Britain in declaring the Western Hemisphere off limits to European expansion. The Monroe Doctrine was proclaimed unilaterally on December 2, 1823. [Ed.]

government, and emancipate a continent at one stroke, which might otherwise linger long in doubt and difficulty. Great Britain is the nation which can do us the most harm of any one, or all on earth; and with her on our side we need not fear the whole world. With her then, we should most sedulously cherish a cordial friendship; and nothing would tend more to knit our affections than to be fighting once more, side by side, in the same cause. Not that I would purchase even her amity at the price of taking part in her wars. But the war in which the present proposition might engage us, should that be its consequence, is not her war, but ours. Its object is to introduce and establish the American system, of keeping out of our land all foreign powers, of never permitting those of Europe to intermeddle with the affairs of our nations. It is to maintain our own principle, not to depart from it. And if, to facilitate this, we can effect a division in the body of the European powers, and draw over to our side its most powerful member, surely we should do it. But I am clearly of Mr. Canning's opinion, that it will prevent instead of provoking war. With Great Britain withdrawn from their scale and shifted into that of our two continents, all Europe combined would not undertake such a war. For how would they propose to get at either enemy without superior fleets? Nor is the occasion to be slighted which this proposition offers, of declaring our protest against the atrocious violations of the rights of nations, by the interference of any one in the internal affairs of another, so flagitiously begun by Bonaparte, and now continued by the equally lawless Alliance, calling itself Holy.

But we have first to ask ourselves a question. Do we wish to acquire to our own confederacy any one or more of the Spanish provinces? I candidly confess, that I have ever looked on Cuba as the most interesting addition which could ever be made to our system of States. The control which, with Florida Point, this island would give us over the Gulf of Mexico, and the countries and isthmus bordering on it, as well as all those whose waters flow into it, would fill up the measure of our political well-being. Yet, as I am sensible that this can never be obtained, even with her own consent, but by war; and its independence, which is our second interest, (and especially its independence of England,) can be secured without it, I have no hesitation in abandoning my first wish to future chances, and accepting its independence, with peace and the friendship of England, rather than its association, at the expense of war and her enmity.

I could honestly, therefore, join in the declaration proposed, that we aim not at the acquisition of any of those possessions, that we will not stand in the way of any amicable arrangement between them and the Mother country; but that we will oppose, with all our means, the forcible interposition of any other power, as auxiliary, stipendiary, or under any other form or pretext, and most especially, their transfer to any power by conquest, cession, or acquisition in any other way. I should think it, therefore, advisable, that the Executive should encourage the British government to a continuance in the dispositions expressed in these letters, by an assurance of his concurrence with them as far as his authority goes; and that as it may lead to war, the declaration of which requires an act of Congress, the case shall be laid before them for consideration at their first meeting, and under the reasonable aspect in which it is seen by himself.

I have been so long weaned from political subjects, and have so long ceased to take any interest in them, that I am sensible I am not qualified to offer opinions on them worthy of any attention. But the question now proposed involves consequences so lasting, and effects so decisive of our future destinies, as to rekindle all the interest I have heretofore felt on such occasions, and to induce me to the hazard of opinions, which will prove only my wish to contribute still my mite towards anything which may be useful to our country. And praying you to accept it at only what it is worth, I add the assurance of my constant and affectionate friendship and respect.

To Major John Cartwright

Monticello, June 5, 1824.

DEAR AND VENERABLE SIR

I am much indebted for your kind letter of February the 29th, and for your valuable volume on the English Constitution. I have read this with pleasure and much approbation, and think it has deduced the Constitution of the English nation from its rightful root, the Anglo-Saxon. It is really wonderful, that so many able and learned men should have failed in their attempts to define it with correctness. No wonder then, that Paine, who thought more than he read, should have credited the great authorities who have declared, that the will of Parliament is the Constitution of England. So Marbois, before the French Revolution, observed to me that the Almanac Royal was the Constitution of France. Your derivation of it from the Anglo-Saxons, seems to be made on legitimate principles. Having driven out the former inhabitants of that part of the island called England, they became aborigines as to you, and your lineal ancestors. They doubtless had a constitution; and although they have not left it in a written formula, to the precise text of which you may always appeal, yet they have left fragments of their history and laws, from which it may be inferred with considerable certainty. Whatever their history and laws show to have been practiced with approbation, we may presume was permitted by their constitution; whatever was not so practiced, was not permitted. And although this constitution was violated and set at naught by Norman force, yet force cannot change right. A perpetual claim was kept up by the nation, by their perpetual demand of a restoration of their Saxon laws; which shows they were never relinquished by the will of the nation. In the pullings and haulings for these ancient rights, between the nation, and its kings of the races of Plantagenets, Tudors and Stuarts, there was sometimes gain, and sometimes loss, until the final reconquest of their rights from the Stuarts. The destruction and expulsion of this race broke the thread of pretended inheritance, extinguished all regal usurpations, and the nation re-entered into all its rights; and although in their bill of rights they specifically reclaimed some only, yet the omission of the others was no renunciation of the right to assume their exercise also, whenever occasion should occur. The new King received no rights or powers, but those expressly granted to him. It has ever appeared to me, that the difference between the Whig and the Tory of England is, that the Whig deduces his rights from the Anglo-Saxon source, and the Tory from the Norman. And Hume, the great apostle of Toryism, says, in so many words, note AA to chapter 42, that, in the reign of the Stuarts, "it was the people who encroached upon the sovereign, not the sovereign who attempted, as is pretended, to usurp upon the people." This supposes the Norman usurpations to be rights in his successors. And again, C, 159, "the commons established a principle, which is noble in itself, and seems specious, but is belied by all history and experience, *that the people are the origin of all just power.*" And where else will this degenerate son of science, this traitor to his fellow men, find the origin of *just* powers, if not in the majority of the society? Will it be in the minority? Or in an individual of that minority?

Our Revolution commenced on more favorable ground. It presented us an album on which we were free to write what we pleased. We had no occasion to search into musty records, to hunt up royal parchments, or to investigate the laws and institutions of a semi-barbarous ancestry. We appealed to those of nature, and found them engraved on our hearts. Yet we did not avail ourselves of all the advantages of our position. We had never been permitted to exercise self-government. When forced to assume it, we were novices in its science. Its principles and forms had entered little into our former education. We established, however, some, although not all its important principles. The constitutions of most of our States assert, that all power is inherent in the people; that they may exercise it by themselves, in all cases to which they think themselves competent, (as in electing their functionaries executive and legislative, and deciding by a jury of themselves, in all judiciary cases in which any fact is involved,) or they may act by representatives, freely and equally chosen; that it is their right and duty to be at all times armed; that they are entitled to freedom of person, freedom of religion, freedom of property, and freedom of the press. In the structure of our legislatures, we think experience has proved the benefit of subjecting questions to two separate bodies of deliberants; but in constituting these, natural right has been mistaken, some making one of these bodies, and some both, the representatives of property instead of persons; whereas the double deliberation might be as well obtained without any violation of true principle, either by requiring a greater age in one of the bodies, or by electing a proper number of representatives of persons, dividing them by lots into two chambers, and renewing the division at frequent intervals, in order to break up all cabals. Virginia, of which I am myself a native and resident, was not only the first of the States, but, I believe I may say, the first of the nations of the earth, which assembled its wise men peaceably together to form a fundamental constitution, to commit it to writing, and place it among their archives, where every one should be free to appeal to its text. But this act was very imperfect. . . .

With respect to our State and federal governments, I do not think their relations correctly understood by foreigners. They generally suppose the former subordinate to the latter. But this is not the case. They are co-ordinate departments of one simple and integral whole. To the

State governments are reserved all legislation and administration, in affairs which concern their own citizens only, and to the federal government is given whatever concerns foreigners, or the citizens of other States; these functions alone being made federal. The one is the domestic, the other the foreign branch of the same government; neither having control over the other, but within its own department. There are one or two exceptions only to this partition of power. But, you may ask, if the two departments should claim each the same subject of power, where is the common umpire to decide ultimately between them? In cases of little importance or urgency, the prudence of both parties will keep them aloof from the questionable ground; but if it can neither be avoided nor compromised, a convention of the States must be called, to ascribe the doubtful power to that department which they may think best. You will perceive by these details, that we have not yet so far perfected our constitutions as to venture to make them unchangeable. But still, in their present state, we consider them not otherwise changeable than by the authority of the people, on a special election of representatives for that purpose expressly: they are until then the *lex legum.*

But can they be made unchangeable? Can one generation bind another, and all others, in succession forever? I think not. The Creator has made the earth for the living, not the dead. Rights and powers can only belong to persons, not to things, not to mere matter, unendowed with will. The dead are not even things. The particles of matter which composed their bodies, make part now of the bodies of other animals, vegetables, or minerals, of a thousand forms. To what then are attached the rights and powers they held while in the form of men? A generation may bind itself as long as its majority continues in life; when that has disappeared, another majority is in place, holds all the rights and powers their predecessors once held, and may change their laws and institutions to suit themselves.

Nothing then is unchangeable but the inherent and un-alienable rights of man.

I was glad to find in your book a formal contradiction, at length, of the judiciary usurpation of legislative powers; for such the judges have usurped in their repeated decisions, that Christianity is a part of the common law. The proof of the contrary, which you have adduced, is incontrovertible; to wit, that the common law existed while the Anglo-Saxons were yet pagans, at a time when they had never yet heard the name of Christ pronounced, or knew that such a character had ever existed. But it may amuse you, to show when, and by what means, they stole this law in upon us. In a case of *quare impedit* in the Year-book 34, H. 6, folio 38, (anno 1458,) a question was made, how far the ecclesiastical law was to be respected in a common law court? And Prisot, Chief Justice, gives his opinion in these words: *"A tiel leis qu' ils de seint eglise ont en* ancien scripture, *covient à nous à donner credence; car ceo common ley sur quels touts manners leis sont fondés. Et auxy, Monsieur, nous sumus oblègés de conustre lour ley de saint eglise; et semblablement ils sont obligé de consustre nostre ley. Et, Monsieur, si poit apperer or à nous que l'evesque ad fait come un ordinary fera en tiel cas, adong nous devons cee adjuger bon, ou auterment nemy,"* etc. See S. C. Fitzh. Abr. Qu. imp. 89, Bro. Abr. Qu. imp. 12. Finch in his first book, c. 3, is the first afterwards who quotes this case and mistakes it thus: "To such laws of the church as have warrant in *holy scripture,* our law giveth credence." And cites Prisot; mistranslating "ancien scripture," into *"holy scripture."* Whereas Prisot palpably says, "to such laws as those of holy church have in *ancient writing,* it is proper for us to give credence," to wit, to their *ancient written* laws. This was in 1613, a century and a half after the dictum of Prisot. Wingate, in 1658, erects this false translation into a maxim of the common law, copying the words of Finch, but citing Prisot, Wing. Max. 3. And Sheppard, title, "Religion," in 1675, copies the same mistranslation, quoting the Y. B. Finch and Wingate. Hale expresses it in these words: "Christianity is parcel of the laws of England." 1 Ventr. 293, 3 Keb. 607. But he quotes no authority. By these echoings and re-echoings from one to another, it had become so established in 1728, that in the case of the King *vs.* Woolston, 2 Stra. 834, the court would not suffer it to be debated, whether to write against Christianity was punishable in the temporal court at common law? Wood, therefore, 409, ventures still to vary the phrase, and say, that all blasphemy and profaneness are offences by the common law; and cites 2 Stra. Then Blackstone, in 1763, IV. 59, repeats the words of Hale, that "Christianity is part of the laws of England," citing Ventris and Strange. And finally, Lord Mansfield, with a little qualification, in Evans' case, in 1767, says that "the essential principles of revealed religion are part of the common law." Thus ingulfing Bible, Testament and all into the common law, without citing any authority. And thus we find this chain of authorities hanging link by link, one upon another, and all ultimately on one and the same hook, and that a mistranslation of the words *"ancien scripture,"* used by Prisot. Finch quotes Prisot; Wingate does the same. Sheppard quotes Prisot, Finch and Wingate. Hale cites nobody. The court in Woolston's case, cites Hale. Wood cites Woolston's case. Blackstone quotes Woolston's case and Hale. And Lord Mansfield, like Hale, ventures it on his own authority. Here I might defy the best-read lawyer to produce another scrip of authority for this judiciary forgery; and I might go on further to show, how some of the Anglo-Saxon priests interpolated into the text of Alfred's laws, the 20th, 21st, 22d, and 23d chapters of Exodus, and the 15th of the Acts of the Apostles, from the 23d to the 29th verses. But this would lead my pen and your patience too far. What a conspiracy this, between Church and State! Sing Tantarara, rogues all, rogues all, Sing Tantarara, rogues all! . . .

To William Ludlow

Monticello, September 6, 1824.

SIR

The idea which you present in your letter of July 30th, of the progress of society from its rudest state to that it has now attained, seems comformable to what may be probably conjectured. Indeed, we have under our eyes tolerable proofs of it. Let a philosophic observer commence a journey from the savages of the Rocky Mountains, eastwardly towards our seacoast. These he would observe in the earliest stage of association living under no law but that of nature, subsisting and covering themselves with the flesh and skins of wild beasts. He would next find those on our frontiers in the pastoral state, raising domestic animals to supply the defects of hunting. Then succeed our own semi-barbarous citizens, the pioneers of the advance of civilization, and so in his progress he would meet the gradual shades of improving man until he would reach his, as yet, most improved state in our seaport towns. This, in fact, is equivalent to a survey, in time, of the progress of man from the infancy of creation to the present day. I am eighty-one years of age, born where I now live, in the first range of mountains in the interior of our country. And I have observed this march of civilization advancing from the seacoast, passing over us like a cloud of light, increasing our knowledge and improving our condition, insomuch as that we are at this time more advanced in civilization here than the seaports were when I was a boy. And where this progress will stop no one can say. Barbarism has, in the meantime, been receding before the steady step of amelioration; and will in time, I trust, disappear from the earth. You seem to think that this advance has brought on too complicated a state of society, and that we should gain in happiness by treading back our steps a little way. I think, myself, that we have more machinery of government than is necessary, too many parasites living on the labor of the industrious. I believe it might be much simplified to the relief of those who maintain it. Your experiment seems to have this in view. A society of seventy families, the number you name, may very possibly be governed as a single family, subsisting on their common industry, and holding all things in common. Some regulators of the family you still must have, and it remains to be seen at what period of your increasing population your simple regulations will cease to be sufficient to preserve order, peace, and justice. The experiment is interesting; I shall not live to see its issue, but I wish it success equal to your hopes, and to yourself and society prosperity and happiness.

To Roger C. Weightman[1]

Monticello, June 24, 1826.

RESPECTED SIR

The kind invitation I receive from you, on the part of the citizens of the city of Washington, to be present with them at their celebration on the fiftieth anniversary of American Independence, as one of the surviving signers of an instrument pregnant with our own, and the fate of the world, is most flattering to myself, and heightened by the honorable accompaniment proposed for the comfort of such a journey. It adds sensibly to the sufferings of sickness, to be deprived by it of a personal participation in the rejoicings of that day. But acquiescence is a duty, under circumstances not placed among those we are permitted to control. I should, indeed, with peculiar delight, have met and exchanged there congratulations personally with the small band, the remnant of that host of worthies, who joined with us on that day, in the bold and doubtful election we were to make for our country, between submission

---

[1] This is the last letter from Jefferson's pen. [Ed.]

or the sword; and to have enjoyed with them the consolatory fact, that our fellow citizens, after half a century of experience and prosperity, continue to approve the choice we made. May it be to the world, what I believe it will be, (to some parts sooner, to others later, but finally to all,) the signal of arousing men to burst the chains under which monkish ignorance and superstition had persuaded them to bind themselves, and to assume the blessings and security of self-government. That form which we have substituted, restores the free right to the unbounded exercise of reason and freedom of opinion. All eyes are opened, or opening, to the rights of man. The general spread of the light of science has already laid open to every view the palpable truth, that the mass of mankind has not been born with saddles on their backs, nor a favored few booted and spurred, ready to ride them legitimately, by the grace of God. These are grounds of hope for others. For ourselves, let the annual return of this day forever refresh our recollections of these rights, and an undiminished devotion to them. . . .

Further Reading on Jefferson

The principal editions of Jefferson's writings are cited in "A Note on the Selections." Mention should be made of the youthful commonplace books edited by Gilbert Chinard: *The Commonplace Book of Thomas Jefferson* (Baltimore, 1926) and *The Literary Bible of Thomas Jefferson* (Baltimore, 1928); *Thomas Jefferson's Garden Book, 1766–1824* (Philadelphia, 1944) and *Thomas Jefferson's Farm Book* (New York, 1953), both edited by Edwin M. Betts; and the *Catalogue of the Library of Thomas Jefferson*, 5 vols., E. Millicent Sowerby, editor (Washington, 1952). Of several editions of bilateral correspondence the most important is *The Adams-Jefferson Letters*, 2 vols., Lester J. Cappon, editor (Chapel Hill, 1959).

The literature on and about Jefferson is immense. No satisfactory bibliography exists, but the reader may wish to consult the Guide to Sources in the present editor's *The Jefferson Image in the American Mind*, cited below. Books alone are included in the selected list which follows.

Adams, Henry, *History of the United States During the Administrations of Jefferson and Madison*, 9 vols. (New York, 1891–1893).

Bear, James A., Jr., ed., *Jefferson at Monticello* (Charlottesville, 1967).

Becker, Carl, *The Declaration of Independence* (New York, 1922).

Berman, Eleanor D., *Thomas Jefferson Among the Arts* (New York, 1947).

Boorstin, Daniel J., *The Lost World of Thomas Jefferson* (New York, 1948).

Bush, Alfred L., *The Life Portraits of Thomas Jefferson* (Charlottesville, 1962).

Caldwell, Lynton K., *The Administrative Theories of Jefferson and Hamilton* (Chicago, 1944).

Chinard, Gilbert, *Thomas Jefferson, The Apostle of Americanism*. Revised Edition (Boston, 1939).

Dumbauld, Edward, *Thomas Jefferson, American Tourist* (Norman, Oklahoma, 1946).

Healey, Robert M., *Jefferson on Religion in Public Education* (New Haven, 1962).

Honeywell, Roy J., *The Educational Work of Thomas Jefferson* (Cambridge, Massachusetts, 1931).

Kaplan, Lawrence S., *Jefferson and France: An Essay on Politics and Political Ideas* (New Haven, 1967).

Kimball, Fiske, *Thomas Jefferson, Architect* (Boston, 1916).

Kimball, Marie, *Jefferson: The Road to Glory, 1743 to 1776* (New York, 1943).

———, *Jefferson: War and Peace, 1776 to 1784* (New York, 1947).

———, *Jefferson: The Scene of Europe, 1784 to 1789* (New York, 1950).

Koch, Adrienne, *The Philosophy of Thomas Jefferson* (New York, 1943).

———, *Jefferson and Madison: The Great Collaboration* (New York, 1950).

Lehmann, Karl, *Thomas Jefferson, American Humanist* (Chicago, 1947).

Levy, Leonard, *Jefferson and Civil Liberties: The Darker Side* (Cambridge, Massachusetts, 1963).

Malone, Dumas, *Jefferson the Virginian* (Boston, 1948).

———, *Jefferson and the Rights of Man* (Boston, 1951).

———, *Jefferson and the Ordeal of Liberty* (Boston, 1962).

———, *Jefferson the President, First Term, 1801–1805* (Boston, 1970).

————, *Jefferson the President, Second Term, 1805–1809* (Boston, 1974).

Martin, Edwin T., *Thomas Jefferson: Scientist* (New York, 1952).

Mayo, Bernard, ed., *Jefferson Himself* (Boston, 1942).

Nock, Albert J., *Jefferson* (New York, 1926).

Peterson, Merrill D., *The Jefferson Image in the American Mind* (New York, 1960).

————, *Thomas Jefferson and the New Nation, A Biography* (New York, 1970).

————, ed., *Thomas Jefferson, A Profile* (New York, 1967).

Randolph, Sarah N., *The Domestic Life of Thomas Jefferson*. American Classics Edition (New York, 1958).

Schachner, Nathan, *Thomas Jefferson: A Biography*, 2 vols. (New York, 1951).

Sheehan, Bernard, *Seeds of Extinction: Jeffersonian Philanthropy and the American Indian* (Chapel Hill, 1973).

Wiltse, Charles M., *The Jeffersonian Tradition in American Democracy* (Chapel Hill, 1935).

THE VIKING PORTABLE LIBRARY

FOR THE BEST IN PAPERBACKS, LOOK FOR THE

In every corner of the world, on every subject under the sun, Penguin represents quality and variety—the very best in publishing today.

For complete information about books available from Penguin—including Pelicans, Puffins, Peregrines, and Penguin Classics—and how to order them, write to us at the appropriate address below. Please note that for copyright reasons the selection of books varies from country to country.

In the United Kingdom: For a complete list of books available from Penguin in the U.K., please write to *Dept E.P., Penguin Books Ltd, Harmondsworth, Middlesex, UB7 0DA.*

In the United States: For a complete list of books available from Penguin in the U.S., please write to *Consumer Sales, Penguin USA, P.O. Box 999—Dept. 17109, Bergenfield, New Jersey 07621-0120.* VISA and MasterCard holders call 1-800-253-6476 to order all Penguin titles.

In Canada: For a complete list of books available from Penguin in Canada, please write to *Penguin Books Canada Ltd, 10 Alcorn Avenue, Suite 300, Toronto, Ontario, Canada M4V 3B2.*

In Australia: For a complete list of books available from Penguin in Australia, please write to the *Marketing Department, Penguin Books Ltd, P.O. Box 257, Ringwood, Victoria 3134.*

In New Zealand: For a complete list of books available from Penguin in New Zealand, please write to the *Marketing Department, Penguin Books (NZ) Ltd, Private Bag, Takapuna, Auckland 9.*

In India: For a complete list of books available from Penguin, please write to *Penguin Overseas Ltd, 706 Eros Apartments, 56 Nehru Place, New Delhi, 110019.*

In Holland: For a complete list of books available from Penguin in Holland, please write to *Penguin Books Nederland B.V., Postbus 195, NL-1380AD Weesp, Netherlands.*

In Germany: For a complete list of books available from Penguin, please write to *Penguin Books Ltd, Friedrichstrasse 10-12, D-6000 Frankfurt Main I, Federal Republic of Germany.*

In Spain: For a complete list of books available from Penguin in Spain, please write to *Longman, Penguin España, Calle San Nicolas 15, E-28013 Madrid, Spain.*

In Japan: For a complete list of books available from Penguin in Japan, please write to *Longman Penguin Japan Co Ltd, Yamaguchi Building, 2-12-9 Kanda Jimbocho, Chiyoda-Ku, Tokyo 101, Japan.*